Studies in the History of Medieval
VOLUME XXV

THE ART AND ARCHITECTURE
OF ENGLISH BENEDICTINE MONASTERIES,
1300–1540

A PATRONAGE HISTORY

Studies in the History of Medieval Religion

ISSN 0955–2480

Founding Editor
Christopher Harper-Bill

Series Editor
Frances Andrews

Previously published volumes in the series
are listed at the back of the volume

To my father, Keith Alexander Luxford,
who first encouraged me to think about medieval art

'Je crois à la nécessité d'une règle at d'un ordre. Je dis simplement
qu'il ne peut s'agir de n'importe quelle règle. Et qu'il serait
suprenant que la règle don't nous avons besoin nous fût donnée par
cette société déréglée…'
Albert Camus, 'L'artiste et son temps', in idem., *Essais*,
ed. R. Quilliot, Bruges, 1965: p. 801.

It be very hard to recover things broken and spoiled.'
–A pearl of Tudor Wisdom
P. L. Hughes and J. F. Larkin, eds, *Tudor Royal Proclamations*,
III vols, London and New Haven, 1964–69: II, p.146.

THE ART AND ARCHITECTURE
OF ENGLISH BENEDICTINE MONASTERIES,
1300–1540

A PATRONAGE HISTORY

JULIAN M. LUXFORD

THE BOYDELL PRESS

First published 2005
The Boydell Press, Woodbridge
Reprinted 2008 and transferred to digital printing
Reprinted in paperback 2012

ISBN 978-1-84383-153-2 hardback
ISBN 978-1-84383-759-6 paperback

The Boydell Press is an imprint of Boydell & Brewer Ltd
PO Box 9, Woodbridge, Suffolk IP12 3DF, UK
and of Boydell & Brewer Inc.
668 Mt Hope Ave, Rochester, NY 14620-2731, USA
website: www.boydellandbrewer.com

A CIP catalogue record for this book is available
from the British Library

Contents

List of Illustrations

Acknowledgements

This book is a revised version of a Cambridge University doctoral dissertation. It is often said that undertaking and seeing through a Ph.D. is a solipsistic and lonely task, even in congenial, collegial Cambridge. My experience could not have been more different. Research has brought me into contact with many generous, good-humoured (and humorous), constructively critical and vastly knowledgeable people, who have helped to make this work whatever it is. I am now happy to call many of them my friends – some even family – and pleased to acknowledge their invaluable support here. If anyone feels him or herself omitted, then I beg their forgiveness, and ask that it be ascribed to an errant brain rather than an ungrateful heart.

Paul Binski supervised the dissertation and has supported me at every step. I owe him a great deal: much more than can be suggested here. Particular thanks are also due to Nigel Morgan, who has given me constant assistance, first at La Trobe University in Melbourne and subsequently at Cambridge. I will always be indebted to these two men. Further, I have received sustained and fundamental scholarly support from my friends Joan Greatrex (who, among many other things, read and commented on a draft of the book), James Carley, Antonia Gransden, and Matthew Reeve; and sustained and fundamental support of all kinds from my beautiful and enthusiastic wife, Claire. Eamon Duffy and Christopher Wilson, to my great good fortune, agreed to examine my doctoral thesis, and have played a significant role in shaping this book: as much through their own scholarship as their analytical comments. Nor may I forget special debts to Alison and Antony Milford; to Paul Crossley and Sandy Heslop; to Linda Monckton and Richard K. Morris; and to Christopher Brooke, who took such an interest in what I was doing from the start. Others have given me significant help, a number of them on multiple occasions: Patrick Dolan, John Draisey, John A. Goodall, Christopher Guy, Michael Hare, Christopher Harper-Bill, Francis Kelly, Simon Keynes, Berthold Kreß, Paul Matthews, David Morrison, Caroline Palmer, Malcolm Parkes, Alan Piper, Kathleen Scott, Kevin Van Anglen, Tessa Webber, and Neil Wright. Further, I am grateful to the staff of the many repositories of manuscripts and artefacts which I have visited, particularly those of the British Library, Cambridge University Library, Duke Humfrey's at the Bodleian, the Wren at Trinity College Cambridge, the Conway Library at the Courtauld Institute of Art, Lambeth Palace Library, and Worcester Cathedral Library.

Two funding bodies have given me substantial grants in aid of publication, and I am indebted to the administrators of both. The Marc Fitch Fund made a very generous award which has paid for much of the illustration. The publication of this book has also been assisted by a grant from the Scouloudi Foundation in association with the Institute of Historical Research. Further, the School of Art History at St Andrews University has provided support. Taking the longer view, I thank warmly the Master and Fellows of Clare College, Cambridge for the award of a post-doctoral Research Fellowship: part of me will always regret leaving them so quickly, despite the weighty compensations offered by life in St Andrews. And at the beginning of it all, the Cambridge Commonwealth Trust flew me over to King's and supported me there, but did not need to fly me back again: to the administrators of this organization go my thanks and my respect.

Finally, I thank my †Mother, who first encouraged me to look at medieval architecture and art, and my Father, who first encouraged me to think about it.

Julian Luxford
School of Art History
St Andrews University
Christmas 2004

The publication of this book has been assisted by a grant from
The Scouloudi Foundation in association with the
Institute of Historical Research

Abbreviations

The following abbreviations are used throughout for manuscript repositories.

BL	British Library
CFM	Cambridge, Fitzwilliam Museum
CUL	Cambridge University Library
DRO	Devon Record Office, Exeter
GCCC	Cambridge, Gonville and Caius College
GCL	Gloucester Cathedral Library
LCA	London, College of Arms
LPL	Lambeth Palace Library, London
OBC	Oxford, Balliol College
OBL	Oxford, Bodleian Library
OCCC	Oxford, Corpus Christi College
OQC	Oxford, The Queen's College
PRO	Public Record Office (The National Archives), London
TCC	Cambridge, Trinity College
WCL	Worcester Cathedral Library

The following abbreviations are used in the bibliography of works cited at the end of the book, and in certain cases in the notes.

AASRP	*Associated Archaeological Societies' Reports and Papers*
AJ	*Archaeological Journal*
Archaeology and History	L. Abrams and J.P. Carley, eds, *The Archaeology and History of Glastonbury Abbey*, Woodbridge, 1991
AoC	*Age of Chivalry: Art in Plantagenet England 1200–1400*, ed. J.J.G. Alexander and P. Binski, London, 1987
BAACT	British Archaeological Association Conference Transactions
Arthurian Tradition	J.P. Carley, ed., *Glastonbury Abbey and the Arthurian Tradition*, Cambridge, 2001
CS	Camden Society
DCNQ	*Devon and Cornwall Notes and Queries*
DR	*Downside Review*
Earliest English Brasses	J. Coales, ed., *The Earliest English Brasses. Patronage, Style and Workshops 1270–1350*, London, 1987
EETS	Early English Text Society
Gothic	*Gothic: Art for England 1400–1547*, ed. R. Marks and P. Williamson, London, 2003
JBAA	*Journal of the British Archaeological Association*
JEH	*Journal of Ecclesiastical History*

PDNHAFC	*Proceedings of the Dorset Natural History and Antiquarian Field Club* (continued as *Proceedings of the Dorset Natural History and Archaeological Society*)
PHFCAS	*Proceedings of the Hampshire Field Club and Archaeological Society*
PHS	Proceedings of the Harlaxton Symposium
PSANHS	*Proceedings of the Somerset Archaeological and Natural History Society* (continued as *Somerset Archaeology and Natural History*)
RGC	*Records of Gloucester Cathedral*
RS	Rolls Series
SDNQ	*Somerset and Dorset Notes and Queries*
SRS	Somerset Record Society
TBGAS	*Transactions of the Bristol and Gloucestershire Archaeological Society*
Tewkesbury Abbey	R.K. Morris and R. Shoesmith, eds, *Tewkesbury Abbey: History, Art and Architecture*, Little Logaston, 2003
TRHS	*Transactions of the Royal Historical Society*
TWAS	*Transactions of the Worcestershire Archaeological Association*
Westminster Abbey	T. Tatton-Brown and R. Mortimer, eds, *Westminster Abbey: The Lady Chapel of Henry VII*, Woodbridge, 2003
Winchester Cathedral	J. Crook, ed., *Winchester Cathedral: 900 Years*, Chichester, 1993

Map of the Region Covered by this Book

The map represents the nine counties covered by this study, and the locations within them of the Benedictine houses mentioned in the text – and only these houses. For a complete list of the houses of the region under review here see appendix 1, pp. 215–17.

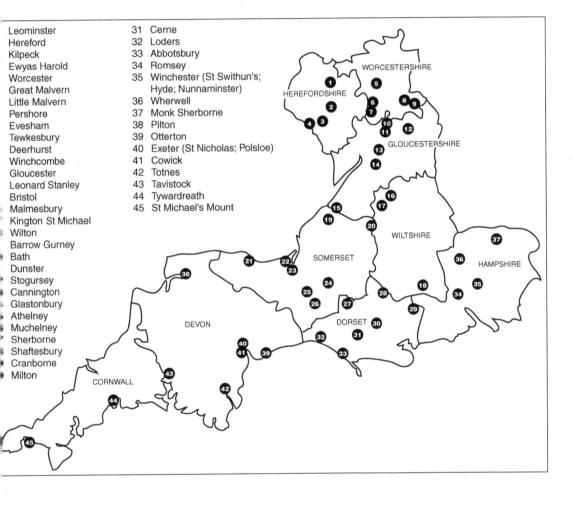

Leominster	31	Cerne
Hereford	32	Loders
Kilpeck	33	Abbotsbury
Ewyas Harold	34	Romsey
Worcester	35	Winchester (St Swithun's;
Great Malvern		Hyde; Nunnaminster)
Little Malvern	36	Wherwell
Pershore	37	Monk Sherborne
Evesham	38	Pilton
Tewkesbury	39	Otterton
Deerhurst	40	Exeter (St Nicholas; Polsloe)
Winchcombe	41	Cowick
Gloucester	42	Totnes
Leonard Stanley	43	Tavistock
Bristol	44	Tywardreath
Malmesbury	45	St Michael's Mount
Kington St Michael		
Wilton		
Barrow Gurney		
Bath		
Dunster		
Stogursey		
Cannington		
Glastonbury		
Athelney		
Muchelney		
Sherborne		
Shaftesbury		
Cranborne		
Milton		

Introduction

Definitions, and the Parameters of the Study

This book analyzes the patronage of Benedictine art and architecture in the west of England from around 1300 until the Dissolution of the Monasteries, a topic not previously addressed. Setting aside the matter of novelty, this introductory statement poses five questions, the answers to which will help to explain the form and constitution of the material that follows. We may be loath to begin with so mundane a task as the stipulation of definitions, and it is hardly a fashionable way to proceed; however, for the sake of clarity it is incumbent upon us to do so before turning to a statement of general objectives.

The first matter requiring definition is the most important: what is to be meant by 'patronage'? If the answer seems obvious, then perhaps it should not. The steady, deliberate march away from traditional art history – Berensonian connoisseurship, Wolfflinian stylistic analysis, Warburgian/Panofskian iconography – that has occurred in British and American universities over the last three decades has benefited the study of medieval art and architectural patronage greatly. However, few writers working with the concept explain what they mean by it. Indeed, scholars are apt to be rather Delphic about the matter, tacitly (and, where documents are lacking, conveniently) accepting not only financial intervention and involvement in commissioning, but also general auspices, as constitutive of patronage. What is styled patronage often turns out to involve little or no direct input on the part of a supposed patron, and to exclude parties – typically less glamorous ones – who also played a part. This can be confusing for the reader, not least because he or she is presented with a core concept that lacks clear parameters.[1]

In fact, the patronage of medieval art and architecture is a more complex and problematic topic than is frequently supposed. Where relevant documentation exists, one must be careful to read it in a manner sympathetic to both the complexities (idiosyncrasies is perhaps a better word) and the unfamiliarity of medieval organizational and financial arrangements.[2] Where such documentation is lacking – the rule in the case of English medieval art and architecture – it is difficult if not impossible to discuss patronage both closely and convincingly. Undocumented objects are not necessarily disqualified from patronage studies: sensible hypothesis can be very useful. However, it is important to know when to step back and admit uncertainty.

This injunction is taken seriously here, restrictive though it can be. Throughout, patronage will be considered to refer to the commission and financing of a given work or works. Gifts and bequests of building materials and works of art will also be recognized as acts of patronage. Where extended programmes of building and embellishment are

---

1   A recent case in point is Gee 2002, a study which otherwise contains much of interest and use.
2   Cf. Baxandall 1972, pp. 1–2 (dealing with the Italian *quattrocento*). The definition of patronage offered here (pp. 1–3) is refreshingly clear.

concerned, the term will also refer to the maintenance of a commission after the initiating patron had ceased to support the work. Conversely, an Olympian, metaphysical concern with a project, involving no demonstrable material input, will not be regarded as patronage. To do so would make the topic impossible to discuss consistently, because while such a concern may be reasonably supposed under certain circumstances (in the case, say, of a bishop's concern with monastic-sponsored rebuilding at a cathedral priory), generally one is not entitled to speculate in this way. We know too little (where we know anything) of the detailed circumstances in which acts of patronage were embedded.

Thus, commission and material support directed expressly towards art and architectural projects are the central concepts to grasp for an understanding of patronage as discussed here. To avoid confusion, 'tutelary patronage' will be used of the guardian-client relationship that is usually intended where church historians refer to 'patronage'.

Patronage can also be understood in another way, and it is convenient to mention this here, although it constitutes a rationale for our general methodology rather than simply for our definition of terms. An act of patronage may be understood as the fulcrum between a work of art or architecture and the dense complex of ideas, circumstances and actions that come under the heading 'history'. It is, with the technical processes of manufacture, the ultimate catalyst: the last denominator in a chain of cause and effect of greater or lesser length. Patronage was not necessary for the existence of a work (works made by monks and nuns for personal use had no patron), but in nearly all of the cases to be discussed here it was the conduit by which ideas were cemented in 'institutional' artistic forms, expressed in stone, wood, paint, parchment, glass, metal, fabric, terracotta etc.[3] Thus, the identification of patterns of history, most immediately inherent in the conditions that influenced patrons to commission and pay for works, but also more broadly, is the overriding object of any broadly based patronage study. Form, materials, and technique can be important for what they reveal about patronage, but matter less than they do in a study of works of art and architecture *per se*.

The second question raised by our introductory statement is easier to deal with. 'Art and architecture' is construed throughout this study in a broad manner; not so broad as to embrace everything commonly included under the euphemistic heading 'visual culture', but not confined, either, to those arts – architecture, sculpture and painting – privileged by scholarly tradition. Nor is it restricted to high-quality works alone. Thus, a dovecot, barn, decorated encaustic tile, item of jewellery, simply incised gravestone, panel of glass with heraldry, or book with illuminated borders or initials will be included, while an undecorated book, earthenware vessel, undecorated item of clothing, quotidian furniture etc. will not. Where art is concerned, the definition is primarily guided by evidence of aesthetic intent. All types of buildings are understood as architecture.

Why focus on the Benedictine order alone? This is a good question to ask of a historically rooted study, for the individuality of English Benedictine houses, epitomized in their art and architecture as much as their liturgical, constitutional and devotional organization, means that they do not immediately recommend themselves to unity of treatment.[4] Nevertheless, the community assumed here is not arbitrary. By and large,

---

3   Cf. Baxandall 1972, p. 3. The term 'preconditioned' may be preferred to 'institutional' here.
4   Cf. Cunich 1997, p. 156.

medieval Benedictines (if not necessarily the laity) understood their order, both in its parts and as a whole, as distinct from others. For Barbara Harvey, this distinction is and was epitomized by their black habits, which affirmed Benedictineness 'in a world where the difference between the several religious orders . . . often seemed quite as great as those separating clergy from laity'.[5] The habit was an important but not unique indication of corporate identification. The triennial chapters of the black monks, which were a later medieval initiative, are perhaps the clearest expressions of such identification; the university colleges founded for Benedictine education another. Lists of Benedictine monasteries that crop up in books formerly belonging to houses of the order bear further testimony to it.[6] Other phenomena – some artistic, some historical – that indicate the distinctness of Benedictinism during the later middle ages will be discussed in due course. It should be added that the edges of the order have been trimmed neatly here: no patronage connected with Cluniac or Fontevrauldine houses will be discussed, even though the practices of these reformed Benedictines were by 1300 similar to those of the black monks and nuns.[7]

The definition of the region to be studied also requires a few words. Throughout, a broad definition of 'the west of England' is assumed, embracing Cornwall, Devon, Dorset, Gloucestershire, Hampshire, Herefordshire, Somerset, Wiltshire and Worcestershire.[8] A signal reason for focusing on this region is simply that the art and architectural patronage of its many and varied Benedictine houses has received less treatment than that of monasteries in the eastern counties. Indeed, the topic has not been pursued in a unified manner for any region of England; but the west offers the least-disturbed ground. This is indicated by the fact that the art and architecture of only three houses within this region – Tewkesbury, Worcester and Winchester (here taken to refer to the cathedral priory of Sts Peter, Paul and Swithun only; Hyde and Nunnaminster will always be identified as such)[9] – have been subject to recent and comprehensive scholarly analysis.[10] It is desirable to include a fair number of counties, rather than taking a narrow definition of the West Country (traditionally Cornwall, Devon, Dorset and Somerset),[11] because although the traditional West Country – Dorset and Somerset anyway – was rich in Benedictine houses, it is comparatively poor in terms of surviving documentation of the classes useful for a patronage study. From time to time, evidence from elsewhere in England will be called on to help substantiate a point at issue, although as a general rule this has been limited.

For what it is worth, the combination of these western counties carries a noteworthy, if from the point of view of monastic studies somewhat lugubrious, historical sanction. The remit of John Tregonwell, William Petre and their assistants, the Dissolution-period commissioners for the West, extended not only to the traditional West Country, but to the five additional counties – and these only – covered by this study.[12]

---

5   Harvey 1988, p. 29.
6   E.g. WCL MS A xii, fol. 116r–v; *Chron.Oxenedes*, pp. 415–17.
7   Although Cluniac (and Cistercian) liturgy was generally more internally consistent of course: see Roper 1993, p. xiii.
8   The term 'West Country' will also be used of this region.
9   Where a distinction is necessary, the cathedral priory will be referred to as St Swithun's.
10 *Tewkesbury Abbey*, Engel 2000 and *Winchester Cathedral* respectively.
11 Purists might even omit Somerset. John Leland's 'west cuntery' included it however: *Itinerary*, I, p. 145.
12 Youings 1971, p. 88 (mentioning all but the 'traditional' West Country); see pp. 78–80, 180, for

The final question raised by our introductory statement concerns the period chosen for analysis. Arbitrariness in the matter of periodization is a perennial bugbear of historians. There is any number of definitions of the 'later' (usually distinguished from the 'late') middle ages currently at large. The tendency in recent years has been to extend the period beyond the reign of Henry VIII: to 1547, 1550, and even to 1558. However, where most aspects of monastic studies – including art and architectural patronage – are concerned, the general Dissolution of 1538–40 constitutes a logical terminus.[13] A starting date of 1300 has been chosen because it allows the comparatively rich documentary source material of the fourteenth century to be examined without, however, encroaching on the thirteenth century, which seems in many ways to represent a separate era where the history of the English religious orders is concerned. That so many studies of English religious life end or begin c.1300 reflects general recognition of this fact.[14] There are a number of ways in which the later thirteenth and early fourteenth centuries may be thought a watershed for English monasticism generally. Most noticeably, the impulse that led to such a proliferation of institutions was by 1300 unambiguously spent. Where the Benedictines alone are concerned, this was true by 1200; but the fact is disguised to some extent by continuing support for the religious orders generally on the one hand and residual loyalties to black monk and nun houses on the other. A drop-off in the number of recruits to monastic life is also noticeable towards the close of the thirteenth century. A raft of economic factors, to be discussed in chapter two, further helps to distinguish the period from c.1300 onwards from the preceding centuries. After the first half of the fourteenth century, no changes that may be identified as watersheds occur. In short, the 240 years from 1300–1540 constitute a relatively self-contained period in historical terms.[15]

Structure and aims

The study is presented in three parts, the first comprising chapter one alone, the second chapters two to four, and the third chapters five and six. There follows a conclusion arranged in two sections. Chapter one has two main functions. First, it introduces the approach to sources that is taken throughout the study. This is done by surveying the categories of primary source available to us, and discussing their relative strengths and weaknesses with reference to the topic of patronage. While there is no secondary source literature survey, chapter one is prefaced by a short discussion intended to locate the study within the context of monastic studies generally. The second main task of chapter one is to survey the material remains of relevant Benedictine art and architecture, in order to demonstrate their importance in the context of later medieval English art and architecture generally (this, it is hoped, adds weight to the study's significance), to

Petre and Tregonwell's activities in Somerset, Dorset, Devon and Cornwall in 1539. All of the houses covered by this study, their county locations, net incomes c.1535, years of dissolution and, where relevant, parent-houses are listed in appendix 1. The map preceding the text indicates the geographical parameters of the study.

[13] Two bequests to the re-edification (not, perhaps, rebuilding) of Glastonbury are recorded during Mary's reign (Dunning 2001, p. 127), but they cannot have been applied to art and architecture.

[14] Although the later middle ages is often dated from c.1250: e.g. Brown 1995.

[15] For a recent argument for 1300 as 'the brink of change' where English, Scottish and Welsh monasticism was concerned, see Burton 2000, pp. 264–8.

impart some notion of the scale on which we are working, and to balance the documentary survey by pointing out the types of non-written source to which the historian of patronage may appeal for information.

Part two presents an analysis of what will be called internal patronage. Here we must pause to introduce some definitions that will be employed throughout. If a patron of a work or works of Benedictine art and/or architecture was Benedictine, then he or she qualifies as an *internal* patron. If the patron was non-Benedictine, however, and either had a work manufactured for a Benedictine context or gave a pre-existing work to a house or individual within the order, then he or she is here classed as an *external* patron. Pinpoint definitions of subclasses within these two categories are given where necessary as the study progresses.

Chapter two begins with a survey of the Benedictine attitude to the patronage of the order's art and architecture. In essence this is a self-contained topic, but is canvassed here at the beginning of the study proper because it highlights aspects of Benedictine understanding that are broadly relevant to the study as a whole. It also represents a concession to a subject which although imperfectly articulated in our source material, and often clouded by conventional terminology, nevertheless warrants some attention. If we are to scour the depleted barrel of Benedictine physical and textual culture for what we can gain from it, then we owe its original proprietors the courtesy of recognition that their conceptions differed significantly from those which the findings of modern scholarship are likely to impart.[16]

It is impossible to explain internal patronage properly without consideration of the historical factors that conditioned it. Theoretically, a great many aspects of history can be identified as 'conditioning' ones here, so it is necessary to be selective about what is discussed. Thus, the bulk of chapter two is devoted to analysis of the historical circumstances that tended to constrain internal patronage during the later middle ages, and the actions taken by the Benedictine order to overcome these constraints. The function of the chapter can be summed up in the question that it poses and answers: How was internal patronage of Benedictine art and architecture possible during the later middle ages?

Chapters three and four survey the practice of internal patronage, chapter three being devoted to superiors and chapter four to all Benedictines below the level of superior, including a separate review of the priorate. The aim here is to examine acts of patronage for what they reveal about the artistic predilections of different classes of monks and nuns, about the meaning and function of art and architecture for them, and about the scope that their respective positions within the conventual hierarchy gave for the practice of patronage. This is a survey that has the potential significantly to inform our broader understanding of monastic art and architecture, the ways it functioned and the manner in which it was appreciated. It also considers a neglected field of art historical inquiry; namely, the purchase and use of works of art and contribution to architectural projects by lower-status monks and nuns.

Part three does for external patrons what part two aims to do for internal ones. Here, however, the three classes into which external patrons are to be divided – royalty,

---

16 It is acknowledged that this concession will be insufficient for those 'indigenous', modern Benedictine historians who consider historical analysis of the 'old congregation' to be their special prerogative: e.g. Bennett 2000, p. 199.

nobility and sub-nobility – are covered in a single chapter, as no one class was demonstrably prolific enough to receive the distinct treatment afforded to Benedictine superiors. Chapter five poses and attempts to answer the same question as chapter two, for external patronage: How was external patronage of Benedictine art and architecture possible during the later middle ages? The question is well asked given the widespread belief that the period from c.1300 to the Dissolution was one of declining external support for English monasticism generally. The factors that recommend themselves immediately for analysis here are more numerous than those relevant to internal patronage, and chapter five is correspondingly longer. The most important of these factors, the adaptability and flexibility of the Benedictines in the face of the conditions that affected patronage, is discussed first.

Chapter six reviews the practice of external patronage at the three socio-economic levels specified above, for the same reasons (*mutatis mutandis*) that chapters three and four survey the practice of internal patronage. It is followed by a concluding section, the first part of which poses what the author identifies as the four most pressing questions raised by the material surveyed in the preceding chapters, plus a fifth which seems to demand address: How does patronage change over the period under review? What does it reveal about the nature of later medieval Benedictine art and architecture? What does it reveal about the Benedictine order during this period? What does it say concerning lay attitudes to the order? And what, if anything, does it tell us about the Dissolution that stops our study in its tracks? These are questions whose answers do not fit succinctly into the main line of argument, but which are nevertheless likely to occur to readers as the study unfolds. It is hoped that the relatively small amount of attention they receive here will go at least some way towards satisfying curiosity about broader issues which for various reasons it is not desirable or even possible to explore at length in this book. These questions and their answers are followed by a short epilogue.

Overall, the study aims to provide an accessible survey of the patronage of Benedictine art and architecture in the west of England during the later middle ages, to suggest the depth and richness of what in a systematic sense is a largely unexplored topic, and to emphasize its importance for our general understanding of later medieval Benedictine monasticism. It may also suggest lines of inquiry which may be followed up in other contexts, not least the Benedictine monasteries of the eastern counties, and houses of other orders.

PART I

1

Materials for a History

It is often proposed that historians are to some extent bound to write the history of their own age, regardless of their particular focus and methodology. Some go so far as to say that history *per se* is invention. 'All history is the creation of historians . . . a new reality, or at worst an unreality, linked to the happenings of the past much as a landscape painting to a landscape': thus the distinguished scholar of Italian medieval art, John White.[1] If such propositions are contentious, they at least draw attention to the advantages and disadvantages of hindsight. The advantages do not need spelling out, and many of the disadvantages are plain to see in the positioning – 'bias' is not always an appropriate term – that has characterized writing on the history of the English religious orders ever since the Dissolution of the monasteries and before; indeed, right back to the time of Gerald of Wales.[2] Inevitably, art historical studies have been influenced by the tenor of prevailing historical scholarship. This is particularly so in England, where the two disciplines have generally shared a closer relationship than on the Continent (especially in Germany). Writing the history of medieval buildings and their embellishments has always been an interdisciplinary affair in this country. More than ever, art history declares its status as a satellite of history (as opposed to a separate planet),[3] a phenomenon encouraged by the growth in historiographical studies of the discipline. 'Positioning' – vocational, political, denominational, and so on – is as influential, if not always as blatant, as it has ever been.[4]

Monastic studies invite interdisciplinary treatment and have usually received it. Regarded from almost any angle, religious houses were highly interdisciplinary organizations. Where art, architecture, books, music and related phenomena are concerned, the peculiar and largely isolated social status of monks and nuns has meant that stylistic issues as well as those of iconography and content have been influenced by awareness of historical context to an unusual degree. Thus, to cite a ready example, early Cistercian architecture is not simply unelaborated but austere, even 'spiritual'; while late Cistercian buildings (say, Abbot Thomas Chard's work of the 1530s at Forde abbey in Dorset) are more than elaborate, they are worldly, even decadent. Most of us are familiar with this sort of thing. Recently, studies of English later medieval religion generally have been marked by a sympathetic (as opposed to apologetic) approach in favour of what is now

---

1 White 1993, p. 289.
2 See GW, p. 101, for Gerald's anti-Benedictine sentiments.
3 See e.g. the papers collected in Bolvig and Lindley 2003.
4 The field of architectural history is less clearly represented by these remarks than other areas of art history. Some reaches of the discipline seem methodologically ossified: no bad thing necessarily.

commonly referred to as 'traditional' religion.[5] Regardless of the extent to which this approach stems from denominational dispositions, it has provided the current genera-tion of scholars with a constructive alternative to the substantially negative viewpoint exemplified in the works of G.G. Coulton and his school, and encouraged by the disap-probation expressed by the vastly influential David Knowles for central aspects of late medieval monastic conduct.[6] (Knowles wrote ironically of 'the exacting critics of to-day', who expect unreasonable things of medieval monastic conduct;[7] but there was no more exacting critic of late medieval monasticism than Knowles himself, precisely because of his intimate personal identification with the subject and – in terms of influ-ence – the fact that this identification was widely recognized and respected by the academic community.) The study of medieval religious art has benefited as a result, which is perhaps understandable given that exploring a topic and its context from a positive viewpoint is, for most, more stimulating than tackling an intrinsically negative phenomenon.

Setting aside monographic treatments of individual monuments, the study of monastic art, architecture and music (books and their texts are another matter) of the later middle ages has been slower to benefit from this revisionist climate than has that of the cathedral, the parish church and the secular domain.[8] The overview provided by this book is intended at least partially to redress the balance. In any event, it may be considered a(n art) history of its time as much as any other.

To the greatest possible extent the discussion that follows has been rooted in primary data. Indeed, this data – both documentary and material – is itself the bedrock of the study, both the means to an end and the end itself; for it goes without saying that the reclamation of patterns of art and architectural patronage derives most of its vitality from the objects themselves (whether or not they survive). At the outset, therefore, it is relevant to review the main categories of primary source material on which it is to rest, and to suggest the manner in which they are approached throughout. This will make clearer the grounds on which certain scholarly conventions concerning monastic patronage are challenged or indeed subscribed to in subsequent chapters. It will also provide some idea (though not a percentage) of the quantity and nature of extant Benedictine art, architecture and relevant documentation, not all of which can be brought into a study as wide-ranging as this one. Although new material – from manu-scripts (e.g. Athelney's fifteenth-century general cartulary, discovered in June 2001; Abbotsbury's previously unknown breviary of c.1400, acquired for Lambeth Palace Library in the summer of 2004)[9] to entire buildings (e.g. the late thirteenth-century infirmary of Wherwell abbey, identified in 1998)[10] – continues to turn up, the gaps in this object domain are and always will be very large; too large, in all but a few cases (e.g. great churches, monastic cartularies), to permit tight systematic analysis of individual classes of object. However, by casting a wide enough net, a profile of both the patronage

5   Not all scholars accept the concept of 'traditional' religion: e.g. French 1997, pp. 216–21.
6   It is also an alternative to the apologetic tone current in later nineteenth-century England (exem-plified among monastic historians by the work of the Benedictine abbot Francis Aidan Gasquet (1846–1929)), and still current due to the large numbers of sources then edited that remain in use. On Knowles's attitude see Greatrex 2002, pp. 36–8.
7   Knowles 1955, p. 130.
8   Indeed, Colvin 1999, p. 52, still writes of the 'infestation' by monks of monastic buildings.
9   Keynes 2001, p. 4 (Athelney cartulary); LPL MS 4513 (Abbotsbury breviary).
10   Roberts and Clarke 1998, p. 137 et passim.

and the functional contexts of Benedictine art and architecture during the later middle ages can be successfully built up.

Documentary Sources

An illustrated book of hours from Shaftesbury, now in the Fitzwilliam Museum at Cambridge, contains the following inscription (Plate 1):

> Iste liber pertinet domine Alice Champnys moniali monasterij Shastonie quem dicta Alicia emit pro summa Decem solidorum de domino Richardo de Marshall Rectore ecclesie parochialis sancti Rumbaldi de Shastina predicta.[11]

> (This book belongs to Lady Alice Champnys, nun of the monastery of Shaftesbury. Alice bought it for the sum of ten shillings from Master Richard Marshall, rector of the parochial church of St Rumbold in the aforesaid Shaftesbury.)

This provenance may be further extended to Abbess Elizabeth Shelford (1505–28), for whom the book was obviously made. It contains her 'ES' monogram (fols 11r, 34r, 105v), her clever rebus (a scallop shell over water – 'shell-ford'), and records of her election as abbess (calendar, June 25) and subsequent benediction (July 12).

Elsewhere, in the obit book of Kington St Michael now in Cambridge University Library, we encounter the following (Plate 2):

> In the dayes of dam Kateryne moleyns priores here, John Baker yaue to thus house at mynchyn kyngton a bone of seint Christofer closed yn cloth of golde a noble relyke. Thus boke for to be there mortilage. A boke of seynts lyves yn Englisshe. A spruse tabell and a cobbord þᵗ be yn there parler. The mendyng and renewyng of a oolde masboke of theres. A ffetherbedde a bolster a pylowe and ij fene coverlettes. The halfe of the money þᵗ was payde for the Image of seint savyor stondyng apon the auter yn there quere. And for the Image of seint myghel and seint katyns yn seint James chapell. Also the awter cloth of the salutacion of oure lady leyng yn seint James Chapell and iij yerdes of canvas annexed thereto to lye apon the auter. A tester and a seler þᵗ hongeth ouer my ladyes bedde. A Greyhale. A ffaire matyns boke wᵗ dirge and many goode prayers. A desen [dozen] of round peuter disshes wᵗ heirs.[12]

A further inscription dates this munificence to 1493,[13] while a third declares that on 25 March 1498, John Baker of Bridgwater (Som.) and his wife were admitted into confraternity at Kington.[14]

This information, respectively from one of the wealthiest West Country Benedictine houses and one of the poorest, is of great value for a study such as this, because it

---

11 CFM MS 2–1957, fol. 132v. On the manuscript generally, see Wormald and Giles 1982, II, pp. 516–21, where it is dated c.1528, the year of Elizabeth Shelford's death.

12 CUL MS Dd 8 2, fol. 11v. See Catalogue CUL, I, pp. 334–6. The 'ffaire matyns boke', bound with the 'mortilage' or obit calendar (fols 21v–38v), contains eight important miniatures in the style of (perhaps by) the Tickhill psalter's first artist: Sandler 1986, II, pp. 34–5. Cf. Jackson 1858, pp. 62–3 note 3.

13 At any rate the book was then written (fol. 9r); and Catherine Molyns did not become prioress until 1492.

14 Fol. 11v.

illustrates patronage at work and examples of art in functional context. Relationships between Benedictines and 'strangers', and the motives and aspirations of both, are candidly revealed: history draws breath. Yet such unambiguous evidence concerning the patronage and functional contexts of Benedictine art in the region and period under consideration is exceptional. For the most part, documentary evidence appears equivocal where patronage is concerned. This is clearest in the case of the richest source of all, monastic historiography; although generally speaking scholars have tended to take the statements of medieval chroniclers (and the testimony of antiquaries who relied on them) at face value. Other types of evidence requiring cautious interpretation (particularly heraldic) have also been used with insufficient caution. While the Marxian admonition to 'doubt everything' is unhelpful – indeed, self-defeating – a study such as this, which seeks to distinguish classes of patron and discuss their activities and motives individually as well as in the broader Benedictine domain, requires a particularly searching examination of the sources in which it is grounded.

Compoti

Obviously, not all sources require equally critical scrutiny. For instance, the data contained in the *compotus* rolls recording the objects and services paid for by obedientiaries can usually be taken at face value. Potentially misleading information does exist: in Glastonbury *compoti* the blanket accounting term 'for building and necessities' may appear where no building was actually paid for,[15] while mathematical errors concerning cost are common.[16] Moreover, as fair copy they may lack details that were included in the original, rough accounts.[17] In what they do contain, however, *compoti* are reliable, their scarcity being their most regrettable characteristic. It is the *compoti* of internal obedientiaries, particularly the sacrist, *custos operum*,[18] *feretrar*, custodian of the Lady chapel and precentor[19] that have the potential to yield most evidence. Unfortunately, such documents survive only from Glastonbury, Pershore, Worcester and Winchester.[20] For Worcester alone are there a significant number of useful rolls: relevant examples for Winchester amount to one sacristan's *compotus* and two for the *custos operum* (although the rolls of other obedientiaries have some relevant information in them). A smattering of useful examples from other houses remains in various Record Offices: one example pertaining to Cowick priory is examined in chapter four. Valuable lost *compoti* sometimes live on through other documents. The Gloucester chronicler records the cost of a major building campaign to the last penny 'prout patet in rotulis . . . operis', while the early sixteenth-century Worcester document headed *Chronologia*

---

15 See for example Keil 1961–67(a), p. 130.
16 On mathematical errors in *compoti*, see CRPer., p. 2 (e.g. pp. 12, 18, 19 etc).
17 E.g. CRWin., p. 111: here are details concerning bells, locks, doors, and the shrine of St Swithun, including artisans' wages, not copied from the (undigested) 'sacristan's book' on to his *compotus* of 1537.
18 Evesham, Gloucester, Winchester and Worcester are the only houses for which evidence of this obedience exists in the later middle ages: Smith 1951, pp. 84–5. Bath had a *custos operum* in 1206: Irvine 1890, p. 87. Cf. *Linc.Vis.*, I, p. 237 *sub magister operum*.
19 For a precentor's role in major building works see *HMGlouc.*, I, p. 54. This was apparently unusual, however.
20 The relevant printed sources are Flower 1912 (Glastonbury); CRPer. (Pershore); CRWin. (Winchester); Acc.Wor., CRWor., 'Catalogue of Rolls' (non-plenary finding list) (Worcester).

ædificorum (of which there will be more to say in chapter four) is clearly based, if at second remove, on *compoti* that no longer exist.[21] The *Chronologia ædificorum* exemplifies the dangers of definitely attributing (as has often been done) the patronage of undocumented works to particular obedientiaries on the basis of general notions of official responsibilities within monasteries. A number of major works, including the vaulting of nave and crossing (1375–77), which apparently fall within the remit of the *custos operum*, are ascribed in this document to the sacrist. Elsewhere we learn that the almoner of Worcester contributed significantly to the building of the west cloister walk: without the evidence of the rolls, who would have supposed it?[22] Finally, the usefulness of *compoti* occasionally extends to evidence of the patronage of individuals other than those whose expenditure they officially record. Thus, we learn through sacrists' accounts that c.1423/4, the prior of Worcester donated an expensive retable ('preciosa tabula') for the high altar.[23]

Inventories and catalogues

Surviving inventories of West Country monastic goods are few and generally disappointing in content. The speed at which Henry VIII's commissioners for the West dispensed their brief apparently did not permit detailed listing of moveable goods:[24] a glance at the inventories for Christ Church Canterbury, Westminster, Peterborough and even ragged Cistercian Rievaulx, so rich in works of art, indicates how much this is to be regretted.[25] Itemized lists of objects annexed to the king's use must originally have been drawn up at the dissolution of every house, but few have come down to us, and those that have are not always plenary (e.g. Tewkesbury's).[26] The inventories of Glastonbury, Pershore, Winchester and Worcester are the most detailed.[27] Typically, such documents say little concerning patronage, although they may name the obediences to which listed items pertained. This is true of pre-Dissolution inventories, as well. One of three to survive for the alien cell of St Michael's Mount (1337), for instance, records items (including silver images) in the possession of the prior, as does the 1338 inventory of another alien house, Tywardreath.[28] A handful of medieval inventories do include the names of donors, although their gifts (almost exclusively vestments or items of plate) are never more than briefly noted.[29] Existing catalogues of

21 WCL MS Axii, fol. 77v. This document has recently been printed: Engel 2000, pp. 235–6.
22 See Harvey 1984, p. 51.
23 The sacrist supplied appurtenances for it: CRWor., p. 65.
24 See Youings 1971, p. 79.
25 See Inv.C.C.Cant. (Canterbury); Inv.Westminster (Westminster); Gunton 1686, pp. 59–63 (Peterborough); Coppack 1986, pp. 103–11 (Rievaulx).
26 Burnet 1865, IV, pp. 264–8; MA, II, p. 58.
27 For Glastonbury's inventory see MA, I, pp. 63–7 (abstracted from the rolls used for *Monastic Treasures*). Not everything listed was Glastonbury's, although some items (e.g. the 'greate Sapphire': p. 65) clearly were. For Winchester see MA, I, pp. 202–3. For Worcester and Pershore, Green 1796, II, pp. ii–iv; Inv.Dioc.Wor., pp. 303–6 (Worcester, 1552), p. 330 (Pershore, 1552). Gross compilations of West Country plate brought to London are printed in *Monastic Treasures*, pp. 23–5, 31, 37–8, 41, 49, 55–6, the latter gilded plate from Glastonbury.
28 Inv.Mic.Mt., p. 5; Oliver 1846, pp. 34–5.
29 For e.g. HMC XIV:viii, pp. 198–9 (Worcester, 1391); BL Egerton MS 2104(A), fol. 209r–v (Wherwell, late fourteenth century).

Benedictine libraries sometimes record the names and status of donors of art works as well.[30] A missal valued at twenty marks, bought for the convent of Evesham by Prior Nicolas Hereford (d.1392), is very likely to have been illuminated, and the remarkable world map, whose purchase (for six marks) is recorded in the same catalogue, survives.[31] Relic inventories, of which a particularly important set survives for Glastonbury,[32] typically reveal very little about art and architectural patronage, although they are, of course, useful sources for the quantity, type and location of reliquaries, and the devotional culture of the houses to which they relate.

Cartularies and registers

Seventy-two cartularies and related registers written post-1300 survive from West Country Benedictine houses.[33] Some are general volumes covering the affairs of whole monasteries, while others pertain to individuals, either superiors or executive obedientiaries. Collectively, they contain a corpus of tangentially relevant information, although direct statements concerning art and architectural patronage are rare. One of the Bath cartularies includes a comprehensive list, compiled c.1340, of royal and episcopal gifts to the priory.[34] The sacrist's cartulary of Wherwell incorporates a *Memorandum de jocalibus* listing forty-eight items of gold and silver plate possessed by the nuns during the late fourteenth century,[35] while the general cartulary of the same house contains a remarkable fourteenth-century eulogy of Abbess Euphemia (1226–57) which ascribes a good deal of art and architectural patronage to her.[36] An instrument in the Muchelney cartulary demonstrates that the sacristan was responsible for paying an unnamed individual (probably a layman) annually for maintaining the roofs of the chapter house, cloister, dorter and frater,[37] while two of the Evesham registers in the British Library are full of interesting titbits concerning monastic expenditure on building and embellishment.[38] Worcester's *Liber albus* is a rich source, containing among its treasures the account of Archbishop Robert of Winchelsey's complaint (1301) concerning Bishop Giffard's ostentatious tomb in the monastic choir, and the prior's response.[39] As a whole, Worcester's later medieval registers are in fact a mixed bag as concerns their usefulness to this study: A v (the *Liber albus*), A xi (William More's 'journal') and A xii are very helpful, while A vi(i), (ii) and (iii) contain hardly anything of use.[40] Indeed, for the art historian, most general cartularies and abbatial registers represent a hard slog for little reward. Of the 728 instruments contained in the registers of

---

30 Existing Benedictine library inventories for the West are printed in *Shorter Catalogues*.
31 BL Harley MS 3763, fol. 191r; *DPP*, pp. 93–7; *Shorter Catalogues*, p. 138; Barber 1995, p. 17; *Gothic*, p. 146. Barber speculates that the map, which is based on a *Polychronicon* world map, may have been produced at Evesham.
32 See *CGA(H)*, II, pp. 445–54; Bird 1994; *GR*.
33 Many survive only as fragments. All except that described in Keynes 2001 are listed in Davis 1958.
34 *Cart.Bath*, pp. 152–60.
35 BL Egerton MS 2104(A), fol. 209r–v.
36 BL Egerton MS 2104(A), fols 43v–44v; cf. *VCH Hampshire & I.W.*, II, pp. 132–3.
37 *Cart.Much.&Ath.*, p. 97.
38 Those contained in Harley MS 3763 (fols 58r–94v) and Cotton MS Nero D.iii (fols 219r–23r, 226r).
39 *Lib.Albus*, pp. 21–3.
40 This variation is largely due to the different functions of these registers.

William Malvern, last abbot of Gloucester (1514–39), only one may be said to concern art and architectural patronage directly – and this is for a chiming mechanism designed to play hymns on the bells.[41] The register of Abbot Walter de Monington of Glastonbury (1342–75), compiled during a period of substantial renewal of the abbey's buildings and embellishment, apparently contains nothing that relates directly to this renovation.[42] Some cartularies and registers contain more works of art than they mention. Among those with coloured illustrations, some of them clearly the work of professional artists, are PRO C 150/1 (Gloucester, c.1300; fol. 18r shows Henry II bestowing a charter on a Benedictine), OBL MS Wood Empt 1 (Glastonbury, c.1340–42; fols 20, 116 have miniatures which will receive further attention in chapter three), BL Egerton MSS 3316 (Bath, fourteenth century; fols 14r, 30v, 31r, 31v etc. have marginal heads of benefactors),[43] Lansdowne 417 (Malmesbury, fifteenth century; fol. 4r has a coloured drawing of the Virgin and Child, fol. 4v heraldic beasts) and GCL Register D (Gloucester, 1514–28; fol. 1v, Malvern's arms, 150x117cm and professionally illuminated).

Examination of cartularies and registers highlights a revealing trend of thought: i.e. that art and architectural description was considered largely *sui generis*, and was unsuited to certain contexts. Such manuscripts contain indentures of many sorts, and descriptions of the objects, lands etc. to which these relate, as well as much of a miscellaneous nature. They are not intrinsically inappropriate places for information about art and architecture, yet leafing through them we could be excused for thinking that the built and embellished environment in which monks and nuns spent virtually their whole lives was of relatively little concern to them.

Histories

Besides the obedientiary *compotus*, the proper place for recording the building and embellishment of monasteries was the domestic history. Such histories were often bound together with cartularies: a place for everything and everything in its place.[44] As their staccato narratives unfold, it becomes clear that art and architecture were very important to Benedictines, not least as vehicles of communal self-promotion. Like *compoti*, however, regrettably few domestic histories exist. This is partially due to losses (chronicles of Abbotsbury, Bath, Milton, Winchcombe and Worcester have all been destroyed since the Dissolution), and partially due to the general decline in both the number and length of monastic histories written in England during the later middle ages.[45] For this study it is significant that major surviving domestic histories for Glastonbury, Malmesbury, Tewkesbury, Winchester and Worcester all fizzle out before or around

---

41 GCL Registers D and E. There are some documents concerning mills and other ephemeral estate architecture. The contract 'to make newe and repayre a chyme gonge uppon viij belles' (plus maintenance of the abbey clock) is GCL Register D, fol. 242r–v; Witts 1882–83(b), p. 130.

42 Monington's register is BL MS Arundel 2, fols 1r–86v.

43 The identities are given in Webster 1943–46, pp. 243–4.

44 See e.g. *HMGlouc.*, *Reg.Malmes.*, *Cart.Bath*, pp. 152–60. The Gloucester chronicle has an index containing charter abstracts that is continually cross-referenced in the historical account: see Brooke 1963, p. 261. Cf. also the cross-referencing in the so-called Founders' Book of Tewkesbury discussed in Luxford 2003(c), p. 57.

45 On this decline, see Gransden 1982, pp. 101–2 and pp. 342–424 *passim*. See also the tables in Gransden 1974, pp. 528–9.

1300, while others for Wilton, Winchester and Hyde, though written or recast in the fifteenth century (and thus of some interest here), break off c.1150 at the latest.[46] The only substantially useful surviving works come from Evesham (to 1412), Glastonbury (to 1342, with a jejune continuation to 1493), Gloucester (to c.1400) and Tewkesbury (to 1494).[47]

These histories are full of interesting information about art and architecture, although major issues (e.g. the extent of royal involvement in the rebuilding of Glouces-ter's abbey church, and the fourteenth-century rebuilding of Tewkesbury's) are often ignored. The 'positioning' of these texts necessitates careful reading, however.[48] In particular, it is important to keep in mind Matthew Paris's well-known statement that works accomplished by monastic obedientiaries and others are frequently ascribed to their superiors 'out of reverence' ('ob reverentiam') for the dignity of higher, paternal authority.[49] The arrangement of their material into demonstrations of superioral (or tutelary patronal in the case of Tewkesbury) achievement and declarations of the bene-fits accruing to the monastic community from these may deliberately exaggerate the importance of the superior as patron of the arts. While this is revealing of the political, utilitarian potential that art and architecture held for later medieval Benedictines (for such accounts were conceived of as quasi-public documents at least),[50] it may mislead. Each statement must be assessed in light of what is known from other sources about the character of the superior in question, his relationship to his convent, his usual responsi-bilities with regard to it etc. As a general rule, there seems less reason for scepticism concerning a chronicler's ascription of a gift of vestments, books or plate to a superior than there is in the case of (say) a major building campaign for which he would not normally have been responsible. The giving of such items by those in high office, which will be examined in some detail in chapter three, was a common convention outside the monastic sphere, and in any case, a superior might be obliged to make such a donation on election.[51] But it was rarely, if ever, his (or for that matter her) job to reconstruct an entire monastery church or claustral complex.

Miscellaneous sources

Alongside these standard primary sources there exist miscellaneous documentary mate-rials differing in value from source to source. Some are extremely rich; for example the account-book (or 'journal') of William More, penultimate prior of Worcester

---

[46] The Wilton chronicle is a reworking of Goscelin's (d. c.1099) Latin Life of St Edith.

[47] The Tewkesbury history is part four of the Founders' Book (OBL MS Top Glouc d 2, fols 8v–42r), printed (from an imperfect manuscript) in MA, II, pp. 59–65. Cf. *Itinerary*, IV, pp. 150–63; Luxford 2003(c), *passim*. The other three texts are CAEve., CGA(C) and HMGlouc., I. CGA(H) contains William Wyche's continuation of the Glastonbury chronicle to 1493. Additionally, short annals exist relating to Sherborne (to 1456), Gloucester (to 1470) and Tewkesbury (to 1471), printed in Kingsford 1913, pp. 346–9, 355–7 and 376–8 respectively. The main general history written in a Benedictine West Country monastery (Malmesbury) post-1300 is the *Eulogium Historiarum* (to 1366).

[48] See e.g. Tout 1921, pp. 92–104; Brooke 1963, p. 260.

[49] GA, I, p. 280.

[50] E.g. John of Glastonbury's chronicle was widely known and owned during the later middle ages. It was a source for the *Nova legenda Anglie*: Riddy 2001, p. 279 note 29; *Jos.Lyfe*, p. xx. Extracts also exist in a York manuscript: Lapidge 2001, p. 119.

[51] An example is given in Britton 1829, p. 9 note 41.

(1518–36), contains many references concerning the commission, manufacture, purchase, cost, and even transportation of art works.[52] From the other end of the monastic hierarchy comes the letter-book of the Evesham monk Robert Joseph, from which we obtain a fascinating picture of the sort of art works that a cloister monk of the early sixteenth century owned, how he obtained and paid for them, and how he used them.[53] Inscriptions in windows, stonework, painting and manuscripts, many of them preserved only in antiquarian writings (e.g. Abbot Malvern's poem on the foundation of the abbey of Gloucester, originally on a mural *tabula* in the nave; the inscription ascribing the paintings of Winchester Lady chapel to Thomas Silkstede) can be of great significance.[54] The letters of Oliver King, bishop and titular abbot of Bath, to Sir Reginald Bray, comptroller of the royal works, shed valuable light on the reconstruction of Bath cathedral priory church.[55] Later medieval miscellanies such as those surviving for Glastonbury and the abbots of Muchelney may not provide details of patronage, but (as with More's journal and Joseph's letters) are important sources for our understanding of the circumstances surrounding it, providing as they do cameo portraits of Benedictine minds at work.[56] The major source for the collective working of Benedictine minds is, of course, the documentation generated by the triennial General Chapters of the order.[57] Although this also contains little or nothing concerning art and architectural patronage specifically, it is a gauge of attitudes and *mores* that are discussed throughout this study, and is used here extensively.

Antiquarian accounts

The classes of documentation discussed above are the main monastic sources on which this study will rely. Of the external sources, the most important are the accounts of antiquaries. Nothing as rich as the *Rites of Durham* survives for the west of England, and although this document is referred to occasionally in coming pages, it has not generally been thought reasonable to use it (as W.H. St John Hope and more recently David Welander have with reference to Gloucester) as a blueprint for the layout, embellishment, conventual and secular life of large monasteries in general.[58] The church notes of Thomas Habington (1560–1647), John Aubrey (1626–97), Ralph Sheldon (1623–84), Anthony à Wood (1632–95), and others contain a great deal of information about buildings, stained glass and sepulchral monuments now destroyed or renovated. In particular, they often record material – inscriptions, heraldry and other iconography – that gives clues about the patronage and function of works. Medieval antiquarian sources, among which the notebook of William Worcestre (composed 1478–80) and the topographical and historical collections of John Leland (*c.*1506–52) stand out, are of

---

52 *Jnl.More*; Knowles 1959, pp. 108–26; Thomson 2001, pp. xxxv–xxxvi.
53 *LBRJ*; Knowes 1959, pp. 100–7.
54 Malvern's poem was copied from an unknown source by Robert Hare (GCCC MS 391, pp. pp. 63–8). *MP* is an annotated edition. Extracts from the poem, abstracted by Leland from 'certayne writyns' on the wall of the north nave aisle, are in *Itinerary*, II, pp. 59–60. The Winchester inscription will be given in chapter four.
55 *Correspondence*, pp. 4–6.
56 *GM*; *Much.Mem.*
57 *Chapters*, I–III.
58 *RD*; Hope 1890(b), pp. 97, 99–101, 102, 106–7, 109–10, 112, 113–14, 115–16, 120, 124, 125; Welander 1991, pp. 302, 321, 325–6, 327. See also Brakspear 1915–16, pp. 192, 196, 203, 204.

particular use. Both men had a special interest in the West Country and in things Benedictine. Worcestre was a native of Bristol, and the burial of his beloved patron Sir John Fastolf in a Benedictine house,[59] coupled with his sophisticated interest in the British History, naturally attracted him to monasteries of the order. Leland's visits to conventual and cathedral libraries, of which the greatest in the country was Glastonbury's (in terms of historiographical manuscripts at least),[60] began in the West in 1533, and included two subsequent visits.[61] As with monastic historiography, however, the truth-value of their statements must be carefully assessed. Their eyewitness accounts, such as Worcestre's observations on the layout of monastic buildings and Leland's description of the tombs at Glastonbury, may be taken as read. However, insofar as their testimony relies (as it often does) on texts perused in monastic libraries and on mural *tabulæ* within churches (to which both frequently referred), they require the same degree of scrutiny as their sources would. Both men also relied substantially on word of mouth for their information.[62] Where this testimony cannot be verified with reference to surviving documents (for example Leland's account of the architectural patronage of Gloucester's fifteenth-century abbots, which he derived around the time of the Dissolution from 'an ould man, made lately a monke'), it demands more searching assessment than it usually receives in published scholarship.[63]

Registers and wills

Besides antiquarian accounts, episcopal registers and wills are the two most important classes of externally generated document for a history of Benedictine patronage. The chief value of the former lies in the contextual material they contain, although entries directly relevant to art and architectural patronage do occasionally crop up. Archiepiscopal registers sometimes include transcripts of West Country wills detailing acts of patronage: for example that of Henry Chichele (1414–43), which is a particularly helpful source. For the most part, however, it is local diocesan registers that are of use, although they tell us nothing of monasteries exempt from ordinary jurisdiction.[64] Such registers provide a picture of the obligations and expectations that Benedictine monasticism entailed which has implications for our view of their forinsec patronage activities, particularly where parish churches are concerned. Episcopal registers would be of greater use had bishops concerned themselves with minor cases of monastic property-owning more often. As things stand, there are apparently no injunctions in printed West Country registers concerning private ownership of works of art by monks and nuns, a characteristic they share with the statutes of the Benedictine General Chapters.[65] Of course, a measure of private possession among monks and nuns was broadly recognized by bishops during the later middle ages, as the widespread practice of fining individuals

---

[59] Albeit not a West Country one (St Benet-at-Holm, Norfolk).

[60] *Commentarii*, p. 41.

[61] See Carley 1985, p. 141; *Lib.Hen.VIII*, p. xliv.

[62] *Itinerary*, I, p. 13 (of the unpaginated foreword); *Itinerary Worcestre*, *passim*.

[63] *Itinerary*, II, p. 61.

[64] These monasteries are listed in chapter two.

[65] Although the Canterbury province General Chapter of c.1363 idealistically required (article 21) that visitors banish expensive bedclothes and 'other ornaments' from monastic cells (*Chapters*, II, p. 85), implying awareness at the highest level of private ownership of art works.

for minor transgressions demonstrates.[66] It may be added here that the same was true of Henry VIII's commissioners, whose visitation reports never mention the ownership of personal works of art among their excuses for dissolving houses; yet as will be seen, the 'straite keppide' brethren of Glastonbury and elsewhere were consumers of art at a personal as well as a collective level.[67] Where episcopal registers do allude to Benedictine art and architecture they require more judicious reading than they have been wont to receive. The choir stalls at Winchester and the rood screen of Totnes priory church, to take two important examples, have both been attributed to the patronage of bishops on the basis of inconclusive statements in episcopal registers.[68]

As with epsicopal registers, historians once extrapolated sweeping conclusions from the contents of wills without acknowledging the hazards of doing so.[69] It has since been pointed out that anxiety concerning death and the hereafter almost certainly caused many testators to make abnormal expressions of piety when bequeathing their worldly goods.[70] The obvious point that a will may say nothing of important benefactions made during a testator's lifetime has also been emphasized.[71] An example relevant to this study comes from Winchester. Were it not for entries in the register of that priory's common seal nothing would be known of the acts of art patronage (including £706 18s 2d *ob*. in gold and silver for the embellishment of St Swithun's shrine and an undisclosed sum for a new high altar frontal of gold and silver adorned with images) for which Cardinal Beaufort was responsible shortly before his death in 1447, for his will does not mention them.[72] The will of Oliver King, bishop of Bath and Wells (dated 1503, the year of his death), further demonstrates how misleading such documents can be. King requests burial in the new priory church at Bath, and bequeaths chantry apparatus including silver-gilt images of Christ crucified and Sts Peter and Paul, and his two best candlesticks; an important act of patronage.[73] But in fact he was buried in a private chantry in St George's Chapel at Windsor, leaving a question mark over whether the images, candelabra etc. ever reached the monks of Bath.[74] Moreover, it is often clear from a testator's requests that arrangements for burial and commemoration (which in all likelihood involved art patronage at one level or another) were made before his or her will was composed. For example, an earl of Devon requesting interment at Glastonbury yet bequeathing that house only 20s may be supposed to have come to a prior under-

66 Knowles 1955, p. 243.
67 Possibly, personal property was secreted at the commissioners' approach: cf. Archbold 1892, pp. 69 (Muchelney), 116 (Glastonbury).
68 *Reg.Woodlock*, pp. v–vi; cf. p. 682; Gibbs 1904–05, p. 118. The attribution of the Winchester stalls to Bishop Henry Woodlock (1305–16) is repeated unquestioned in subsequent literature: e.g. Tracy 1993(a), pp. 194–5. There is documentary evidence, however, for collaboration between the bishop and the prior and convent on other, contemporaneous, works in Winchester's presbytery: see Harvey 1984, p. 339.
69 E.g. Jordan 1959; Rosenthal 1972 (although see the token acknowledgement on p. 98); Tanner 1984.
70 For a rejoinder to this point, see Burgess 1988, pp. 57–8; Harper-Bill 1996(a), pp. 72–3. However, Norman Tanner showed that eighty per cent of later medieval Norwich wills were proved within a year of making, suggesting that most were certainly composed under conditions of anxiety. See further Marks 2004, pp. 7–8, 170.
71 Burgess 1987, pp. 841–2; Marks 2004, p. 7.
72 RCSWin., pp. 102–4; *Royal Wills*, pp. 321–41.
73 SMW(b), pp. 44–5.
74 Hope 1913, II, pp. 413–14 and pl. LVII.

standing with the convent, not least concerning the location and construction of his tomb.[75]

Notwithstanding these caveats, wills remain fundamental sources of data about patronage by individuals at most levels of the social hierarchy.[76] The symbolic and utilitarian importance of wills for Benedictine houses as evidences of lay support is also interesting. Like a sealed charter, a signed will was an affirmation of irrevocable support on the testator's part (if not on that of his or her executors). This symbolic significance is epitomized in the Founders' Book of Tewkesbury, which includes a miniature of Isabella Despenser (d.1439) on her deathbed, bestowing on Abbot William of Bristol a document symbolizing both the reconfirmation of time-honoured privileges and the gifts (including vestments, jewellery and metalwork) which her will assigned to the convent.[77] These gifts are described in the text immediately below the illustration. Elsewhere, the fifteenth-century *Liber de Hyda* includes transcripts of wills of past monarchs who had given generously to the three Benedictine monasteries of Winchester. For example, that of the 'clementissimus rex' Eadred (946–55), who gave items of pure gold to St Swithun's, appears consecutively in garbled Anglo-Saxon, Middle English, and Latin.[78]

Heraldry

These, then, are the most useful categories of primary source material for this study. Before turning to surviving works of art and architecture, however, heraldic evidence must be considered. It is a source of particular importance for patronage studies, and one that has been widely misused in the past. Heraldry (along with rebuses and other personal insignia) spans the divide between documentation and artwork, appearing as it did in almost all contexts and media. It was ubiquitous, prolix, and promiscuously (which is not to say randomly) applied, here for decoration, there for commemorative or political purposes; now to denote ownership and involvement in patronage, now to pretend to the same; or it might signify a combination of these things. To say the least, its meaning is often ambiguous. Decorative application can be especially misleading. Some of the fifteenth-century tiles at Tewkesbury, for example, contain combinations of shields that testify not to acts of patronage but simply to enthusiasm for the most popular decorative idiom of the age.[79] With reference to encaustic tiles in particular (which were not tinctured or metalled, of course), it has been pointed out that 'copyrights' did not exist on coats of arms, and that craftsmen and patrons were free to employ

---

[75] SMW(a), p. 96.

[76] Although Benedictines did not ordinarily make wills, references to a number do exist. For West Country examples, see Power 1922, pp. 337 (nuns of Romsey), 338; Anon. 1924–26, pp. 94–5 (abbesses of Shaftesbury); CGA(C), pp. xxxi, 254–7 (abbots of Glastonbury); Carley 1996, p. 45. William of Wykeham warned Romsey's nuns against the sin of propriety demonstrated by wills: Power 1922, pp. 337–8.

[77] OBL MS Top Glouc d 2, fol. 31r; cf. Blunt 1898, pl. facing p. 80: a copy c.1550 from BL MS Additional 36985, fol. 32r.

[78] L.Hyda, pp. 153–61.

[79] Hall 1904, p. 59; Vince 2003, *passim*. For other decorative arms see Goodall 1997, pp. 184–90; Tolley 1988, *passim*. Armorial decoration often derived from widely circulated heraldic rolls: see e.g. Backhouse 1999, p. 24; Marks 1993, p. 87; Vince & Wilmott 1991, p. 146.

them in whatever context they wished.[80] Beauchamp, Mortimer, Berkeley and Despenser patronage have all recently been claimed for Malmesbury abbey on the strength of the heraldic tiles from the cloister, however.[81] Other circumstances also shake our faith in heraldry's usefulness. For example, the last abbot of Glastonbury demanded that his coat of arms be placed on the house of a debtor in recompense for non-payment,[82] and would thus certainly be regarded as that building's patron did written evidence to the contrary not exist. Only when an independent connection between its bearer(s) and the context in which it appears has been established is it safe to consider heraldry a signification of patronage. Even then they may mislead: the shields of Cardinal Hadrian de Castello on the west front and in the vaults of Bath abbey are most unlikely to denote assistance with the rebuilding of the church even though Castello was bishop of Bath and Wells (1504–18).[83] He never visited his see, let alone Bath, and no record of interest in the project appears in his slim register.[84] In this case the arms are more likely to have been erected by monks keen to demonstrate the status of their titular abbot. Elsewhere, the south transept vault of Pershore has long been attributed to Abbot Newnton (1413–57), and thus ascribed a fifteenth-century date, simply because that prelate's rebus appears on one of its bosses. For the same reason, the lierne vault of Milton's north transept is almost always identified as a product of Abbot Middleton's (1492–1525) renovations. From a stylistic point of view both date spans are intrinsically unlikely; and indeed, the two projects have now been convincingly assigned much earlier dates.[85] Notoriously, the great east window at Gloucester has been supposed the gift of Thomas, Lord Bradeston, because his arms occupy the extreme right of the lowest register (sometimes loosely referred to as the 'donor' position). Yet the escutcheons here have probably been reset.[86] Thus, while heraldry can be a useful tool for identifying patronage, it requires judicious reading.

Surviving Art and Architecture

As with documentation, the surviving corpus of later medieval Benedictine art and architecture reflects the priorities of its post-Dissolution owners rather than monastic ones. Just as ongoing legal considerations ensured a relatively high survival rate for cartularies,[87] so the desire of communities for grand parish churches and of the gentry for

---

80 Eames 1980, I, pp. 282–3; cf. Astill and Wright 1993, p. 127. The right to *bear* a given coat, fully blazoned and tricked, was of course taken very seriously: see e.g. *Foedera*, IV:ii, p. 201; Keen 2002, pp. 25–58.

81 Brown 1995, p. 27; cf. p. 41 for an analogous case.

82 Dunning 2001, p. 117.

83 For Castello's arms see Britton 1825, p. 81.

84 *Reg.King*, p. xx. Maxwell-Lyte says that Castello valued his episcopate 'only as a source of revenue': while things are rarely that simple, his point is well taken in this instance. See also Shickle 1907, p. 75.

85 Andrews 1932, pp. 82–3 even cited documentary 'evidence' for assigning the Pershore vault to Newnton: cf. Thurlby 1996, p. 184 (vault redated to c.1325–75). A date c.1500 has always been accepted for the Milton vault: e.g. Pevsner & Newman 1972, p. 287. Cf. Monckton 2000, p. 111 note 38.

86 Kerr 1985, pp. 125–6. On the 'donor' position see Bond 1916, p. 27.

87 Davis 1958, pp. xiv–xv.

ready-made, ostentatious accommodation and utilitarian buildings ensured that many conventual churches, domestic complexes and barns were spared (albeit more or less dismembered) even when 'deemed superfluous' by Henry VIII's commissioners. The romantic love of fragments has preserved in part many defaced buildings, such as the imposing eastern crossing piers and south east aisle wall at Glastonbury, the exquisitely carved chapter house vestibule doorway at Evesham (the sculpted archivolts of which may provide a key to the design of the abbey church's pre-1395 Decorated tracery),[88] and the east wall of the Guesten Hall at Worcester, with its curvilinear tracery.[89] The medieval stained glass of Great Malvern, Gloucester and Tewkesbury owes its survival at least partially to the unpalatable cost of replacing it.[90] And the perceived worthlessness of the broken tiles, glass and sculpture that have been excavated by the thousand on former Benedictine sites has allowed them to lie undisturbed, increasing their value for the modern historian.[91] On the other hand, the poor survival rate of illuminated Benedictine manuscripts from the area covered by this study demonstrates their relative lack of importance as works of art following the Dissolution; while, as everywhere, ecclesiastical and domestic metalwork and high-status liturgical vestments are wanting due to wholesale Crown appropriation and destruction.

Thus, the balance of surviving post-1300 Benedictine material from the West Country is both uneven and unrepresentative of monastic priorities.[92] However, what remains constitutes a significant chunk of all extant English later Gothic art and architecture. Without it, the origins and development of many diverse and important phenomena would be considerably murkier: the Perpendicular style (the south window of Gloucester's south transept, c.1335–36, constitutes its earliest surviving manifestation proper),[93] the canopied wooden choir stall (Winchester's, c.1308, are 'unique' and 'the finest set of choir furniture in Europe for their date': Plate 3),[94] fan vaulting (the prototype of which, c.1351–64, spans the east walk of Gloucester's cloister),[95] the stone-cage chantry chapel (over half of the surviving examples, including the earliest, stand in churches covered by this study: Plates 4, 5),[96] the monumental illuminated missal (Sherborne's being one of only three remaining examples: Plates 6, 7),[97] the hammer-

---

[88] Built between 1296 and 1318: Cox 1980, p. 8. The abbey church's chancel was rebuilt from 1395: Cox 1990, p. 128.

[89] On the value of monastic ruins for post-Dissolution generations, see Aston 1973, pp. 246–54 *et passim*.

[90] Rushforth 1936, p. 6.

[91] Although the claim that such things, when discovered *in situ*, can yield substantial patronage information (Astill & Wright 1993, *passim*) is largely incorrect.

[92] Indeed, it is claimed that a balanced history of fourteenth-century English art generally is impossible due to the vast losses: Sandler 1986, I, p. 48. The same seems true for the later middle ages as a whole.

[93] Wilson 1990, pp. 206–7; Harvey 1978, pp. 77, 79.

[94] Tracy 1987, p. 16. The stall canopies are unique, as was the sculpture these carried until the mid-seventeenth century. For the latter see *Short Survey*, pp. 44–6.

[95] AoC, p. 417. Cox 1990, p. 131, speculates that Evesham abbey church possessed the first fan vault. The other early candidate is the canopy of Hugh Despenser's tomb (d.1349), which in any case is at Tewkesbury. However, this is hardly a fan vault proper: Wilson 1980, p. 315; cf. Leedy 1980, pp. 3, 38; Morris 2003(c), p. 15.

[96] The earliest is Bishop Edington's at Winchester, perhaps built soon after 1345. For brief notes on the chapel see Cook 1947, pp. 89–90; Harvey 1978, pp. 85, 90; Pevsner & Lloyd 1967, p. 682.

[97] See Backhouse 1999, pp. 7–12.

beam roof (the monastic guest house called 'Pilgrims' Hall' at Winchester, c.1330, has the earliest English example),[98] fourteenth-century stained glass (Gloucester and Tewkesbury have two of the three most important extant ensembles),[99] fifteenth-century stained glass (Great Malvern's is of great importance: Plate 8), fifteenth-century encaustic tiles (Great Malvern has the largest collection of any),[100] the alabaster sepulchral effigy (Edward II's of c.1330, once again at Gloucester, is the first significant instance: Plate 9),[101] later medieval figure sculpture in general (Winchester retains perhaps the largest collection outside Westminster),[102] and even furniture (Gloucester has two of only seven remaining medieval cope chests, while the armoire in the Venerable chapel at Winchester is of unique design, and one of very few such survivals).[103] While not the main focus of this study, the intrinsic historical importance of these survivals deserves emphasis, not least for the weight it lends to the related issues of patronage and function that are examined below.

Conventual churches

Twenty-one of the sixty-three churches relevant to this study survive, in part or, in the cases of Dunster, Totnes and the cathedrals, in whole.[104] The cathedrals are Gloucester (Plate 10), Winchester (Plate 11) and Worcester. Milton functions as a public school chapel, while the other eighteen are now parish churches, with Bath, (Plate 12) Great Malvern, Malmesbury, Pershore, Romsey, Sherborne, and Tewkesbury standing out among these for their size and architectural importance. The others are Bristol (St James),[105] Deerhurst, Dunster, Leominster, Little Malvern, Monk Sherborne (Pamber End), Leonard Stanley, Pilton, Stogursey and Totnes. Some of these, for example Bristol, Deerhurst, Monk Sherborne, and Romsey, retain few later medieval additions; or, in the case of Stogursey (priory dissolved 1442),[106] received their later medieval additions when no longer monastic, and therefore (architecturally at least) fall outside this study. Others, such as Bath, Gloucester, Great Malvern and Tewkesbury, were substantially rebuilt after 1300, and are thus central to it. Only at Glastonbury does a significant portion of a destroyed conventual church survive, although the sites of a number of others (e.g. Athelney, Evesham, Muchelney, Shaftesbury) have been excavated, yielding significant information about later medieval building work. Some sites, Cerne for instance, have never been excavated; but it is probable that the Perpendicular east window (c.1480) of St Mary's parish church at Cerne, which is an imperfect fit, was taken from the dismantled abbey church, a situation paralleled at All Saints Hilton

---

98   The hall is now incomplete: see Crook 1991, p. 130 (reconstruction). The roof timbers of 1324–30 on dendrochonological evidence: Crook 1982, pp. 87, 100; Crook 1991, p. 129 (stressing the architectural importance of the hall-range entire). See also Greatrex 1993, p. 151.
99   Alongside York Minster, of course. See Rushforth 1922; Rushforth 1924; Kerr 1985; Brown 2003.
100   Molyneux and McGregor 1997, p. 2.
101   Stone 1972, p. 161. For an isolated example of c.1300 see Gardner 1940, p. 45 and fig. 117.
102   Lindley 1993(a), p. 97. On the sculpture generally see Lindley 1986, pp. 604–15; Lindley 1993(b), *passim*.
103   Hewett 1988, pp. 105, 121; Jervis 1993, pp. 211–13.
104   At Totnes, the outer north aisle and east window are nineteenth-century work: Pevsner & Cherry 1989, p. 868.
105   The monastic part of this church is almost entirely lost.
106   Ballard 1992, pp. 13–14; K&H, p. 92.

(Dor.), whose five Perpendicular north aisle windows come from a walk of the now lost cloister of nearby Milton.[107] In fact, many fragments of destroyed conventual churches have found their way into existing buildings.

Superiors' and priors' residences

Of conventual buildings, the commonest survivals are former superiors' and priors' residences.[108] These were easily adapted to suit the requirements of their post-Dissolution purchasers, for whom they often represented a considerable advance in living standards. The fluidity of fashions in domestic architecture has resulted in the destruction of certain examples which survived the Dissolution (as at Milton), or else such great modification that they are now scarcely recognizable (as at Little Malvern and Cannington).[109] Elsewhere, new residences were built from the materials of demolished monastic ones (for example, Delacombe Manor, Milton Abbas, c.1750; Winchcombe).[110] A fair number of superiors' and priors' residences, or components thereof, do survive in something like their later medieval form, however. Examples include those at Deerhurst, Dunster, Exeter (Polsloe and St Nicholas), Gloucester, Kington St Michael, Pilton,[111] Tewkesbury (with a fine fan-vaulted oriel), and Winchester, none of them particularly outstanding from the point of view of architectural history.[112] More remarkable are the abbatial remains at Cerne (the gateway at the northern end of the hall, with its fan vaulting, complex heraldry and magnificent oriel), Glastonbury (the freestanding kitchen), Milton (the hall), and Muchelney (the entire complex). Parts of the abbatial residence at Sherborne also survive. These domestic buildings belong more wholeheartedly to the later middle ages than do the surviving conventual churches, although some (for example Deerhurst, and particularly Gloucester) incorporate older elements. Muchelney, the most complete, is also the most recent, dendrochronological analysis suggesting completion as late as the early 1530s.[113] In the abbot's parlour stands one of England's finest surviving late medieval fireplaces, decorated above the lintel with a frieze of sub-cusped and foliated quatrefoils, octagonal capitals and lions *couchant guardant*. Another exceptional fireplace (c.1475), also with a rich quatrefoil frieze (each quatrefoil impaled by a *bouché* shield), remains in the renovated prioress's house at Cannington, while further particularly noteworthy examples survive in the almonry at Evesham and the abbatial chamber at Meare.[114]

---

[107] Dorset 1901, pp. xxxix–xl; Dicker 1908, p. 6; Monckton 1999, p. 222 note 133 (Cerne). Newman & Pevsner 1975, p. 228 (Hilton).

[108] These buildings and their embellishment are discussed as a class in chapter three.

[109] The late medieval hall incorporated into Little Malvern Court may perhaps have served the convent generally rather than the prior in particular: Pevsner 1968, p. 214.

[110] Delacombe Manor even incorporates a date-stone (1515) from the abbey: RCHM *Dorset* 1970, p. 198. For the reconstituted building at Winchcombe, see Brock 1893, p. 166.

[111] The survivals at Pilton may conceivably belong to the guest house: Pevsner & Cherry 1991, p. 629.

[112] The former prioress's lodging at Polsloe is distinguished by the first known instance of a double splayed and halved scarf in English timber architecture, however: Everett 1934–35, pp. 170–1. This apparently dates to c.1300.

[113] The analysis of roof timbers in the west range provides a felling date c.1513–30. Information from Mr Francis Kelly of English Heritage.

[114] Wood 1994, pp. 269–71; Luxford 2002(e), fig. 39 (Muchelney); Vivian-Neal 1959–60, p. 75 (Cannington); Ridsdale 1884–85, p. 128 (Evesham).

Other conventual architecture

Other classes of conventual building survive in greater or lesser numbers, depending on their adaptability. The only cloisters remaining are those at Gloucester (Plate 13) and Worcester, the former substantially (if not wholly) of the fourteenth century, the latter mostly of the fifteenth.[115] A cloister walk of the late fifteenth century, un-vaulted, also survives at Muchelney, while significant traces are visible, or have been excavated, at Glastonbury, Malmesbury, Milton, Sherborne and Tewkesbury. There are no complete post-1300 chapter houses, although as mentioned, an arched doorway stands at Evesham, the east end of Gloucester's was updated during the later fifteenth century, and the external cladding and window tracery of Worcester's Norman chapter house is of the period c.1386–92.[116] Dormitories, with the exception of the modest building at Polsloe which served both prioress and nuns, and the fragments at Sherborne, are also wanting. Refectories and more exclusive dining halls (Exeter St Nicholas, Worcester), guest houses (Cerne, Kington St Michael, Exeter St Nicholas, Sherborne, Winchester), almonries (Evesham), libraries (Gloucester, Worcester), reredorters (Leominster, Malmesbury),[117] infirmary chapels (Tavistock), dovecotes (Dunster), well-houses and lavatoria (Dunster, Gloucester, Sherborne) are, however, all represented by later medieval survivals. There are sections of precinctual wall at Cowick, Evesham, Polsloe, Shaftesbury, Tavistock and Winchester. A relatively common survival is the conventual gateway. Tavistock retains three, the main (Perpendicular) gates of Hyde abbey, Great Malvern and Worcester (the Edgar Tower) still stand, albeit variously restored, while other gates remain at Dunster, Glastonbury, Gloucester, Tewkesbury, and Winchester. There are also surviving fragments of the main gate at Abbotsbury. Some of these gates (e.g. Gloucester, Worcester) incorporate twelfth- and thirteenth-century elements. The great foregate at Evesham, called in the seventeenth century 'as large and stately as any . . . in England', has been converted into a house (that immediately north of the almonry), and is now unrecognizable as a conventual gateway.[118] From the same abbey survives the magnificent Perpendicular campanile-cum-gate-tower, raised on the eve of the Dissolution (Plate 14).[119]

Surviving forinsec architecture

Surviving forinsec Benedictine buildings have usually been heavily renovated. Parish churches and chapels partially (and occasionally entirely) constructed at monastic expense are numerous, although deciding where rectorial and parochial contributions start and finish is an inexact science, as in most cases the only evidence of division of responsibilities lies in the fabrics themselves. Churches such as St Benignus at Glastonbury, St Peter at Winchcombe, St Lawrence at Evesham, and the chancel of St Peter at Northleach (Gloucs.) are substantially of monastic patronage. The latter (its

---

115 The east walk was begun c.1385. The south and north walks date to 1404–8 and 1421–28 respectively, while the west walk was underway in 1435/6: Engel 2000, p. 27.

116 Harvey 1957, p. 24.

117 The most complete surviving reredorter is at Muchelney. It dates from the later thirteenth century.

118 Cox 1980, p. 4. Cf. CAEve., pp. 191–2.

119 McAleer 2001, pp. 67–9.

tithes impropriate to St Peter's, Gloucester) displays crozier-heads at the entrance to its chancel (north and south walls) which declare not only ownership but also the concomitant responsibility to build and embellish which is too generally and too often said to have been ignored by corporate rectors. St Catherine's chapel above Abbotsbury, built during the later fourteenth century, is the best-preserved example of a monastic extra-precinctual ecclesiastical building.[120] The reasonable survival rate for manor houses, not surprising given the assimilation (at the wealthier monasteries) of Benedictine living standards to those of the gentry during the later middle ages, demonstrates less about these standards than one may wish, for most have been thoroughly renovated. The residences of Glastonbury at Meare (Som.), Gloucester at Frocester (Gloucs.) and Prinknash (Gloucs.), Pershore at Broadway (Worcs.) and Tavistock at Morwell (Dev.), along with a number of others, may still be recognized for what they were.[121] Others, Glastonbury's Mells (Som.) for example, are unrecognizable beneath post-medieval accretions.[122] At Meare there also exists a stone fish-house of the fourteenth century, where the abbot of Glastonbury's fisherman lived, and in which his catches were processed.[123] Such utilitarian buildings normally survive only where their form allowed them to be easily converted; thus, the early fourteenth-century priest's house at Muchelney and the impressive fifteenth-century Pilgrims' Inn at Glastonbury still stand.[124] Bradford-on-Avon and Tisbury (both Wilts.) have substantial remains of large granges formerly belonging to the nuns of Shaftesbury that were rebuilt during the fourteenth and fifteenth centuries.[125] These are rare survivals, however; of mills, stables, dovecotes and bridges, so often mentioned in *compoti*, chronicles and inquisitions *post mortem*, there is little (there are dovecots at Frocester and Leonard Stanley, and monastic stables at Winchester). No town houses built for superiors survive (the Exeter house of the abbot of Tavistock, 'de novo reaedificatum' in 1481, was destroyed in 1942),[126] and other urban monastic properties, of which there were once many (institutions such as Bath and Gloucester were the largest landlords of their respective towns) have with rare exceptions (e.g. the Talbot Inn at Mells (Som.), built c.1470 as a house)[127] been rebuilt or destroyed. The proudest and in terms of condition most authentic forinsec Benedictine buildings surviving are the stone corn barns that dot the West Country.[128] The architecture of some is not particularly distinguished (e.g. Barrow Gurney, Dunster, Muchelney, Leonard Stanley, Polsloe, Sherborne (porches only), and West Pennard (Som.)). However, that of others, such as Shaftesbury's fourteenth-century barn at Bradford-on-Avon (Wilts.) and its colossal fifteenth-century barn at

[120] *RCHM Dorset* 1952, pp. 3–4; Hutchins *Dorset*, II, pp. 721–2; Newman & Pevsner 1972, p. 72.
[121] Meare, Prinknash and Morwell will come up again in chapter three. On Broadway see Platt 1976, p. 193. Regarding Frocester Court, now extensively renovated, see Price 1980, pp. 75–8.
[122] Pevsner 1958(a), p. 226.
[123] Gray 1926(a), p. xli.
[124] Glastonbury's 'Tribunal' was secular: Dunning 1991, p. 92. Nevertheless, its window-glass contained the arms of abbots, founders and benefactors of the abbey: Collinson 1791, II, p. 263; Woodforde 1946, p. 94. See Pantin 1957, pp. 121–4 on the Muchelney priest's house.
[125] Platt 1969, pp. 190–1, 240–2; Pevsner and Cherry 1975, pp. 137, 523; Dufty 1947, pp. 168–9.
[126] The abbot of Tavistock's house in Exeter is mentioned by Oliver 1846, p. 93.
[127] See Dunning 2001, colour pl. 16.
[128] Beacham 1987, the finding-list for barns (not all for tithe corn) for Gloucestershire, Somerset and Worcestershire, demonstrates how difficult it is to be certain concerning the date and original patrons of many fragmentary survivals.

Tisbury (also Wilts.), Gloucester's at Frocester (c.1300), the 272 foot long barn at Abbotsbury (c.1400), the now-truncated barn at Cerne, and the Glastonbury barns at Glastonbury, Pilton (Som.), and Doulting (Som.), is significant, in terms of structure, symbolism and space.[129] In terms of the latter alone, it is worth noting that Abbotsbury's is the longest medieval barn in England, while that at Tisbury is the largest in area.[130]

Sepulchral monuments and micro-architecture

Not surprisingly, works of micro-architecture and art survive best in church buildings, museums and libraries. Where micro-architecture is concerned, the greatest monuments are the stone-cage chantry chapels at Bath (one), Gloucester (two: Plate 10), Great Malvern (one), Tewkesbury (three: Plate 4), Winchester (five, all episcopal) and Worcester (one: Plate 5).[131] Outstanding free-standing canopied tombs survive at Tewkesbury (four: Plate 15), Gloucester (two), and Dunster (one), and there are effigies on chests at Gloucester, Malmesbury, Pershore, Tewkesbury and Worcester, some of which may once have been covered by canopies or testers. Important wall monuments exist at Dunster, Romsey, Tewkesbury, and Worcester. Of other sepulchral furniture there is relatively little outside excavated fragments. Whole later medieval effigies excavated on Benedictine sites are rare, but the single examples at Wherwell (now in parish church) and Muchelney hint at what may have been. Incised gravestones from conventual churches survive at Dunster (two), Romsey, Tewkesbury and Tywardreath, but brasses are wanting. Milton has a minor monastic brass, to which may be added fragments such as those excavated at Glastonbury and existing beneath Wykeham's chapel at Winchester; but the lack is practically total.[132] There are, however, numerous indents which at least adumbrate the lost richness. These include three important pre-1350 examples, at Askerswell (Dor.) and Whitchurch Canonicorum (Dor.) (a double 'Camoys'-style indent with two foliated crosses and an individually lettered Lombardic inscription commemorating Thomas and Eleanor de Luda, formerly at Abbotsbury, c.1320), Milton (figure with the same style of inscription commemorating either Abbot Walter of Corfe or Walter of Sydling, also Camoys-style, c.1315) and Tewkesbury (figure beneath elaborate canopy, of Maud de Burgh, with four saints and a Coronation of the Virgin over, c.1320).[133] At Winchester there is a large indent, of the late fourteenth or the fifteenth century, of a mitred figure to the west of the site of St Swithun's shrine in the retrochoir, which is important as a documented example. It is almost

---

129   The Glastonbury barns are thoroughly discussed by Bond & Weller 1991. On the Frocester barn, burnt and restored during the early sixteenth century, see Rigold 1965, pp. 209–11.

130   Pevsner and Cherry 1975, p. 523.

131   These are noted in Cook 1947, pp. 89–93 (Winchester), 96–7 (Worcester), 142–4 (Gloucester and Tewkesbury), 146 (Bath); VCH Worcester, IV, p. 130; Leedy 1980, p. 170 (Great Malvern). On the chapels of Prince Arthur (Worcester) and Bishop Fox (Winchester), however, see respectively McClure 1912; Smith 1988(a), passim; Smith 1988(b), pp. 192–232.

132   The minor Milton brass is discussed in chapter four.

133   For the De Luda indent, see Binski 1987, p. 80; Blair 1987, pp. 145, 147, 185–6; and below, p. 183. The Milton casement, whose inscription reads simply 'Abba Waltere', is usually ascribed to Walter of Sydling (1291–1314): e.g. Blair 1987, p. 186; cf. Binski 1987, pp. 92, 94. On the Tewkesbury indent see Rogers 1987, p. 26; Binski 1987, pp. 77–8; Blair 1987, p. 189.

certainly the 'tumba unis episcopi' close to the shrine repaired at a cost of 10 shillings by the *custos operum* in 1532–33;[134] for the other tombs nearby are of bishops who were well known (i.e. Beaufort and Waynflete). The entry in the *compotus* suggests that it had a canopy or railings.

Screens and woodwork

The only monumental transversal screens that survive are Malmesbury and Milton, the first incomplete[135] and the second an eighteenth-century assemblage of fragments of the original. The rood screen at Totnes (c.1460) is outstanding – George Gilbert Scott called it 'one of the finest [screens] in the world'[136] – but is essentially an enriched version in stone of the wooden screens for which Devon parish churches are renowned. Dunster also retains its late medieval timber rood and aisle screens (c.1498), as do (in part) Monk Sherborne and Pilton. Abbot Middleton's hall at Milton has a massive oak screen (dated 1498), pierced by three doorways and topped off by incongruous Gothick arches. Besides these, most of the larger churches retain parclose screens of stone and/or wood, some of them (e.g. Bishop Langton's chapel at Winchester, and screens at Gloucester, Malmesbury, Tewkesbury, and Worcester) fine. Presbytery screens survive at Gloucester and Winchester. Both churches also retain their medieval choir stalls – Winchester has a complete set of Lady chapel stalls of the early sixteenth century as well[137] – as do Great Malvern, Little Malvern, Milton (much restored),[138] Tewkesbury,[139] and Sherborne, the latter an incomplete set, but with sculpted misericords. The stalls of c.1430–50 at St Peter's church in Hereford may come from St Guthlac's priory in the same town, although this is apparently incapable of proof.[140] Winchester and Gloucester (Plate 16) have, moreover, important sets of misericords, and their stalls carry medieval canopies (Plates 3, 10).[141] Worcester also has an important series of thirty-seven fourteenth-century misericords, now reset in Victorian stalls. The fourteenth-century abbatial 'throne' from Evesham (now in the almonry heritage centre) does not seem to be choir furniture.[142] Other timber seating, of the early sixteenth century, survives at Winchester (south transept) and Totnes (what is possibly the prior's throne, in the chancel), while Kingweston (Som.; parish church) and Wells (bishop's palace) hold chairs or parts thereof made for Glastonbury monks, including Richard Whiting, the last abbot (1525–39).[143] Of pulpits, there are examples at Cranborne, Glastonbury (St Benignus; much-restored), Long Sutton (Som.), St Mary's

134 CRWin., p. 219.
135 On Malmesbury's screen see Brakspear 1913, p. 422 and pl. LVI; Hope 1917, p. 98.
136 Gibbs 1904–05, p. 118.
137 On the Winchester Lady chapel stalls see Tracy 1993(b), *passim*.
138 See Long 1922(b), pp. 28–9.
139 Tewkesbury's (incomplete) stalls, mentioned in Tracy 1987, p. 25 note 1 (where they are dated c.1340–44) and Morris 2003(b), 139–41, have never been thoroughly studied.
140 Warren n.d., p. 7. RCHM Hereford, I, p. 122 does not mention this tradition.
141 Only forty-six of Gloucester's fifty-eight misericords are medieval. All are ill. in Farley 1990, *passim*. On the stalls see Tracy 1987, pp. 44–8.
142 Originally, perhaps, from Worcester: see CAEve., p. 302; MA, II, p. 7 note a. The arms of Evesham on the back are manifestly a later addition.
143 For another Glastonbury chair see Horne 1943–46, pp. 19–21; Carley 1996, p. 78. Only the Kingweston chair's back panel can date to Whiting's period.

at Meare, Milton (now at Winterborne Whitechurch (Dor.)), St Catherine (Som.), and Totnes. Stone preaching lecterns from Evesham, Gloucester and Pershore also survive.[144]

Non-sepulchral sculpture

Of non-sepulchral sculpture there are a great many examples, mostly fragmentary. Vault bosses and corbels aside, only minor relief sculpture, such as the *Annunciation* of the Winchester screen and the survivals on the reredos of Abbot Butler's chapel at Gloucester, remains *in situ*.[145] Larger pieces carved in the round, such as the headless seated figure on Bishop Fox's chantry chapel at Winchester and the St James Major at Milton, have been re-established in unauthentic contexts.[146] The quality of these survivals differs: the Winchester Madonna of the later fifteenth century was for Lawrence Stone 'one of the major achievements of medieval art',[147] and the head of a bishop-saint belonging to the same ensemble 'one of the most sensitive pieces of late medieval art in northern Europe' for Phillip Lindley.[148] Although broken and weathered, the archivolt figures at Evesham are also clearly of high quality. The Milton St James (probably early fifteenth century), however, is more workmanlike, and there is plenty of lesser merit than this. Bath (west front: Plates 12, 17), and Gloucester (south nave aisle) have monumental external sculpture, and Worcester has a large surviving ensemble of internal sculpture on Prince Arthur's chantry chapel (Plate 5). There is a sizeable collection of fragments for Glastonbury, too.[149] Well-preserved programmes of roof-bosses survive, the best being those of Worcester (cloister), Tewkesbury (nave), Winchester (nave aisles, Lady chapel, and particularly, the presbytery), Gloucester (presbytery) and Sherborne (presbytery, nave): other bosses survive in monastic-sponsored parish churches. *Ex situ*, the fullest collection is that now in the lapidary collection at Winchester, while Shaftesbury, Sherborne, Tewkesbury (Plate 18) and Worcester hold significant assemblages of fragments, some retaining much of their medieval polychromy. Those of Tewkesbury will receive more attention in chapter six.

Stained and painted glass

West Country Benedictine houses hold three of England's most important later medieval collections of stained glass. In addition to that of Gloucester (presbytery (Plate 10), Lady chapel) and Tewkesbury (presbytery), alluded to above, Great Malvern is well known for its ensemble of fifteenth- and early sixteenth-century (Plate 8) glass, although not all that survived the Dissolution and Reformation has come down to us.[150] This also holds true for Little Malvern, whose east window retains only a fraction of

---

144 Little or no documentation exists for these furnishings.
145 Lindley 1993(b), p. 797 and ill. 2 (Winchester); Luxford 2002(e), fig. 109 (Gloucester).
146 See Stone 1972, p. 225; Smith 1988(a), p. 28; Jones and Traskey 1997, p. 10. For the Winchester Madonna see now Deacon and Lindley 2001, p. 64.
147 Stone 1972, p. 225. Surely too enthusiastic a judgement.
148 Lindley 1989, p. 612.
149 See *AoC*, p. 323 (many are pre-fourteenth century); Stratford 1983, *passim*.
150 Rushforth 1936, *passim*; Marks 1973–74, pp. 199–202.

what the seventeenth-century antiquary Habington saw there.[151] Otherwise, Winchester preserves components of two late medieval programmes by Flemish glaziers (heavily restored), and there are interesting remains at (among other things) Abbotsbury (parish church), Barrow Gurney (in Barrow Court), Deerhurst, Sherborne, Muchelney (parish church) and Melcombe Bingham (from Milton). Heraldic glass (including *arma Christi*) of Benedictine provenance survives at Beer Hackett (Dor.),[152] Glastonbury (St John the Baptist),[153] High Ham (parish church), Milton, Muchelney (parish church), Pancrasweek (Dev.; from Muchelney),[154] and Shaftesbury (parish church). At St Catherine (Plate 19) and Holloway (both Som.) are survivals that will be discussed in chapter four. There are fragments of domestic glass at Gloucester (from Prinknash Park),[155] Milton (abbot's hall), Muchelney (abbot's house) and Winchester (prior's hall). From Glastonbury come lozenge-shaped leaden ventilating panels that qualify as works of art in their own right.[156]

Panel and wall painting

There is considerably less by way of panel painting. The most important examples (historically, if not artistically) remaining are the monumental panels representing the Twelve Apostles at Hilton, brought from Milton at the Dissolution, and the Romsey retable, also a monumental work. Both date to the early sixteenth century, and neither is complete in its current condition.[157] At Gloucester, the panelling on the north side of the choir stalls has a fourteenth-century *Reynard the Fox* sequence remarkable for its quality and narrative length (it is the most extensive English *Reynard* sequence outside manuscript painting), if not for its condition.[158] Above this are painted two large figures of saints (Margaret of Antioch and Antony the Hermit) of the fifteenth century: their quality leaves more to be desired.[159] There is a second fragmentary work at Romsey, representing a kneeling cleric,[160] and single panels at Milton of King Æthelstan (founder: Plate 20) and his mother Queen Egwynna (buried in the church): both of these have been truncated and subjected to repainting. The Milton examples may have come originally from the choir stalls. Otherwise remarkably little survives, a situation probably reflecting the national taste for altarpieces and private devotional images in alabaster as much as the thoroughness of iconoclasm. Surviving wall paintings are almost as scarce. The Miracles of the Virgin episodes of the early sixteenth century in

---

[151] Habington, II, pp. 190–2; *Gothic*, p. 176 and pl. 19.

[152] The arms of Sherborne abbey (Beer Hacket's corporate rector) in the porch were originally in the east window: Long 1922(a), p. 50.

[153] Some of it from elsewhere: Woodforde 1946, pp. 45, 110.

[154] Woodforde 1946, p. 51.

[155] Welander 1985, pp. 53–5.

[156] See Woodforde 1946, p. 278.

[157] Originally, there were six additional saints (Bartholomew, Benedict, Martin, Nicholas, Sampson and the Virgin Mary) from Milton at Hilton: Hutchins *Dorset*, IV, pp. 357–8; Lee 1908, p. 115. The Romsey retable once had two upper registers showing the Nine Orders of Angels and God the Father or the Trinity: Anon. 1829, p. 584; Green 1933, p. 307.

[158] Rouse and Varty 1976, *passim*; Welander 1991, pls 13, 14.

[159] Rouse and Varty 1976, p. 106 and pl. IX. The paintings are now very faint.

[160] This possibly belonged to a gild based in the parish church (i.e. the north nave aisle), however: Walker 1999, pp. 33–5.

Winchester's Lady chapel are easily the most important (Plate 21).[161] There is an interesting representation of the Throne of Grace Trinity with supplicants, Resurrection of Christ and Coronation of the Virgin in the Trinity chapel at Tewkesbury (c.1400), and some chancel wall paintings in parish churches (e.g. Cerne, a John the Baptist cycle) that may have been executed at monastic expense. In the south transept at Winchester and the chancels of Leonard Stanley and Monk Sherborne there are remains of important fourteenth-century paintings (a sequence involving Benedictine monks, two founders, and angels respectively).[162] Former monastic domestic buildings at Gloucester also retain traces of fifteenth-century iconographic mural painting (a Throne of Grace Trinity and shield-bearing seraph).[163] Much that the county antiquaries describe has subsequently been lost. John Hutchins recorded an Annunciation on the north side of the choir at Milton and a 'history of the seven charities and seven deadly sins' in the south transept, the merest traces of which are visible today.[164] Positively, however, Benedictine wall paintings continue to turn up: several late medieval examples have come to light in the past two decades in Winchester cathedral.[165]

Manuscript decoration

The work of West Country provenance that best epitomizes later medieval Benedictine *mores* and aspirations is the Sherborne missal, illuminated by the Dominican John Siferwas and his workshop (Plates 6, 7). It is also the most complex work of art (not architecture) relevant to this study, and overshadows all other manuscript survivals. A Glastonbury manuscript decorated more modestly by Siferwas also exists.[166] The Hyde abbey breviary is exceptionally important for liturgists and art historians alike, and the section of the book of offices given in 1493 to Kington St Michael (c.1300–10) contains miniatures of exceptional quality. The artistically outstanding components of the latter manuscripts were apparently not produced in the West Country, however;[167] and the same may be said of the border-work in the Gloucester *Polychronicon* now at Oxford, which is likely to be an East Anglian product.[168] Otherwise, there is a series of lesser illustrated manuscripts; two books of hours from Gloucester and one from Shaftesbury, psalters from Evesham, Hyde, Nunnaminster, Shaftesbury, and Wherwell (Plate 22), and a fifteenth-century miscellaneous book from Glastonbury with significant

---

161 BL MS Additional 29943, fols 19r–22r; James & Tristram 1928–29, pp. 13–35 and pls XXI–XXIII; Park and Welford 1993, pp. 133–5.

162 For the Leonard Stanley paintings, now whitewashed over, see Tristram 1955, p. 251. Monk Sherborne's paintings (north wall) are possibly fifteenth century: *VCH Hampshire & I.W.*, IV, p. 238.

163 See Welander 1991, pp. 510–11.

164 Hutchins *Dorset*, IV, pp. 355, 357; Long 1928(b), p. 193.

165 See Park and Welford 1993.

166 TCC MS B 3 7, Stephen Langton's commentary on the Pentateuch. It contains one historiated initial (fol. 1r) and two inhabited borders (fols 1r, 8r). See Scott 1996, I, p. 54; James 1900–02, I, pp. 106–7.

167 The Hyde breviary's (OBL Raw liturg e1) Queen Mary psalter-style miniatures are post-medieval additions: Sandler, II, p. 72; Pächt & Alexander 1966–73, III, p. 50. The miniatures of CUL MS Dd 8 2 are too close to those of the Tickhill psalter's first master to originate from the West Country: Sandler 1986, II, pp. 34–5.

168 Dennison and Rogers 2002, pp. 89–90, 93–4.

miniatures by the 'Oriel Master' (Plate 23).[169] A Winchester *Golden Legend* of the early fourteenth century has a good Last Judgement miniature (Plate 24),[170] another *Golden Legend* of a century later from the same house has significant red, white and blue initials with grotesques,[171] and a *Gesta Pontificum* from Sherborne includes a distinctive initial containing the Virgin and Child, with supplicating Benedictine monk.[172] From Tewkesbury comes a remarkable pair of manuscripts (a roll with fifty-three miniatures and armorials of exceptional quality plus the so-called 'Founders' Book' of c.1500–10) commemorating the founders and benefactors of the abbey, works that will receive further attention below. Another roll from Evesham has a world map, as does the Gloucester *Polychronicon*.[173] The main subject of the Evesham roll is a series of genealogies (including the succession of the monastery's superiors from St Ecgwine), dating to c.1450 and including 'portraits' of prominent individuals past and present.[174] Discounting those with flourishing only, there are at least fifty other manuscripts containing minor decoration of art historical interest. As mentioned, these include cartularies and other utilitarian books, as well as liturgical and devotional manuscripts. A number are mentioned in the coming pages.

Textiles, tiles, seals and other objects

Examples of embroidery that can be tied down to particular Benedictine houses are almost non-existent. The church of St John the Baptist at Glastonbury retains a chasuble said to have belonged to the last abbot of Glastonbury,[175] and there is a fragmentary cope preserved at Winchcombe. A late fifteenth-century cope from Othery (Som.) displaying the Assumption of the Virgin, now at Glastonbury abbey museum, may also be of Benedictine patronage, and the sixteenth-century cope embellished with fourteenth-century figures at Minsterworth (Gloucs.) is said to have come from Gloucester at the Dissolution.[176] Excellent encaustic tile pavements, or sections thereof, remain at Gloucester, Great Malvern (approximately 1300 tiles, 100 designs),[177] Shaftesbury, Tewkesbury, Winchester and Worcester. Muchelney parish church has iconographic encaustic tiles excavated on the site of the abbey presbytery. Digs at Evesham (fifty-nine designs), Malmesbury, Tavistock and Glastonbury (over 100 designs) have also yielded many tiles, while lesser quantities exist for nearly all houses. Later medieval bells survive from Worcester, Gloucester, Malmesbury, Milton,

---

[169] Excepting the Shaftesbury hours (aforementioned), these manuscripts are discussed in due course.

[170] CUL MS Gg 2 18, fol. 1r (discussed chapter four).

[171] TCC MS B 15 1, fols iv verso, 1r, 138r, 165r, 169r, 219v, 243v, 288r.

[172] TCC MS R 7 13, fol. 123r. Folios 1r and 58r also have fine illuminated borders and initials. See Luxford 2002(c), pp. 287, 292 note 16; Luxford 2002(e), fig. 130.

[173] The Evesham world map is LCA muniment 18/19, sixth membrane, dorse: *Gothic*, p. 146. The Gloucester example is OCCC MS 89, fol. 13v.

[174] *HCE*, p. 59 and pl. XLI.

[175] Carley 1996, p. 78.

[176] Glastonbury abbey was corporate rector of Othery, but this does not prove a Benedictine provenance for the cope. See Luxford 2002(e), fig. 133. The Minsterworth cope (Verey 1970, I, p. 299), which appears incomplete, has long been ascribed to Gloucester (e.g. *Catalogue Exhibits 1883*, p. 87), but this cannot be confirmed.

[177] Molyneux and McGregor 1997, pp. 7–8, 11, 14, 17–18, 21–2, illustrate and discuss forty-nine individual designs. See also *Gothic*, p. 363.

Sherborne (a sacring bell, c.1350) and Winchcombe.[178] Seal impressions exist for most houses, although it seems unlikely that the number of impressions of personal and special jurisdictional seals remaining represents a large percentage of the original total. The iconography of some (e.g. the common seals in use at Evesham (Plate 25), Milton and Pilton (Plate 26) during the later middle ages) is sophisticated and highly suggestive, and as such will receive further attention below. Finally, there is a flotsam and jetsam of objects which, in their rarity (e.g. the organ chamber at Malmesbury;[179] the sacrament tabernacles at Milton (c.1500) and Tewkesbury;[180] the dorter lantern from Evesham now in the almonry museum) or their incompleteness (the fifteenth-century font step from Milton), epitomize the vicissitudes to which all things Benedictine have been subjected, and the insubstantial nature of the ground on which historians of the order's art and architecture stand: the tip of a lost iceberg.

178 Two Winchcombe bells are now at Stoneleigh (Warwickshire): Witts 1882–83(a), p. 59. On Gloucester's bells see Witts 1882–3(a), pp. 62–7; Witts 1882–3(b), passim; Thurlow 1979, pp. 5–7.
179 On its function, see Brakspear 1913, pp. 422, 424; Hope 1917, p. 98.
180 RCHM Dorset 1970, p. 188 and pl. 167 (Milton). Tewkesbury's tabernacle is mounted on a bracket on the north wall of the chancel.

PART II

PRECEPT AND PRACTICE:
INTERNAL PATRONAGE IN FOCUS

The following three chapters discuss the internal patronage of Benedictine architecture and art, beginning with an examination of historical context. This will analyze the conditions necessary for the existence of internal patronage and consider the main ways in which these conditions were fulfilled in light of the challenges facing the Benedictine order during its last 240 years. A systematic review of the historical factors which influenced monastic patronage has not been attempted in published scholarship, yet it is of obvious importance for a balanced understanding of what was, after all, a fundamentally economic activity. Prefacing this review is a brief consideration of the Benedictine concept of art and architectural patronage, which is necessary in order to explain why some of the conventional assumptions concerning monastic patronage are being set aside here. As noted in the general introduction, it is also relevant, before embarking on the broader study, to examine what may be said about the Benedictine view of the phenomenon with which this book is concerned.

Chapter three discusses the patronage of Benedictine superiors, the ways in which their profiles as patrons have been exaggerated by monastic chroniclers (and also by subsequent scholarship), the reasons they had for buying art and commissioning architecture, and the classes of objects which can be safely ascribed to their munificence. Chapter four considers obedientiaries and cloister monks and nuns as patrons, dividing their patronage into 'official' and 'unofficial' activity, depending on its function and the capacity in which it was exercised. Superiors, obedientiaries and cloister monks and nuns represent the three basic classes (for classes they had become by the later middle ages) into which the monastic personnel of most houses were divided. Of course, this is a simplification of a complex and fluid set of vocational and social relationships: for one thing, a distinction between novices, juniors and seniors, all represented among the 'cloisterer' class, should be acknowledged as one that has received recent scholarly attention.[1] Barrie Dobson has justifiably called cathedral priories (three of which come into this study; Bath, Winchester and Worcester) 'the most formidably complex institutions [existing in] late medieval England', and the larger monasteries examined here

---

[1] See e.g. Clark 2002(b).

were no less complicated in their organization.[2] Each house possessed its own internal hierarchy which fluctuated over time according to financial pressures, changes in numbers of monks or nuns, in temporal and spiritual responsibilities etc.; a fact thrown into ever sharper relief by the increasing scholarly concern with the personalities not only of particular monastic communities, but also of individual religious.[3] However, in the current context, this can be but heeded, for apart from the fact that resources do not exist for the construction of more than a handful of individual patronage portraits (e.g. the Worcester monks William More and John Lyndsey), cataloging isolated instances of patronage demonstrates little of substance concerning Benedictine approaches to art and architecture generally. In a broad-based study such as this, the old truism that the parts may be noted but the whole must be observed holds good.

[2] Dobson 1990, p. 151.
[3] See e.g. *BRECP*; *HRH*; Thomson 2001.

2

The Historical Context of Internal Patronage

The Benedictine Concept of Patronage

Isolating the threads of both internal and external patronage as they actually existed – the sort of thing that Sir Richard Southern called 'the poor old facts'[1] – from the tangle which the combination of post-Dissolution destruction and monastic invention has created is part and parcel of this study. However, it should be acknowledged that the Benedictines had their own ideas about art and architectural patronage, which come through strongly in their historiography. An act of patronage – at any rate, a major one – had for them a symbolic importance and utilitarian value over and above its mundane status as a social and financial transaction. On the one hand, it had an explicitly religious significance that was both generic, in the sense that all objects of patronage were effectively oblations to the one God, and particular, insofar as they pertained to the patron saint(s) of particular houses. The formula of donation (for instance) 'to God and St Ecgwine' expresses this. On the other hand, it provided an opportunity to enhance the reputation of a given monastery, and the Benedictine order as a whole (a reciprocal benefit), first and foremost by association with high-status individuals. This is perhaps the main reason underlying a phenomenon to be discussed further in chapter three, i.e. the willingness of Benedictine convents to ascribe communally funded works to superiors alone.[2] Even when kings, queens and princes had ceased to participate in extensive programmes of monastic building and embellishment, the head of a wealthy house remained a prestigious personality whose generosity was worth boasting about.[3]

The construction or renovation (whether partial or complete) of a monastery and its decoration with ornamental and utilitarian works of art was important, and worth publicizing, for other reasons. It endowed monks or nuns with a physical and spiritual home in which the monastic vocation could be realized, and affirmed the popularity and strength supporting both themselves and their order. When the building and embellishment had occurred long in the past, it acquired additional significance as a proof of the

---

1 GRA, II, p. vi.
2 The other main reason was rooted in St Benedict's Rule: the superior, as *pater* or *mater familias* (on the latter see *RBFox*, pp. 89–94), was theoretically responsible for everything that occurred in the monastery he or she governed. This was acknowledged and respected; hence Matthew Paris's *ob reverentiam* statement.
3 The lists of items attributed to superiors' patronage in later medieval chronicles, often savouring of greater concern for quantity than quality, are reasonably and perhaps best understood holistically, as collective statements of the munificence of heads of houses. Taken together, they compare with the great acts of refoundation etc. of individuals past.

community's antiquity. Such an important task was not to be ascribed to a gaggle of obedientiaries and lay benefactors with the support of a superior, even though this is probably how most major projects of building and embellishment were accomplished. Rather, it was to be attributed to a single individual (or, as at Tewkesbury, a coalition of patrons) of powerful or holy estate, association with whom would carry the maximum prestige possible.[4] These were the great patrons, typically kings and saints, who loomed so large in the mental landscape of Benedictine monasticism during the later middle ages, but who had by then virtually ceased to exist. In their memory were countless armorials displayed, retrospective tombs built, effigies installed in windows and historical epitomes penned during the two and a half centuries before the Dissolution.

It must be said that, as a rule, there is no reliable evidence for the sweeping acts of patronage ascribed to these individuals. Even the patrons themselves may be spurious: the colourful figures of the Mercian 'dukes' Oddo and Doddo with which the Founders' Book of Tewkesbury opens, for example (Plate 27).[5] In fact, the whole great patron class is decidedly nebulous. As suggested above, the actual responsibility for works of construction and embellishment is likely to have lain with a complex of individuals, just as it did during the later middle ages. Great benefactors founded monasteries, gave them lands, privileges, and other gifts, thus endowing communities with the means to build. The process is illustrated with great clarity on the reverse of Evesham's common seal (engraved after 1274, in use 1538), where in the lower register three kings of the Golden Age (Coenred and Æthelred of Mercia, Offa of the East Saxons) present a sealed charter of liberties to Bishop Ecgwine (d.717), while above, the charter appears transmuted into a sumptuous church, which Ecgwine hands on to the Virgin and Child (Plate 25).[6] However, this is not quite what is meant by art and architectural patronage.[7] It would obviously be wrong to deny to founders patron-status altogether (apart from anything else, there will have been many grants of timber and stone), although the true nature of their contributions is almost always obscure.[8] It is their role as patrons to the exclusion of others that is usually questionable. That monks and nuns sought to include their founders and important benefactors in the building histories of their houses (as Matthew Paris did so effectively with King Offa of Mercia) is understandable,[9] for a charter of foundation without the physical presence of buildings, litur-

---

4   A point perfectly illustrated with reference to the East Anglian houses of Bury St Edmunds and St Benet-at-Holm. Both claimed King Cnut (d.1035) as first founder, although less illustrious individuals seem to have been responsible: Gransden 1985, pp. 11–12 (Bury), 18 (Holm).

5   OBL Top Glouc d 2, fol. 8v. On the actual Mercian *earls* Odda and Dudda, see Blunt 1898, pp. 16–17, 23–4; Basset 1997, p. 12; Heighway 2003, pp. 5–6.

6   See Birch 1887, pp. 546–7 (no. 3113); Williams 1993–98, II, pp. 30–1.

7   A distinction between foundation and actual construction is important here. *Facta* and *constructio* are used in medieval sources to denote foundation alone: e.g. UANG, p. 164; BL MS Stowe 1047, fol. 126r (*facta*); TCC MS R. 5. 33, fol. 20v; OBL MS Gough Essex 1, fols 13r–14v; *Mem.Bury*, III, p. 150 (*constructio*).

8   'Founder' here refers to a monastery's tutelary patron. First founders – what Leland called 'very original founderes' (*Itinerary*, IV, p. 22) – will be described as such. On the term generally see Holdsworth 1991, p. 5; Thompson 1994, p. 104.

9   Matthew Paris depicts Offa, king of Mercia (d.796), personally directing construction in the role of founder and builder of St Albans: Lowe, Jacob and James 1924, p. 33. In fact, the evidence for Offa's involvement at any level at St Albans hangs by a thread: see Crick 2001, pp. 82–3 *et passim*.

gical vessels, stained glass and statuary was a hollow document indeed.[10] A physical monument, or a publicly displayed picture or description of such a monument, established a particularly powerful link between a founder or great benefactor and a monastery, backing up the documents contained in cartularies in a way that could be accessed and understood by all who saw (or heard) it. In the figural arts this link is rendered explicit in the ubiquitous practice of representing founders and benefactors holding model churches. Gloucester (fourteenth-century stained glass now in the Lady chapel and sixteenth-century effigy of 'King' Osric: Plate 28), Leonard Stanley (fourteenth-century wall paintings), Milton (fifteenth-century panel painting: Plate 20), Muchelney (fifteenth-century statue), Shaftesbury (sculptural fragment in the abbey museum), Tewkesbury (the Founders' Book: Plate 27) and a number of other houses have later medieval iconography of this kind, and it need not be doubted that it once existed at most, perhaps all, of the houses covered by this study.[11]

The *Capella argentea* supposedly built by Ine, king of Wessex (d. *c.*726), at Glastonbury exemplifies this concern to link great founders and benefactors with the physical construction of monasteries. The matter has been part of Benedictine lore well-nigh continuously from William of Malmesbury's day to this: Clement Reyner cited it in the early seventeenth century, and one finds it discussed in the most recent histories of monasticism.[12] The dedication and liturgical function of this chapel (i.e. its *raison d'être*) are ignored in the surviving descriptions of it, and it is thus particularly interesting as evidence of monastic concern with patronage, art and architecture specifically. It is also, of course, a self-consciously ostentatious display of wealth, albeit wealth past (but then, the past was where Glastonbury stored up much of its treasure). Charter evidence and historical accounts demonstrate that during the later middle ages, association with Ine was exceptionally important for religious houses in what had been the kingdom of Wessex.[13] The description of the silver chapel thus recommended itself as the perfect act of patronage by the perfect patron – John of Glastonbury's 'gloriosus rex'.[14] Ine, promoted as Glastonbury's fourth founder, was said to have extensively rebuilt the abbey church, and to have annexed to it a remarkable chapel 'constructed . . . of gold and silver, with ornaments and vessels of the same materials'.[15] The latter included images of Christ, the Virgin Mary, and the Twelve Apostles, together cast from 175 pounds of silver and twenty-eight pounds of gold. All of the chapel vestments, along with its altar-frontal, were interwoven with gold and precious stones. The chapel itself was constructed of 2,640 pounds of silver, and contained an altar made of 264 pounds of gold: a true mansion of Paradise, founded upon the holiest ground in England. Glastonbury's monks not only had a comprehensive description of this astonishing act of largesse

---

10 For a post-1300 e.g. (Austin Friars, Sherborne), see Fowler 1951, p. 188.

11 See Rushforth 1921, p. 217 (Gloucester Lady chapel); Tristram 1955, p. 251 (Leonard Stanley); *RCHM Dorset* 1970, p. 188 (Milton). The Muchelney statue and Shaftesbury fragment are unpublished.

12 Reyner 1626, p. 44; Dunning 2001, p. 79 (the latter, like the current author, is sceptical). Descriptions of the silver chapel all derive from William of Malmesbury: *DA*, pp. 96–9. For an explicitly similar, obviously fantastic, example given by William, see *GRA*, I, pp. 284–7; II, p. 157.

13 On the charter evidence, see Davidson 1884, *passim*; Finberg 1953, p. 123; Abrams 1991, *passim*. Non-monastic houses, outstandingly Wells cathedral (see *Ecclesiastical Docs*, pp. 11–14), also sought association with Ine.

14 CGA(C), p. 18. John also styled Ine a *post mortem* miracle-worker (p. 104).

15 'Construere . . . ex auro et argento cum ornamentis et vasis similiter aureis et argenteis.'

inserted into their fourteenth-century domestic chronicle, but they also advertised it at length on a *tabula* set up in their church c.1400 for the edification of visitors.[16]

There remains no independent evidence for the existence of the silver chapel, and it would be unprofitable to look for it. Of most interest here is what the preservation and public promotion of the tradition tells us about the Benedictine concept of major art and architectural patronage. Clearly, such generosity ranked among the most important events of a house's history, constituting as it did a joint gift to God and community which underscored both the sanctity of Benedictinism and the esteem in which that sanctity was regarded by the rich and powerful. It was an incitement to potential patrons, an invocation to them to follow an illustrious lead and give generously (in whatever kind).[17] It was also an opportunity to demonstrate the sagacity and holiness of a celebrated benefactor with the dual aim of garnering him or her commemoration and, as mentioned above, enhancing the house's reputation. Thus did Alfred the Great build the remarkable cross in square-plan church of Athelney (more appropriate to Byzantium than the Wessex marshes) and Bishop Walkelin, leading an army of carpenters, cut down all the trees of Hampage Wood in just four days for the reconstruction of Winchester. Thus did Abbot Serlo rebuild the conventual church of Gloucester from its foundations in only eleven years, King Cnut plumb the royal treasury for the sumptuous shrine of St Edith at Wilton, and King Eadred bestow an altar and a cross fashioned of gold upon the monks of St Swithun's – his especial beloved.[18] Thus did the great patrons continually.

By 1300, however, the great patron class (whatever its actual historical status) was clearly a thing of the past.[19] Legal, financial and other constraints on the aristocracy had increased to the extent that foundation and rebuilding on anything other than a modest scale were beyond the ability of all but the most powerful. Fashions in religious endowment had also changed; as discussed in chapter five, friaries and parish churches were now the object of many would-be patrons. Excepting the aberrant Upholland (Lancs.), no Benedictine houses were founded in England at all after the death of Henry III.[20] There were Benedictine rebuildings of course, but these (with the possible exception of Tewkesbury) were substantially of communal patronage. Being accomplished within living memory, they were not credibly attributable to anyone more prestigious than superiors, who themselves suffered a collective reduction in prestige during the later middle ages commensurate with the loss of Benedictine hegemony over the religious affinities of the public.[21] The fourteenth century also saw the aforementioned decline in

[16] CGA(C), pp. 94–7; *Mag.Tab.*, p. 518; MA, I, p. 23.

[17] Matthew Paris's manuscript with Offa depicted as builder of St Albans was shown to Henry VI in 1441: Lowe, Jacob and James 1924, p. 15; Clark 2001, p. 222. Here is the principle in action.

[18] For Alfred's patronage see GP, p. 199; HKW, II, p. 12. Alfred was also credited with founding the University of Oxford ('as trewe story telleth wel': CV, p. 19; also TCC R 7 13, fol. 30r; MMBL, III, p. 358 etc.), an example which puts much of the 'great patron' tradition into proper perspective. For Walkelin's patronage (partially royal patronage, as Hampage was a royal wood) see *Annales*, II, pp. 34–5. See also HMGlouc., I, pp. 10–11 (Serlo); CV, pp. 95, 98 (Cnut); L.Hyda, p. 151 (Eadred).

[19] Henry V's patronage of Sheen and Syon was quite exceptional: see below, p. 152.

[20] See the tables in Tanner 1787, pp. vi–viii; MA, IV, pp. 409–12 (Upholland). Augustinian Spinney (Cambs.) became dependent upon Ely, and thus Benedictine, in 1449 (K&H, p. 77), but this was not a refoundation. Excepting Syon and five charterhouses, no houses of monks, nuns or canons were founded in England after 1377. On Bisham (Berkshire), an exceptional case, see below, p. 211.

[21] For the reduction in monastic superiors' political importance, see chapter six. This reduction in importance coincides with the decline in new foundations.

the Benedictine historiographical tradition. As the order became increasingly retrospective, the copying and collation of older histories took precedence over the drafting of
new ones, and these traditional authorities (and the uses to which they were put), as the
public display of King Ine's generosity suggests, are the most significant gauge of later
medieval Benedictine attitudes to patronage. The post-1300 identification with the
pre-1100 Benedictine Golden Age, which may be likened in certain respects to the
Renaissance longing for classical antiquity, embraced art and architecture as readily as
anything else. This illustrious past was to be 'aestheticized' in a manner commensurate
with the heroism of its patrons.

Benedictine attitudes to the more modest acts of art and architectural patronage that
were forthcoming throughout the later middle ages are harder to recover. Such acts
rarely rate a mention in the older chronicles: to record the gift of an item of plate or a
vestment alongside King Edgar's foundation/reconstruction of forty-seven monasteries
or King Æthelstan's gift of twenty-six towns to the city of Exeter might have seemed
trivial, and in any case, memory of small benefactions was not preserved unless the giver
had been particularly important. A suggestion of Benedictine attitudes is found,
however, in the aesthetic language used in chronicles and occasionally in other sources.
The Founders' Book of Tewkesbury may speak for all here, for there is nothing unusual
in the rhetoric of its writer. Moreover, the monuments he describes survive (albeit
without most of their paint and statuary), and this breathes a life into his words which
ordinarily is missing. The chantry chapel of Robert Fitzhamon, built in 1397 (Plate 4,
left), was 'satis mirifice tabulatam'; that built for Edward Despenser (d.1375) by his wife
'ex lapidibus arte mirifice constructam', and that of Richard Beauchamp (d.1422)
'pulchram capellam arte mirifice fabricatam' (Plate 4, right). The tomb of Hugh
Despenser III (d.1349) was, moreover, 'satis praeclara' (Plate 15).[22] In other sources,
such terms as *decenter* (with or without the qualification *valde*), *pretiosus* (with or
without *satis*), *magni pretii*, *sumptuosus*, *splendidus* (often in conjunction with *ornatus*), *de
opere speciosissimo*, *perpulchram*, *pulcherrima*, *de sumptibus depinxerunt* and so on are
commonly found.[23]

There is, of course, nothing especially Benedictine nor particularly later medieval
about such terminology. Ancient authorities had used it – Julius Caesar wrote of a 'turris
mirificis operibus exstructa' (in the *Bellum Civile*, a copy of which existed at Bath in the
1530s) – and what was good enough for classical authorities was usually good enough for
medieval writers in Latin, regardless of the cut of their cloth.[24] More than information
concerning attitudes to patronage, such usage conveys the stylization of aesthetic
language so notable in the gleanings of Otto Lehmann-Brockhaus.[25] It does, however,
demonstrate appreciation of art for more than its utilitarian and symbolic values, which
in turn implies an attitude to art patronage which differed from that of, say, financial or
real estate patronage. A gift of art or architecture, even a minor one, was in a mean-

22 OBL Top Glouc d 2, fols 14r, 25r, 28r, 23r.
23 Some of these terms apply to value as well as appearance, of course. These two things were inti-
    mately if not always consistently related in Benedictine minds.
24 *Bellum Civile*, III:12. For Bath's copy see *Shorter Catalogues*, p. 18.
25 *LSK, passim*. Aesthetic language of the period bears profitable comparison with the contemporary
    terminology of decay (the *imo funditus dirutam* used of Bath, mentioned below, is entirely typical)
    everywhere found in petitions for tax breaks, parish church appropriations, legal suits etc. One
    could further extend this to the later medieval rhetoric of praise and blame.

ingful sense special (if not necessarily more esteemed than other sorts of gifts). The enthusiasm conveyed by adjectives in the superlative degree (*pulcherrima, pretiosissima* etc.) evinces appreciation which it is reasonable to suppose extended to donors. In a small house such as Tywardreath, such appreciation might be enough to get a patron enrolled as a confrater. During the fifteenth century, Robert Pedder and his wife received this honour at the price of four service books, John Nyvet for a set of vestments and a silver chalice.[26] This is not surprising, for such gifts were of relatively high value to a small, cash-strapped monastery, and must have added considerably to its ornamentation.[27] Proportionately, John Baker's generosity towards Kington St Michael mentioned in chapter one stands alongside the silver chapel of Ine, for by the end of the middle ages, the nuns of Kington subsisted on an annual income totalling approximately three quarters of one per cent of Glastonbury's.[28] The discrepancy which existed between the two conventual churches in terms of art and architectural embellishment was no doubt of commensurate order.

Finally, the fact that Benedictines might distinguish carefully between different modes of patronage should be recognized. One of the cartularies of Bath contains a list recording items given to the monks by their bishop and titular abbot Robert Burnell which will serve as an example.[29] Burnell died in 1292, but the list is of the fourteenth century, and may thus be cited here. It includes objects such as a frontal with the Annunciation and a cope with the Tree of Jesse that he gave ('dedit'), plate and vestments he bequeathed ('legavit') and items he obtained for ('procuravit') the priory. These last include sumptuous vestments embroidered with imagery and the arms of England and Spain ('Hispaniae') from the chapel of Eleanor of Castile (Burnell had been one of the queen's executors), of which Bath's monks were no doubt very proud.[30] This precision, a typical instance of Benedictine tidy-mindedness – 'eny thynge withoute discrete ordre may not long contynew ne endure', as the last abbot of Gloucester wrote[31] – displays a less idealized facet of Benedictine conceptions of patronage than that which is usual in monastic historiography. The 'poor old facts' were not lost on the Benedictines, but neither were they always what mattered most.

Challenges to Conventual Prosperity

Broadly stated, the main conditions necessary for the existence of internal patronage during the later middle ages were sustained financial prosperity at an institutional level and a relaxation of official strictures concerning ownership of private property and communal living arrangements at an individual one. Of course, these conditions were not unique to the later middle ages, and although the means needed to fulfil them differed slightly from house to house, the main strategies remained constant: legal action

[26] Oliver 1846, p. 37. See under 9 August and 7 December respectively.
[27] See for example the 1338 inventory of Tywardreath's property: Oliver 1846, pp. 34–5.
[28] Around 1535, Kington's annual income was estimated at £25, Glastonbury's at £3311 (see below, appendix 1).
[29] *Cart.Bath*, pp. 156–8; *LSK*, I, pp. 63–4.
[30] 'Unam casulam decenter ornatum, cum vestimento cum targiis regis Angliae et Hispaniae, et unum amictum de secta cum alio amicto brendato de ymaginibus valde decenter consutis'.
[31] *HMGlouc.*, III, p. lxxxv.

(usually but not always defensive) and the appropriation of parish churches on the one hand, and appeals to the broad scope for abbatial discretion built into the *Rule* of St Benedict on the other.[32] However, a number of more or less novel factors combined with local pressures to make the period from 1300 until the Dissolution one in which the maintenance of prosperity and individual freedom became more challenging and complicated than had previously been the case. These included the effects of the Statute of Mortmain, competition for public support from other religious institutions, the Black Death and subsequent epidemics, inflation (a factor during the early Tudor era), and a series of papal, metropolitical and royal attempts to reform Benedictine monasticism to the exclusion of personal property. Most of the chief income-sapping factors are epitomized in petitions to appropriate parish churches, of which the three following examples are entirely typical. In 1314, Great Malvern cited poor relief, hospitality charges, war, papal fees, and 'extortion by secular princes'; in 1334/5 Hyde pleaded all of these plus bad harvests, livestock murrain, litigation and royal taxation; while in 1379, Winchcombe embellished the litany with the recent pestilence, reduced rents and services arising there from, and the demands of corrodians.[33] Here are the economic constraints with which the internal patronage of art and architecture had to compete – more or less – in a nutshell.

Mortmain

The statute *De viris religiosis* (Mortmain), published in 1279 and augmented by six subsequent parliamentary statutes, is often cited as a major turning point in the fortunes of English monasticism.[34] Certainly, aggressive campaigns of land acquisition by wealthy Benedictine houses such as Glastonbury were to some degree its immediate catalyst.[35] In fact, however, Mortmain only exacerbated an already extant trend which, since the proclamation of Henry III against selling or alienating land to religious houses (1228), had seen the capacity of Benedictine communities to acquire new real estate-derived revenues diminished.[36] At a popular level, the clause *exceptis religiosis et judæis* was finding its way into an increasing number of testaments relating to real estate bequests as time progressed.[37] More broadly, the trend embraced the loss of Benedictine hegemony in the provision of spiritual services to the laity. The number of institutions vying for benefaction increased exponentially between 1200 and 1300, as did the variety of 'spiritual services' on offer, and the Benedictines were forced to promote themselves with renewed vigour in order to compete. Their competitive strategies are discussed in chapter five; for the moment, the effects of the Statute of Mortmain and the ways in which these were mitigated are the focus. In fact, these effects are rather difficult to isolate from those which other pressures exerted on Benedictine prosperity. Occasionally they can be gauged at a local level, where communities purchased the licences

---

32 See in particular *RB*, chapters II, LIV.
33 *Lib.Albus*, p. 42; *Cart.Winch.*, p. 176; Haigh 1950, p. 135.
34 On Mortmain, see the work of Sandra Raban: Raban 1974; Raban 1982. The statutes augmenting that of 1279 are listed by Tanner 1787, p. vi note a. The major one was 15 Rich. II, *cap.* 5: Raban 1974, p. 16.
35 See Postan 1975, p. 181; Raban 1974, p. 4.
36 On this proclamation see Raban 1982, pp. 16–17.
37 Kennett 1818, II, glossary, under *religiosi* (unpaginated).

necessary to amortize parcels of land, as at Evesham during Roger Yatton's abbacy (1379–1418);[38] or where royal action is recorded against a house for accepting lands not legally alienated, as at Athelney and Winchcombe in the fourteenth century and Barrow Gurney in the fifteenth.[39] Moreover, that the imposition of Mortmain was considered a significant and negative event is demonstrated by the notice it receives in monastic chronicles.[40] However, in the main the evidence is negative, and the most that can be said is that the heavy fines payable under this statute for authorization to alienate lands to ecclesiastical uses are likely to have caused many would-be benefactors to think again.[41] Thus, the acquisition of new income-generating properties needed to offset the loss of old ones through legal challenges, and to finance rising living-costs, became an unreliable prospect for Benedictine houses throughout England.

Overwhelmingly, the answer was sought in the appropriation of ever more parish church revenues.[42] Fifteen per cent of all parish churches across England had their greater tithes appropriated between 1291 and 1535, the vast majority of them by religious houses.[43] Episcopal registers contain hundreds of examples relative to the abbeys and priories covered by this study, and monastic chroniclers (always expert at making virtues of necessities) reckoned churches successfully appropriated among the most laudable of abbatial achievements.[44] The fact that the rectorships and revenues of so many churches were granted to prosperous Benedictine houses during the later middle ages illustrates both the centrality of this form of revenue-raising in the maintenance of their prosperity and the relative ease with which the requisite royal and episcopal permission could be obtained.[45]

Litigation[46]

Litigation by a range of individuals and corporations seeking to annex monastic property presented another serious challenge to the prosperity of many Benedictine houses during the later middle ages. Neighbouring landlords and the heirs of benefactors

---

[38] CAEve., p. 306.

[39] Hugo 1897, p. 123 (Athelney); Landboc, I, p. xxxiii (Winchcombe); Hugo 1863–64, pp. 75–6 (Barrow Gurney).

[40] For example, HMGlouc., I, p. 33; see also CAEve., p. 306.

[41] A Mortmain licence typically cost several times the annual value of the land alienated, although the system was liable to Crown experimentation. The alienating party also paid for an assessment of the land's value. See Raban 1974, pp. 18–20; Raban 1982, pp. 29–71; Wood-Legh 1934, pp. 62–5.

[42] Although advowsons of parish churches came under Mortmain, the appropriation of the greater tithe, which made of the appropriator rector as well as tutelary patron of institutions to the cure, did not. A monastery appropriating the major tithe would often hold the advowson already.

[43] On Benedictine appropriations see Elliott 1986, p. 21. By 1535, thirty-seven per cent (or c.3900) of England's parish churches had been appropriated, overwhelmingly by religious houses. In 1291–92, the figure had been only about twenty-two per cent: Knowles 1955, p. 291; cf. Harper-Bill 1996(b), p. 95, where lower estimates are preferred. See also Elliott 1986, p. 23.

[44] E.g. HMGlouc., I, pp. 49, 56; CAEve., pp. 290–1; CGA(C), pp. 264–5.

[45] The chief grounds for any grant of appropriation were indigence and dilapidation. However, even wealthy monasteries usually experienced few difficulties in the matter. Papal sanction could always be solicited if a bishop declined: Wood-Legh 1934, pp. 127–8. For an e.g. of episcopal refusal based on wealth see Reg.Swinfield, p. 433.

[46] Knowles 1948, pp. 322–3, estimated that almost sixty per cent of Christ Church Canterbury's income went on taxation and litigation combined between 1285 and 1318 (Henry of Eastry's priorate). This is by no means an extraordinary figure.

seeking to contest endowments were the most vociferous parties, and accordingly, reconfirmations of past gifts were eagerly sought and copied into cartularies. Pershore claimed to have lost twenty-seven manors to litigation since its foundation, and Great Malvern also suffered 'devastation of property'.[47] Glastonbury considered itself and its lands in a state of perpetual siege throughout the later middle ages, while the Evesham chronicler repeatedly mentions the heavy burden that litigation placed on his house.[48] The writer responsible for recasting the *Chronicon Vilodunense* (c.1420), who selected only the most immediate issues for his moralizing cameos, colourfully represents the Benedictine case.[49] One Bryxyn, cousin of a nun of Wilton, 'dyd to ʒat abbay gret ouʒtrage/ For a parcell of londe he toke away'. He died contumacious and went to hell for his crime, whither his tortured spirit arose to frighten his relatives into making restitution (a reversal of the usual process of endowment and reclamation that the Second Statute of Westminster so cooly facilitated).[50] However, just recompense brought Bryxyn no relief; he remains in hell 'for ev'more', and the author reminds readers that this will be the fate of all who so behave.[51]

As the same author laments elsewhere, however, men no longer fear divine retribution for such crimes, an assertion amply endorsed by circumstances.[52] The old, appalling anathemas seem to have been useless by the later middle ages: the world had moved on.[53] Where *timor Dei* was lacking, demonstration of legal proprietary rights was essential, and Benedictine convents throughout the west thus set about copying old cartularies and compiling new ones, fabricating records of endowment where original charters were wanting, and retaining secular lawyers.[54] University monks, too, took degrees in canon law, acquiring skills which must often have been useful to their communities in litigious circumstances.[55] Books of current parliamentary statutes and civil law were also purchased for Benedictine libraries, demonstrating widespread concern with keeping abreast of changing legal rights and obligations. Gloucester's abbot John de Gammages (d.1306) is said to have purchased a volume of 'Constitutiones Domini Regis Edwardi', while at the other end of the period Prior

---

[47] Pershore's chief bugbear was another Benedictine house, Westminster: *Cart.Beau.*, p. xvii; *VCH Worcester*, II, p. 129. On Great Malvern, see *Lib.Albus*, p. 138.

[48] CGA(C), pp. 8–9, cf. pp. 182–5. Professor Carley calls John of Glastonbury's claims against the bishops of Bath and Wells 'almost paranoid': CGA(C), p. 272 note 8. Regarding Evesham, see CAEve., pp. 309–10, for an exemplary case (early fifteenth century).

[49] Cf. *Chapters*, II, p. 54, for a more prosaic Benedictine assessment of the situation.

[50] CV, pp. 110–14 (quote at 110). Among Edward I's Second Statute of Westminster (1285) was a clause permitting heirs to reclaim possessions alienated to religious institutions if the grantees misapplied them. What constituted misapplication was no doubt hotly contested: Pantin 1955, pp. 126–7; Platt 1984, p. 98.

[51] 'For Goddus mercy passeth all þe gode werk þt he dude wyrche/ Bot depe dampnacyon God he byhetuth all ʒo/ þt by revy [i.e. take away] the ony possession from holy chirch': CV, p. 113.

[52] CV, p. 139.

[53] The traditional Benedictine anathema was not dead post-1300, however. For a wonderful later fifteenth-century example from Deerhurst see James and Jenkins 1930–32, p. 188.

[54] For fabricated records pertaining to the real estate of West Country Benedictine houses, see e.g. *Cart.Bath*, p. xxxiv; Graham 1927, p. 60.

[55] On monastic lawyers generally see Coulton 1936, p. 40. Note, however, that only between five and ten per cent of Benedictines ever went to university: Pantin 1929, p. 208. Moreover, while the study of canon law was popular among the monks of some houses (e.g. Ely, where half of the monks with first degrees took them in law) those of others (e.g. Worcester) studied it little or not at all: Greatrex 1999, pp. 322–3.

William More gave a 'little bucke of þᵉ statutes of yngland' together with a 'bucke of þᵉ late statutes' to the monks of Worcester in 1519.[56] In 1533, More provided a 'greate bucke of statutes of yngland from þᵉ furst yere of Edward the thyrd till þᵉ parliament holden after Cristmas in þᵉ xxv yere of kyng henry þᵉ Eyght', lest his previous purchases prove inadequate.[57] During the fourteenth century, Abbot Walter de Monington of Glastonbury and Prior John of Worcester of Evesham both purchased volumes of civil law for their communities.[58] In a general sense, the legal rights of monasteries were also reinforced by the promotion of founder cults (e.g. Sts Coenwulf and Kenelm at Winchcombe, St Wulsin at Sherborne, Sts Ecgwine and Odulf at Evesham) and the production, display and dissemination of chronicles advertising venerable origins, and describing the ancient gifting of contested lands. After all of this, however, some monasteries still found it expedient to cut their losses and pay large sums to be rid of drawn-out, expensive and morale-sapping litigation. The abbot and convent of Malmesbury, for example, paid Edward III £500 just to ensure that a case concerning former Despenser lands (which had already been tried with a favourable verdict for the abbey) was not raised again.[59]

Chronic debt and taxation

Royal exactions, hospitality charges and inflation all took their toll on Benedictine prosperity during the later middle ages, reducing the capacity of convents to commission, contribute to and purchase works of art and architecture. Between 1388 and 1463, the income of Pershore's obedientiaries fell by one fifth, mirroring circumstances elsewhere in the West Country.[60] Other convents got themselves into serious debt, and chroniclers were not slow to praise superiors who pulled their houses back into the black.[61] Not all did so successfully, however, and debt often became chronic. The list of Athelney's fifty-seven debtors, and the abbot's undertakings to Thomas Cromwell in the matter of restitution, make pathetic reading, and things were clearly little better at Bath and Muchelney by the 1530s.[62] Certainly, care is required when interpreting the effects of this apparent reduction in disposable income on patronage. The monks of Bath and Muchelney were both involved in large-scale building campaigns during the period of their greatest financial embarrassment, and among Athelney's debtors one 'John goldyssmythe' of Taunton appears. On the whole, however, there is little doubt that pressures on the economies of most Benedictine houses during the later middle ages did place restrictions on internal patronage of art and architecture. During the fourteenth century, financial crises obviated (or so it was claimed) routine repairs at both Hyde and Nunnaminster.[63] Under such conditions, new building and embellishment were clearly out of the question.

---

[56] HMGlouc., I, p. 40; Shorter Catalogues, pp. 672–3.
[57] Jnl.More, p. 335.
[58] Shorter Catalogues, p. 133; cf. pp. 146 (Evesham), 224–8 (Glastonbury).
[59] Luce 1979, p. 48.
[60] CRPer., p. 21.
[61] For e.g. HMGlouc., I, pp. 39, 57; CAEve., p. 339; CGA(C), pp. 250–1.
[62] Archbold 1892, pp. 29–33; Hugo 1897, pp. 151–5 (Athelney); Archbold 1892, pp. 34–5 (Bath), 69 (Muchelney).
[63] VCH Hampshire & I.W., II, p. 123; Cart.Winch., p. 176.

As founder of all independent Benedictine houses of the West except Tewkesbury, the king was entitled to demand a range of fees, taxes and services from each. That he exercised these entitlements freely has become all but proverbial. 'Our abbeys and our priories shall pay this expedition's charge', Shakespeare has King John declare; but he might just as appropriately have put the same words into the mouth of any English monarch from Edward I to Henry VIII.[64] Royal expeditions affected all houses, even those usually exempt from taxation due to poverty,[65] and the rejoicing described by the Gloucester chronicler when tenths were waived in 1378 was no doubt symptomatic of the drop in living standards they must have occasioned.[66] Such payments were, however, irregular (which is not to say uncommon). The relentless annual tax of scutage, paid in lieu of the knight service for which all tenants holding in chief were liable, was the greatest blight, and was much resented by the ancient foundations, which in the pre-Conquest Golden Age had held their lands in frankalmoign. Scutage was calculated according to the quantity of land held rather than the income that land generated. It was thus crippling for monasteries holding large and inefficiently exploited estates – Tavistock, for example, whose annual scutage consumed the income of twelve of its manors.[67] The other major royal exactions were occasional, but still a severe drain on the monastic purse. During voidances in superiorships, the king was entitled not only to annex the abbot or abbesses' income, but also to exact a heavy fee for rubber-stamping the convent's choice of successor (as was the pope).[68] Wealthy houses paid vast sums for the privilege of retaining the abbatial *mensa* during voidances, and regarded gaining this right as a hard-won victory, while for his part the king considered it an act of abnormal royal generosity.[69] Parliaments and routine (if increasingly occasional) royal visits typically cost a great deal. The monks of Glastonbury spent £800 on the brief royal sojourn of 1331, a fact worthy of record in their chronicle.[70] While less formal visits such as the 'gistes pour les chaces du roy' at Milton, Shaftesbury and Wilton recorded on the flyleaf of a fifteenth-century French *Brut* chronicle will have been cheaper, they must still have stung, prestige notwithstanding.[71] A raft of other royal charges also spasmodically blighted the collective Benedictine purse, the last being appointed portions of the £200,000 fine imposed generally on the churches of the convocation of Canterbury after prosecution under the praemunire statutes in 1531. This cost each house according to its means: thus Gloucester, with a net annual income of £1430, paid £500, while Evesham, whose income was £1183, paid 500 marks.[72] Finally, the right of feudal overlords to

---

64 *The Life and Death of King John*, Act I, line 48.
65 For e.g. the nuns of Barrow Gurney (income c.1535, £24 p.a.) had to pay Henry VI 2d in 1445 'against the Saracens and Turks': Hugo 1863–64, p. 82.
66 *HMGlouc.*, I, p. 54.
67 Finberg 1951, pp. 227–8.
68 In 1354, the monks of Evesham obtained papal rights to free abbatial election. This was estimated to save at least £500 on each occasion: *CAEve.*, p. 297. Episcopal charges were also incurred at a new abbot's confirmation. Oliver 1846, p. ix, gives a breakdown of these (totalling c.£32) for Exeter diocese.
69 E.g. CGA(C), pp. 262–3; cf. *CFR*, IV, pp. 123–4.
70 CGA(C), pp. 262–3.
71 TCC MS R 7 14, fol. 148v. Partially printed by James 1900–02, II, pp. 229–30. This is a fifteenth-century list, perhaps pertaining to Henry VI, although not corresponding precisely to any part of his known itinerary: cf. Wolffe 1981, p. 367.
72 On the praemunire incurred in 1531, see *Concilia*, III, pp. 746–8. For Gloucester's payment, see MA, I, p. 536; for Evesham's portion, *CAEve.*, p. 340; MA, II, p. 9.

nominate corrodians of their choice effectively constituted another form of royal taxation for the Benedictine houses of the west.[73] Glastonbury supported three royal
corrodians continuously during the later middle ages, two of whom were replaced as they
died, the other nominated whenever there was an abbatial vacancy.[74] This latter
arrangement was paralleled at Malmesbury.[75] At other times the king attempted to institute corrodians at random, a practice strenuously but respectfully – and sometimes
successfully – resisted. The attempt by Edward II to foist Alicia Conan, one of Queen
Isabella's ladies-in-waiting, upon the monks of Worcester, which occupies fifty-one
letters in the *Liber albus* of the priors, was ultimately thrown out of court.[76]

Hospitality and alms

Hospitality charges, for which the Benedictine *Rule* made all houses liable, were
ongoing and heavy throughout the period.[77] Petitions for tax relief and permission to
appropriate parish churches cited them as a matter of form. With characteristic orderli-
ness, Glastonbury set aside the revenues of an entire manor (Domerham, Wilts.) valued
(in 1535) at £139 11s 6d *ob.* exclusively for this purpose, but other houses, such as Bath,
which could hardly afford such a luxury, are likely to have attracted equally large
demands due to their location.[78] Hospitality charges contributed to the dissolution of
some small houses: Ewyas Harold (1359) and Kilpeck (1428), Herefordshire cells of
Gloucester, were both terminated partially for this reason. In the abbot of Gloucester's
words, 'because of the excessive flow of people to its table' Kilpeck in particular was no
longer viable.[79] The enormous quantity of food recorded as consumed in the surviving
Tewkesbury *coquinarius's* roll of 1385/6 – including seventy-three bullocks, 216 sheep,
224 pigs and over 70,000 eggs – bears vivid testimony to the demands made on the
kitchens of larger monasteries.[80] The burden of poor relief (a related issue) was also
unrelenting.[81] The poor came in many guises (travelling poor, naked poor, resident poor
etc.), and most had some claim on monastic alms. By the later middle ages, those
Benedictine houses able to do so institutionalized a given (often symbolic) number of
paupers, providing them with accommodation, a chapel for worship, food and even
livery. Thus, they dispensed with their obligation in a way which might be of maximum
benefit to them. The 'Peterysmen' of Gloucester (established 1516), for example, were
obliged to go abroad in the town displaying the abbey arms on their right shoulders
while ostentatiously bidding their bedes.[82] At Glastonbury a similar arrangement was

[73] Keil 1964(a), pp. 119–31, lists the ninety-six corrodians (royal and otherwise) resident at later
medieval Glastonbury. The total number of corrodians at Benedictine houses declined late in the
middle ages: Knowles 1959, pp. 266–7; Keil 1964(a), pp. 114–15. For Winchester's corrodians see
CRWin., pp. 159–70.
[74] Keil 1964(a), p. 115 note 6.
[75] Luce 1979, p. 47.
[76] See *Lib.Albus*, p. 86.
[77] RB, chapter LIII.
[78] *Collectanea*, p. 14; *Valor*, I, p. 144; *Cart.Bath*, p. xvi. Bath received a continual concourse of visitors,
due to its site on major commercial and pilgrimage routes.
[79] 'Propter excessivum concursum populi ad eorum mensam': Bannister 1902, pp. 64–5. Cf. Heale
2004, pp. 137, 152.
[80] *Kitchener's Roll*, p. 319 *et passim*.
[81] In general see Harvey 1995, pp. 16–23.
[82] GCL Register D, fol. 1v; *HMGlouc.*, III, pp. lxxxiv–lxxxv.

instituted in 1512: here the almswomen – all of them widows – wore black livery embroidered with the arms of Joseph of Arimathea. Their chapel, with some of its stained glass, survives in the abbey precinct.[83] The nuns of Wilton maintained thirteen 'poor Magdalenes', as well as bedesmen supplicating perpetually for the souls of the abbey's founders.[84] The monks of St Swithun's at Winchester, too, maintained twenty-two 'poor sisters', the cost of whose maintenance was calculated from one feast of St Scholastica (10 February) to the next, thus placing emphasis on the female Benedictine component of the alms.[85] Less wealthy houses might still organize poor relief along these lines to some extent, by maintaining greater or lesser numbers of bedesmen and women.[86] While such arrangements were often the catalyst for a measure of building and embellishment, they were a drain on the communal purse which obviated patronage in other areas.

Inflation

The 'ravages' of 'rampant inflation' only really set in during the early sixteenth century, although 'dere yeres' due to crop failures and murrains (e.g. 1315–22, 1371, 1437–40, 1482) were always in the offing.[87] Inflation particularly affected houses that derived their incomes from real estate leasehold, for leases were commonly long-term and at fixed rates, while the price of food (which had to be bought in) was anything but fixed. By the turn of the sixteenth century, Glastonbury operated on an almost wholly rent-based economy, a situation paralleled at most substantial English monasteries.[88] This form of management was dictated by a combination of royal restrictions limiting the methods by which religious houses might exploit their lands (for houses with an annual income of over £533, this extended to the growing of corn for sale at market),[89] and by the small size of their resident communities: direct estate management required (in the generic sense) manpower. In this regard at least, Benedictine finances were a victim of the order's own administrative success.

Epidemics

In addition to these restrictions on the Benedictine capacity to finance art and architecture came the Black Death, the 'secunda pestulentia' of 1360/1 so well remembered at Evesham, and a raft of other epidemics.[90] These continued throughout the later

---

83 Carley 1996, p. 71. On top of this charitable provision, the abbey still parted with approximately £150 per annum in arms during the 1530s: Heale 1997, p. 141.

84 Nightingale 1881, p. 261.

85 CRWin., p. 139. Normally, accounts at Winchester were calculated Michaelmas–Michaelmas.

86 Great Malvern, for example – hardly a wealthy house – had thirty resident poor in 1314: Lib.Albus, p. 138.

87 On inflation in the early Tudor period generally see Lander 1983, pp. 10–11; Harper-Bill 1996(a), pp. 45, 71. The significance of 'dere yeres' we perceive in the accounts of lay chroniclers: see for example Three Chron., pp. 41–2, 46. See also Dyer 1998, p. 265, and (for the 1315–22 crisis particularly) Kershaw 1976, passim.

88 Carley 1996, p. 59; Keil 1961–67(b), p. 183. Obedientiaries still managed Glastonbury's home farm, however.

89 Knowles 1959, p. 249 note 3.

90 See in general Black Death; Harper-Bill, 1996(b); Holt 1985; Fletcher 1922. The Evesham reference is BL MS Cotton Nero D. iii, fol. 222r.

middle ages, and the fifteenth-century *Tractatus pestilencialem* in the Muchelney breviary, the prayer to the Virgin Mary against the plague (*Stella celi extirpavit*) in Elizabeth Shelford's book of hours of the 1520s, and the prominence given Sts Roche and Sebastian on the Romsey retable (also probably 1520s) lend enduring immediacy to a threat especially menacing for enclosed communities.[91] The chroniclers of Evesham and Gloucester do not mention these epidemics, which, particularly in light of the general medieval belief that the Black Death exterminated ninety per cent of England's population, seems nothing short of a conspiracy of silence.[92] Perhaps this was because the epidemics implicated Benedictines in what was generally considered divine retribution.[93] But the devastation was appalling. Athelney (twice), Malmesbury, Muchelney, Pershore, Romsey and Tavistock all lost their superiors, and at Bath, Glastonbury and Winchester, around half of the monks are thought to have died in 1349–50.[94] On monastic estates, as everywhere, the loss of rent-derived income and rising labour costs caused already straitened convents further difficulties, and, as has been noted, the plague became a standard apology in petitions to appropriate parish church revenues (no conspiracy of silence here). While conventual populations did recover to a certain degree, they never regenerated completely, hovering at between sixty-five and seventy-five per cent of c.1320 levels.[95] The implications of this for patronage of art and architecture are clear – a smaller community simply did not need to go on building. Indeed, the cost of repairing superfluous fabric constituted a drain on the conventual purse which seems to have militated against new building and embellishment in certain cases (e.g. Bath, pre-c.1480).[96] 'The shell', as A.G. Dickens observed, 'had become too large for the oyster.'[97]

These represent the main economic constraints on the patronage of art and architecture by Benedictine convents during the later middle ages. Of course, the broader picture was not one of total economic gloom. The measures taken by the Benedictines to mitigate these drains on their wealth included retrenchment (of both religious and servants),[98] advertisement and sale of spiritual services and corrodies (the latter often a false economy), promotion of cults and other attractions designed to draw paying crowds (both considered further in chapter five), sale of real estate and moveable property, constant pleas for exemption from taxes and hospitality obligations, diversification of capital investments (Bath got involved in weaving, Tavistock in tin-mining and

---

91 BL MS Additional 43405, fols vii verso–ix recto (printed in *Much.Mem.*, pp. 8–9; see also Singer and Anderson 1950, pp. 32–3); CFM MS 2–1957, fols 52v–53r (a regular feature in primers). See further the image of St Roche mentioned in *LBRJ*, p. 79.

92 On the ninety per cent estimate see *Black Death*, p. 3.

93 See *Black Death*, *passim*; Fletcher 1922, p. 6. St Albans (GA, II, pp. 369–70; *Black Death*, pp. 252–3) and Cistercian Meaux (see *Black Death*, pp. 67–70), however, were not in denial: we must look to them for an informative gauge of monastic feeling on the matter.

94 Knowles 1955, p. 11. The lists in *HRH* suggest how many superiors died in the epidemics.

95 Harper-Bill 1996(b), p. 98. Glastonbury was, however, successful at keeping numbers up: see e.g. *List Admissions*, pp. 306–15; Carley 1996, p. 49.

96 Luxford 2000, p. 315.

97 Dickens 1972, p. 80.

98 Widespread retrenchment ('discouragement of novices' as Dyer 1998, p. 98, has it, was only part of the strategy) had begun before the Black Death: Dyer 1998, p. 98; Knowles 1955, pp. 8–13; Snape 1926, pp. 21–2. See Brown 1995, p. 33, for an e.g. (Milton, 1344).

printing),[99] and loans, in addition to the appropriation of parish church revenues and legal engagement already mentioned. Such expedients kept the Benedictine ship afloat tolerably well during the last 240 years of its voyage. At any rate, no house actually disappeared due to insolvency, and the large ones with diverse interests remained quite comfortably positioned; although it is important not to be mesmerized by Glastonbury's wealth when making general judgements about the financial health of West Country Benedictinism. Nevertheless, the maintenance of standards (of living, liturgy, prestige etc.) was a continual struggle, and was first and foremost a pragmatic enterprise. The mindset, too, was emphatically pragmatic: one need only study the aspects of monastic life which the chroniclers chose to commemorate to realize this.[100] This is understandable, for (and this is a commonplace) as well as being centres of prayer and commemoration, religious houses were multifarious business enterprises competing in a tough, unstable market-place.[101] It ought not to be supposed that Benedictine attitudes to art and architectural patronage were somehow independent of the same pragmatic concerns: the later medieval cloister had little room for art for its own sake.

Challenges to Individual Autonomy

What has been said so far primarily concerns patronage at the institutional level. Internal patronage on a private, individual basis was subject to other constraints, and it is to a consideration of these that we now turn. In fact, the main barriers – personal poverty, the stern injunctions prohibiting private property written into the Benedictine *Rule* and the requirement to live, eat, sleep, pray, work, and do everything else in common – had been successfully overcome by 1300. That the Benedictines, within the closed ranks of the order, recognized this for the contradiction of official policy that it was is seen in the reforming articles agreed to by the General Chapters of 1343 and 1444.[102] That they were not deeply concerned about it is demonstrated by the ubiquitous flouting of these articles; and that they considered it nobody's business but their own emerges in their defensive responses to external criticisms, particularly those of Henry V.[103] In fact, it is obvious that individual religious did not recognize personal ownership of small items to be the 'execrable and detestable crime' decried by the king.[104] Robert Joseph, monk of Evesham and self-styled 'little Benedict' ('Benedictiaster'), could declare himself devoted to virtue and highly moral while thumbing through his own illustrated Bible,[105] while Alice Champnys, nun of Shaftesbury, had no qualms about recording her private ownership – in rubric – of the

---

99 However, Henry VIII made it illegal for religious to act as middle men in commercial ventures: Knowles 1959, p. 249 note 3.
100 Not simply the chroniclers of the West Country. The Evesham chronicle, however, provides a paradigm of the domestic historiographical tendencies of the age.
101 Cf. Harvey 1995, p. 1.
102 *Chapters*, II, pp. 28–62, 187–220. Part of the function of such injunctions must have been to publicly demonstrate official recognition of a perceived problem, whether or not anything could be done to deal with that problem.
103 *Chapters*, II, pp. 116–34.
104 *Chapters*, II, p. 113: 'proprietas religiosorum execrabile et detestabile scelus [est]'.
105 *LBRJ*, pp. 198 ('Benedictiaster'), 188–9 (devotion to virtue), 213 (elevated morality), 46 (his illustrated Bible).

book of hours into which she also copied private prayers (Plate 1).[106] The informal, touching declaration 'ego sum bonus puer quem deus amat' found (twice) among the accretions to the surviving breviary of Muchelney (a house whose monks slept in beds 'like tabernacles', and kept personal items of 'silly ornamental' furniture) does not strike one as the product of a guilty conscience.[107] A few Benedictines became Carthusians after 1300, but on the whole there is little besides visitation depositions made under duress to indicate internal dissatisfaction with the later medieval Benedictine status quo: and an order-wide status quo it was on the evidence of external criticisms and visitation reports.[108] Conscience, then, was no constraint on personal patronage, regardless of what St Benedict had said about personal property.[109] However, the external attempts to enforce reform at a general level (in themselves an indication of the ubiquity of property owning and other supposedly nefarious practices) were a potential constraint, for all that they were successfully negotiated.

External attempts to enforce personal poverty

Between 1281 and 1284, Archbishop Peckham (d.1292) introduced measures designed to enforce centralized control of finances (the *Regimen scaccarii*) at Benedictine houses throughout the province of Canterbury.[110] This was a direct response to the private and often wayward administration of funds by obedientiaries. From this time on, popes, kings and prelates issued articles of reform at more or less regular intervals.[111] The common assumptions underlying these proposed reforms have never been properly analyzed, but it seems that breaches of Benedictine decorum were embarrassing and worrying to Church and State alike, both of which had vested interests in the popularity of traditional religion. In any case, the criticisms imply a broad-based conception of what ideal

---

106   CFM MS 2–1957, fol. 78r. This prayer is in the same hand as the note of ownership on fol. 132v. Other prayers were added after the book's manufacture (see fols 1v, 9r (a psalm), 10v, 77v), though not certainly by Alice Champnys.

107   BL MS Additional 43406, fols x recto, 330v; cf. *Much.Mem.*, p. 47. The same or a similar inscription occurs in many other monastic manuscripts: e.g. LPL MS 259, fol. 1r; TCC MSS B 5 21, end flyleaf (from Glastonbury); O 2 38, fol. 334r; BL MSS Royal 3 B I, fol. 84r; 11 C III, fol. 249r; Oxford, St John's College MS 1, fol. 121r. While it may have originated as a school mnemonic (cf. the e.g. at *MMBL*, III, p. 639), its widespread use by adults and non-pedagogical, personalized variants such as 'Daniel puer bonus' (LPL MS 377, fol. 166v), 'Iohannes Vyall est bonus filius amen' (Hereford Cathedral Library MS P 1 9, fol. 154r), and 'Thomas Taylor est bonus' (London, Westminster School MS 1, written inside front cover: from Worcester), demonstrate that it was adopted as a devotional saying (cf. the commonly encountered *Ihesus est armor meus*). For the complaints about living arrangements at Muchelney (1335), see Hugo 1858, p. 100; *VCH Somerset*, II, p. 105.

108   For Benedictines who became Carthusians see Rowntree 1981, p. 143. Understanding of this phenomenon may be nuanced with reference to Carthusian letters of confraternity to Benedictines, for which see Clark-Maxwell 1929, p. 208.

109   *RB*, chapter XXXIII: 'It is of the greatest importance that this vice should be totally eradicated from the monastery.' See also chapter XXII.

110   On the *Regimen scaccarii* see Smith 1942. At some houses there were minor common funds comprising unassigned revenues which might go towards building (e.g. Evesham: appendix 2, p. 219).

111   The progenitors of these later medieval reform proposals were the edicts of Innocent III concerning Benedictine reform issued at the Fourth Lateran Council: *EHD*, III, pp. 643–76, particularly 669.

monasticism was; or at least of what it was not.[112] Naturally, nobody expected Benedictine communities to revert to the letter of their rule in all respects, but in certain regards this was advocated. One of these was personal ownership of property, which was, as the reforming rhetoric suggests, widespread. Benedict XII's constitutions of 1336, proclaimed under the decree *Summi magistri* and directed explicitly at the Benedictines (this pope himself had been a Cistercian), unambiguously outlawed it.[113] The English Benedictines acknowledged these edicts, and acted on them at a general level,[114] but they must have proved very difficult if not impossible to implement on the ground. Further papal interest in English Benedictine reform particularly was registered as early as 1238, in a directive aimed at nuns as well as monks.[115] A directive of Urban VI (1378–89), issued shortly before 1385 at the instigation of the former Norwich monk Adam Easton (d.1391), fell victim to skulduggery and never reached its intended audience, although the abbot of Malmesbury for one had a rough idea of its contents.[116] Henry V's articles (1421), which did reach their intended audience, also singled out the Benedictines, as the largest and most influential monastic force in English religion. In article nine, the king mentioned silver cups and spoons, other items (*jocalia*) of gold and silver,[117] and books as objects which individual monks and nuns should be forbidden to possess. Needless to say, this itemization is excellent (if negative) evidence for the widespread ownership of such things.[118] Royal edicts were not to be taken lightly, for the king was founder and feudal overlord, reconfirmer of rights and privileges and the ultimate resort for Benedictine houses in times of trouble. The abbots, sitting in a specially convened General Chapter, reworked the royal edicts tactfully and legalistically, excusing personal property with reference to the discretionary powers that the *Rule* of St Benedict placed in the hands of the superior.[119] Understandably, they saw themselves as masters of their own rule, and they argued accordingly. By the time Wolsey promulgated his criticisms (in 1520 or 1521) the response from the heads – among them highly respected abbots such as Richard Kidderminster of Winchcombe and William Malvern of Gloucester – was a less idealistic (but no less pragmatic) one. The times, they said, were 'unhappy' ('infelici'), and Benedictine monks 'feeble' ('infirmi'): let the order remain as it was or many religious would simply run away.[120] Independently, Kidder-

---

112 The interest in Benedictine reform was not simply a manifestation of the 'alarm' occasioned by the widespread religious 'disunity of the age' (Catto 1985, p. 100), for this disunity was not a pan-European phenomenon. *Summi magistri* was perhaps most influential in countries where there was relatively little religious (i.e. doctrinal) strife (e.g. Italy, Spain; see Lunn 1973, *passim*). However, Henry V's desire for a straighter-kept, more primitive monasticism (and thus a more popular one) may be seen in this light, and also in that of his own desire to 'place the monarchy at the spiritual centre of English life': Catto 1985, p. 110.

113 *Concilia*, II, pp. 585–651, especially 604–5. See also Knowles 1955, pp. 3–5.

114 *Chapters*, II, pp. 230–2; III, pp. 3–11.

115 CM, III, pp. 499–517.

116 HMC XII:ix, pp. 394–5.

117 The word *jocalia* usually refers to plate, but items such as silver rosary beads may possibly be meant here as well.

118 Henry V's injunction reads: 'ciphum argenteum seu coclearia vel alia iocalia aurea vel argentea seu libros': *Chapters*, II, p. 114. D.C. Douglas renders 'libros' as 'illuminated books' (*EHD* (III), p. 789), which seems unjustified.

119 *Chapters*, II, pp. 116–34; regarding property specifically, see 118–19, 123, 132.

120 *Chapters*, III, pp. 123–4; Harper-Bill 1996(a), pp. 102–3. Wolsey's articles to the Benedictines are lost.

minster observed with a mixture of fascination and sorrow that the Benedictine monks of the past 'could live on what seems incredible now'.[121] Wolsey's response (assuming that he made one) is not recorded, but it is clear that his demands were ignored in practice. The ownership of personal property was successfully defended against its most powerful opponents throughout the later middle ages. To unofficial calls for abolition of personal property, such as that contained in Reginald Pecock's mid-fifteenth-century *Reule of Crysten Religioun*, Benedictine convents were not obliged to respond.[122]

The silence of episcopal registers on the subject of private ownership of devotional objects such as painted, drawn, printed or sculpted images, prayer beads and decorated prayer books (e.g. psalters and books of hours) suggests strongly that these were widely tolerated, as part of a monk or nun's personal spiritual armoury. Indeed, Edmund Audley, bishop of Salisbury (1504–24), gave his niece Anne, a nun at Shaftesbury, a delightful little fifteenth-century psalter (of Sarum Use, not that of the nunnery). This contains eight historiated initials, copious gilding, and an inscription of ownership proudly naming the donor as well as the recipient (Plate 29).[123] That private possession of such things existed will be further demonstrated in chapter four: the use and ownership of personal devotional images in continental convents during the later middle ages has received some attention,[124] but the situation in England remains unstudied, and thus the point requires emphasis. Other reasons for lack of episcopal notice may exist, most obviously the fact that for much of the time, bishops had larger fish to fry than minor cases of property owning. There is also the fact that a number of Benedictine houses were exempt from visitation altogether: Evesham, Great Malvern, Malmesbury and (from 1517) Tavistock enjoyed this status.[125] Other houses made much of supposed exemption to deter visitation, or at least to delay it. John of Glastonbury copied a supposed charter of Henry II into his domestic history which included the clause '[the abbey] should be entirely free from all jurisdiction of the bishop of Bath, just as is my own crown', a component of the abbot and convent's claim that their monastery deserved greater freedom than any other ecclesiastical institution in England on account of its status as the realm's *fons et origo religionis*.[126] Many other houses must have wished that they possessed the wherewithal to follow suit. Of course, official visitors knew of the resort to the letter of the Benedictine *Rule* that might be made where property was concerned, and in any case, a humane bishop would recognize a degree of personal ownership endemic to human nature: he might even endorse it outright.[127] Art historians may regret that more was not made of the issue.

---

[121] *Landboc*, II, p. xiv. Cf. CM, V, pp. 243–4: ' "O quam venerabiles extitere priores ac patres nostri preambuli, dum talibus uterentur quæ indicia sunt sanctitatis, religionis, et humilitatis!" ' (etc.)

[122] RCR, pp. 418–19.

[123] LPL MS 3285, measuring 11½ × 7 cm. Illustrations at fols 7r, 42v, 61v, 79v, 95v, 115r, 132r, 150r. An inscription on fol. 191r reads: 'Liber iste pertinet domine Anne Awdeley moniali monasterij Shaston. Ex dono Reuerendi domini domini Edmundi Awdeley sarum episcopi ac Avunculi predicte domine.' (Plate 29.)

[124] See in particular Hamburger 1997.

[125] Tavistock dated its exemption to 1191 (Radford 1932–33, p. 201), but this was not generally recognized. Oliver 1846, pp. 103–4 prints Leo X's bull of exemption for 1517: see also Finberg 1951, p. 236. Evesham's exemption was only finally settled in 1336: VCH Worcester, II, p. 119. Great Malvern's exemption was unofficial but effective: VCH Worcester, II, p. 141.

[126] CGA(C), pp. 176–7; Raban 1982, pp. 105–6.

[127] See e.g. *Linc.Vis.*, I, p. 4.

Means to the end of personal patronage

Just as later medieval Benedictines were allowed to own works of art and other personal items, so also were the means by which they could obtain these things countenanced. Opportunities were not wanting, for practically all religious had multiple channels of contact with the world beyond the cloister. Indeed, in most Benedictine houses up to half the religious were regularly at large in an official capacity, and in any case there were many lay people working, trading and living within the precincts of larger monasteries.[128] Robert Joseph's letters demonstrate how broad a monk's network, in other houses and *in saeculum*, might be. If he was atypical, then this was only in the number of his contacts, not the fact that he had them in the first place. Neither was money a problem. Cloister monks and nuns received regular income – wages, as David Knowles has it – from a number of sources.[129] The *peculium*, in lieu of clothing and other necessities, pittances in cash (rather than food, ale or spices), customary stipends (called *salaria*, *stipendia* or similar) paid by superiors and/or obedientiaries,[130] labour performed in the service of superiors and obedientiaries, and money distributed at funerals and anniversaries could net each individual £5 annually and more.[131] The staff of the smallest priories might be paid in cash: in 1317, the little West Country and Welsh satellites of St Peter's at Gloucester rose of one accord and demanded wages of Abbot Thoky, which were soon forthcoming.[132] Legacies were another source of income, and also of works of art. William of Wykeham bequeathed 100 shillings to Felicity Aas, nun of Romsey (1404); and a monk of Glastonbury, John Benet, received a handsome endowment of plate and other goods by his mother's will (1507). Walter Lucas, citizen of Salisbury, left silver plate to his Benedictine daughter at Wherwell.[133] Moreover, some individuals retained external sources of income after entering the monastery. In a house such as Shaftesbury, among whose nuns practically all the great Dorset and Wiltshire families were represented, such external support is not surprising.[134]

Finally, as a matter in which the Benedictine *Rule* placed discretion in the hands of the superior (in practice, female as well as male), gift-giving was widespread.[135] Robert Joseph received 'a bundle of presents' ('zeniolorum fasciculo') from a fellow monk at

---

128 Durham had a parlour between the chapter house and church door for 'marchannts to utter ther waires' in (*RD*, p. 44), and a public library above the charnel chapel at Worcester was occasionally run by the sacrist of the cathedral priory, on the authority of the bishop: *BRECP*, p. 856 (sole known instance at Worcester); Wilson 1911, p. 7.

129 Knowles 1955, pp. 241–2; for nuns, Power 1922, pp. 322–3. Even the monks of a small priory such as Cowick received 5s per week during the later fifteenth and early sixteenth centuries: Yeo 1987, p. 25. Accordingly, religious could be taxed individually: see Lega-Weekes 1906–07(a), pp. 273–8 (temp. Richard II).

130 See e.g. *Linc.Vis.*, III, p. 301 (1446/7). Stipends paid by obedientiaries are found in most *compoti*. At early sixteenth-century Muchelney, 12½ per cent of the monastery's total income went on stipends: Almond 1903, pp. 11–12.

131 *SMW*(a) and *SMW*(b) are replete with examples of money bequeathed to monks and nuns. An outstanding example is Wykeham's own will: he left five marks to every Winchester monk in orders, and 40s to each not ordained: *Test.Vet.*, p. 768. One is invited to suppose that other superiors made like arrangements.

132 *HMGlouc.*, I, pp. 42–3.

133 *Test.Vet.*, p. 770; *SMW*(b), p. 106; Brown 1995, p. 31.

134 Power 1922, p. 324; Sayers 1990, p. 537; Baskerville 1937, p. 207.

135 *RB*, chapter LIV. For its application to the Benedictine abbess see *Reg.Godstow*, p. lxxxvii (1432).

Oxford,[136] and generally, routine contact with family and friends plus bonds of union between many houses (a tangible reminder of which survives in the heraldry of the nave at Sherborne, the gateway at Cerne and the Sherborne missal) provided ample opportunities for the exchange of more than greetings and prayers.[137] Bequests of works of art, particularly decorated books, must have found their way into the order: those bequeathed by John Baret to monks of Bury St Edmunds will have had their West Country parallels.[138] To all practical extents, the conditions necessary for Benedictine ownership of personal property had been well and truly fulfilled by 1300.

Conclusion

The foregoing discussion covers the salient aspects of the historical context in which the internal patronage of Benedictine art and architecture was set. Ideological constraints have emerged as a major theoretical consideration, and financial constraints as a major practical one. However, it is clear that the latter – like the former – did not always curb the ambitions of convents and their superiors. One of the most remarkable aspects of art and architectural patronage by Benedictines during the later middle ages was their commitment to maintaining it even in the teeth of financial hardship. While, as suggested, houses might be so straitened that they simply could not afford to build and to embellish, lack of sufficient funds was not generally thought an obstacle to pressing ahead with some project or other. The scale on which the conventual church of Milton abbey was conceived following the fire of 1309 illustrates this. The building is full of memorable elements (particularly in the vaulting and window tracery), obviously carefully conceived and achieved at what can only have been great expense. Yet behind these lurk unmistakable signs of economy. The great blank arcades of the presbytery, which minimized the need for moulded stone; the bands of flint showing through the plaster of the interior walls, knapped square to be sure, but nevertheless, not ashlar; and above all, the truncated appearance of the whole, its lack of a nave due not to post-Dissolution destruction but to a patronal concern with building and embellishment that overreached itself. The level to which Milton was reduced post-1309 is considered in the introduction to part three. Here it is sufficient to note that for that house's monks, as for their colleagues elsewhere, art and architecture mattered so much that it was thought worthwhile suffering privation and disruption for. As non-monastic great church building projects suggest, this was true in a general sense, but for monks and nuns, confined for much of their lives within the high walls and among the complex masses and volumes of the claustrum, buildings and their embellishments were of more than usual significance. They were part of what it meant to be Benedictine, and while this is undeniably a truism, it is one which stands reconsideration each time an act of monastic patronage is assessed. It is itself part of the context which has been considered here.

---

136 *LBRJ*, p. 86. For other examples of gift-giving, see pp. 12–13, 37–8, 46–7, 83, 139–40, 204–5, 252–3.
137 For confraternity between West Country houses see e.g. Goodall 1997, p. 190; *Landboc*, II, pp. 548–50; *Brev.Hyde*, V (calendar, unfoliated), under 9, 15 March, 20 April, 22 September, 5 October; OBL MS Bodley 543, fol. 13v (Worcester and Thorney; an 11th-century confraternity re-founded); *VCH Wiltshire*, III, p. 219; Walcott 1866, p. 576 and note 1.
138 *Bury Wills*, pp. 15–16.

3

The Patronage of Superiors

The Superior *sui generis*

Etymology notwithstanding, monasticism as St Benedict and his followers understood it was a communal experience as much as an individual one.[1] That it continued to be regarded as such throughout the middle ages is evident in both Benedictine rhetoric and the expectations of those looking in on the monastic world from without: patrons, testators, critics, supporters and so on. Many surviving aspects of Benedictine art and architecture are metaphors for this corporate identity, conventual churches, chapter houses, cloisters, retrospective founders' tombs, institutional heraldry (every independent house had its coat of arms),[2] common seals, and bells among them. Accordingly, many aspects of monastic art and architectural patronage may be seen as communal, and indeed, are only fully intelligible in this light.

However, it needs to be recognized that monasteries, like all institutions, were only conceptually greater than the sum of their parts. The idea of community as an autonomous entity helped to determine thought, outlook and action, but had no quantifiable existence beyond the constituent members of a given institution at a given point in time. Monastic communities continued across centuries, but ultimately disappeared overnight. Acts of communal patronage were grounded in the body corporate, and the body corporate consisted of individuals whose autonomy was everywhere confirmed in Benedictine monasteries of the later middle ages: in work places, the dorter, the infirmary, and even the cloister.[3] Benedictine art provides paradigms here as well, none sharper than the division of the liturgical choir into so many self-contained stalls, each surmounted by its own elaborate canopy (Plate 10). This arrangement was reflected throughout the church, in reredoses and retables, the sculpted facade, the stained glass windows: the saints themselves set the example, their abode understood as a honeycomb of individual mansions.[4] Benedictine monasticism was a communal phenomenon, but it would be wrong to suppose (as it is frequently supposed) that the individual monk or nun, backed as he/she was by the financial means and official sanction defined above, did not enjoy a meaningful autonomy as well.[5]

---

1 *LDO*, pp. 18–19.
2 See Reyner 1626, pp. 214–16, Tanner 1787, pp. 45–7, and the various entries in *MA* for the shields of the armigerous houses covered by this study.
3 For example, the partitioned carrels in the south cloister walk at Gloucester (Plate 13). On the partitioning of Benedictine dorters see Brakspear 1915–16, pp. 191–2.
4 John 14:2, cf. Summerson 1963, pp. 1–28; Wilson 1990, pp. 130, 168.
5 Later medieval Benedictine habits of dress, too, demonstrate 'the extent to which the common life of the medieval monastery was undermined by the pursuit of individuality': Harvey 1988, p. 29.

The most obviously autonomous monk or nun was the superior. Here, the term 'superior' will refer to the titular head of a Benedictine house, an abbot or abbess, prior or prioress in the case of an independent priory or, where Bath, Winchester and Worcester are concerned, a bishop. Admittedly in the case of the cathedral priories, the principal prior was effective head of house. However, as patrons of art and architecture, priors belong to a separate category: this is discussed at the beginning of chapter four. Moreover, in terms of ultimate authority they were subordinate in most matters to their diocesan. The treatment of John Cantlow, prior of Bath, by Bishop Oliver King discussed below is a strong reminder of this. The superior was the public face of his or her monastery, an authority invested with great spiritual and temporal responsibility: at once shepherd and the wall of the sheepfold.[6] If the illustration of the apotheosized John Islip (abbot of Westminster 1500–32) in his mortuary roll is broadly representative, then he or she was also considered (internally, at least) the seat of conventual virtue, strength, wisdom and piety (Plate 30).[7] Islip is represented within an ornamented arch surrounded by symbolic flowers identified by the following labels: 'fortitudo', 'consilium', 'intellectus', 'sapiencia', 'timor domini', 'sciencia', 'pietas', 'prudencia', 'iusticia', 'temperencia', 'constancia', 'fides', 'spes', and 'caritas'. The chroniclers of Evesham, Glastonbury and Gloucester clearly believed that their abbots also embodied these qualities.

To a large extent, monastic communities were defined with reference to their superiors, in the eyes of both their individual members and the wider world. This is reflected in the arrangement of domestic chronicles (*Gesta abbatum* would in fact be a fitting title for many), and was once manifest in the series of abbatial monuments and figures in paint and glass (a glimpse of which survives in the great east window at Gloucester) that existed at many houses.[8] The autonomy of the superior, defined by St Benedict, was thus maintained in history writing and art as well as in practice. By 1300 it had come to embrace private residential complexes (including chapels for worship) within and without the monastery, large, liveried *familiae* (Richard Whiting is said never to have left Glastonbury on official business without a personal retinue numbering over 100),[9] pontifical regalia in church and a lordly port, charge and countenance out of it. The illustrated parliamentary rolls of the fifteenth and early sixteenth centuries that were owned by various convents, decorated with shields of lords spiritual and temporal, provide a vivid demonstration of the social context of the most powerful Benedictine superiors.[10]

Most significantly for art and architectural patronage, this autonomy also extended to

---

6   RB, chapters II, LXIV. For use of the 'wall' topos see CGA(C), pp. 182–3; VitaES, pp. 40–1; HMGlouc., I, p. 13.

7   On this illustration generally, see Hope 1906, p. 46.

8   Rushforth 1922, pp. 300–2; Kerr 1985, pp. 123–5; Marks 1993, p. 89. The series alternates bishops (presumably of Worcester) with abbots.

9   MA, I, p. 8. Among Henry V's proposed reforms was the curbing of 'costly and scandalous' abbatial trains (including sumptuous 'phaleratura equorum').

10   HCE, pp. 33–4 and pl. XXX, nos 13, 14. That no. 13 (a parliamentary roll of 1513/14) was monastic property is suggested by a list of Anglo-Saxon kings and their monastic foundations (third membrane, dorse). This begins 'Rex Yna fundavit monasterium de Glastonia.' For contemporary, iconographically similar manuscripts with West Country Benedictine shields, see LCA MS Vincent 153, p. 37 (paginated ms.) and LCA MS M 2 G 4, fol. 6r: see Campbell and Steer 1988, pp. 392–3 for short descriptions.

an income that was in every practical respect completely separate.[11] Although a supe-rior's portion of his or her house's income could be modest, as at Gloucester (pre-c.1330) and Tewkesbury (1535), it was usually large: at Malmesbury (1539) in comprised sixty-three per cent, at Sherborne c.1400 it was seventy per cent, and at Tavistock ninety-three per cent.[12] A bishop-superior's income (which was not calculated as a percentage of monastic revenues) could be many times the annual value of the convent's. At Winchester, for example, the discrepancy c.1535 was £4038 against £1507 in favour of the bishop.[13] The degree of financial detachment often strikes one as emblematic of the personal detachment that must, in practice, have obtained between many superiors and their communities, as when Abbot William de Chiriton (1317–44) of Evesham gave the monks under him the revenues of a parish church and an annuity of £13 'to be divided among them as they saw fit.'[14] This and many other acts recorded by Benedictine chroniclers read more like *noblesse oblige* than the beneficence of a loving father. While John Lydgate's *Daunce of Machabree* reminded readers that the abbot (with 'great head [and] belly rounde and fat') and abbess (with 'mantelles furred large and wyde' and 'ryng of gret riches') would 'as a cloystrer dye', there was no question of the Benedictine superior *living* after the same fashion.[15]

The autonomy of the superior was further underscored by frequent absences from the monastery, at parliaments (eight West Country superiors were lords spiritual),[16] coun-cils, visitations, and (most often) on his or her estates – Henry V unsuccessfully sought to limit sojourns on the latter to three months annually.[17] Telling of this is an entry in the Evesham chronicle, stating that Roger Yatton had a great gradual of fine and expen-sive workmanship made for the use of the abbots in choir 'whenever they are present there'.[18] The administrative apparatus of the later medieval Benedictine monastery took this absence for granted: important decisions aside, the superior was not essential for the day-to-day functioning of a house. His or her symbolic status as *pater* or *mater familias* always remained explicit, however, and was often spelled out in acts of art patronage. The pontifical regalia bought by Abbot William Boys (1344–67) of Evesham for the use of himself and his successors (mitre, crozier, rings, gloves, almuce – of grey fur, we are told,[19] rochet, tunicle, dalmatic, sandals and a pontifical) were apposite purchases for one styled 'good shepherd' and 'ruler of souls' by St Benedict.[20] Indeed, these were the very items that Abbot Samson of Bury (1182–1211) had defined as the most appropriate

---

11 On division of monastic incomes between superior and convent, see Howell 1982, pp. 173–4; Knowles 1948, pp. 270–80; Knowles 1950, pp. 404–6.

12 Tavistock represents a case of almost complete centralized control by the abbot over coventual finances (for the figure given see Finberg 1951, p. 238). See also *VCH Gloucester*, II, pp. 59 (Glou-cester), 64 (Tewkesbury); *VCH Wiltshire*, III, pp. 226–7 (Malmesbury); BL MS Cotton Faustina A ii, fols 29v–30v (Sherborne).

13 Cf. Davis 1993, p. 118 and appendix 1.

14 *CAEve.*, p. 291.

15 *Fall of Princes*, III, p. 1032.

16 The abbots of Evesham, Glastonbury, Gloucester, Hyde, Malmesbury, Tavistock, Tewkesbury (from 1514), and Winchcombe.

17 *Chapters*, II, pp. 110–11. Cf. *Suppression Letters*, p. 85, where an abbot's lying 'moche forth in his granges' is cited as a vice.

18 'Quum ibi præsentes fuerint': *CAEve.*, p. 305.

19 Cf. Rushforth 1936, p. 27; Woodforde 1946, pp. 27–8 note 3.

20 *CAEve.*, p. 296. For the abbot as good shepherd and ruler of souls, see *RB*, chapter II, vv. 7–8, 37. All typology with Christ is omitted from translations of the *Rule* for nuns.

gifts that a superior could bestow on his monastery.[21] Another lord of Evesham, John de Brokehampton (1282–1316), had his personal chamber painted with the story of Joseph,[22] whose status as patriarch and type of Christ was too well known for the significance of the scenes to have been lost on visitors. Brokehampton's use of the Joseph narrative (Genesis 37–50) recalls its appearance in Henry III's palace at Westminster, and especially in the contemporary Queen Mary psalter.[23] In both of these cases it has been regarded as, among other things, an allegory of conjugal fidelity,[24] and it may be that the abbot of Evesham also wished to advertise the fidelity represented in his vows of office: to community, rule and God. Elsewhere, and with unambiguous intent, Abbot John Chinnock (1375–1420) had himself buried in the chapter house at Glastonbury in a tomb sporting a fashionable alabaster effigy.[25] He thus maintained a perpetual abbatial presence at the heart of his convent. Ultimately, indeed, the superior was thought closer to God than those he/she ruled. John de Gammages (1284–1306) and John Thoky (1306–29), abbots of Gloucester, were both styled prophets by the domestic chronicler (perhaps an abbot himself). Because of his holiness, the former is even said to have been vouchsafed an epiphany which attendant monks were unable to see.[26] When the abbot of Tewkesbury was placed on the high altar on the day of his installation he occupied the symbolic lap of God:[27] parallels with the eucharist, and perhaps also the familiar image of the Throne of Grace Trinity, must surely have occurred to many of those present. Finally, Richard Beere, penultimate abbot of Glastonbury (1493–1524), constructed a chapel of the Holy Sepulchre, in which he had himself buried.[28] St Benedict's conflation of Christ and abbot was never less ambiguously interpreted than this.

Motives and Misconceptions in the Patronage of Superiors

In terms of both material self-sufficiency and paternal obligation, then, Benedictine superiors were well placed to operate as patrons of art and architecture in their own right. The reasons they had for doing so defy comprehensive categorization, but a number will have been common to most, if not all. *Ut in omnibus glorificetur Deus* runs the Benedictine motto, and if superiors be credited with the degree of religious integrity attributed to them by chroniclers, then this would have provided them with all the motivation they needed to update and beautify their convents' buildings, and commission works like the Sherborne missal.[29] Vocational pride and obligation played their part, and when Bishop Simon de Montacute of Worcester (1333–37) spoke of the rebuilding of his 'spouse' the cathedral church, the figure of speech, though formulaic, is infused with definite strength of feeling.[30] Similarly, Thomas Seabroke (1450–57) had a

---

21 CABury, p. 87.
22 CAEve., p. 287.
23 BL MS Royal 2 B VII, fols 14v–20r.
24 Binski 1986, p. 88 (Westminster); Smith 1993, pp. 154, 156.
25 Itinerary, I, p. 289.
26 HMGlouc., I, pp. 38, 39, 44. On Abbot Walter Froucester (1382–1412) as this chronicle's author, see Brooke 1963, p. 260 and note 3; Gransden 1982, p. 391 and note 4; cf. Sharpe 2001, pp. 734–5.
27 See Haines 1989, p. 19.
28 Itinerary, I, p. 290.
29 On the Benedictine motto see *Benedictines in Britain*, p. 52.
30 Lib.Albus, p. 277.

new pavement of encaustic tiles laid in the presbytery at Gloucester, each nine-tile design bearing his name and the first verse of Psalm 133, 'Behold what a good and joyful thing it is, brethren, to dwell together in unity.'[31] Seabroke himself may not always have participated bodily in this unity, but his gift of tiles expresses his belief that it represented a vocational ideal: the inscription ends with an 'Amen', and he had himself buried in a chantry chapel abutting the liturgical choir to the south-west.

Abbots and abbesses had licence for a good deal of pomp, and beautiful buildings and luxury embellishments were commissioned as showpieces that would demonstrate the taste, wealth, piety and dignity of their proprietors. The great hall of the abbots of Glastonbury cost John of Breynton (1334–42) £1000 simply to complete from the tops of the windows.[32] Therein, Richard Whiting is recorded to have entertained up to 500 'persons of fashion' at once.[33] Next to it stood a sophisticated complex of abbatial buildings, mostly erected during the course of the fourteenth century,[34] of which the abbatial kitchen with its four fireplaces, stone-vaulted octagonal roof and ostentatious lantern (the work of either John Chinnock or Nicholas Frome, 1420–56) is the only substantial survival.[35] Here was a display to impress the most important visitor, not least the heads of other houses. The spirit of emulation must often have played its part in stimulating patronage, just as it influenced the substance of Benedictine historiography. Conversely, because the physical condition of a religious house reflected on its head, dilapidation might provide reason enough for a superior's patronage. Bath cathedral priory church (to be examined presently) is the outstanding West Country example here.

It often appears as though contribution to a monastery's fabric (or that of its satellite buildings) was a rite of passage for superiors, undertaken even when not strictly necessary. Abbots (and abbesses, no doubt, though less indications survive of this) thought it important to make their own personal mark on the institutions they ruled, and what one considered worth starting the next might not trouble to finish.[36] For example, we are told that Abbot John Morwent (1421–37) began to update the nave at Gloucester with the intention of making it completely Perpendicular (no doubt he was aware of contemporary developments at Winchester, Christ Church Canterbury and Westminster, not to mention local churches in and around Gloucester itself), but that he died before realizing his ambition.[37] Subsequent abbots ignored the project, instead concentrating their energies on the crossing-tower and the Lady chapel. At Glastonbury, Adam of Sodbury (1322–34) vaulted (we are told) much of the nave, filling in the severies with representations of saints, kings and benefactors.[38] The eastern bays of the nave had to wait until Richard Beere's abbacy (1493–1525) to receive their vaults, however.[39] The abbots in between turned their attention to other projects: cloister, chapter house, presbytery and superior's apartments.

---

31 'Ecce quam bonum et quam jocundum habitare fratres in unam fiat: amen': see Kellock 1989, pp. 172–3; Eames 1980, I, p. 247.
32 CGA(C), pp. 266–7.
33 MA, I, pp. 7–8; *Short Survey*, p. 79.
34 See MA, I, p. 8 (not a plenary list).
35 The building is difficult to date precisely on stylistic grounds. Carley 1996, p. 59, prefers Frome as the patron.
36 Cf. the notorious case recorded in GA, II, p. 283.
37 *Itinerary*, II, p. 61.
38 Collinson 1791, II, p. 254.
39 CGA(H), I, p. 263; CGA(C), pp. 260–1; Collinson 1791, II, pp. 254–5.

This desire to make one's mark ties in with the commemorative motive. *Post mortem* commemoration was an incentive for patronage at all levels, and many records survive of its influence on superiors. Besides tombs, donor portraits such as those of Robert Brunyng (1385–1415) in the Sherborne missal and Elizabeth Ryprose (1523–39) on the Romsey retable reminded posterity of acts of patronage, and continue to do so.[40] Walter de Monington (1342–75), abbot of Glastonbury, is recorded to have left to his convent a silver-gilt pyx weighing seven pounds with an image of himself engraved on it, thus ensuring his 'perpetual presence' before generations of users (Plate 31, lines 13–14).[41] Inscriptions, particularly where 'suggestively' located, performed a similar task. Roger Yatton gave to Evesham six mass chalices, 'of both good and middling quality', but all alike engraved with his name, that he might be commemorated even at the lesser altars.[42] With similar intent, Clement Lichfield (1514–39) had a window installed in the abbey church at Evesham declaring that he had presided over the construction of the Perpendicular gate tower.[43] This makes the commemorative motive underlying the art and architectural patronage of superiors every bit as explicit as the vermin-infested *transi* upon the so-called Wakeman cenotaph at Tewkesbury.[44] The moral of Lydgate's *Daunce of Machabree* was one that later medieval Benedictine superiors scarcely needed to be taught.

From motives, then, to misconceptions, a subject which the historian of art and architectural patronage is bound to linger over. It cannot be doubted that, collectively, the Benedictine superiors of the west of England were responsible for a great deal of patronage during the later middle ages. Theoretically, they had a stake in all building projects concerning the houses they ruled (embellishments were another matter),[45] and while this did not translate into practice during the later middle ages, they maintained their traditional status alongside the episcopacy and the royal court as one of the most important collective patrons of art and architecture in the country. However, to some extent their reputation as patrons has been exaggerated, first by chroniclers and antiquaries and subsequently by most of the standard secondary sources. As will be shown, the issue of over-attribution touches on some of the most important Benedictine projects carried out in the west during the later medieval period. While a simple lack of supporting evidence often means that one's suspicions cannot be confirmed, there are instances in which it is possible to demonstrate that the actual extent of a superior's responsibility was less than has been assumed. The historical importance of the topic lies as much in its implications for our understanding of monastic organization of, and participation in, matters of building and embellishment in general as in our conception of individual projects. Over-attribution to superiors helps to sustain the historical illu-

---

40 Brunyng appears 'about a hundred' times throughout the Sherborne missal: Backhouse 1999, p. 48. If the Romsey reredos pre-dates 1523, then the abbess represented thereon will be Ann Westbroke (1513–23). The Renaissance-style candelabra dividing the figures are exceptionally unlikely to predate 1513.

41 'Unum pixidem argentis et deauratis cum ymagine abbatis pro nuncio, ponderis in grocis vij li.': TCC MS R 5 16, p. 255 (paginated ms.).

42 'Tam bonos quam mediocres': BL Harley MS 3763, fol. 191r; printed in MA, II, p. 7 note d.

43 'Orate pro anime domini Clementis Lychfeld sacerdotis, cujus tempore turris Eveshamiæ ædificata est': MA, II, p. 8.

44 King 1985, pp. 141–8 sees in the *transi* an allegory of the Seven Deadly Sins. However, cf. Lindley 2003(b), pp. 181–2.

45 Smith 1951, p. 49.

sion (first propagated by the Benedictines themselves) that convents were dependent on their abbots and abbesses as young children are on their parents. (Cf. appendix 2.)

The remodelling of the nave at Winchester is a convenient place to begin (Plate 11). Setting aside the limited amount of remodelling accomplished during William of Edington's episcopacy,[46] the whole is usually attributed to William of Wykeham (1367–1404), and has been so since the fifteenth century.[47] This is due to the great sum (2500 marks, or about £1666) which he bequeathed to the project's completion, the position of his chantry chapel, and the involvement of the master mason William Wynford, who had worked for Wykeham on previous occasions.[48] The contribution of the convent is ignored, yet in financial and organizational terms it was highly significant. In 1394, when Wykeham initiated the project, he extracted from the monks £1340 towards it, to be paid over seven years, plus (as his will explains) supply of all scaffolding, lime and sand, and comprehensive supervision of the project. All forty-three brethren of Winchester were obliged to sign up to this agreement, which saw their corporate contribution recompensed by restoration of certain privileges removed by Wykeham himself in 1387.[49] The convent continued to fund the project for some time after their superior's death: an entry in the *custos operum*'s account of 1409 lists £2 16s 8d paid to his executors for timber.[50] Thus, though the superior played a leading role in the project, its patronage was partially due to the convent, which played an important organizational role as well as a financial one.

The remarkable campaign of building and embellishment carried out at Evesham between 1295 and c.1317 and attributed more or less wholesale to Abbot Brokehampton represents an even clearer example of the tendency to overemphasize the patron status of the superior.[51] The abbey's chronicler, looking back a century and more, vividly describes the panoply: a new Lady chapel, one of England's most beautiful chapter houses, a dorter, frater, misericord, farmery, seyney and much other building, sculpture, painting and metalwork.[52] This is woven into a general description of Brokehampton's achievements, and the majority of the works mentioned individually are attributed directly to his patronage. Yet if the reader's suspicions are aroused by the claim that he built far more than a superior would normally have been responsible for (e.g. the private apartments of certain obedientiaries), then they are confirmed by a less eulogistic document implicating the entire convent in the project (see appendix 2). Here is recorded in detail the amount that each obedientiary was bound to contribute annually, as well as the fact that the pittances of the cloister monks were appropriated to the works. Moreover, the manner in which the project was to be administered is set out, with direct input on the part of Brokehampton conspicuous by its absence. Effectively, all of the monks contributed to the rebuilding, and the whole project emerges as an

---

46 Crook and Kusaba 1993, p. 217–21.
47 *Anglia Sacra*, I, p. 229.
48 *Test.Vet.*, pp. 763–76 is a translation from the will. For Wynford's previous work for Wykeham, see Harvey 1984, pp. 353–4.
49 Greatrex 1977, pp. 244–5.
50 This may have been for scaffolding: *CRWin.*, p. 114.
51 For the date of 1295 see Tindal 1794, pp. 120–1 note. The tower collapsed in a storm in 1291: *Collectanea Leland*, I, p. 248. BL MS Cotton Nero D iii, fol. 221r, states that the chapter house was built in 1317 (i.e. presumably completed); so work continued well into the fourteenth century.
52 *CAEve.*, pp. 286–7; Salzman 1997, pp. 387–8 (with misleading dating).

example of communal patronage, with the abbot playing an important but far from lone-hand role.[53]

Other well-known projects which have been too generously ascribed to the munificence of superiors include rebuilding programmes at Bath and Worcester. Oliver King, bishop of Bath and Wells (1496–1503), has always been regarded as the instigator and chief patron of the reconstruction of the cathedral priory church of Bath (from 1499: Plate 12).[54] In the literature on the subject he cuts quite a historical dash: a no-nonsense, reform-minded superior (acting, we are told, under the influence of divine inspiration) determined to get the job done at any cost, and to reform a chapter of loose-living monks into the bargain.[55] The reality is different. Successive bishops of Bath and Wells had overseen the deterioration of the church without contributing anything substantial towards its upkeep, and its condition no doubt caused King much embarrassment when he first troubled to set foot in it, over three years after his investiture. Blaming Prior John Cantlow (1483–96), whom he described as 'slack' and 'not well disposed to the repair or [re]building of the church', as well as previous priors, King appropriated £300 of the annual conventual income of £480 towards the works.[56] The stipend and pittances of every monk were sacrificed to the cause, and after King died in August 1503 (bequeathing no money to the project), the convent was left to sustain a burden that by the bishop's own admission would take them over a century to relieve themselves of.[57] While King certainly did play an important role in the reconstruction – for one thing, it was through his agency that the royal masons William and Robert Vertue were contracted to build a fan vault than which 'ther shal be noone so goodely neither in england nor in france'[58] – he spent only four years at it, while the monks, who in that time contributed £1200, went on contributing to, and what is more directing, the works for another thirty-five years.[59] The project may never have come to the fruition that it did in the seventeenth century if not for King, but the monks (as at Evesham, all of them) were its patrons to a critical extent.

Worcester provides a further case. Here, Bishop Thomas de Cobham (1317–27) has been held up by Robert Willis and subsequent authorities as patron of the north nave aisle vaulting.[60] This attribution rests partially on stylistic analysis of the architecture, but mostly – again – on Leland's testimony, which simply states that Cobham 'made the vault in the north nave aisle of the church'.[61] Yet Leland's reason for saying this was

---

53 The actual extent of his input is lost in the minutiæ of the instrument detailing conventual contributions. See below, appendix 2.

54 See most recently Dunning 2001, pp. 73–4.

55 See King's injunctions in MA, II, p. 270; Cart.Bath, p. lxviii. For his active personal involvement in the project see Correspondence, pp. 4–6. On the circumstances surrounding the issue of King's injunctions, see Luxford 2000, pp. 314–15.

56 'Remissum non benevolum ad dictæ ecclesiæ refectionem seu edificationem': MA, II, p. 270. However, see below, p. 85.

57 MA, II, p. 270; SMW(b), pp. 44–5.

58 Correspondence, p. 4; Harvey 1984, pp. 306–8. The same letter (of 1501/02), to Sir Reginald Bray, mentions 100 cases of Norman glass, presumably for windows. This suggests a remarkable degree of building in only two years. Cf. Dr Monckton's opinion, that rebuilding actually commenced c.1480: Monckton 1999, pp. 268, 288.

59 Even then it was incomplete: Cobb 1980, pp. 24–8; Luxford 2000, pp. 324–5.

60 Willis 1863, p. 108. For a critique of Willis's dating methods, see Bond 1899, pp. 17–18, 29–30.

61 'Fecit testitudinem borealis insulae in navi ecclesiae': Itinerary, V, p. 227. See also Willis 1863, p. 108 note 9.

premised on a mistake. Leland thought Cobham to have been buried in the north aisle: thus, he was regarded (in Willis's words) 'as a benefactor [buried] in the midst of his own work'.[62] However, his tomb was relocated to the north aisle at some time during the late middle ages.[63] He was originally buried in the Jesus chapel adjoining this aisle, and while he probably did renovate this, the vaulting of the aisle, though it may have been initiated c.1327,[64] is not necessarily to be ascribed to him at all. Indeed, Ute Engel has recently supposed that the fourteenth-century architectural campaigns at Worcester were primarily chapter-driven projects, citing the reconstitution of the fabric confraternity in 1302 by Prior John de Wyke as indicative of a fact underscored by the *Chronologia ædificorum* (to be examined in chapter four).[65] Similarly, the cathedral's west window and north porch are usually assigned to the patronage of Bishop Henry Wakefield (1375–94), whereas the *Chronologia* suggests that the sacrist was responsible.[66] This brings Winchcombe to mind, where the vault of the presbytery is held to have been the responsibility of Abbot Walter de Wykewan (d.1308). Here, too, we discover a sacrist underpinning the project.[67]

That contemporaries (monastic or otherwise), as opposed to later observers, recognized conventual enterprise in works ascribed to superiors out of reverence is strongly suggested by a statement in the unpublished *Ostensa* of Glastonbury's Abbot Monington.[68] After describing the forty-foot, two-bay extension of the presbytery and new eastern ambulatory commissioned by Monington, the reader is told that the abbot received no contribution from the convent or the obedientiaries towards the work – all was achieved at his personal charge.[69] The document goes on to mention the high altar reredos of twenty-two statues ('ymagines') in tabernacles that formed an integral part of the new east end, suggesting that this, too, was a purely abbatial enterprise.[70] There seems little point in questioning the claim, especially given Monington's reputation for integrity (he has been likened to Thomas de la Mare, abbot of St Albans 1349–96).[71] What is striking about the statement in this context is the awareness of the *Ostensa*'s author that readers may well assume such a large and costly undertaking to have been a product of collective enterprise rather than solely abbatial, and his consequent concern that posterity give the abbot his full due.

The point regarding over-attribution of patronage to superiors has been made at some length, because it has important implications for the way in which Benedictine patronage in general has been conceived and written about. If it be argued (perhaps with Matthew Paris's *ob reverentiam* caveat in mind) that the problem is mostly one of definition, then it may be urged that current working definitions of superiors-as-patrons are in

---

62 Willis 1863, p. 108. It may be noted that Cobham willed only £20 to the fabric of the church: Thomas 1736, p. 103.

63 O'Grady 1901, pp. 234–5.

64 Morris 1978, p. 123. Dr Morris has demonstrated that deliberate anachronism in the architecture of Worcester's nave makes dating it hazardous: Morris 1978, pp. 116–18.

65 Engel 2000, p. 231.

66 Willis 1863, p. 316; WCL MS A xii, fol. 77v.

67 *Landboc*, I, p. cvii note 1; II, p. lx.

68 The *Ostensa* is TCC MS R 5 16, pp. 215–31 (the pagination jumps from pp. 224–8).

69 TCC MS R 5 16, p. 219: 'Nulla ad tantum opus a *conventum* vel obedienciariis contribuicione accepta'. This work, probably begun during the early 1360s, is analyzed in Wilson 1980, pp. 319–23.

70 TCC MS R 5 16, pp. 219–20.

71 Carley 1996, pp. 51–2; Heale 1997, p. 141.

need of the scrutiny to which other nostrums concerning later medieval monasticism have been subjected in recent scholarship. Further examples of over-attribution could be produced, from other parts of England as well as the west, although to do so would labour the point unnecessarily. Suffice it to add that many acts of patronage tradition-ally attributed to superiors and less sweeping than those reviewed above will actually have benefited from significant communal input, whether or not the abbot or abbess played a decisive role in them. A case described in the Gloucester chronicle spells out circumstances which were no doubt common. During the abbacy of Thomas Horton (1351–77), it is recorded, two sets of expensive mass vestments were bought 'by the community, [Horton] himself ordering their purchase and procuring them'.[72] As we have seen in the cases of Winchester and Bath, the intervention of a superior could be crucial for recruitment of outstanding architects and artists. This was not, however, where things rested, for a project had still to be directed and financed. It was here that the convent typically lent a substantial hand.

The Superior's Contribution

Conventual architecture

When considering instances of patronage that can be safely attributed to superiors, it should be recognized that a 'safe' attribution is not necessarily one that can be proven. Lack of documentation and the vagueness of a superior's responsibilities where monastic art and architecture was concerned make the science in which we are dabbling inexact.[73] For bishop-superiors, patronage at the regular cathedrals they governed was purely voluntary: the monks of Bath became well aware of this after Oliver King's untimely death. The only definite responsibilities lay with the convent.[74] The indenture of 1513 made between Richard Fox (1500–28) and the monks of Winchester states that only those of his funds (if any) left over after completion of the construction and embel-lishment of Corpus Christi College Oxford may be annexed to a proposed programme of revaulting in the cathedral (retrochoir, transepts and presbytery aisles).[75] Given the cost of setting Corpus up, the nature of what he left to pay for it (largely plate and chattels) and the spiralling inflation of the early Tudor period, only a fraction of this ambitious programme was ever realized. Yet the superior did not thereby default in his legal or moral obligations, for the former were non-existent, and the latter would have been satisfied with much less than the reconstruction, paving and vaulting of the presbytery aisles that was actually achieved with his support.[76] Circumstances were little different

---

[72] HMGlouc., I, p. 49: 'dua secta vestimentorum . . . tempore suo fuerunt empta de communi [i.e. of their mensa], ipso ea procurante et ordinante'.

[73] Occasionally patronage-generating obediences were concentrated in a superior's hands; e.g. the abbot of Cerne occurs as sacrist in 1396: Cart.Cerne, I, p. 78. This is a different matter, however.

[74] See Smith 1951, p. 38; Graham 1960, p. 66. It is sometimes stated, apparently on no reliable authority, that bishops did have predetermined patronage responsibilities: e.g. Bugslag 1980, pp. 73–4; Knowles 1955, p. 32 note 1.

[75] The indenture is printed in full in Smith 1988(b), pp. 378–413.

[76] Smith 1988(b) also credits Fox with rebuilding the eastern gable and great east window of the cathedral (pp. 154–9), installing much of the east end's stained glass (pp. 236–50), finishing the high altar reredos (p. 278), and patronizing the choir screens (pp. 278–85). None of the work is

where abbeys and priories were concerned, although modest agreements such as that between the abbot and convent of Evesham stating that the former would make up shortfalls in the sacrist's budget when expensive building campaigns were undertaken, were probably not unusual.[77] After all, the vocational brief that St Benedict defined for superiors obligated them morally to do a certain amount of building for the good of those they ruled. This is exemplified in the practice of prioritizing the reconstruction of dorters and fraters over conventual churches. Bath provides a good example here. William Worcestre tells us that its titular abbot, Thomas Bekynton (1444–65), paid for a new dorter, ignoring the church that Bishop King was shortly to find 'ruined to its foundations'.[78]

Where primary sources do yield trustworthy evidence of superiors contributing to the renovation of conventual churches, the idiosyncratic nature of such patronage is underscored. The indistinctness of the superior's brief in this area, coupled with the great variety in the matter of distribution of finances at Benedictine houses (as we have seen, the superior might control a small or a large percentage of total revenues), means that no clear patterns of responsibility emerge. Besides the aforementioned examples of William of Wykeham at Winchester, Oliver King at Bath, and Walter de Monington at Glastonbury, the Gloucester chronicler's testimony that Abbot Thomas Horton contributed £444 0s 2d of the £781 0s 2d needed to remodel the north transept of the abbey church may be considered sound, both because it cites *compoti* as evidence of the information and because it admits a substantial non-abbatial contribution.[79] The Evesham chronicler's account of the reconstruction of his church's presbytery and the erection of a new campanile (from 1395) also describes the sort of joint patronage which must have been common. Abbot Yatton, it says, was 'doubtless the greatest benefactor in the transportation of stone and other essential matters' with respect to the campanile, while 'with the help of master Robert More he put his kind, helping hands' to the presbytery, specifically in the 'haulage of stone and timber, as well as with the windows'.[80] The tenor of this description is notably different to the hyperbole of this chronicler's overgenerous attributions to John de Brokehampton, perhaps because the works carried out under Yatton were accomplished within living memory (the chronicle was written c.1418).

John Leland records that at Glastonbury, Abbot Richard Beere 'cumming from his embassadrie out of Italie made a chapel for our Lady de Loretta'.[81] The remains of this

documented, however, and the choir screens were manifestly the result of joint patronage. She also ascribes, cogently, the presbytery vault-bosses to Fox's munificence (pp. 162–79). There is independent evidence for Fox's patronage of the presbytery aisle vaults: see *CRWin.*, p. 217.

77 *VCH Worcester*, II, p. 121.
78 *Itinerary Worcestre*, pp. 294–5; Dunning 2001, p. 73. Bekyngton was also involved in ('fecit fieri') erection of a new dorter at Witham charterhouse: *Itinerary Worcestre*, pp. 294–7. King's 'imo funditus dirutam' (*MA*, I, p. 270) should not be understood literally: cf. its use in *HKW*, II, p. 655. See also Monckton 1999, p. 255 note 51.
79 *HMGlouc.*, I, p. 50.
80 *CAEve.*, p. 305: 'Item campanile de Evesham fuit constructam tempore suo, ad quod sine dubio maximus adjutor et benefactor fuit tam in cariagio lapidum quam in aliis necessariis multis. Postea presbyterium istius loci factum fuit in tempore suo, ad quod gratiosas manus adjutrices apposuit, tam in cariagio lapidum [et] meremii quam ad fenestras, cum adjutorio magistri Roberti More'. Cf. Cox 1990, p. 128.
81 *Itinerary*, I, p. 290.

chapel have been excavated immediately to the west of the north transept.[82] Beere went to Italy at the behest of Henry VII in 1503/4, passing through Urbino on official business en route to Rome.[83] Here he encountered the cult of Our Lady of Loreto, and it is thus reasonable to suppose that he was responsible for the chapel which Leland ascribes to his munificence. Was it built in the form of the *Casa Santa* (as it existed prior to Bramante's remodelling)?[84] It is impossible to be sure, as so little of it has been discovered in excavations.[85] What has come to light is embellished with Renaissance ornament, however: precocious for England, let alone the West Country. All this smacks of someone who had visited Italy personally and had a strong interest in both the visual idioms of humanism (as Beere undoubtedly did) and the cult of the Virgin Mary; and here it is noteworthy that Beere promoted the intrinsically related cult of Joseph of Arimathea with great energy, and built lodgings for the seculars who staffed the Lady chapel.[86] As an act of patronage *per se*, it also appears somewhat arbitrary,[87] as are other good works that Leland attributes to Beere: a chapel of the Holy Sepulchre, an *antependium* of gilded silver for the high altar, the chapel of King Edgar at the east end of the church (finished by Richard Whiting), the infrastructure for a community of bedeswomen, strainer arches beneath the crossing tower *à la* Wells, sumptuous guests' lodgings, and much else besides.[88]

Domestic architecture and its embellishment

Richard Beere also rebuilt the abbatial manor house at Sharpham park (about a mile from the abbey), transforming what Leland described as a 'poore lodge' into what Henry VIII's commissioners (Layton, Moyle and Pollard) were to call 'the goodliest house of that sort that ever we have seen' – and they had seen a few.[89] Grand though Sharpham undoubtedly was, its general layout was not unusual: a great hall and chapel, with a two-storey arrangement of parlour, chambers, storehouses, offices and other appurtenances, the whole encircled by a perimeter wall made of stone on its 'display' side and oaken pales on the other. This wall enclosed a park stocked with 400 deer and forty large cattle, as well as orchards and fishponds.[90] Morwell, a retreat of the abbots of Tavistock on the Cornish border, is an example of what might be accomplished where funds were more restricted. Here, a late fourteenth- and early fifteenth-century remodelling is indicated by the issue in 1391 of an episcopal licence to construct a chapel, and by surviving fenestration.[91] The house, of four ranges enclosing a large central courtyard,

[82] Bond 1919, pp. 76–85.
[83] Carley 1996, p. 66.
[84] Bramante commenced his remodelling c.1509: Weil-Garris 1977, I, pp. 12–13.
[85] Bond 1915, p. 131; Bond 1919, p. 85, anachronistically assumes that it imitated Bramante's *Casa*. The walls of the medieval *Casa* were, however, refaced in the fifteenth century (Weil-Garris 1977, I, p. 10), presumably in an early Renaissance idiom.
[86] Lagorio 2001, pp. 78–9; *Itinerary*, I, p. 289. On Beere's interest in humanism, see Carley 1996, pp. 66–7.
[87] Unless the intention was to imitate the cultic house at Walsingham. This, too, was being renovated during the early sixteenth century: Marks 2004, p. 195.
[88] *Itinerary*, I, pp. 289–90. The arches were clearly necessary additions.
[89] *Itinerary*, I, p. 290; MA, I, p. 10; *Suppression Letters*, p. 256.
[90] Collinson 1791, II, p. 268.
[91] Oliver 1846, p. 91.

was encircled by a perimeter wall incorporating a rib-vaulted, crenellated gateway resembling the main gate of the abbey.[92] Around 1420, the abbatial complex within the abbey at Tavistock was also completely rebuilt.[93] With projects such as these more confidence about a superior's acts of patronage is possible, for both within the monastic precinct and without, abbots and abbesses were responsible for works pertaining to their private domestic complexes.[94]

Only certain manor houses were modelled to accommodate a superior's *familia* (although others were expanded to accept various obedientiaries and their retinues), and these may be reckoned among the most important instances of patronage by the heads of religious houses. A definite pattern of patronage now emerges, which is best illustrated with reference to Glastonbury. Spurred by the desire to remain abreast of rapidly developing trends in baronial standards of living (which in turn impressed the importance of both abbot and abbey on outsiders), successive abbots rebuilt favoured manor houses (typically those close to the mother church) in grand style. If they did not compete with the grandest 'trophy houses' going up elsewhere in England at the time, then this was substantially because they maintained multiple forinsec seats.[95] Adam of Sodbury (1323–34) erected domestic chambers, chapels and outbuildings at Meare, Pilton and Domerham.[96] He and the following four abbots reconstructed the abbatial buildings within the monastery, as well as augmenting the buildings on various manors; the austere and practical Walter de Monington built a fish-house at Zoy and a *cameram necessariam* at Doulting;[97] while John Chinnock (1375–1420) reconstructed the manor house at Pilton, with its hall, 'long chapel', ten chambers and many other appurtenances.[98] John Selwood (1456–93), whose rebus is practically as common as Richard Beere's on buildings and furnishings in which Glastonbury had a proprietorial interest, substantially rebuilt the manor house at East Brent, and also patronized works at Ditcheat, High Ham, Ivy Thorn Manor and Norwood.[99] Beere completed Norwood, updated Meare and, as noted, renovated Sharpham, in addition to having new royal chambers built onto the state lodgings within the abbey.[100] When Richard Whiting began his reign in 1525, he had at his disposal these lodgings, two park houses, a London house at Smithfield (apparently Chinnock's acquisition),[101] plus ten manor houses built largely of freestone fit to receive him and his considerable retinue.[102] It is to such projects that a great deal of the art and architectural patronage of superiors was directed during the later middle ages, and if Glastonbury's abbots were atypical in this regard

---

92 For Morwell (Barton) today, see Pevsner and Cherry 1989, pp. 579–80. The house has been enthusiastically Victorianized.
93 Finberg 1951, p. 222.
94 Though an obedientiary might still oversee the works, of course: e.g. MA, II, p. 6; HMGlouc., I, p. 46.
95 On the late medieval 'trophy house' see Emery 1996–2000, II, pp. 494–8.
96 *Rentalia*, p. xxiii; Carley 1996, p. 42; cf. CGA(C), pp. 262–5. On Meare see Gray 1926(b), p. xlii.
97 Carley 1996, pp. 51–2 (Monington's austerity), p. 107; TCC MS R 5 16, p. 221 (*necessarium*).
98 *Itinerary*, I, p. 290; cf. the survey in Platt 1969, p. 227.
99 *Rentalia*, p. xxiii.
100 *Itinerary*, I, p. 289. The royal apartment is called the 'high chamber' in the Dissolution inventory: MA, I, p. 8. Apparently, Beere (or perhaps Selwood) also updated the abbatial great hall: Anon. 1910–11, pp. 114–15.
101 CGA(H), p. 279; cf. *Star Chamber*, II, p. 199 note 22.
102 *Rentalia*, p. xxiii.

then in all likelihood it was only in the total amount paid out, rather than the proportion of abbatial revenues thus spent.

Most of these residential complexes have been either renovated beyond recognition or razed completely: even Sharpham, fit for kings, was not splendid enough for its owners in the time of George III.[103] Consequently, fewer indications of their decorative schemes and furnishings survive than we would like, but it is reasonable to suppose that superiors' patronage of domestic complexes extended to embellishments commensurate with the pretentious scale and quality of the architecture. The highly ornamented fireplaces installed by the abbot of Muchelney and the prioress of Cannington in their private apartments have been mentioned in chapter one, and it is interesting to note that the Muchelney example was designed to incorporate a painting (or a tapestry) over its mantelpiece. That there was a fashion for embellishing abbatial apartments with painted and woven iconographic schemes is apparent from the descriptions of John de Brokehampton's aforementioned Joseph cycle, the many tapestries ('dorsalia') that Adam of Sodbury supplied for Glastonbury's abbatial hall (the best of them representing the Tree of Jesse),[104] and the genealogy of the English kings that adorned John Thoky's private hall at Gloucester.[105] The latter suggests that such embellishments were commissioned by superiors to advertise their personal allegiances and the historical associations of their convents. An example from Abbot Monington's *Ostensa* reinforces this impression. We are told that the abbot provided two hangings for his newly built hall at Glastonbury, the first and better of which, of woven work, displayed the Nine Worthies, the second a painted image of Edward III (i.e. Edward as the tenth worthy) within fine borders.[106] For apartments on his manors he purchased two hangings, one of them white with indigo embroidery displaying a description of the arms of King Arthur – which were also Glastonbury's arms – in French. The other was of red, with yellow butterflies on it.[107]

Muchelney also retains traces of two other embellishments that must have been common in superiors' residences; decoratively carved timber wainscoting (here the linenfold so popular during the sixteenth century) and stained glass (in the heads of windows in the abbot's parlour), apparently the product of Thomas Broke's patronage (1505–22).[108] When Evesham's abbot William Boys purchased the timberwork and windows of the royal hall at Feckenham manor (Worcs.) from the queen in 1354, he must have obtained some luxury fittings, no doubt including panelling (Feckenham's chapel at least was wainscotted).[109] Such royal appurtenances are most likely to have

103 Carley 1996, p. 73.
104 CGA(C), pp. 262–3; cf. p. 252 where 'dorseer' (i.e. *dorsalium*) is used for *tapecia*.
105 HMGlouc., I, p. 44.
106 TCC MS R 5 16, p. 230: 'Pro aula abbatis dorsalia duo prouidit quorum primum operis textrinus continet nouem trine fidei milites meliores sine costis. Secundus tinctus cum costiis bella continens Regis Edwardi tercij a conquestum.' Edward III's epitaph puts him in similar company: Binski 1995, p. 197.
107 TCC MS R 5 16, p. 230: 'Dedit et alia duo [dorsaliæ] pro manerijs quorum primum album cum frecto indico continens in summitate descripcionem armorum Regis arthuri in gallico cum costis secte eiusdem. Secundum rubeum cum papilionibus crocei coloris et costus secte consimilis.' The description in French may have been derived from that in *HRB*, pp. 103–4, or the *Quedam narracio de nobili rege Arthuri* for which see Carley 2004, pp. 58–9. A 'tapestry poem' (see Hammond 1910–11, *passim*) may even be indicated.
108 See Woodforde 1946, pp. 272–3 and pl. XLVIII.
109 HKW, II, p. 938.

gone to the abbot's own apartments. The abbatial chambers at Gloucester, renovated by William Malvern (1514–39), contained especially fine wooden panelling, a piece of which (bearing Malvern's device of a buck *trippant*) survives as a sideboard in the episcopal palace.[110] Superiors' chapels were handsomely appointed, more so at richer houses than were the entire conventual churches of poorer ones. John of Ombersley, abbot of Evesham (1367–79), stocked his with two pairs of altar cruets, two candlesticks, a *salsorium*, a holy-water vessel with aspergillum, and a pax-brede, all silver gilt, the pax also enamelled; this compares favourably with the inventories of St Michael's Mount and Tywardreath taken during the same period.[111] For the table of the abbatial hall he procured twenty-four plates, a salt cellar and spoon for each, six serving platters, two large salt cellars and two alms dishes, all of silver.[112] There is no reason to suppose that this was unusual for a superior of his means.[113]

William Malvern installed high quality armorial glass in the abbatial residence at Gloucester, and also in the drawing room at his favourite external residence, Prinknash Park.[114] What survives of the Prinknash glass – a mere six pieces – has now been inserted into a window of the south cloister walk at the cathedral, and provides an example of one of the commonest objects of a superior's art patronage in the domestic context: the heraldic programme. Here are the arms of Henry VIII and Catherine of Aragon, Malvern's own arms and his personal badge, Catherine's pomegranate badge (which also appears on Malvern's tomb) and the arms of the abbey's seventh-century first founder, Osric (as both viceroy of the Hwicce and king of Northumbria).[115] The scheme illustrates more than a concession to contemporary fashion; it encapsulates the complex concerns and *mores* of a major Benedictine superior at the end of the middle ages, the requirement to juggle such weighty issues as royal favour, appropriate commemoration of founders (for here are the Alpha and the Omega of Gloucester's royal overlords), personal prestige, and the antiquity of the institution which he ruled, the latter such an important plank in the defence of the abbey's traditional rights and privileges. The glass has an obvious aesthetic function, too, but above all it reminds one that even in a superior's domestic environs art patronage was a serious, often pragmatic business.

Similar concerns are demonstrated by the heraldic decoration of Abbot William Middleton's hall at Milton (completed 1498).[116] Here the porch, the corbels and hammer beams of the magnificent roof, the great screen and the string courses are carved with demi-angels holding oval-shaped fields charged with the armorials of the king, local aristocratic families, other Dorset abbeys with which Milton enjoyed confraternity (Abbotsbury, Cerne, Sherborne and Cistercian Bindon), Milton itself, Abbot Middleton (arms and rebus), and King Æthelstan (Milton's first founder). More heraldry survives in the hall windows, and once filled the glass of the abbatial solar,

110   Chandler 1979, p. 81.
111   Cf. *Inv.Mic.Mt.*, p. 5; Oliver 1846, pp. 34–5.
112   *CAEve.*, p. 303.
113   Cf. CGA(C), pp. 260–3; HMGlouc., I, p. 46.
114   Malvern renovated Prinknash c.1520: Bazeley 1882–83, p. 273.
115   Welander 1985, pp. 53–5; Bazeley 1882–83, pp. 275–6. The surviving pieces date to c.1520–25. The glass in the abbatial apartments at Gloucester included Malvern's initials and the arms of Osric: Chandler 1979, p. 81.
116   Hutchins *Dorset*, IV, pp. 393–4; Oswald 1966, p. 1718; Jones and Traskey 1997, p. 19.

known as the 'star chamber' for its rich decorative scheme (vermilion, speckled with gold stars).[117] An even more complex programme is found at Cerne (fifteen coats, plus one blank escutcheon) on the fan vault and oriel window of the gateway which formed part of the abbatial residence reconstructed by Thomas Sam c.1505–08.[118] Elsewhere, Abbot Richard of Tavistock (1491–2) had armorial glass (including the attributive arms of Ordulf, his abbey's first founder) installed in the 'great window' (presumably an oriel) of his town residence in Exeter.[119] By the turn of the fifteenth century, heraldry had become a major (if relatively inexpensive)[120] object of every superior's art patronage. Certainly, it is one of the best-known today, thanks to its iconographic innocuousness and also its utility for post-Reformation heralds and antiquaries. Yet it formed only one element of a panoply which, with the exception of a few items (e.g. the back panel of Richard Whiting's chair) has vanished. The armorials of William Middleton's hall only stand out as they do because they no longer compete for attention with the tapestries that must once have cloaked the walls to the level of the string course.[121]

Forinsec non-domestic architecture

Patronage by superiors outside the monastery extended beyond the manor-house wall (or moat), embracing parish churches whose greater tithes were annexed to the abbatial *mensa*,[122] 'public works' in which the superior had an interest (at Evesham, we are told, Roger Yatton built the main span of the bridge over the Avon and also paved the town, while Glastonbury's Abbot Sodbury built a stone dyke near Brent Knoll (Som.) against inundation by the sea),[123] and quotidian erection and maintenance of estate buildings (the Evesham chronicler baulks at recording all of these 'because it is tiresome to write them down').[124] Much information relating to the latter is found in abbatial registers as well as chronicles. Occasionally, surviving buildings provide evidence: the rectorial barn at Church Enstone (Oxon.), for example, carries the ostentatious inscription 'Ista grangia facta & fundata fuit aº dⁱ mº cccº lxxxiiº per Walterum de Wynforton abbatem de Wynchecumbe ad exoracionem Roberti Mason ballivi loci istius.'[125] Mills (wind and water) are a particularly prominent feature, as is housing for secular employees. Nicholas Bubwith, bishop of Bath and Wells (1407–24), gave the monks at Bath 320 marks for the erection of houses to be built on their land, and Leland tells us that Glastonbury's Abbot Selwood built many houses at Mells during the mid-fifteenth century, wishing to reshape the plan of the village into that of a tau cross.[126] He was also responsible for the

---

117 Hutchins *Dorset*, IV, p. 395.
118 Oliver 1937, pp. 18–22 and pl. facing 22.
119 Oliver 1846, p. 93. As noted in chapter one, the town house was 'newly rebuilt' in 1481, hence the attribution to this abbot.
120 Cf. *Jnl.More*, p. 219 (see below, p. 198).
121 Pevsner and Newman 1972, p. 289, write of 'a principle of increasing decoration with increasing height'. This ignores the use of tapestries. Cf. Wilson 2003(b), p. 105.
122 E.g. CGA(C), pp. 262–3; Lewis 1926, p. xxxvi; Thompson 1926, p. xliv; CAEve., p. 287.
123 CAEve., p. 305; CGA(C), pp. 262–3. Walter de Monington also built sea walls: TCC MS R 5 16, p. 221.
124 'Propter tædium legentis': CAEve., p. 305. This expression was a commonplace: cf. GA, II, p. 283; OBL Top Glouc d 2, f. 5v; BL Cotton Domitian A iv, f. 226v; *Suppression Letters*, pp. 72, 175.
125 Wood-Jones 1956, p. 43. Wynforton ruled at Winchcombe 1359–95.
126 *Reg.Bubwith*, I, pp. xxxvii–xxxviii; *Itinerary*, V, p. 105.

Pilgrims' Inn in the shadow of his own abbey.[127] Educational facilities also attracted abbatial munificence, both at Oxford, which for some was *alma mater*, and closer to home. Abbot Breynton, for example, contributed £40 towards a new hall and chambers for Glastonbury monks at Gloucester College,[128] while the free-school porch at Evesham still carries the inscription 'orate pro anima Clementis Lichfield' (d.1539).[129] Presumably because they owned property therein, the abbots of Malmesbury and Glastonbury and the prioress of Kington St Michael were obliged to contribute to the upkeep of Malmesbury's town walls, otherwise a royal responsibility. Here was joint patronage on the part of superiors at work to an unglamorous and (one suspects) irksome end: not all art and architectural expenses were matters of choice, nor of apparent benefit to the patron. Indeed, one wonders what benefit Glastonbury's Walter de Monington derived from providing the dean and chapter of Wells with seventy cartloads of freestone (plus carriage) 'ad *reparacionem magni campanile ecclesie Wellensis*' from his quarries at Doulting (Som.) between 1355 and 1356.[130] The second of the two transactions is specified 'concessionem', suggesting that the stone was a handsome gift. If so, then the abbot of Glastonbury was a patron of the central tower of Wells cathedral; a fact which, incidentally in this context, sits uneasily with John of Glastonbury's contemporary account of the enmity between the two institutions.

Conventual art

Within the monastic precinct, almost any project of building or embellishment might attract a superior's generosity, and although reliable evidence exists for only a fraction of what was accomplished, the wide range of objects which can be attributed with confidence show that the wind of a superior's patronage blew very much where it listed. Richard of Bromsgrove (1418–35) had the Lady chapel reredos at Evesham repainted,[131] while William Middleton performed a similar service with respect to the high altar at Milton.[132] Walter de Monington donated to his convent a silver-gilt image of the Virgin, with the child held in her left arm, of 59s 2d weight.[133] Henry Farley, abbot of Gloucester (1472–98), contributed to a nave clerestory window at Great Malvern in which he was represented kneeling in prayer,[134] and William Malvern commissioned a mechanism for playing hymns (*Christe redemptor omnium* and *Chorus novæ Ierusalem*, according to the contract) on the abbey bells at Gloucester.[135] William Boys, too,

---

127 Dunning 2000, p. 398.
128 CGA(C), pp. 266–7. Walter de Monington also contributed to Glastonbury's quarters at Oxford: TCC MS R 5 16, p. 221.
129 From 1444 Benedictine houses were required to establish buildings for the teaching of 'primitive sciences': Pantin 1929, p. 199.
130 BL MS Arundel 2, fols 18v (twenty cartloads, to canon William de Camell), 27r (fifty cartloads, plus carriage, to dean and chapter, *ad campanile*). Draper 1981, pp. 24, 29 note 54, notices one of these instruments.
131 BL MS Cotton Nero D. iii, fol. 223r (printed in CAEve., p. 286 note 1, incorrectly citing fol. 246), records verses inscribed on the reredos.
132 See the inscription in *RCHM Dorset* 1970, p. 189. This does not necessarily refer to anything more than polychromy.
133 TCC MS R 5 16, p. 254.
134 Rushforth 1936, p. 245.
135 GCL Register D, fol. 242r–v; cf. Witts 1882–3(b), pp. 130–1; Thurlow 1979, p. 6.

recognized in its bells the public voice of his abbey, and commissioned the founding of 'Great Ecgwine', with thunderous verses and 'Dompnus Willelmi Boys abbas fieri fecit' inscribed thereon; Ralph of Shrewsbury gave Bath two bells worth 100 marks; while Richard Kidderminster had a treble bell decorated with crowned heads in relief cast for Winchcombe.[136] At the other end of the financial spectrum, Richard Stoke, prior of Totnes (1439–58), contributed £10 in 1449 to the construction of a new campanile, while Prior Richard Marston (d.1506) paid for a seven-light window to be installed in the frater at Tywardreath (1504), a luxury embellishment which suggests that house's attempts to remain abreast of contemporary artistic fashions as effectively as its ambitious musical culture does.[137]

Four categories of art for use within monasteries stand out as objects of superiors' patronage with particular prominence: illuminated books, decorated liturgical vestments, metalwork and personal sepulchral monuments. These invite separate discussion, for they constitute the clearest artistic (as distinct from architectural) expressions we have of the values, priorities and perhaps also the aesthetic predilections of the heads of Benedictine houses after 1300. To some extent, the patronage of such objects was 'standardized' in that superiors were obliged to purchase them, for the health of their souls, and perhaps – morally at least – for the spiritual and financial good of their communities. Books, whether illuminated or not, carried symbolic connotations both biblical and specifically Benedictine, and items incorporating precious metals had a special prestige, which made them particularly suitable acquisitions for superiors.[138] The giving of books, vestments and metalwork was also influenced by the weight of a tradition that was actively promoted: here was the stimulus of precedent, that anchor to which so many Benedictine aspirations were bound during the two and a half centuries before the Dissolution. Benedictine monasteries, particularly the larger ones that had a vested interest in advertising long and illustrious histories, contained and what is more displayed many items said to have been bestowed on them by great superiors past. It has been pointed out that medieval authorities recommended the display of these 'props in the theatre of memory' as the visual counterpart to cartularies and chronicles (which were particular responsibilities of superiors); they complemented perfectly the pictorial iconography covering the walls and windows of the church.[139] Glastonbury, Winchester and Worcester all preserved significant collections of such antiques (as they were called) alongside their more conventional relics. Cambridge, Trinity College MS R 5 33 contains a list of items said to have belonged to St Dunstan (abbot, c.943–56) which were in the hands of the treasurer at Glastonbury in 1289, including jewels, a cup, gold rings, spoons and two gilded images, one of the Virgin Mary, the other of St Joseph.[140] This list reads just like an extract from the good works of some later medieval abbot as contained in the Glastonbury or Evesham chronicle. Another Glastonbury manuscript at Trinity contains a copy of John of Glastonbury's chronicle that has a fifteenth-century sketch of a thurible, altar cross and cruet in the margin alongside a description of the items with which Dunstan enriched the abbey: 'altarcloths, crosses, thuribles,

136 BL MS Cotton Nero D.iii, f. 223; *Cart.Bath*, p. 159; *Landboc*, II, pp. xli–xlii.
137 Watkin 1914–17, II, p. 956; Oliver 1846, p. 35. On Tywardreath's ambitious early sixteenth-century musical provisions, see Orme 1987–91(a), pp. 277–80.
138 On metalwork's special prestige, see e.g. Wilson 1990, p. 130; Binski 1995, p. 153.
139 Clanchy 1999, p. 38 (quote); cf. Michael 1997, p. 73.
140 Printed in CGA(H), II, p. 369; Bird 1995, p. 356.

phials, chasubles and other vestments'.[141] Glastonbury also held manuscripts that had belonged to Dunstan, the best known being the polyglot 'Classbook' (actually a suite of manuscripts bound together in the early fifteenth century),[142] with its frontispiece representing the abbot prostrate at the feet of Christ. During the early sixteenth century, a stylistically archaizing inscription was added to this image (probably at the direction of Richard Beere) identifying it as the work of Dunstan himself.[143] Worcester, where Dunstan had reigned as titular abbot from 957 to 959, held other books once owned by the saint, some of them illuminated,[144] and the same convent also retained the pastoral staff of another West Country Benedictine hero St Wulfstan (d.1095), which was displayed at fund-raising events.[145] At Winchester (St Swithun's and Hyde) manuscripts such as the Benedictional of St Æthelwold (963–84) and the Winchester Bible (c.1155–85) were preserved with particular reverence (as witness their condition), while the 'great cross [with] an image of Christ, and Mary and John . . . of plate silver and partly gilt' which still dominated the nave of the cathedral at the Dissolution was almost certainly that given by Bishop Stigand (1043–70).[146] More recent advertisements of gifts of plate, vestments and books in chronicles and inventories, as well as on the items themselves (Roger Yatton's six 'good and middling' chalices, for example), underscored the strength of this tradition. The fact that acquiring such items was and always had been simply part of what a superior *did* could not have been more obvious.

Illuminated books

Where the patronage of illuminated books by superiors is concerned, the west of England offers lamentably slim pickings. The chroniclers of Evesham, Glastonbury and (to a lesser extent) Gloucester were obsessed with cataloguing but not with detailed description, and to read that Adam of Sodbury acquired for the library at Glastonbury 'Biblam preciosam . . . duo psalteria preciosissima et vnum benediccionale perpulchrum' is for the art historian more tantalizing than informative.[147] While it is eminently likely that these were highly decorated works of art, further conclusions are impossible on the basis of such information.[148] Most of the surviving Benedictine manuscripts which qualify as works of art were either demonstrably the property of obedientiaries, and thus probably products of their patronage, or of uncertain ownership: the psalters of Evesham and Nunnaminster, and the two books of hours from Gloucester (mentioned in chapter four) are cases in point. Where ownership by a superior can be demonstrated, it may say nothing about a book's patronage. British Library MS Harley 960, a small (approxi-

---

141 TCC MS R 5 16, p. 54; Carley 1996, p. 115 (ill.).
142 OBL MS Auctarium F 4 32: see Pächt & Alexander, III, pp. 2, 3, 4.
143 Parkes 1997, p. 103. Such an addition to such a book surely required abbatial authorization. For another example see Dunning 2001, p. 93 ill. 42.
144 Pächt & Alexander 1966–73, I, pp. 32, 33 and pl. 34; III, p. 4.
145 See *Annales*, I, p. 211; Mason 1984, pp. 159–63; *Lib.Albus*, p. 121.
146 Francis Wormald's provenancing of the Benedictional (Wormald 1959, p. 9) to Hyde is entirely convincing. Further evidence in Deshman 1995, pp. 74–5. See also *MLGB*, p. 201; Zarnecki 1984, p. 121 (Winchester Bible); *MA*, I, p. 202; Oman 1957, p. 71; cf. *Annales*, II, pp. 25, 30 (Winchester rood).
147 CGA(C), pp. 262–3.
148 A benedictional 'perpulchrum' was surely illuminated, although Deshman 1995, p. 3, points out that illumination was rare in this class of manuscript.

mately 17½ × 12½cm) and much-used psalter from Hyde abbey made during the last quarter of the fourteenth century and containing eight illuminated initials,[149] illustrates this point. The only indication of ownership is the 'constat Ricardo abbate' written on fol. 246r, which must refer to Richard Hall (c.1488–1530): the earlier owners are unknown.[150] Like the (undecorated) Muchelney breviary, it may have been passed down from abbot to abbot, but there is no hard evidence either way. However, widespread commission and purchase of decorated bibles, psalters and books of hours by Benedictine superiors need not be doubted: Elizabeth Shelford's book of hours was not a one-off. In the surviving portrait of Avelina Cowdrey, abbess of Wherwell (1518–29), the sitter holds a small devotional book, with gilt clasps and gilt stamped binding.[151] Devotional considerations aside, the article was simply *de rigueur*.

The greatest of all late medieval Benedictine books, the Sherborne missal (BL MS Additional 74236), contains mixed messages concerning its patronage. Was it a product of joint patronage, or (like the Lytlyngton missal) an individual initiative? The latter is hardly certain, although the many portraits of Abbot Robert Brunyng, and the ubiquity of his motto (*Laus sit Trinitati*), surely denote a controlling interest on his part. However, the portraits of Richard Mitford, bishop of Salisbury (1395–1407) – there are eight, each one juxtaposed with a portrait of Robert Brunyng (e.g. Plate 6) – and the addition of his arms, need not indicate that he contributed.[152] The Benedictines of Sherborne, and particularly their abbot (who was a prebendary of Salisbury), were too aware of their abbey's status as an ancient episcopal seat (former bishops of Sherborne were painted on the vault of their chapter house)[153] to ignore the 'typology' of their superior with his secular colleague. Typology does seem to be the main idea expressed in the paired portraits (whether or not Mitford was a patron), and it is reinforced throughout the manuscript, most strikingly in the *bas-de-page* representation (p. 397) of the historical progress of the see, from Sherborne to Salisbury via Old Sarum: the latter is represented by a lugubrious castle, beslimed by a gross snail and overshadowed by a crane on one leg, symbolizing the vigilance of the castellan.[154] The relationship between monastery and episcopacy was, moreover, refreshingly good. The bishop of Salisbury was a strong supporter of the convent, as Leland's account of the ructions of 1437 makes clear,[155] and his appearance in the missal may simply betoken due gratitude and respect. If the project was one of joint patronage, then the convent – either as a whole or through one or more obedientiaries – seem more likely allies of Brunyng than Bishop Mitford. Here, it will be acknowledged that the Sherborne missal must have cost significantly more than the £25-odd spent on the missal commissioned a few years previously by Nicholas Lytlyngton, abbot of Westminster.[156] Moreover, Robert Brunyng did not command the disposable income of Lytlyngton, and (unless he played no part in it) the

---

[149] See fols 8r, 39v, 59r, 78r, 118v, 160r, 175r, 230v.
[150] *Constat* is unlikely to signify a loaned book in this case (as it may in other cases: cf. MLGB, p. xxvi). Hall, a parliamentary abbot, need not have borrowed such a book.
[151] Coldicott 1989, p. 87 (ill.).
[152] Mitford's involvement is usually assumed: Herbert 1920, pp. 12–14; Tolley 1988, p. 122; Scott 1996, II, p. 57; Goodall 1997, p. 189. Backhouse 1999, p. 49, is more judicious.
[153] *Itinerary*, I, p. 153.
[154] Backhouse 1999, p. 56 (ill.).
[155] *Itinerary*, I, p. 152.
[156] Backhouse 1999, p. 12.

major campaign of architectural reconstruction at Sherborne during his abbacy must have placed constraints on his purse.[157] Above all, the *spirit* of this remarkable work of art is as emphatically communal as its likely repository, the high altar: p. 524, with its ranks of monks in adoration of the Virgin Mary (to whom their abbey was dedicated), exemplifies this.[158] However, staying with the issue of superiors' patronage in particular, Brunyng's involvement here was clearly decisive, and the manuscript stands towards the end of a long line of great Benedictine books stamped with an abbatial *persona*. One can only imagine that it found an equal in the 'missale perpulchrum pro magno altari' which Walter de Monington commissioned for Glastonbury.[159]

Liturgical books were not the only decorated manuscripts commissioned and paid for by superiors. The abbatial copy of the general cartulary of Glastonbury abbey, the *Secretum Abbatis* commissioned by either John of Breynton or Walter de Monington,[160] includes among its 1335 documents three professionally executed miniatures contained in initials, and a number of interesting images added by the scribe.[161] As one would expect, the miniatures relate to the charters they appear alongside. Folio 20r has two miniatures, the first of a bishop (it could be any one of a number mentioned in the charter) in pontificals with two seculars in train speaking to a group of Benedictines, the second representing the same bishop handing a sealed charter to a monk. They relate to the episcopal sanction of a monastic archdeaconry at Glastonbury, a special privilege possessed by only five religious houses.[162] The archdeaconry was a source of great tension between bishop and convent (it interfered with episcopal jurisdiction and dignity),[163] and these miniatures were thus politically sensitive. The third miniature, on fol. 116r, heads the section of the cartulary comprising deeds connected with Glastonbury estates. Here a nobleman with two attendants kneels before a mitred abbot and donates a sealed charter. This charter might, as the adjacent text explains, relate to a single messuage only,[164] but it was worth illustrating for the statement that it made about the legal basis of abbatial (and by extension conventual) authority and privilege. Similar thinking underlies the miniature representing Henry II bestowing a charter of reconfirmation of liberties and entitlements on a kneeling Benedictine in the general cartulary of Gloucester commissioned by John de Gammages (c.1300).[165] Such pictures, strategically positioned and iconographically loaded, told a thousand words.

157 Monckton 2000, pp. 100–1.

158 Backhouse 1999, p. 58.

159 *Shorter Catalogues*, p. 231.

160 Cf. Aelred Watkin's supposition that Breynton was patron (*Cart.Glaston.*, I, p. xi) with the *de perquisitio* inscription implying Monington's patronage (OBL MS Wood Empt 1, fol. 1r).

161 Brief notes on the (professionally executed) miniatures in Pächt & Alexander 1966–73, III, p. 55; Luxford 2002(e), fig. 156 (fol. 20r). For scribal illustrations see fols 12v, 32v, 68v, 71r.

162 Sayers 1976 discusses only four (Glastonbury, Westminster, Bury and St Albans). For the obedience at Evesham see Knowles 1950, p. 606 note 5.

163 Keil 1961–67(a), p. 129.

164 *Cart.Glaston.*, II, p. 249.

165 PRO C 150/1, fol. 18r: illustrated in Welander 1991, pl. 3. Two similar professionally executed examples from Malmesbury, slightly pre-1300, are in PRO E 164 24, fols 44, 64. Noticed in *Reg.Malmes.*, II, p. xxv.

Liturgical vestments

Turning from books to vestments and metalwork taxes the imagination still further, for here nothing of substance survives.[166] However, this is greatly compensated for by the attention which chroniclers and inventorizers paid to the acquisition of these items by superiors. The provision of basic liturgical vestments and metalwork for communal use was usually the responsibility of the sacrist, and a proportion of the items attributed to abbots in chronicles is likely to have been due to this obedientiary,[167] perhaps with the assistance of the prior or prioress. Moreover, because a domestic chronicle, like an artistic 'relic' of the sort considered above, was in part an exhortation to future superiors and their convents to emulate good works and deeds past,[168] some of these attributions may be overgenerous: to properly appreciate this, modern readers must forget about the Dissolution and envisage the chronicler recording for a dim and distant monastic posterity. However, for a number of reasons over and above the goad of precedent discussed above, there is less cause for suspicion about the recorded generosity of superiors here than there may be where architectural patronage is concerned. As stated previously, the *Rule* of St Benedict cast the superior as a type of Christ, and thus, donation of plate and vestments, which were necessary appurtenances of the mass, was highly appropriate. It constituted a particularly salient example of the pastor endowing his flock with the material means to their spiritual salvation (for which the superior would be accountable on the Last Day).[169] Items of plate and other valuables that could readily be sold were occasionally necessary for a convent's temporal salvation, as well.[170] Further, because of their actual and symbolic value, metalwork and fine vestments (remembering that copes and chasubles might contain almost as much gold and silver as fabric) were obvious indicators of a superior's piety and wealth, the well-endowed treasury, like the well-repaired monastery, being an unambiguous symbol of good governance. Philippa of Hainault received a guided tour of the treasury at Glastonbury during the royal visit in 1331, as much to impress on her the wealth and propriety of Adam of Sodbury – here reflected in his convent's prosperity – as to satisfy her curiosity.[171] Costly liturgical paraphernalia, which exceeded a certain minimum standard (set according to the income of the relevant obedientiary), could not as a rule be covered by the monastic *mensa*,[172] which in most cases was sufficient for comfortable subsistence but not superfluity. A financially free agent was in a better position to pay for it. Finally, the lasting impression which gold, silver and jewels made on contemporary minds (the best witnesses being the chroniclers themselves), together with the contexts of their use,

[166] However, Christie 1938 and Williamson 1996, pp. 187, 191–2, 199, 202, 205, 217, 231, 233 illustrate useful comparative material.

[167] For example, the section of the Evesham chronicle devoted to Roger Yatton reminds readers that 'before [becoming abbot], when he served as sacrist, he did much that was commendable in the matter of vestments and other things' ('antea plura dignæ memoriæ commendanda operatus est in officio sacristariæ, ut in vestimentis et aliis': *CAEve.*, p. 303).

[168] Cf. the observations in Heslop 1987, p. 31.

[169] *RB*, chapter II; *RBFox*, p. 90.

[170] Knowles 1959, p. 246 speaks of accumulation of metalwork as 'banking', but to alienate such items permanently was considered disgraceful: e.g. *Vis.Nor.*, pp. 62, 284; *Linc.Vis.*, III, p. 291; GA, II, pp. 141–2; *Star Chamber*, I, pp. 24, 27.

[171] *Cart.Glaston.*, I, pp. 194–5.

[172] Occasional examples are forthcoming, however: e.g. *HMGlouc.*, I, p. 49.

made the products of the whitesmith and the fine embroiderer more than usually effective vehicles for commemoration, a fact as clear to superiors as it was to wealthy lay patrons. Shortly before his death, when Thomas Horton established an anniversary for himself at Gloucester, he ordained that the mass be celebrated 'in vestments provided by himself, of blue velvet embroidered with small moons and little golden stars'.[173]

When asked by the monk-historian Eadmer how St Benedict appeared in heaven, the spirit of Foldbriht, first abbot of Pershore (c.970–88), is supposed to have answered that he was 'the most nobly clad of any, shining with precious stones'.[174] This points up a Benedictine identification with high-status liturgical vestments which forms one of the most important and pervasive artistic themes of the order's post-Conquest historiography, and which existed prior to this: magnificent copes, 'incomparable' chasubles and related items were a part of Anglo-Saxon monastic culture as well, as the 'great black chasuble' given by King Cnut (1016–35) to Evesham and still used for high mass on Christmas day during the later fourteenth century testifies.[175] While Cnut's gift matched the penitential cast of the cloisterer's tunic and cowl, it was an anachronism in the later medieval Benedictine choir, where more vivid colours, embroidered with imaginative iconographic schemes, were fashionable. Huge sums were spent on such items: the inextricable link between price and worth which was as evident in medieval society as it is today is handsomely manifest where liturgical vestments are concerned. The 300 marks devoted to the 'Jesse vestment' by the Benedictines of Crowland (Lincolnshire) in the early fifteenth century – one fifth of their annual income – must have been paralleled at Glastonbury and Winchester.[176] Successive superiors acquired dazzling collections of ceremonial vestments, and although some were more enthusiastic than others, most seem to have contributed to what by the Dissolution were rich and enormous collections: the capacious fourteenth-century cope chests surviving at Gloucester bear mute witness to this.[177] Winchester, for example, possessed 188 copes of varying quality, some of 'bawdkyne' others of 'tisshew', others yet of silk. The cataloguer singled out one 'principal' embroidered cope 'wrought with gold and pearles', as well as vestments given by cardinal (and titular abbot) Beaufort (1404–47). There were forty-eight chasubles as well.[178]

Glastonbury, with its larger population, may have had even more than this (for extraordinary ceremonial and liturgical feasts celebrated in cappis), although its superior was not so wealthy. Collectively, however, his taste for iconographic display could hardly have been more extravagant. Geoffrey Fromond (1303–22), gave a grey velvet

173 HMGlouc., I, p. 51.
174 Quoted in Andrews 1901, p. 7.
175 Off. Eccl. Eve., p. 166; cf. CAEve., p. 83. For all but penitential occasions, 'ferial black' (see e.g. Gunton 1686, p. 59) was an anachronism by the fourteenth century: Off. Eccl. Eve., p. 165. Thus the customary's editors suppose the 'great black chasuble' mentioned therein as used at Christmas to have been Cnut's gift.
176 VCH Lincoln, II, p. 114.
177 Hewett 1988, pp. 118, 121. Peterborough's inventories include 328 albs and 168 copes, along with many other vestments: Gunton 1686, pp. 59–63. The greatest documented collection of such vestments at an English Benedictine house post-1300 is apparently that for Christ Church Canterbury in BL MS Cotton Galba E iv, fols 112r–121v (compiled in 1315, and including jocalia).
178 MA, I, pp. 202–3. These figures include Lady chapel vestments. In 1552, the cathedral still held ninety-nine copes, including five 'for children' (boy bishops?), and ten chasubles: Inv.PRO , pp. 235–7.

cope with moons and stars (evidently a popular theme), and another of red powdered with little parrots, while the next abbot, Walter of Taunton (Dec. 1322–Jan. 1323), gave among ten copes of 'feathered work' one embroidered with a Passion cycle against a gold and diapered field, another with a Crucifix and the stories of Sts Catherine and Margaret, a third with the Twelve Apostles and their attributes, a fourth of deep red samite displaying the stories of Sts Dunstan, David and Aldhelm etc. etc. As though not to be outdone, Adam of Sodbury acquired a collection copes and chasubles displaying an astonishing array of subject matter, from 'white rams and black horses' on red to 'red griffins and peacocks on a green field' to the 'majesty of Mary on a field of gold'. His political colours, and perhaps also the general advance in the popularity of heraldry as decoration, is seen in his gift of a cope of indigo samite 'with the English arms embroidered large' and another 'sewn all over with the arms of various magnates'.[179] Walter de Monington, too, commissioned a cope with the royal arms, and another, of green velvet, with gold leopards' heads and silver woodwoses all over it. The Ostensa of this abbot, which contains the richest of all West Country enumerations, lists the vestments that he left to his convent first and at much the greatest length.[180] Everything else is subordinate: other classes of ornament, internal building, external building, and books bequeathed follow in that order. A stronger indication of the importance of high-status liturgical vestments for Benedictine superiors could hardly be given.[181]

Metalwork

In the pontifical ornaments (mitre, tunicle, dalmatic, ring, sandals, gloves, and pastoral staff), which most later medieval male Benedictine superiors were entitled to use, the boundary between vestments and metalwork is crossed.[182] Insofar as they carried pastoral staffs, abbesses also shared in this display. The wholesale loss of these items is to a slight degree compensated for by the information that effigies such as that of William Malvern at Gloucester supply (Plate 32). In this case, the jewelled mitre (clearly of the *preciosa* type) replicates the sort of item Malvern thought it appropriate to go abroad in, and while the head of the crozier is missing, enough survives of the knop to show that it was of the octagonal variety embellished with miniature figures painstakingly wrought in gabled niches: an approximation of Wykeham's and Fox's croziers, which have remained intact.[183] Abbatial *pontificalia* are also represented in manuscript and glass painting. Malvern's first register is prefaced by a full-page representation of his arms, incorporating a crozier and highly ornamented mitre.[184] The acquisition of pontifical ornaments such as these is recorded fairly often in surviving sources, for they had a high

[179] CGA(C), pp. 252–3, 256–9, 260–1. Fromond also gave a green tapestry 'cum diuersis armis': CGA(C), p. 252. Walter de Monington gave three red tapestries with green borders, in the corners of each being the arms of King Arthur: TCC MS R 5 16, p. 219.
[180] This is a common characteristic of such lists.
[181] The Sherborne missal contains the largest surviving pictorial catalogue of high-status liturgical vestments from the West Country. There is no certainty, however, that any of these are 'portraits' of vestments actually existing at Sherborne: it may be noted that none of them have figural iconography. Some or all may be inventions of the artists.
[182] Certain priors were also entitled to wear *pontificalia*, which led to friction with Worcester's superiors: Marret 1970–72, pp. 61–2; *Lit.Can.*, II, p. 329 (both cases involving the prior of Worcester).
[183] Hope 1907; *Gothic*, p. 241.
[184] GCL Register D, fol. 1v; Welander 1991, pl. 16 (top).

'turn-over' rate: the use of episcopal vestments and insignia was a particular point of prestige, and no superior would wish to be seen by his peers in anything less than pristine garb. Abbots were also buried in pontifical regalia, though whether of their own patronage or older stock is uncertain, as almost everything has subsequently been dispersed. In support of the latter notion, perhaps, is the fact that the small figure of St Peter in the head of the crozier from the tomb of Thomas Seabroke (d.1457) would be better placed in the mid-thirteenth century than the mid-fifteenth,[185] notwithstanding the fact that the abbot of Gloucester was only granted the *pontificalia* in 1381.[186] The first set of ornaments which the abbey of St Peter possessed was donated by the duke of Gloucester, and thus it cannot be assumed that abbots were the patrons of these items wherever they appear. Furthermore, once purchased, responsibility for their repair lay with the sacrist.[187] However, shortly afterwards, Walter Froucester acquired four mitres (one 'preciosa' and three 'minoris pretii'), a pastoral staff and other appurtenances, reflecting a circumstance often met with in the chronicles of Evesham and Glastonbury.[188] John of Ombersley even purchased an episcopal throne ('sedile episcopale') complete with canopy and hangings from the executors of a late bishop of Worcester c.1373; the perfect prop for domestic appearances in the episcopal regalia which he obtained at the same time.[189] While few of the recorded items will have matched the quality of William of Wykeham's crozier, there must have been many mitres like his. The monastic treasury at Winchester contained thirteen mitres at the Dissolution, at least three of gilded silver and all covered with pearls and precious stones.[190]

According to surviving inventories, Glastonbury had five mitres, and Tewkesbury two, 'garnished with gilt, ragged pearls and counterfeit stones'.[191] The stones may have been counterfeit – and this, as the Westminster retable demonstrates, was not necessarily an economy[192] – but the pearls were no doubt real enough: Abbot Ombersley of Evesham spent fifty marks on pearls alone for the manufacture of a *mitra preciosa*, which he did not live to wear.[193] Such items were not always simply bought in complete, but (like sumptuous service books) were conceived of, planned and executed by degrees (a process illustrated in William More's account-book),[194] as might be expected of such important components of a superior's public image. It is worth pointing out that the fifty marks (about £33 6s) spent by John of Ombersley on pearls quite overshadows the £25

---

185 See the illustration in Welander 1991, p. 258.
186 The crozier may have been purchased or donated second-hand (cf. CAEve., pp. 301–2) and may thus pre-date 1381.
187 E.g. CRWor., p. 65. All of Winchester's pontifical ornaments were in the sacrist's keeping.
188 HMGlouc., I, p. 57; cf. CAEve., pp. 296, 302, 305; CGA(C), pp. 250–1, 266–9.
189 CAEve., p. 302, reading 'coopertoriis' as 'canopy and hangings'. For a notion of such hangings cf. CAEve., p. 296, where it is recorded that Abbot Boys purchased 'unum tapetum de blodio cum mitris intextis pro sede abbatis ad altare'.
190 MA, I, p. 202. On Wykeham's crozier and (reconstructed) mitre see Hope 1907, *passim*; AoC, pp. 471–3. William of Edington may actually have been the crozier's patron: Hope 1907, p. 472.
191 MT, p. 25; Burnet 1865, IV, p. 267.
192 On the retable and its high-status function, see Binski 1995, pp. 152–67, especially (in this context) 159–61. However, such imitations might be recognized for what they were: cf. e.g. *Suppression Letters*, p. 218.
193 CAEve., p. 302.
194 Jnl.More, pp. 163–4.

that the Lytlyngton missal is recorded to have cost some two decades later.[195] Presumably, the finished product would have matched in expense that recorded in the account-book of Prior William More of Worcester, under 1521: 'Item this yere I made þᵉ New Myter that cost in every charge, 50*l*.'[196]

Another aspect of metalwork particularly associated with superiors was the reliquary. Large Benedictine churches contained a great number of these: Winchester's Dissolution inventory mentions forty containing silver and/or gold, including four head and two arm reliquaries, and Glastonbury, the self-styled 'tomb of saints', could rival this.[197] Many were small and probably ancient, such as the ivory reliquaries at Winchester, and Hyde's 'Greek shrine' ('scrinio greco'), mentioned during the Anglo-Saxon period and subsequently in the fifteenth century.[198] As such, they would have received little attention once they had been established. However, shrines in the devotional spotlight might be more or less regularly updated.[199] This was an abnormal expense, which superiors and wealthy external patrons were better placed to bear than the obedientiaries (sacrist and feretrar) charged with basic shrine maintenance.[200] The fact that a number of important shrines held the relics of past superiors, for example those of Sts Patrick and Dunstan at Glastonbury, St Aldhelm at Malmesbury, St Edith at Wilton, St Swithun at Winchester and Sts Oswald and Wulfstan at Worcester, provided extra incentive for the head of the house to make a contribution.[201]

Three examples are relatively well documented. The first is recorded in the catalogue of episcopal gifts and commemorative entitlements written into the general cartulary of Bath. Ralph of Shrewsbury, bishop of Bath and Wells (1329–63) and former monk of the priory, gave his erstwhile colleagues a silver-gilt reliquary three feet in length, 'in all parts well-ornamented'.[202] This is simply designated 'for holy relics': no specific saint is mentioned or implied. Unfortunately, we are told no more about it, although other gifts of the bishop are listed. The second example, the benefaction made by Cardinal Beaufort to the feretory of St Swithun, has already been noticed in passing in chapter one. He gave, as we have seen, £477 15s in gold and £229 3s 2d *quart.* in silver for the re-edification of St Swithun's shrine, which was subsequently set up in the retrochoir alongside his burial chapel.[203] In this instance, the motive underlying the patronage

---

[195] Backhouse 1999, p. 12.

[196] *Jnl.More*, p. 179. The total cost as itemized at pp. 163–4 was £49 15s.

[197] MA, I, pp. 202–3. The mid thirteenth-century relic list in CGA(H), II, pp. 445–54, mentions twenty-three reliquaries, a number augmented by the early fourteenth-century list printed in GR.

[198] MA, I, p. 202. Glastonbury also had ivory reliquaries: Bird 1994, p. 318. For Hyde's 'Greek shrine', see Wormald 1959, p. 9.

[199] See Coldstream 1976, pp. 22–6 for post-1300 examples.

[200] Which is not to deny obedientiaries involvement altogether. The initials of Ralph Whitchurch, *thesaurius* at St Albans, are prominent on the post-1323 base of St Amphibalus's shrine: see Coldstream 1976, p. 20.

[201] The shrines of Sts Patrick, Aldhelm and Edith are practically undocumented during the later middle ages, however.

[202] *Cart.Bath*, p. 159: 'sanctarum reliquiarum [word missing: ed., p. 159 note 1, suggests *cuspam*] trium pedem longitudinis, argento ex omni parte decenter ornatam, et deauratam'.

[203] RCSWin., pp. 103–4. The shrine was ultimately valued at 2000 marks: *LPHVIII*, XIII:ii, pp. 401–2. It was not translated to the retrochoir until 1476. John Crook suggests that Beaufort (d.1447) had foreknowledge of the translation (Crook 1993, pp. 64, 68 note 29), however, which seems likely given the location and design of his chantry chapel.

seems to have had more to do with commemoration than with the fact that both saint and benefactor had been rulers of the same house.

In the third case, however, that of the shrine of St Dunstan at Glastonbury, the connection between saint and superiors appears more intimate, for St Dunstan had been the paradigmatic good shepherd, metaphorical and physical rebuilder of Glastonbury during his abbacy, and subsequently (along with King Edgar and St Æthelwold) of English monasticism generally. Though eclipsed in the popular imagination by Becket, he always retained a particular importance for the English Benedictines. All subsequent rulers of the abbey in whose shadow he grew up, and which he later ruled, were bound to identify with him to some degree. Ignoring the claim (historically more cogent) of Christ Church Canterbury to the relics, a succession of abbots set about installing Dunstan at the head of a long list of Glastonbury saints.[204] His primacy was declared in no uncertain terms on the reverse of Glastonbury's common seal (made c.1300–25), where he appears flanked by Sts Patrick and Benignus, the abbey's chief luminaries prior to the recovery of his relics after the fire of 1184.[205] His first shrine was built immediately after the fire,[206] and was subsequently embellished by Michael of Amesbury (1235–52), who separately enshrined St Dunstan's head, just as the heads of (for example) Sts Oswald and Wulfstan at Worcester had been separated from their bodies. The experience of Canterbury showed how popular, and thus remunerative, this might be.[207] During the first half of the fourteenth century, the shrine – which must have been large, as the monks claimed to possess Dunstan's body entire – was further embellished by three abbots. Walter of Taunton donated a large quantity of silver plate towards its renovation, Adam of Sodbury spent 'a large amount of treasure' on it, while his successor, John of Breynton, contributed a further 500 marks. The process was chronicled by John of Glastonbury,[208] and in the margins of Cambridge, Trinity College MS R 5 16, an early sixteenth-century annotator has illustrated it with five small drawings of the feretory,[209] each one placed next to a passage in the text recording abbatial munificence (Plate 33). These drawings are significant, for they provide the only known visual evidence for the appearance of St Dunstan's feretory.[210] They are also important for the evidence they yield concerning later abbatial attitudes towards it, for they were probably added at the behest of Richard Beere.[211] Beere also did a certain amount of work on the shrine (although he did not, as is sometimes stated, rebuild it), setting it up in a more honourable position than that it had previously occupied. This was, he said, to obviate theft of precious metal from it;[212] but in fact, the reasons went deeper than this, for soon a concourse of enthusiastic visitors came to worship at it, strengthening Glastonbury's

204 Dunstan's relics always remained Glastonbury's most important primary relics, Joseph of Arimathea's bones never being found: see Carley 2001, *passim.*
205 Birch 1887, pp. 564–5 (no. 3189); VCH *Somerset,* II, pl. 1, fig. 2.
206 CGA(C), pp. 180–1.
207 CGA(C), pp. 218–19 (head shrine), 220–1 (embellishment of main feretory). A 'keeper of St Dunstan's head' appears in 1525: *Reg.Wolsey,* p. 85. On Becket's head-shrine see Nilson 1998, pp. 211–15.
208 CGA(C), pp. 180–1, 221–2, 258–9, 264–5, 266–7.
209 Pp. 117, 161, 199, 207, 211.
210 On the drawings and their historical context see Luxford 2002(a), *passim.*
211 Beere pushed Glastonbury's claim to custodianship of St Dunstan's relics in the face of strong archiepiscopal opposition: *Mem.Dunstan,* pp. 432–4; Luxford 2002(a), pp. 115–17.
212 *Mem.Dunstan,* p. 433.

claim to Dunstan's relics in the face of mounting objections from the monks, and eventually, the archbishop of Canterbury.[213] Richard Beere was as conscious of his obligations to his great forebear (whom he calls 'Sancti Patroni nostri')[214] as his fourteenth-century colleagues had been; and as silver and gold were the appropriate materials for his own regalia, so were they all the more for the relics of St Dunstan.[215]

Other items of metalwork, in particular statuary, liturgical ornaments and domestic plate, are attributed to the patronage of superiors more or less frequently in surviving sources. Abbesses, we learn, commissioned items that would not have disgraced their most prosperous male counterparts. For example, Maud de Littleton of Wherwell (1333–40) contributed to the sacristy a gilded silver cup, with thirteen gold rings attached to the bowl, and precious stones encrusting the foot.[216] The Leominster chalice – which if not actually Benedictine was certainly in use in a Benedictine context – and the modest fourteenth-century processional cross now displayed in All Saint's church, Evesham, may be set alongside Seabroke's crozier, Wykeham's pontifical ornaments, and the sketches of St Dunstan's shrine in order to provide at least some idea of what existed before the descent of Messrs Pollard, Tregonwell and company.[217] Gold and silver were perhaps the principal aesthetic leitmotifs of the later medieval Benedictine church. They were to be found everywhere, from the espousal ring of the poorest nun to feretories such as St Swithun's, into which grown men might bodily climb.[218] Vestments and hangings were often sewn with gold and silver thread, and stone and woodwork often gilded. Leland reports that parts of the piers in the east end at Worcester were gilded; and the cathedral's lapidary store holds a fifteenth-century polygonal micro-architectural fragment sculpted with angels to which substantial quantities of gold still adhere. The choir stall canopies at Winchester (Plate 3) were also originally gilded.[219] As such, these things said a good deal about Benedictinism and its values, and it is to be expected that superiors would play a key role in the provision and renovation of objects plated with and cast in them.

Sepulchral monuments

We turn now to the final class of object to recommend itself as an unproblematic example of the patronage of superiors, the (personal) sepulchral monument. This might take any form, from a simple gravestone to an ostentatious chantry chapel, depending on personal predilections. The variety is remarkable, and cannot be sufficiently accounted for in terms of income, for the wealthiest of abbots sometimes chose for themselves modest stones, as Richard Beere did. Leland records that Beere was interred

---

213 For the shrine's popularity following its relocation, see *Mem.Dunstan*, pp. 426, 434. For the gist of the archiepiscopal objections, see *Mem.Dunstan* pp. 436–7.

214 *Mem.Dunstan*, p. 432.

215 St Dunstan's feretory was, as Beere wrote to the archbishop, 'ducentis annis in ecclesia nostra per religiosos patres antecessores erectum auroque et argento pulcherrime fabricatum': *Mem.Dunstan*, p. 432.

216 BL MS Egerton 2104(A), fol. 209r.

217 On the Leominster chalice, see Oman 1957, p. 45. The cross at All Saints, Evesham, is apparently undocumented, and the local ascription to the abbey thus conjectural.

218 *Reg.Morton*, I, pp. 52–3.

219 *Itinerary*, V, p. 227: 'Columnellis marmoreis cum junctures areis deauratis' (Worcester piers); Tracy 1993(a), p. 199 (Winchester stalls). The gilded fragment is unpublished.

'sub plano marmore', and though this was presumably incised or inset with a brass, Leland's silence in the matter of a three-dimensional effigy makes it clear that the abbot did not have one.[220] Essentially, then, the greatest West Country head of all chose a memorial similar to that which an abbess of middling means such as Joan Icthe of Romsey (1333–49), or even a poor superior such as Prior Thomas Colyns of Tywardreath (1506–38) might consider appropriate.[221]

Like his contemporary Thomas Ramryge, abbot of St Albans (d.1521), who also chose a flat slab for his tomb,[222] Beere was buried in a chapel of his own making, and this may explain the relative plainness of his monument. Leland wrote that Beere's chapel of the Holy Sepulchre was located to the west of the south nave aisle. Frederick Bligh Bond thought that this perhaps indicated an annexe chantry chapel of the sort that Clement Lichfield had built for himself on the south side of All Saint's church at Evesham,[223] but it seems more likely, given the nature of the church involved, to have been a stone-cage chapel; just the sort of monument which Ramryge had erected over his grave.[224] With a monumental canopy of such grandeur, an ostentatious tomb-chest and effigy were unnecessary. Indeed, they were a disadvantage, as they limited the number of people who might fit into the chapel during masses, which in turn reduced the number of prayers that might be said for the repose of the abbatial soul.[225] Thomas Seabroke seems to have realized this. His stone-cage chapel at Gloucester was supplied with a wall-niche that allowed his effigy to rest as unobtrusively as possible.[226] Abbot Malvern, who had a stone-cage chapel constructed on the north side of the presbytery one bay west of Edward II's tomb (Plate 10), was less concerned about providing space for a congregation. Approximately half of the available floor space within his chapel is taken up with a high freestone tomb-chest, richly embellished with heraldry and devotional motifs – the Five Wounds, the *arma Christi*, and a Crucifixion on a raguly cross, now defaced – and heraldry, and topped with the alabaster effigy examined above (Plate 32). What floor space is left free remains embellished with encaustic tiles displaying a variety of motifs, including his device of a buck *trippant* between broad arrow heads (*pheons*) and the arms of the abbey he ruled.[227] The abbatial chantry chapel was a *Gesamtkunstwerk* no less than the monastic church of which it was a microcosm.

Shrines such as those of Sts Dunstan and Swithun aside, the grandest superiors' monuments of all are the five chantry chapels at Winchester, in which bishops Edington (1345–66), Wykeham, Beaufort, Waynflete (1447–86) and Fox are buried. They reflect

220 For he otherwise lists many sculpted abbatial effigies: *Itinerary*, I, pp. 289–90. Cf. Cardinal John Morton's (d.1500) choice of a 'marble stone' set with a brass for his tomb in Canterbury cathedral: Wilson 1995, p. 485.

221 Liveing 1906, pl. facing p. 120; Perkins 1907, p. 61; Walker 1999, p. 44 (Joan Icthe's stone and inscription); Lake 1867–72, IV, p. 273; Luxford 2002(e), fig. 91 (Colyns's gravestone).

222 See Wooley 1930, pp. 31–6 for Ramryge's monument.

223 See Bond 1913, pl. between pp. 56 and 57; for Lichfield's chapel see Harvey 1984, p. 307; Cox 1980, pp. 16, 23–4; Monckton 1999, p. 284. Lichfield had another chapel constructed, apparently by the same architect (identified by Harvey as Robert Vertue junior) on the south side of the adjacent parish church of St Lawrence.

224 For a precedent stone-cage chapel at the west end of a Benedictine nave, see Wilson 1995, p. 475.

225 For public (in this case largely, but not necessarily completely, monastic) attendance at private chantries see Wood-Legh 1965, p. 294.

226 Chapel noted in Cook 1947, p. 142.

227 Illustrated in Welander 1991, p. 291.

the status of their patrons, their desire for commemoration, and the jealousy with which they maintained their hegemony over burial rights within the cathedral. There are remarkably few high-status sepulchral monuments within the cathedral at Winchester besides these chapels; all of the royal remains, with the possible exception of William II's, are relegated to the chests atop the choir screens.[228] This jealousy was no doubt injurious to the monks, reducing as it did their capacity to generate income via chantries. Less possessive superiors might still build visually dominant tombs for themselves, however, and on at least one occasion this led to problems for the monks. One case which is quite well known is documented in both archiepiscopal and conventual registers.[229] Around 1300, Godfrey Giffard, bishop of Worcester (d.1302), built himself 'a great monument for his own burial, quite close to the great altar of the church . . . that . . . [had] certain pinnacles upon it constructed after the fashion of a tabernacle – a lofty and sumptuous erection of carved stone.'[230] (A free-standing canopy tomb of the type coming into fashion at Benedictine houses such as Ely and Westminster is probably to be envisaged here.)[231] These are the words of Robert of Winchelsey, visiting archbishop, whose objections to the tomb – that it interfered with the honour due to the saints whose shrines were located close by, prevented sunlight from reaching the high altar, interrupted the usual disposition of a cathedral choir, and got in the way of lay people visiting the incorrupt body of one John de Constantiis – highlight the lengths to which Giffard was prepared to go in his quest for commemoration. In his response to these objections the prior alluded to the frailty of his superior, writing that to remove the tomb would hasten an already imminent death. His delaying tactics seem to have worked, for it appears that the tomb was not removed until the erection of Prince Arthur's chantry chapel on the site, early in the sixteenth century.[232] The superior remained in the bosom of his flock, a focus of their attention each time they entered the choir.

As patrons and rulers, Godfrey Giffard, William Malvern, Richard Beere and other Benedictine superiors were unusually well placed to annexe the premium locations available for their burials and to commission monuments befitting their social and religious status. Where a superior might choose to be buried differed from individual to individual: at Evesham, a number of abbatial tombs were clustered around the font,[233] while at Glastonbury, Winchester and Gloucester they were spread throughout the church. Often, an influential factor was the desire to be buried in proximity to a work for which they had been responsible. Malvern presided over works in the presbytery at

---

[228] For the 'mortuary chests', renewed c.1525 under Richard Fox, see Crook 1994, pp. 165–73, 186–8. On the so-called 'Rufus' tomb, more probably that of Henry of Blois, see Crook 1999, pp. 207–8 et passim; Gardner 1951, p. 162 note 2; Duffy, M. 2003, pp. 46–7.

[229] Reg.Winchelsey, II, pp. 761–2; Lib.Albus, pp. 21–3. See also Hutchinson 1942, pp. 29–31; Rogers 1987, pp. 24–6.

[230] Lib.Albus, p. 21; MacKenzie 1997, pp. 24–6.

[231] See Binski 1995, pp. 176–8 (Westminster); Lindley 1995, pp. 85–96 (Ely). For Giffard's probable cognizance of Westminster's tombs see Wilson 1995, p. 452 note 2; Park 1996, p. 20. No architectural element of Giffard's tomb survives.

[232] What is said to be Giffard's effigy now lies in the chapel's undercroft: see Park 1996, pp. 20–1 and fig. 6. The infrequency of archiepiscopal visitations and constant interruptions caused by deaths and translations of Worcester's bishops (in 1302, 1307, 1313, 1317, 1327, 1333, 1337, 1338, 1349 etc.) suggest how such grave injunctions could be flouted.

[233] CAEve., pp. 289, 293. Cf. Romans 6:3–4.

Gloucester,[234] Walter de Wykewan was buried in a chapel on the north side of the presbytery at Winchcombe beneath a vault reconstructed at his behest,[235] Walter of Taunton lay in the shadow of the great rood he had erected,[236] and Bishops Edington and Wykeham of Winchester were buried in the nave which they had helped to rebuild.[237] Moreover, it is possible that some tombs were built with the goal of consoling convents over the death of their patrons: indications of this motive exist for medieval prelates' tombs, though not Benedictine ones.[238] In each case, however, the principal rationale underlying the patronage of a given superior's sepulchral monument was the annexation of the maximum possible amount of intercessory prayer. In this regard it was important, for abbots and priors at least, to choose tombs that would remind their convents (whose prayers were, after all, unusually effective; most Benedictine monks being priests) of their former status: as loving father, good shepherd, generous benefactor and tireless defender. If, as St Benedict suggested, the superior would be brought to book for the shortcomings of those he or she ruled, then the need of intercessory prayer was surely believed greater in this quarter than anywhere else in the monastery. When the prophetic London Carthusian John Homersley was asked why a former prior of upstanding life had not yet escaped purgatory, he is reported to have answered '*Saunce doute*, he takes a dangerous work upon himself, whoever takes upon him the office of prelate.'[239] There is nothing specifically Carthusian in this pronouncement: theoretically, it might just as appropriately have been said of a Benedictine abbot or abbess. We should consider this awareness of responsibility carefully in the current context, because although it sits uncomfortably with some heads of houses – the 'pessimus, quasi hereticus' Abbot Bonus (1327–33) of Tavistock, for example[240] – it throws an informative light on the patronage of most Benedictine superiors.

Conclusion

The superior was the dominant personality in any Benedictine house, casting a long and influential shadow over most aspects of conventual life even when absent. Only the priors of Bath, Winchester and Worcester, whose art and architectural patronage will be considered in the following chapter along with that of monastic obedientiaries, commanded commensurate influence and prestige. An important aspect of this *persona* was the material embellishment for which a given superior was responsible: cloister monks and nuns remembered their ruler not only for the pittances of food, clothing, spices and money which he or she provided, but also for the great mass-book lying on the high altar, the portrait in stained glass, the grandeur or humility of the tomb, and the voice (for so it was understood) of the bells, from treble through to tenor. On the patron's part, the effect was deliberate, and sought for the most practical of all ends: for

---

234 See below, p. 167.
235 Although as noted previously, not at his charge: *Landboc*, II, pp. lvii–lviii, lx.
236 CGA(C), pp. 256–7; cf. *Itinerary*, I, p. 288; Henderson 1937, plan between pp. 108 and 109.
237 Wykeham even had a relatively recent tomb (it had a brass: Stephenson 1926, p. 167) removed that his own (of c.1400) might occupy his preferred location.
238 See e.g. *Cart.Chichester*, p. 48.
239 Hope 1925, p. 63.
240 *HRH*, p. 73.

the superior's soul endured purgatory alongside those of humbler religious. As has been shown, there were other reasons for patronage as well: the patronage of art and architecture was an ideologically and psychologically complicated business. With the tomb, however, the signal rationale is candidly exposed. Ultimately, the patronage of art and architecture offered escape, and thus, it was in the interests of all heads of monastic houses to fund – or at least gain the reputation for funding – as many works of benefit to the community as possible. Over-attributions, ambiguities and uncertainties aside, they were the most significant class of patron of Benedictine art and architecture during the later middle ages, in terms of quality if not quantity.

That Benedictine monks and nuns of lower station also understood the potentially redemptive nature of patronage is apparent from the quantity and nature of the art and architecture which they purchased and contributed to. As with superiors, commemoration was not the only reason for acting as a patron, but it was clearly influential. Many obedientiaries were bound to act as patrons, of course, in particular (as noted previously) the sacrist, *custos operum*, precentor and *feretrar*, to whom it is time to add the principal prior. However, many obedientiaries paid for works of art and contributed to campaigns of rebuilding over and above those covered by their occupational briefs. Insofar as means and circumstances permitted, cloister monks and nuns also acted as patrons. Although this fact has been ignored in studies of English monastic art, recent consideration of the production, purchase and use of artworks by the lower orders of religious in Germany during the later middle ages have suggested how much there is to be unearthed in this regard.[241] In the next chapter, which addresses the patronage of art and architecture by those below the level of superior, we will scratch the surface at least.

[241] Particularly Hamburger 1997. See also Driver 1995, *passim* (on English Brigittine woodcuts).

4

The Patronage of Obedientiaries and Cloisterers

Patronage on the part of those beneath the level of superior is best designated 'official' and 'unofficial'. Official patronage covers commission of and payment for building and embellishments according to the remit of a given obedience. As such, it was not practised by cloister monks and nuns, except where they were obliged to agree and contribute to a programme of works such as those mentioned above at Bath, Evesham and Winchester. Most of the items recorded in obedientiary *compoti* qualify as examples of official patronage. Unofficial patronage includes all items purchased or contributed to that were not sanctioned by office (although they might still find their way onto *compoti*). Personal devotional objects are the most obvious example. Both obedientiaries and cloister monks and nuns (the distinction between these classes will be drawn in due course) practised unofficial patronage, although because it usually went undocumented, evidence of it is scarce. Indeed, a considerable amount of the evidence lies in surviving, undocumented objects (or descriptions of such), and these carry only suggestion, not demonstration.

Take, for example, the little psalter from the nunnery of the Holy Cross at Wherwell, now in the British Library, made during the early fourteenth century but still in use late into the fifteenth.[1] A well-drawn, characterful series of labours of the months and signs of the zodiac illustrating the calendar, and illuminated initials on fols 12v (King David as psalmist) and 31v qualify it as a work of art (Plate 22).[2] What is more, an identity can be attached to it thanks to an inscription on fol. 131v: 'Iste liber constat dompne Johanna Stretford monasterij Werwellensis *sancti* cruce.' A clear-cut example, it may be thought, of unofficial patronage on the part of Joan Stretford, Benedictine nun of Wherwell.[3] But a moment's consideration, and a closer look at the manuscript, induce doubts. 'Johanna Stretford' has been written over another name, now illegible. Did she buy the psalter from another nun or receive it as a gift? If the latter, then she – like Shaftesbury's Anne Audley – can hardly be regarded as the book's patron. Further, did the original owner purchase it while a nun, or before she entered the monastery? The inscription may have been added later on. These uncertainties do not debase the psalter's value as evidence of private ownership of art by Benedictines, but they do demonstrate its limitations as a document of patronage, and similar caveats apply to other surviving artefacts lacking the sort of detailed information found in Elizabeth Shelford's

---

1   BL MS Additional 27866. The calendar includes 'Deposicio *sancti* Osmundi' (fol. 11v).
2   The calendar is at fols 6–11v.
3   Here, the rubricated textura of the inscription indicates that *constat* denotes ownership, not temporary possession.

book of hours. The history of unofficial patronage is thus bound to be based largely on possibilities rather than proofs.

The Patronage of the Priorate

As discussed in chapter three, the patronage obligations of superiors were not, in general, clearly defined. Insofar as their obedience was unceasing and, in theory at least, might embrace any aspect of conventual life, all of their expenditure was 'official'. As the *persona* of his or her house, the superior's brief was always active, and thus even works of art for his or her private use might serve official functions. When we read that Edward II noticed and remarked on the paintings of kings in the abbot's hall at Gloucester, we comprehend works of art functioning to maximum effect, realizing the ideal end to which they were commissioned.[4] This decoration of an exclusive space in a private set of apartments was as much the product of official patronage as abbatial construction of a new conventual presbytery, for whether officiating at a high mass or entertaining in seclusion, the superior was acting in an official capacity.

To a considerable extent, the same may be said of the priorate (here referring to principal priors and prioresses only),[5] especially the priors of Bath, Winchester and Worcester, who, as acknowledged above, were effectively the heads of their houses. They are not considered along with superiors here because they were distinct in important ways: politically (they did not regularly sit in parliament,[6] and their election was not subject to tutelary-patronal prerogative); financially (a prior's *mensa* was not legally distinct from conventual finances, nor was it proportionately large);[7] in terms of dignity and decorum (for example, the head of a cathedral priory was constrained to use a plain mitre and unornamented bourdon rather than a pastoral staff in the presence of higher ecclesiastical dignities).[8] Admittedly, however, the distinction is not consistently clear where art and architectural patronage is concerned. One need only look to monuments such as William Birde's sumptuous chantry chapel (begun 1515) at Bath to gain an impression of this.[9] Like a superior, but unlike a lesser monk, a prior (or a prioress, although information here is scarce) remained at all times representative of the convent to which he belonged. The cathedral priors, who considered themselves in all meaningful respects to be the heads of their houses,[10] were important feudal lords in their own

---

4   *HMGlouc.*, I, p. 44.
5   Larger Benedictine houses had up to four 'priors': see for examples *BRECP*, p. 848; *CRWin.*, p. 221; Harvey 2002, pp. xix note 20, xx note 26.
6   Coventry's prior excepted.
7   E.g. at Glastonbury (1538/9) the prior received £50 1s 2d: cf. the cellarer, £611; sacrist, £311 12s 6d; chamberlain, £158 18s 9d *ob. quart.*; medar, £93 16s: Flower 1912, pp. 51, 54. At Milton (1344) the abbot had £200, the prior and convent £100 between them, an extra £1 betokening the dignity of the prior: Traskey 1978, p. 116. At Worcester (1523/4), the prior got £147 12s 6d: cf. the cellarer, £368 3s 5d *ob*; kitchener, £134 8s 2d; precentor, £118 4s: Noake 1866, p. 270. See WCL MS A xii, fol. 12v, for similar figures in 1513.
8   Atkins 1951, pp. 14–15.
9   Bird's stone-cage chantry chapel is the grandest surviving free-standing sepulchral monument to a prior: see Davis 1834, *passim*.
10   Dr Greatrex has impressed this on the author.

right, and may even be said to have 'personified' their monasteries in the manner of an abbot. Thus, when Oliver King complained of the dilapidated state of the church at Bath, he held Prior Cantlow (1483–99) and Cantlow's predecessors to account, both for the condition of the building and the 'superfluity' that he claimed characterized the life of the chapter.[11] The titular superiors had nothing to do with it, and the lesser monks were hardly to blame. And indeed, Cantlow was a prior who maintained the port and countenance – if not the charge – of a superior to a high degree. In a case involving him brought before the Court of Star Chamber in the mid-1480s, which concerned (among other things) the alienation of plate and liturgical vestments from Bath, it was revealed that he 'commonly rideth with xviij horses or therabout and his seruantes all in one lyverey or clothyng'.[12] This testimony was submitted by the abbot of St Augustine's, Canterbury, who probably saw his own arrangements for progress outside the precinctual wall reflected here. Cantlow looked like an abbot; and the historian of patronage reviewing the prior's deeds but ignorant of his name or rank might be excused for mistaking him for one.

All things considered, however, it is both justifiable and expedient to discuss the patronage of the priorate separately from the official and unofficial patronage of other classes of monk and nun. John Cantlow is a good subject with whom to begin, because the art and architecture that he chose to commission and pay for illustrate a number of important points concerning priors' patronage in general. If it is accepted that the rebuilding of Bath cathedral priory church began c.1480, as Linda Monckton proposes (the hard evidence, which is wholly architectural, suggests that she is correct), then it can no longer be assumed that Cantlow ignored it completely.[13] What may still be said is that it was not a patronage priority for him. He surely realized – his superior certainly did[14] – that rebuilding the church was too great an undertaking given the funds at his disposal. The limited amount that he may have achieved, and whatever improvements to the claustral complex he oversaw,[15] were insufficient to give King any pause, and thus probably relatively insignificant. In general, his patronage concerns seem to have lain with buildings outside the monastery. Evidence survives of his involvement in the reconstruction and embellishment of a number of churches on the outskirts of Bath. On the tower of St Thomas Becket, Widcombe, his device, station and name are present, along with the arms of Bath priory, and the east window retains part of a black-letter inscription including the name 'Cantlow' and the date 1492. Given that parts of the tower and the tracery of the east window (the rest of the chancel has been thoroughly Victorianized) are clearly late medieval, these indications strongly suggest the prior's involvement in a campaign of renovation.[16] At St Catherine to the north-east of Bath, the evidence of patronage is clearer. Here, in the church (formerly chapel) of St Catherine, the four-light east window of the chancel retains its principal subjects: (from

---

11 MA, II, p. 270. Cantlow himself had earlier blamed the church's condition on his predecessors: Manco 1993, p. 91.
12 *Star Chamber*, I, p. 34; PSC, p. 49. The items included 'unum par vestimentorum quondam ex dono recolende memorie domini Thome Bekynden nuper Bathoniensis & Wellensis Episcopi [i.e. Bath's titular superior] valoris iiij marcarum': *Star Chamber*, I, p. 27.
13 Monckton 1999, pp. 233–89; *Gothic*, p. 361.
14 MA, II, p. 270.
15 See Manco 1993, p. 91.
16 Devenish 1924–26, pp. 50–1; Woodforde 1946, p. 29.

north to south) the Virgin Mary, Christ Crucified, St John the Evangelist and St Peter.[17] Beneath the Virgin are the arms of Bath priory, below Christ, England and France quarterly, under St Peter, those of Cantlow (*argent, on a fess azure a mitre or,* with the monogram 'I C' *or* thrice), while beneath St John is a representation of Cantlow himself, kneeling and clad in pontifical regalia (purple dalmatic, fur almuce, indigo cope, golden mitre and crozier: Plate 19). He directs the usual petition to the Crucified: 'O fili dei miserere mei.' A black-letter inscription reading '*Domini* Johannis Cantlow quondam prioris. Hanc cancellam fieri fecit anno domini mcccclxxxxix' once underlined these figures,[18] while the borderwork surrounding the main panels of glass contains a series of crowned letters which make up Cantlow's name once more. Further, the south window of the chancel retains two roundels displaying his device of an eagle and 'Prior Cantlow' in black letter, while the east window and two in the nave have rose and sun motifs belonging to the same period which hint that this glazing scheme was formerly more extensive. Here inscription and iconography (remembering that Christ as well as St Peter was a spiritual patron of Bath priory),[19] the architecture of the chancel and the Perpendicular pulpit installed at the same time, go together to demonstrate Cantlow's concern with advertisement of self and institution, with personal commemoration, and with fulfilment of obligation to those whose tithes sustained his office.

The commemorative motive was emphatically underscored in another example of Cantlow's patronage, the chapel of St Mary Magdalene at Holloway, again in Widcombe parish.[20] On 19 June 1678, Anthony à Wood copied the following inscription which he found incised in stone on the east wall of the porch:

> Thys chapell florysschyd w[t] formosyte spectabyll
> In the honowre of mary magdlen prior Cantlow hathe edyfyde
> Desyring yow to pray for hym w[t] yowre prayers delectabyll
> That sche wyll inhabyt hym in hevyne ther evyr to abyd.

The inscription still exists.[21] Wood also noticed the arms of Bath priory in the porch roof, and further, that 'the windows of this chapel are full of painted effigies . . . the two Maries, St. Peter, St. Barthelmew, St. Philip, St. James'.[22] To either side of the east window was a 'neach in which probably had been the images of the two maries'. A century later, John Collinson noted in the east window the Virgin and Child, a figure with a crozier (which he supposed might represent Cantlow), Christ crucified, Sts Bartholomew and Mary Magdalene, and a 'monkish figure'.[23] What survives of this scheme – a haloed ecclesiastic, a figure of St Leonard and part of the Bartholomew along with miscellaneous smaller fragments – is datable to the late fifteenth century, and demonstrates obvious stylistic affinities with the glass at St Catherine. Indeed,

---

[17] Woodforde 1946, pp. 27–8; Devenish 1924–26, p. 50. The heads of all but Christ are modern replacements.

[18] Collinson 1791, I, p. 138. The glass has been restored, and the date 1490 anachronistically inserted.

[19] See Luxford 2000, p. 321. The iconography thus follows the patronal prerogative rather than the church's dedication. St Catherine appears in a roundel in the south chancel window: ill. in Manco 1998, p. 43; apparently Flemish, but not noticed in Cole 1993. While this is contemporary with the glass of the east window, it was conceivably installed at a later date.

[20] On this chapel see Manco 1998, pp. 44–8. Pevsner 1958(a), p. 107, dates the rebuilding to 1495.

[21] It is represented in Manco 1998, p. 47.

[22] OBL MS Wood D 11, fols 147r–148r.

[23] Collinson 1791, I, pp. 173–4.

Christopher Woodforde supposed that the two schemes were executed by the same glazier(s).[24] This undertaking was apparently part of a larger scheme of good works on Cantlow's part, including the refoundation of a hospital for lunatics to which the chapel was annexed (which explains the figure of St Leonard, for the lunatics were presumably under lock and key).[25] The verse commemorating the rebuilding is an unusually candid demonstration of the desired end of these works: the chapel has been built and decorated in surpassing fashion ('florysschyd with formoyste spectabyll') in honour of the Magdalen, yes; but also that the nature and quality of the embellishment might garner prayers for its earthly patron. The utilitarian intent is emphasized by the inscription's use of the vernacular, and of rhyme (for mnemonic purposes). Its nature and location – black letter set in an eye-catching banderole by the chapel entrance – is also relevant, reminding visitors to be truly thankful for what they were about to receive. That future priors recognized the potential of the hospital chapel to attract worshippers and their prayers is suggested by the burial therein of Prior William Gibbs's (1525–39) parents, their tomb also inscribed with a petition in English.[26]

Commemoration can nearly always justifiably be assumed as a motive for patronage of religious art and architecture, regardless of the patron's social status. In Cantlow's patronage another ubiquitous motive, the pious urge to honour saints to whom one (personally and institutionally) was beholden, also stands out. The images described by Wood and Collinson and still displayed in the chancel window at St Catherine tell part of a devotional story that can be properly understood only with reference to other, related phenomena: the monumental effigies of Sts Peter and Paul flanking the west door of the priory church,[27] the statue of Christ proffering the Charter of Human Redemption on the central mullion of the north aisle window (Plate 17),[28] the comb of St Mary Magdalen preserved among the convent's treasures,[29] and the chain which bound St Peter in prison, 'counted a great relic', fastened around local women in the *extremis* of childbirth, and carried by the prior in procession through the town on Lammas day, to be kissed in its silver basin by every monk in turn.[30]

It is some jump in terms of status and financial wherewithal from the prior of Bath to the last French prior of Cowick, Robert of Rouen, elected in 1446 to govern a community of just three monks. Yet the devotional element in the patronage of priors can be illustrated as clearly with reference to him as to John Cantlow. The case to be discussed

---

24 Woodforde 1946, p. 40.

25 The original foundation, for lepers, predates 1100: K&H, p. 341.

26 OBL MS Wood D 11, fol. 147v notes this inscription in a stone pavement slab: 'Robert Gibbes & hys wife/ 1525/ I desyre yow yowre charite for the soules above writen praye ye.' Cf. Collinson 1791, I, p. 172.

27 Stylistically these statues appear post-medieval. They are perhaps products of Bishop Montague's early seventeenth-century building campaign at Bath. Cf. Pevsner 1958 (a), pp. 101–2, where they are dated to the early sixteenth century. It need not be doubted that they replace earlier statues representing these same saints, however.

28 On this statue, and the only other known example of the iconography (BL MS Additional 37049, fol. 23r), see Luxford 2003(a), pp. 307–10. No Charter of Human Redemption exists for Bath, but there are fifteenth- and early sixteenth-century copies of the so-called Short Charter from Muchelney, St Albans and Winchester, and lost copies are known to have existed at Christ Church Canterbury and on a gravestone in 'an abby in Kent': Spalding 1914, pp. xx, xxv, xxviii, 11, 15; *Winch.Anth.*, fols 114v–115r; James and Jenkins 1930–32, p. 134.

29 *LPHVIII*, II, p. 42.

30 *LPHVIII*, II, p. 42.

also suggests other possible motives for priors' patronage. Robert of Rouen arrived to find Cowick at a low ebb. Much of the priory had been gutted by fire in 1443, and a repair estimate of over £177, together with the hostile rumblings emanating from Westminster, effectively precluded rebuilding:[31] a sad end to the English dominions of the great Norman abbey of Bec, of which Cowick was the last. And it was the end; for on 29 May 1451 Henry VI suppressed the monastery, together with tiny Cistercian Begare in North Yorkshire, to the advantage of Eton College.[32] Robert of Rouen resigned in November of that year, and within six months the last monk had left Cowick and returned to France. (The house remained vacant until its reconstitution as a cell of Tavistock Abbey in 1462.)[33]

However, immediately before his resignation, the prior was involved in a substantial act of joint architectural patronage. In 1451 he contributed to the renovation of the chancel of St Michael's at Spreyton, a church impropriated to Cowick.[34] The evidence for this is a remarkable fifteenth-century inscription, refreshed in the late eighteenth century, still visible on the timbers of the elaborate chancel roof. This testifies that the work was done at the behest of the vicar Henry de Maygne, and that Robert of Rouen, with the lord of the local manor, contributed: 'Henry de Maygne, priest [and] vicar of this church, had me made in the year of the Lord 1451. Robert of Rouen of Becdenne, prior of Cowick, and Richard Talbot, Lord of Spreyton, gave of their goods towards my making. Pray for their souls. This Henry was born in the land of Normandy, and wrote all of this with his own hand.' The disclosure that the vicar personally composed the inscription and the verses that follow it is exceptional, and emphasizes the extent to which our knowledge of patronage at any level often depends on the vagaries of recordation as well as survival.[35]

Given his tenuous position in England and the utter poverty of his own house, it is remarkable to encounter Robert of Rouen contributing to such an enterprise. Commemoration, coupled with his customary duty as head of the church's corporate rector and, possibly, patriotic affinity with Henry de Maygne, may all have influenced this act of patronage. Perhaps most clearly, however, the case is suggestive of the piety underpin-

---

[31] Yeo 1987, pp. 20–1.

[32] CPR 1446–52, p. 429. K&H, p. 130 calls Begare a grange rather than a priory.

[33] Yeo 1987, p. 22. Concerning Cowick, Yeo's dates are always to be preferred to those of K&H.

[34] It is just possible that the roof alone is designated by the pronoun (me) occurring in the inscription: see Yeo 1987, p. 21. However, the Perpendicular chancel of Spreyton sits happily c.1450. On the church generally see Pevsner and Cherry 1989, p. 757.

[35] The entire inscription reads thus: 'Henricus le Maygne Presbyter Vicarius istius ecclesiæ me fecit fieri anno Domini 1451. Robertus de Rouen de Becdenne, Prior de Cowyk, et Ricardus Talbot, armiger, Dominus de Spreyton, dederunt de bonis suis ad me faciendum. Orate pro animabus eorum. Normanniæ terra Henricus hic natus fuit, et ipse scripsit hæc omnia manu sua propria. Dulcis amica dei vernans et stella decora/ Tu memor esto mei, mortis dum venerit hora/ Jesu parens refove gentes quæ corde precantur/ Labe carens renova mentes quæ sorde ligantur: Hæc domus [domus] orationis vocabitur/ in ea omnis qui petit accipit qui quærit invenit et pulsanti aperietur [cf. Isaiah 56:7; Matthew 7:8.]: Testis sis Christe/ quod non hæc scriptitat iste/ Corpus ut laudetur/ sed spiritus et memoretur. Orate pro nobis Sancte Nicholæ, Sancte Martyr Edwarde, intercede pro nobis. Stultum sit peccatum/ perpetuo reputatum/ Pro solo pomo/ perditur omnis homo/ Virgo deum perpetit/ sed si quis quomodo quærit/ Non est nosse meum/ sed scio posse Deum.' See Jones 1889, p. 23. It is the verses' composition rather than the physical act of painting the inscription (for which he is unlikely to have been responsible) that Henry le Maygne wanted recognized as his own work.

ning monastic expenditure on art and architecture. Robert of Rouen must have foreseen the imminent suppression of his monastery, and the return of himself and his convent to France: practically every other alien house, and all of Bec's possessions, had either disappeared or been appropriated. But rebuilding a chancel, which contained and dignified the high altar, represented to him an intrinsically worthy cause, even though he would never inspect it or be involved with his fellow patrons again.

Not all motives were as universal as religious devotion. The desire for career advancement (to return to the mundane), while not a documented incentive for the patronage of art and architecture, nevertheless deserves consideration as such where senior Benedictine obedientiaries are concerned. In particular, this applies to the priorate: one need only consider the great number of superiors who had previously been priors to see why.[36] That sponsorship of building and embellishment over and above the obligations imposed by office might under certain circumstances be recognized and acknowledged financially is shown by the annuity of 50s with which Adam of Cheddar, prior of Bath's cell at Dunster, was rewarded in 1345 for his 'sumptuous building'.[37] However, financial reward, which in any case could never be particularly great in the monastic context, is unlikely to have been as significant an incentive for ambitious Benedictine priors as the opportunity to climb the final rung of the hierarchical ladder they had often spent years ascending. (This ambition, it will be observed, was perfectly compatible with the pious urge to serve one's community as fully as possible. It need not be interpreted as particularly self-seeking.) Wolstan de Braunsford, prior of Worcester from 1317 to 1339, distinguished his priorate with construction of the Decorated Gothic 'Guesten' Hall (known in the late middle ages as the Prior's hall), a grand addition to the precinctual architectural ensemble.[38] This was largely demolished in 1862, but its eastern wall with some residual tracery still stands, and its roof is preserved elsewhere,[39] providing a strong impression of its patron's taste and ambitions. For the Guesten Hall was an ambitious building, a sumptuous and fashionable set piece in which high-status guests could be entertained: fit for any bishop. It also served as monastery courtroom, and an impressive, intimidating place it must have been.[40] Of five bays, some sixty-four feet in length and thirty-four in width, it stood thirty-six feet eight inches high to the top of the wall plate, its arch-braced roof opening out above this in a profusion of moulded purlins and serrated ogee-cusped wind-bracing.[41] Corbels sculpted in human form (two of which survive) and an elaborate programme of wall painting were also incorporated.[42] The windows of the three southernmost bays stood over twenty-five feet in height, and those

---

36 A model case is John de la Moote's rise to the abbacy (1396–1401) of St Albans: GA, III, pp. 441–7.

37 Cart.Bath, p. 175.

38 For Braunsford as patron, see Itinerary, V, p. 227; Willis 1718, II, p. 262; Noake 1866, p. 92. This is attested by medieval sources: see Strange 1904, p. 13; VCH Worcester, IV, p. 395; also Engel 2000, p. 237, reproducing a post-Dissolution source. Emery 1996–2000, II, p. 461, dates the hall c.1320–30, while Morris 1978, p. 42, puts it in the 1330s on the basis of window tracery design. That the hall was a component of the prior's lodgings (Leland thus calls it 'magna aula Prioris') buttresses the attribution.

39 Now at the Avoncroft museum, Bromsgrove (Worcs.): Emery 1996–2000, II, p. 461; Barker 1994, fig. 82.

40 Noake 1866, pp. 92, 277.

41 Strange 1904, pp. 94–5; Emery 1996–2000, II, p. 461.

42 Park 1998, pp. 18–19, figs 13, 14.

of all five had complex patterns of flowing tracery in the heads. Surviving rebates, and antiquarian illustrations, show that the glazing extended the full height of the windows.[43] Enthroned on the dais within, Braunsford – who could be very fierce when occasion required[44] – must have looked like episcopal material. In 1327, his convent elected him bishop, and although the appointment was immediately quashed, he was re-elected in 1339, and held the office until his death ten years later.

If John of Glastonbury is to be believed, Abbot Walter of Taunton (1322–23) ranked alongside other abbots of Glastonbury as a patron of art and architecture, despite the fact that he died less than two months after taking office, and was never in receipt of the temporalities pertaining to his *mensa*.[45] Among the items that the chronicler ascribes to his patronage are the pulpitum of the abbey church 'with ten images', the monumental rood group located above it, ten embroidered copes, two chasubles and many other rich vestments (their vivid colours and picturesque iconography are described at length), two altar-frontals, two tapestries (a red one with leopards and a second one, indigo with parrots), a quantity of books and plate, and a handsome contribution to St Dunstan's shrine.[46] The rood group alone lives on, through an early sixteenth-century pen sketch in the margin of p.198, TCC MS R 5 16.[47] Taunton had himself buried in its shadow: 'Gualterus de Tantonia . . . Abbas Glaston ante imaginem Crucifixi', Leland tells us in his description of the tombs.[48] Clearly, few of these things were achieved while Taunton was abbot. In that capacity he can have been responsible for almost nothing as a patron, particularly not a pulpitum with monumental statuary carved along and above it. Yet the fact that he could be buried before the choir door (in the midst of his own work, as it were), a location regarded as a patronal prerogative in other Benedictine houses during the fourteenth century (e.g. Ely, Prior Alan of Walsingham; Gloucester, Abbot John Wigmore), tends to support John of Glastonbury's claim that he was the patron of the screen and its imagery.[49] It is thus to be assumed that these things were done while he was serving as prior under Geoffrey Fromond (1303–22), in support of which James Carley observes that Taunton 'seems to have been taking over abbatial duties' for some time before his election.[50] Patronage of a new pulpitum and monumental rood, and annexation of a prime burial space in the midst of the abbatial mausoleum, are good indications of Taunton's ambition.

Many cases are susceptible to similar interpretation, although the desire to emulate a superior and the more serious ambition of succeeding him often stand in danger of being confused. The patronage of the grisaille wall paintings of Winchester cathedral's Lady chapel highlights this. The paintings were executed c.1510–20 (largely on costume evidence),[51] at the behest and charge of Prior Thomas Silkstede (1498–1524). The

---

43 The bottom third of each tall window has been filled in with rubble, so that no rebate is visible. However, see the internal elevations as illustrated before demolition in Barker 1994, fig. 80; Park 1998, fig. 17.

44 E.g. *Lib.Albus*, p. 172.

45 *HRH*, p. 47; Keil 1964(b), p. 337.

46 CGA(C), pp. 256–9.

47 On this sketch see Luxford 2002(b), *passim* (with ill.).

48 *Itinerary*, I, p. 288; cf. Henderson 1937, plan, p. 10. Further, Leland notes that 'hic fecit frontem Chori cum imaginibus *lapidus* id est [word(s) missing] stat Crucifixus'.

49 BRECP, p. 454 (Walsingham); HMGlouc., I, p. 47 (Wigmore).

50 Carley 1996, p. 40.

51 Park and Welford 1993, p. 134.

attribution is substantiated, for among the twenty stories (in twenty-two pictures) involving miracles of the Virgin, deriving from the *Speculum historiale* of Vincent of Beauvais and the *Golden Legend*, is a portrait of Silkstede which was formerly accompanied by an inscription declaring that in honour of the Virgin (mankind's intercessor, whom he cherished), he has ornamented at great expense the pure stones of the chapel walls (Plate 21).[52] It is no coincidence that a slightly earlier, fuller (thirty-two scene) grisaille cycle of miracle stories, among which almost all of the Winchester iconography is represented, is to be found on the walls of Eton college chapel.[53] The patron of these paintings was William Waynflete, bishop of Winchester from 1447 until 1486 and comptroller of the king's works at the college.[54] That Silkstede, who had been a monk at St Swithun's since 1468 at least,[55] wished to succeed his superior Richard Fox (1501–28), who was at the height of his governance of England's richest and (with the exception of Canterbury) most politically important bishopric, cannot be entertained.[56] His patronage here is an example of emulative spirit rather than careerism. Once again it also smacks of sincere devotion, and the desire for commemoration, for the portrait is an ostentatiously pious one, painted directly over the piscina where all using the chapel would see it. Silkstede kneels at a prie-dieu, dressed in the black cowl of his order with mitre set aside (but still present), prayer book open before him, and a statue of the Virgin on the wall. To the latter he offers words which he must have repeated many thousands of times during his life: 'Benedicta tu in mulieribus'. If, as current scholarship supposes, he contributed to the late stages of the Lady chapel's reconstruction (c.1490–c.1510), to its sumptuous timber stalls and to its stained glass, then the pious commitment made by the paintings was heavily underlined in art and architectural terms.[57]

In William More, penultimate prior of Worcester, David Knowles found his paradigmatic late medieval straw-monk. Equipped with rich primary sources and a surpassing genius for historical biography, he painted an engrossing portrait of a senior Benedictine turned country gentleman: mild-mannered, possessed of a generosity befitting his station, proud, fond of good food, entertainments and glittering ornaments, deeply involved in social and familial affairs outside the monastery, and not over-zealous in the matter of religion. 'His inclusion [here] . . . is due primarily to the aptness with which his

---

52 Partially recorded in copies of the paintings by the antiquary John Carter (1748–1817), now BL MS Additional 29943, fols 19r–22r: '. . . hominum mediatrix/ . . . Silkstede [diva maria colit]/ Has . . . iussit quoque saxa polita/ Sumptibus ornari . . . Maria suis'. See also James & Tristram 1928–29, p. 35; Park and Welford 1993, p. 133.

53 James & Tristram 1928–29 (p. 14 for the number of scenes at Eton). On Eton see further Martindale 1998, *passim*.

54 James & Tristram 1928–29, p. 2. The paintings were executed between 1477 and 1488. Waynflete, and the college, rather than the Crown, commissioned and paid for them: Davis 1993, p. 55.

55 *BRECP*, p. 735.

56 Post-Conquest, Henry Woodlock (de Merewelle) was the only prior of Winchester (1295–1305) to become bishop (1305–16).

57 Silkstede's involvement in the Lady chapel's reconstruction is predicated on the presence of his rebus (with those of his predecessor) on the severies of the vault: *Short Survey*, p. 48; Lindley 1993(a), p. 114; Smith 1996, p. 14. Some involvement on his part does seem probable, although note that obedientiaries (CRWin., p. 300), and probably the whole convent, shared the task. Tracy 1993(b), p. 233, associates the Lady chapel stalls with Silkstede, although they lack the prior's rebus (cf. the canopied seats in the south transept, c.1520–24, which have it). See Marks 1993, p. 212, for a 'probable' representation of Silkstede in the chapel's glass.

career at all points illustrates the [monastic] trend of the age', Knowles observed.[58] Due to the survival of his 'journal' (WCL MS A xi), almost as much can be said about More as a patron of art and architecture as about his status as a lukewarm monk. Indeed, the relationship between one status and the other, which it is natural to posit, can be neatly illustrated with the decoration prefacing another of his registers.[59] The great (30cm^2) capital 'R' of 'Regestrum' (sic), executed in black ink and displaying the ornamental interlace characteristic of the early sixteenth century, has in the upper compartment the Virgin Mary holding the Christ child, in the lower St Catherine enthroned, to the left a swordsman approaching, and to the right a lute-player seated, strumming, on a three-legged stool with his instrument's case hanging casually from one of its legs (Plate 34).[60] Prior More did love his music.[61] However, whether or not it is correct to assume a link generally between patronage of the arts and a decline in monastic rigour is a murkier issue, for the 'journal' (basically an extended *compotus*, covering the period 1518–36) from which his activities as a patron are substantially derived is unique. Benedictine priors to whom posterity has been kinder – Henry of Eastry, say, or Alan of Walsingham – will have supported relations and paid for fine clothes, sweetmeats and entertainments as well. The fact that there is no *magnum opus* to offset More's petty expenditure does not of itself permit us to consider his patronage indicative of religious laxity. What the account-book does underline is the point made at the beginning of this section concerning the relative autonomy of a prior's expenditure, and the fact that any such expense in the matter of art and architecture could at once be considered both 'official' and 'unofficial'.

More was patron of many works for his own use, which nevertheless could be observed by those coming into contact with him and taken as a reflection of conventual as well as personal dignity. It is worth citing a number of examples, for the variety and concerns they evince: two illuminated missals costing £6 1s 5d and £6 6s 2d respectively;[62] a 'grete grayle [i.e. gradual] for þe priur in þe quyer', cost £6;[63] a 'peynted clotth of þe ix wurdyes [i.e. worthies], xiiij yeards & iij quarters long', cost 10s;[64] a crozier ('croystaff') of gilded silver, weight 115 ounces, cost £28 15s, along with the precious mitre costing £50 mentioned in chapter three;[65] a gilded silver chalice for the prior's chapel, 'þe trinite in þe patten', weight 22½ ounces, cost £2 9s 9d;[66] two tailor-made tabernacles for the manor chapel at Grimley, with images of the Virgin Mary and St John the Evangelist, cost £3 5s;[67] two ready-made gilded tabernacles with images of the

[58] Knowles 1959, pp. 108–26 (quote at 108). For a kinder assessment, and full documentation of his career, see *BRECP*, pp. 848–50.
[59] WCL MS A vi(ii), fol. 111r.
[60] The illustration is inscribed 'Thomas blokley' ('R', lower compartment). Cf. *Jnl.More*, p. 74: 'Item payed to Dan Thomas blockeley for makyng & floresshyng of þe begynnyng of þe register 12d.' For a full discussion see Luxford 2004(b), *passim* (note addendum on p. 248).
[61] See e.g. *Jnl.More*, pp. 88, 102, 354, 399.
[62] *Jnl.More*, pp. 99, 116.
[63] *Jnl.More*, p. 116. Thomson 2001, p. xxxvi, points out that the gradual was not complete when this cost was recorded.
[64] *Jnl.More*, p. 132.
[65] *Jnl.More*, pp. 144–5, 179. The crozier was purchased in London of one John Crancks, goldsmith. Its carriage cost 28d. A leathern case cost 4s 4d extra, plus 5s 4d for a linen lining.
[66] *Jnl.More*, p. 190. Made by one John Pynson (in Worcester?), rather than Crancks.
[67] *Jnl.More*, p. 183. Carved by one Robert Penrise for 9s each.

Virgin Mary and St Catherine for the manor chapel at Crowle, cost £1 6s 8d;[68] glass with 'xij skochions of my arms' (this is one of many references to glass patronage);[69] and – neither last nor least – 'a beryles [i.e. burial] ston . . . that is leyde before Johns Awter for me to be beryde under . . . with þᵉ garnesshyng of hym', cost £10. This last is perhaps to be identified with the recumbent effigy built into the rear of the Victorian high altar reredos.[70] He also purchased items for the use of the convent, including many of the eighty-seven books listed in his accounts (among them '3 boks of seynt Benetts Rewle in Englisshe'),[71] two eagle lecterns, one for the choir, the other for the high altar, cost £15 13s 3d;[72] a suit of vestments (cope, chasuble, two tunicles 'with þᵉ albes and makyng'), cost £90 18s 4d;[73] the gilding and painting of all the images of St Cecilia's chapel, a cloth to protect the gilt frontal, and curtains, cost £11 14s 4d;[74] a seal die in silver, weighing three ounces, 'to serve hym that shalbe priur hereafter, the scripture of the seyd seale is on þᵉ on side *Sigillum prioris Wigornie*', cost 20s.[75] Projects undertaken by other houses (e.g. 3s 4d to the prior of Great Malvern towards the 'construction' of Malvern parish church; 5s to the prior of Little Malvern for replacing stolen chalices)[76] and charitable causes (e.g. 10s 'ex devocione' towards the rebuilding of the anchoress's cell by the priory charnel house; 'a seale for beggars to have Auctorite to begge', 12d) also benefited from his considerable generosity.[77]

In More's provision for his convent of copies of St Benedict's *Rule*, the problematic nature of the distinction between prior and superior being drawn here arises again. The miscellaneous register WCL MS A xii, which is closely related to the account-book (it lists many of the works of art mentioned in the accounts, with their cost),[78] contains a series of inventories detailing the layout and chattels of Crowle, Grimley and Batnall manors that further blurs it.[79] Here are items that would not have been out of place at the abbot of Glastonbury's Sharpham. Crowle, for example, had a 'lord's chamber' with

---

68 *Jnl.More*, p. 300.

69 *Jnl.More*, p. 266.

70 *Jnl.More*, pp. 211, 217. Made in London. Transport to Worcester cost 26s 8d, setting 16s 7d. On the effigy, see Atkins 1951, *passim*. While Atkins's argument that More's account pertains to this effigy is strong, £10 seems remarkably little for a monument of this sort. Moreover, it lay before an altar: a gravestone, incised or with a brass, is perhaps more likely. Ultimately, More (d.1558) was not buried in the cathedral: Noake 1866, p. 205.

71 *Shorter Catalogues*, pp. 664–73; *Jnl.More*, pp. 409–15. He also gave a copy of the *Rule* 'cum comento': *Shorter Catalogues*, p. 667.

72 *Jnl.More*, p. 153.

73 *Jnl.More*, p. 116. These vestments (along with a bolt of cloth of gold with red velvet ground, cost £65 16s 8d) were London purchases, too; as were most of his books.

74 *Jnl.More*, p. 420: further, see Noake 1866, p. 188. The images of Christ and the Virgin Mary 'in þᵉ midd of þᵉ awtur' are especially mentioned. These statues were probably instituted in 1382 by a former prior (see below, p. 103).

75 *Jnl.More*, p. 365. The entry ends 'And the scripture on the other side . . .', without stating what this was. John Crancks made the die.

76 *Jnl.More*, pp. 168 (to the sacrist), 377.

77 *Jnl.More*, pp. 136, 334.

78 Fegan considered WCL MSS A xi and A xii companion volumes: *Jnl.More*, p. 416. The latter contains much concerning the sacrist as well (e.g. fols 35r (receipts), 36r–36v (payments by), 51r (churches in gift of)), plus much miscellaneous material: Engel 2000, p. 236, prints a précis. The information recorded begins before More's election. Indeed, the regnal list (fol. 103r) has no burial place or length of reign for Henry VII, so may predate 1509.

79 WCL MS A xii, fols 1r–12r.

a magnificent bed covered with a cloth of green, scattered with representations of animals, 'dog, catt, connys, &c.' There was also 'a pillow of selke with lyons'. In a second chamber was another great bed, with 'a bedcloth of ymagery', while the guest chamber was hung with painted cloths 'of foliage with beasts and fulls'.[80] Grimley was possessed of similar, while at Batnall the walls and galleries of both the great chamber and great parlour were hung with painted cloth with 'beests, byrds, folorii, &c.' The priors of Worcester may not have commanded the income of a superior ruling a house of comparable wealth (Worcester's income c.1535 was £1290), but as mitred priors who considered themselves abbots in all but name, it suited them to appear as though they did.

Official Patronage

Collectively, official patronage on the part of obedientiaries was responsible for more Benedictine art and architecture than any other category. Most of its major products cannot be discussed individually here for want of hard evidence, but it should be acknowledged at the outset that such monuments as Gloucester's cloister, stained glass and west front, a certain amount of the mid to later fourteenth-century work at Tewkesbury (architecture of the abbey church, cloister, glass, sculpture etc.), the cloister, chapter house, dorter, frater and at least some of the architecture of the abbey church at Glastonbury, the great fourteenth-century chapel on the north side of the abbey church of Shaftesbury (probably a Lady chapel), the fourteenth- and fifteenth-century church, cloister and conventual complex at Milton, the fifteenth-century church of Great Malvern, the cloister at Worcester, and many other major projects will have been, substantially if not wholly, products of official patronage by monastic officers below the level of prior.

Where hard evidence is lacking, and in view of the danger of assigning the patronage of given projects to particular obedientiaries on the basis of general notions of responsibility, it is naturally tempting to attribute such projects to collective enterprise, for modern scholarship is almost as uncomfortable with a patronless masterpiece as it is with an authorless one. In the case of grand (i.e. expensive and disruptive) designs, for which a measure of preliminary discussion and agreement in chapter was mandatory, this notion receives at least some support. It is also broadly valid where more modest expenditure by small convents of half a dozen or so religious is concerned. In such houses, where means were restricted and obediences spread across a larger percentage of the inmates, art and architectural patronage that could have passed unnoticed by many elsewhere must in most cases have been, to all practical extents, a collective responsibility. A surviving record of Cowick priory's expenses from Michaelmas 1484 to Michaelmas 1485 helps to make the point (Plate 35).[81] Here a year's worth of expenditure on architectural repairs and new buildings (e.g. 'j camere de nouo factis vocatur le parler'), both claustral and forinsec, is rehearsed together with the purchase and repair

---

80 These hangings, bought in London, cost 5d ob. per yard. Cf. *Jnl.More*, p. 263. Inventories partially printed in *Jnl.More*, pp. 416–18.

81 DRO W1258M/G4/53/2, one of a bundle of some fifteen documents containing accounts relating to Cowick and other institutions. A number of the others, e.g. W1258M/G4/53/1, 3, also contain small quantities of patronage information.

of unspecified books, 'the making and painting of one image called the Jesus with one crucifix' and 'numerous ornaments bought, namely cloths for the altar [and] the purchase of one book called the bible'.[82] The ornaments alone came to 116s 11d, or almost £6. The account is based on a *compotus* generated by Cowick's receiver, the obedientiary responsible for administering the returns from the priory estates on behalf of the abbot of Tavistock (by this time Cowick's overlord). This monk paid for all building, repairs and embellishments out of that fraction of his priory's income not diverted to the mother house.[83] However, his patronal autonomy was apparent rather than real. Such expenditure inevitably had a knock-on effect for the basic standard of maintenance experienced by the handful – typically five or six – of resident monks. It also covered buildings and work of art which benefited all: the new parlour, crucifix, altar-cloths, bible and other books must have made a general impact and been generally employed in this 'household' environment. It is inconceivable that the abbot's receiver took all decisions affecting art and architectural patronage at Cowick without consultation with and financial support (implicit or direct) from his fellow monks. Such patronage may properly be called collective.

On the whole, however, it is worth stressing the broad autonomy with which official patronage was exercised. In most cases, obedientiaries personally decided what needed purchasing or commissioning, hired the necessary artisans, and paid for their labour and the materials used out of separately administered incomes.[84] While these incomes were not, strictly speaking, private, they were first and foremost an obedientiary privilege, and accordingly, any surpluses might be counted as perquisites.[85] The communal prerogative was recognized mainly in the production of *compoti*, which were available if required for scrutiny and the annual audit. This independence was both cause and effect of a broader autonomy, according to which most later medieval Benedictine obedientiaries worked alone, either outside the monastery or in private checkers (regular attendance at chapter and choir being excused where necessary). They frequently lived apart, as well: surviving sections of the hordarian and guestmaster's house at Winchester remind us of this. Some, for example the sacrist, kitchener and pittancer of Malmesbury, maintained private residences outside their monastery.[86] Those with major briefs not only had separate cartularies but personal seals of office.[87] They could often borrow from external sources at their own discretion, and might be separately taxed – Henry IV solicited the sacrist of Worcester directly for £100 in 1400.[88] The treatment of official patronage as an enterprise determined largely by individuals thus has historical foundations. It is even supported by monastic

---

82 'Pro facturis et picturis j ymaginis voc*atur* le ihc cum j crucifixe ac pro diversis ordnuamentis [sic] emptis videlic*et* in tuell*is* pro altar*is* [et] in acquietanc*is* j libr*um* voc*atur* le bibell ut pat*et* pro bill*am* suam.'
83 Yeo 1987, p. 23.
84 See the valuable discussion in Smith 1951, p. 74. Most recently, see Harvey 2002, pp. xxii–xxvii (on the obedientiaries of Westminster, but with broader implications).
85 Knowles 1955, p. 243. Obedientiaries paid themselves allowances from their incomes: e.g. CRWin., pp. 55–6, CRPer., p. 12.
86 *Star Chamber*, I, pp. cxxx, 45–9 (for the practice at Abingdon see cxxx); Luce 1979, p. 40.
87 *Benedictines in Britain*, p. 36.
88 Greatrex 1980, p. 13. Also HMGlouc., III, p. lxvi; CRWin., p. 94; Harvey 1984, p. 62 (private borrowing); Keil 1963(b), pp. 159–61; Gasquet 1892, pp. 151–2; MA, II, p. 360 (individual taxation).

historiographers, who despite their preoccupation with abbatial personalities occasionally singled out obedientiaries for special recognition: particularly if they subsequently became superior.[89] The case of John Lyndsey, sacrist of Worcester, and his colleagues will be examined below.

Apart from the individualistic nature of its exercise, official patronage of art and architecture in Benedictine houses during the later middle ages may be generally characterized in four ways: ongoing, broad-based, complicated and largely unremarkable. That it was ongoing is self-evident. A large, lead-covered, well-fenestrated and glazed freestone church and conventual complex required constant attention. Here, the architectural ambitions of one generation could be the curse of the next, and where projects were left unfinished, as at Bath and Milton, intensive maintenance was required to avoid a 'melt-down' of the sort that occurred at St Albans during the early thirteenth century.[90] Moreover, the conventual complex was only the central element of a much broader network of buildings within the monastic purlieu. Together, the obedientiaries of each large monastery had literally hundreds of agricultural, commercial and domestic edifices to maintain.[91] The scope of this responsibility can be appreciated only where a representative sample of *compoti* survive: in the case of Norwich, for example, where it has been admirably analyzed by Claire Noble.[92] Although such comprehensive documentary evidence is lacking for the monasteries covered by this study, it is safe to assume that the region's larger Benedictine houses were responsible for the maintenance of just as much utilitarian architecture as Norwich. With increasing appropriation of parish church revenues came increasing obligation to maintain and embellish fabrics, notwithstanding the fact that many responsibilities in this area were transferred to the laity after 1300.[93] Far from diminishing, maintenance requirements grew as Benedictine communities shrank during the later middle ages, a circumstance echoed in countless pleas for tax breaks and licences to appropriate. The complaint voiced against the obedientiary system in John Gower's *Mirour de l'omme* (c.1376–79) describes the typical monastic official 'riding about his lands, spending liberally'.[94] This, indeed, he (or, less often, she) was obliged to do, if not to the ends implied by the pietistic poet.[95]

That official patronage was broad-based and complicated is demonstrated by a glance at the surviving *compoti* of Pershore, Winchester and Worcester. As pointed out in chapter one, some obedientiaries had more to do with patronage of buildings and embellishments than others, but all who drew significant revenues from tithes and landed

---

[89] The chronicles of St Albans, in many ways more candid than existing West Country ones, include many examples. See also *CAEve.*, pp. 264–72 (early thirteenth century); CGA(C), pp. 266–7.

[90] GA, I, p. 219 (the west front). Cf. GA, II, p. 283: 'It happens, unfortunately, at almost all monasteries that each successive abbot initiates new building works . . . [while] practically ignoring maintenance of the works of his predecessors.'

[91] The rent-based economy did not eliminate obedientiary bills for renovation: cf. McFarlane 1973, pp. 229–31.

[92] Noble 2001, pp. 91–132.

[93] For lay responsibilities see Archbishop Winchelsey's promulgations (1305) in *Councils & Synods*, II, pp. 1385–6; CWA *Somerset*, pp. 243–4. BL MS Additional 43405, fols 6r–7r, has a fifteenth-century copy from Muchelney – the monks were well aware of them. Winchelsey's successor, Walter Reynolds, augmented these: *Councils & Synods*, II, pp. 1387–8.

[94] Gower, p. 236 (lines 20,956–8: 'Car lors luy falt selle et chival/ Pour courre les paiis aval/ Si fait despense au large mein'). By no means a unique witness: see e.g. Clark 2002(a), p. 3.

[95] On the whole, nuns had more resort to lay obedientiaries for affairs outside the monastery than did monks. Tombs of such officials will be noted in chapter six. Cf. Power 1922, pp. 131–60.

possessions – and this was the majority – had some obligation to organize and pay for building and maintenance. In the Winchester rolls such activity is recorded under the heading *Emendatio domorum cum necessariis* – necessary expenditure. (The heading covers new building as well as repair work.) Typically, an obedience was financed by one (or more, depending on specific requirements) core source – e.g. a manor, the tithes of a relatively prosperous parish, the proceeds of some commercial enterprise utilizing built infrastructure – which required more or less constant upkeep, as well as various less important sources. Not all of the latter involved the obligation to build and embellish, of course, but a certain percentage (to estimate a general figure would be misleading) did. This is where matters start to look complicated. Sometimes, one obedientiary would be responsible for works on a property from which a number of his or her colleagues drew resources, while in other cases a number would pay for maintenance of a property on which only one drew.[96] All manner of other arrangements were exercised, and, as in matters liturgical, each house had its own idiosyncratic customs. This complexity, and the complexity of later medieval conventual management and finances more broadly, are reflected in the compilation and content of obedientiary cartularies. As noted in chapter one, even the sacrist of a modest-sized house such as Wherwell possessed an independent cartulary.[97] Similar volumes survive for Evesham (sacrist, various), Glastonbury (almoner, pittancer, various), Gloucester (various), Malmesbury (sacrist, custodian of the Lady chapel), Shaftesbury (various), Tavistock (various), Winchcombe (various), and Worcester (almoner).[98] While their contents do not detail individual acts of building and embellishment, they impart some impression of the web of patronage obligations in which later medieval obedientiaries were caught up.[99]

That official patronage was largely unremarkable is again a straightforward matter. Routine repairs and the construction of quotidian buildings qualify as acts of patronage but, naturally enough, did not and do not stir the imagination greatly. What is more, few very informative details emerge from surviving accounts. For example, to read that the receiver of the prior's treasury at Winchester spent £32 and a penny on construction of a new grange (1334/5) reveals little of substance. It is not even clear how many buildings went up.[100] In 1408/9, Winchester's *custos operum* bought a great quantity of lead, tin, slates, and other items, including 43,500 pegs and nails.[101] Much of this must have been required for ongoing work on the nave (scaffolding as well as actual building), but some is likely to have been used for other, now obscure projects, within and without the monastery. The nuns of Romsey spent over £120 in 1411/12 on repairs to mills and manor houses, but though we know the latter's names, we cannot pinpoint the

---

96   See Haigh 1950, p. 109, for an example.
97   Wherwell's income c.1535 was £339 annually. The fullest set of obedientiary cartularies and registers surviving is for Bury St Edmunds: Davis 1958, pp. 13–17.
98   See Davis 1958, pp. 44, (nos 383, 384: Evesham); 50 (nos 439–41: Glastonbury); 51–2 (no. 456: Gloucester); 73 (no. 647: Malmesbury); 101 (no. 887: Shaftesbury); 109 (no. 950: Tavistock); 119–20 (no. 1037: Winchcombe); 124 (no. 1073: Worcester). For examples which epitomize the complexity of these documents see *Landboc*, I, p. cvii note 1.
99   Far from producing chaos, however, the systems in place apparently worked remarkably well. The *minutiæ* of cartularies are admirable testimony to the organizational capacities of the later medieval convent.
100 CRWin., p. 121. The reference is to a grange, not to a barn (*grangia*) on its own.
101 CRWin., pp. 114–17.

projects.[102] They are likely to have been equally as mundane as the repairs to the pigsties of Tewkesbury abbey recorded in the kitchener's roll of 1385/6, and the small amounts spent on nails, stone and erection of a partition ('sepe') in the conventual tailor's shop and elsewhere by the chamberlain of the same abbey in 1351.[103] Occasionally, it is possible to draw an important conclusion from such mundane details. Rod Thomson has recently identified the hitherto disputed location of the library at Worcester, which the *Chronologia ædificorum* informs us was completed in 1377, by calculating the area that would have been covered by the 2000 roof-tiles purchased by the cellarer in 1376/7.[104] If he is right then we know not only the location of the library but also have confirmation of its patron. At other times, a significant work of art can be glimpsed among commonplace details. For example, context (Quidhampton (Hants) estate's chapel chancel) and cost (6d per foot, thus relatively expensive)[105] suggest that the forty feet of glass purchased for 20s by Winchester's almoner in 1514/15 was for iconographic windows – though little more than this may be said.[106] Usually, however, the objects and exercise of patronage appear humdrum. The construction, embellishment, maintenance and use of conventual churches, superiors' residences and sumptuous cloisters relied on a vast and largely mundane infrastructure, and it was to the upkeep of this that the majority of official patronage was directed.

Caution, as ever, is required when interpreting official patronage, for the holes in our knowledge of monastic organization are gaping, and one frequently encounters some piece of information that suggests the folly of filling them in with supposition. For instance, in 1360, Abbot Boys assigned £8 6s 8d in rents to the establishment and maintenance of a chantry for the souls of kings, abbots, monks and benefactors in the newly built charnel chapel at Evesham. Rather than administering this through his household, however, he diverted the money via the almoner.[107] Thus, while the chapel was apparently maintained by the almoner, the responsibility was actually borne by the abbot. A silver plate 'in qua est sculptum nomen domini prioris' for the high altar retable at Worcester was commissioned by the sacrist and recorded on his *compotus* (1423/4), although, it transpires, the prior requested and paid for it.[108] Again at Winchester, the hordarian's *compotus* of 1484/5 records the obligatory construction of a new mill on a property at Exton (Hants) annexed to his office. It also lists contributions made by other obedientiaries towards this, and one from the convent as a whole, totalling £4. This was an annual payment: the eventual total donated was £31 15s.[109] At some stage a joint decision to assist the hordarian's office, which was deeply in debt, in the matter of the mill's construction (rather than in some other way) was taken. Thus, in terms of deter-

---

[102] Coldicott 1989, p. 41.
[103] *Kitchener's Roll*, p. 323; *Tewkes.Comp.*, pp. 253–5.
[104] Thomson 2001, p. xxxiv. Window-bars and 1000 nails are recorded in the same account.
[105] Contemporaneously, William More paid 'for glaysing þe lower windowe with Mary and John in þe chapel at Crowle, conteynyng ix foots & halff', 4s 12d, i.e. approximately 6d *quart.* per foot (*Jnl.More*, p. 194), not counting labour. Cf. white glass, which he bought at between 10s per 100 feet (in bulk) and 5d per foot (pp. 262, 312), painted roundels at between 6d and 8d each (pp. 219, 312), and panels of glass with armorials (approximately one foot each: cf. p. 222), 8d each (e.g. pp. 219, 266).
[106] *CRWin.*, p. 461.
[107] *CAEve.*, p. 299.
[108] *CRWor.*, p. 65.
[109] *CRWin.*, p. 296; cf. Smith 1951, p. 92.

mination and payment, the patronage was a product of many rather than one; yet if the hordarian's scribe had not recorded this extra information, we would be none the wiser, and an attribution of Exton mill to the hordarian alone would seem perfectly reasonable. Monastic records contain many similar cases.

The point being made here is not to be considered a superfluous caution. It goes to the very heart of the subject of monastic (not only Benedictine) patronage obligations, and the scholar who ignores it and tries to synthesize in a general manner is likely to fall into error straight away. In current scholarship, this occurs often in the unquestioned attribution to monastic (or indeed secular) rectors of the construction or renovation of parish church chancels on the basis of ecclesiastical legislation,[110] variously reinforced at a diocesan level by declarations such as (to take a West Country example) that issued by Thomas Brantingham, bishop of Exeter 1370–94. 'The work of constructing and repairing the chancels of all mother churches', he ordained, 'belongs to the rector of the parishes, but that of the nave pertains to the parishioners, without regard to any contrary custom.'[111] Obviously, such pronouncements did not fall from a clear sky, and in Brantingham's declaration may be read official recognition of the widespread existence of contrary custom late into the fourteenth century (in the diocese of Exeter at least). It is a simple fact that where no definite composition existed concerning the division of patronage responsibilities, specific, local arrangements frequently obtained.[112] That parishioners might build chancels, in part or in whole (e.g. Totnes),[113] as well as embellishing them, and monastic rectors contribute to naves (e.g. High Ham, Meare, Cerne),[114] porches (e.g. Evesham, All Saints)[115] and towers (e.g. Glastonbury, St John the Baptist; Bristol St James),[116] is shown by many examples.[117] Cambridge University Library holds a late fourteenth-century missal with many high-quality illuminated capitals and borders, inscribed 'Notandum quod venerabilis in xpisto pater dominus Willelmus More prioris ecclesie Cathedralis beate marie Wygornie hoc missale ecclesie Bromisgrove dedit Anno domini M.ccccc.xxi' – in spite of Archbishop Winchelsey's ordinance of 1305 designating provision of the missal a parish responsibility (Plate

---

110 *Councils & Synods*, I, pp. 82 (dioceses of Durham, Salisbury), 512–13 (diocese of Salisbury); II, pp. 1005–8 (diocese of Exeter), 1385–8 (province of Canterbury).
111 Cook 1956, p. 23.
112 *Linc.Vis.*, III, p. 282 and note 6.
113 Pevsner and Cherry 1989, p. 868; Watkin 1914–17, I, p. 407; II, p. 967; Rea 1924–25, pp. 307–8.
114 *Schaell's Memoir*, pp. 114–15; Dobson 1950, p. 71; CGA(C), pp. 262–3. The initials of Thomas Corton (1525–39), last abbot, are ostentatiously displayed in the stonework surrounding the two south-west nave clerestory windows at St Mary's, Cerne. Admittedly this is not definite proof of patronage.
115 Cox 1980, p. 24.
116 Lewis 1926, p. xxxiv. The abbot is also said to have contributed to the nave of the Glastonbury parish church (p. xxxvi), although this is undocumented. At Bristol St James it was agreed in 1374 that the prior and convent would supply all mortar for the new tower, and contribute to hanging the bells therein: Barrett 1789, p. 386. This was usually a parochial responsibility: French 1997, p. 223.
117 For recent recognition of this see Pounds 2000, p. 385; Dunning 2002, p. 51; Marks 2004, p. 82. It is reasonable to suppose that in many instances, the devotional enthusiasm that played such an important part in late medieval parish church rebuilding generally stimulated parochial involvement in work on a stunted and, from a communal point of view, unedifying chancel: cf. Duffy 1992, pp. 132–4.

36).[118] The point requiring emphasis is not that the standard assumptions concerning official patronage responsibilities are always incorrect, but rather that they are usually insufficiently sensitive to the detailed and site-specific arrangements concerning patronage responsibilities which obtained both within convents, and between convents (whether represented by an individual or corporately) and external parties.

Selected examples will flesh out what has been said so far. In some cases, enough material survives to produce quite an interesting and lively patronage portrait. The *compotus* of 1423/4 of John Clyve, sacrist of Worcester, shows him receiving £148 12s 8d and spending £166 2s 8d.[119] His expenses in the matter of patronage are a typical *mélange*: a good deal of money was spent on routine repair works to buildings within and without the monastery, on a second-hand clock purchased from Gloucester, on maintenance of the bells in the great tower, and on wages for masons working on the cloister. A red silk ('tartre') curtain for a high-altar retable supplied by Prior John of Fordham cost the large sum of £4 13s 4d (the retable was 'preciosa'), two silver-gilt and enamel shields with the arms of Richard earl of Warwick and his wife Isabella Despenser, weight 13 ounces, cost £1 5s,[120] repair of one of the prior's mitres cost 2s 8d and part of an altar-cloth for Bishop Cobham's chapel (the expense was shared with one Marian Bureford) cost 3s 4d. A further 2s 6d was spent on banners ('vexellis') for the church's dedication day. A century later, a sacrist's roll compiled for Robert Alchurch provides a reassuring impression of continuity.[121] In 1522/3, he received £168 5s 6d, and was required to spend £154 5s 10d. This went towards repairing and purchasing liturgical vestments (£3), tiles and shingles (£1 11s 8d), bricks (£2 19s 9d), his carpenter's stipend (£3 18s 8d) and employing a plumber (£1 3s 6d). The most attractive item for the art historian is the £4 8s 11d paid for gilding part of the altar dedicated to St John the Baptist, and providing three new images for its reredos.

The surviving sacrist's rolls for Winchester (1536/7) and Glastonbury (1538/9) demonstrate no more compelling concern with patronage than those reviewed here.[122] It should be noted that this has nothing to do with any supposed prescience of the Dissolution. Glastonbury's sacrist still paid for new stained glass windows, repaired liturgical vestments (at the formidable cost of £7 13s), erected a new gate in St Patrick's chapel and had church plate mended. Only slightly earlier (1532/3), Winchester's *custos operum* rebuilt his monastery's infirmary hall, spending on it £29 19s 1d *ob*.[123] These accounts lack more than superficial art historical interest simply because, like those of John Clyve and Robert Alchurch, they do not coincide with any major programme of works. *Compoti* recording official patronage at obedientiary level on a grand scale are wanting for the west of England.

In the *Chronologia ædificorum*, however, something of their substance, albeit condensed and redigested, survives. The *Chronologia* is an enigmatic and exceptionally

---

118 CUL MS Additional 6688, fol. 372v. For examples of excellent borderwork, see fols 150v, 179v, 184v, 192v, 194r, 229v, 234r, 244r etc. Cf. *Councils & Synods*, II, p. 513. St John the Baptist at Bromsgrove was appropriated to Worcester in 1236 for the maintenance of candles around King John's tomb in the cathedral: *EEA* XIII, pp. 26–7 (no. 36).

119 *CRWor.*, pp. 63–9.

120 Richard Beauchamp, earl of Warwick, and Isabella Despenser were married on 26 November 1423: these jewels may have been wedding gifts.

121 *Acc.Wor.*, pp. 36–40.

122 *CRWin.*, pp. 109–11; Flower 1912, p. 56.

123 *CRWin.*, pp. 219–20.

interesting document (Plate 37). It is a piece of historiography no less than the continuation (1314–77) of the *Annales de Wigornia*,[124] but rather than taking the conventual life of the monastery as its subject, it focuses on Worcester's architectural profile. It is manifestly a fragment, describing only the building accomplished in the cathedral, the priory and at the manor of Batnall between 1372 and 1386 (there are eleven annals in all).[125] A lacuna occurs between 1382 and 1386, the latter annal (simply 'Eodem anno perfectus est opus porticus ecclesie supradicte') citing an 'above-mentioned porch' that in fact does not appear anywhere in the text.[126] As previously noted, the *Chronologia* occurs in the miscellaneous register WCL MS Register A xii at fol. 77v, written out in a decent hybrid hand of the first third of the sixteenth century.[127] In light of the register's contents, it seems to have been copied at the behest of either William More or Robert Alchurch the sacrist, although why it was copied is less obvious. Where it was copied from is also unclear. The possibility that it is a product of antiquarian research conducted on the eve of the Dissolution and based on *compoti*, like the so-called annals of Augustinian Thornton (Lincs.),[128] is improbable due to its irregular nature, although the notion cannot be discounted if it is assumed that Worcester possessed an incomplete set of *compoti* for the period covered. It is perhaps more likely to derive from a chronicle based partially on muniments (as domestic chronicles often were), perhaps that 'pendens in ecclesia' and updated on a regular basis between 1346/7 and 1467/8.[129] Certainly, this 'hanging' text is a prime candidate, for it covered the period of the works in question, and must, like the *Chronologia*, have been annalistic in arrangement. The issue is of some importance, because the *Chronologia*, besides providing a précis of the work accomplished during a 'heroic' period of construction, is also a glorification of the patrons of this work: the senior obedientiaries of Worcester. As such, it attests the prestige of obedientiary patrons and official patronage more forcefully than any other document surviving from the period and region addressed by this study. If this information was indeed part of a chronicle, *pendens* or *non pendens*, then the attestation is all the stronger.

Of the obedientiaries mentioned in the *Chronologia*, the sacrist John Lyndsey is afforded the most attention. Lyndsey was a prolific personality at Worcester, twice being nominated for the priorate.[130] As sacrist, he enjoyed a peculiar, controversial and prestigious status, namely, that of selection and appointment by the bishop rather than the convent.[131] His name appeared in a window in the west walk of the cloister ('Orate pro

---

124 *Annales*, IV, pp. 561–2.
125 The works at Batnall are attributed 'ex voluntate conventus'.
126 Moreover, during this period the east cloister walk was begun, yet it is not mentioned.
127 Folio 77 is integral to its gathering, and the text was never continued on fol. 78r. So the *Chronologia* was itself probably copied from a fragment.
128 Partially printed in Major 1946, from OBL Tanner MS 166. Like the *Chronologia aedificorum* this is a record of the art and architectural patronage of the monastery's obidientiaries copied out just before the Dissolution. However, it covers three centuries, and is clearly not a fragment of anything longer.
129 Gransden 1992, pp. 330–2; Thomson 2001, p. xxxi. Antonia Gransden argues persuasively for a codex rather than a *tabula*. Cf. Pantin 1950, pp. 207–8, Piper 1998, p. 307, *MMBL*, III, p. 358, and GCCC MS 391, p. 108 (paginated ms.), for hanging 'tabular' chronicles in later medieval Benedictine houses (including one at Winchester 'pendet super sepulchrum vel feretrum sancti Swythuni'). Augustinian Stone priory in Staffordshire also had one (Gerould 1917, p. 325): they were indeed quite common, although the type of information they contained differed.
130 In 1370 and 1388: *BRECP*, p. 841.
131 See Greatrex 1980.

anima Johannis Lyndsey monachi') and on one of the bells of the central tower ('Johannes Lyndesey hoc opere impleto Christi virtute faveto'),[132] and given the quantity of work with which he is credited in the *Chronologia* it need not be doubted that he ran a higher profile than this. The opening annal introduces him as though he were an abbot:

> John Lyndsey [becomes] sacrist, A.D. 1372.
> Around the end of this year, John Lyndsey was made sacrist. He finished the work at which his predecessors had laboured long and hard, and in a short period of time made it prosper, although only a small amount of money ['bona'] was left in the office [when he was elected].[133]

That he was dedicated to his job is certain. In 1374, he uncovered a cache of gold coins while digging foundations in the monastic cemetery, and straightway applied the £84 windfall (which he must have considered divine providence) to the task in hand.[134] The second annal of the *Chronologia*, which is for 1374, explains that he completed the central tower of the cathedral, hung the great bells therein (which had for seventeen years resided ignominiously in the nave), and provided a clock. In 1375 he made a new vault and windows in the chapel of St Mary Magdalene (perhaps the north-west transept),[135] and, on the first of October, began work on the choir stalls. The following year he built the central tower vault ('voltam supra chorum'), and the vault and windows of the chapel of St Thomas, while in 1377 he vaulted the nave.[136] In 1379 he finished the choir stalls and ornamented (presumably with encaustic tile) the pavements of the choir and the aforementioned chapels, while 1380 saw him erect a screen between the choir and presbytery, build the episcopal throne, screen the chapels of St Edmund of Abingdon and Holy Cross, and erect the Perpendicular west window – a magnificent eight-lighter with through reticulation in the head.[137] For the latter chapel he also provided a painted altarpiece.[138] The chapel of the Virgin Mary 'juxta rubeum hostium' was screened in 1381 (the door itself being removed and placed elsewhere), and a new pulpitum was built. The following year Lyndsey had two new bells cast, one at least, as noted, inscribed with his name. Finally, in 1386, the work of the 'church porch' (i.e. that at the north-west end of the nave) was completed – by Bishop Henry Wakefield (1375–95), Leland tells us,[139] and if this is so then it is noteworthy that the *Chronologia*

132 'May Christ favour and fill with virtue this work of John Lyndsey.' Thomas 1736, p. 30; Strange 1904, p. 82. The bell still exists.

133 'Johannes Lyndsey sacrista. Anno domini CCClxxij. Circa finem istius anni Johannes Lyndsey fit sacrista/ qui opera in quibus predecessores sui diu desudaverant atque fecerant modico temporis spacio/ respective graciose ac prospere consummavit licet in dicto officio paucissima bona fuerit/ sibi relicta.'

134 An explicitly similar story exists concerning John of Wisbech and the Ely Lady chapel: *Anglia Sacra*, I, p. 691. Wisbech found 'urnam æneam pecuniam plenam'. Lyndsey did, however, actually find the coins: see *BRECP*, p. 841.

135 Thus Brakspear in *VCH Worcester*, IV, p. 395.

136 No particular section is specified. 1374 saw the completion of the central tower, however; and the remodelling of the transept and vaulting of the nave was, according to Engel 2000, p. 231, begun around the dates cited in the *Chronologia*.

137 Schematically illustrated in Cobb 1980, p. 170; Barker 1994, fig. 102L.

138 Or perhaps had a pre-existing *tabula* repainted ('Tabulam etiam illam ad altare sancte crucis fecit depingi').

139 *Itinerary*, IV, p. 227.

avoids mentioning him. Unlike other written evidences of significant acts of official patronage by obedientiaries (for example the inscription commemorating Robert Tulley's involvement in the crossing tower at Gloucester,[140] and that naming John Dunster, sacrist of Sherborne, as builder of the chancel in St Cuthbert's church at Oborne (Dor.)),[141] there is no superior present to steal the thunder. Nor is the principal architect, John Clyve, mentioned.[142] John Lyndsey, sacrist, is the celebrity here.[143]

Not that Lyndsey is the only obedientiary mentioned. William Power, cellarer, is also singled out for his role in conventual building. In 1377 he appears as patron of a new dorter equipped with beds, a new treasury and library, while in 1378 it is stated that he made a floodgate ('portam aqueam') on the Severn.[144] The following year he built a shaving-room ('domum rasture') in the monastery infirmary. The dorter, it is recorded, had been initiated by Richard Wenlock, also called cellarer, in 1375.[145] The only other figure to appear is Prior Walter de Legh, who had been unanimously elected bishop by the chapter in 1373, but who was never provided. In 1382 he furnished the altar of St Cecilia's chapel with alabaster images (from Prior More's accounts we learn that these included statues of Christ and the Virgin Mary), wishing to be buried therein after death.[146] Alongside Lyndsey's heroics, and given Legh's status, this contribution appears slight and self-interested. It may be that the prior's sponsorship of works outside the cathedral and claustral complex are overlooked, however.

There is no apparent reason to question the attributions made by the *Chronologia ædificorum*, as there might well be if Worcester had been an abbey and Lyndsey its abbot. No ulterior motive recommends itself. Like Ely's great fourteenth-century builder-officials, Alan of Walsingham and John of Wisbech, we have here a Benedictine obedientiary whose responsibilities were so important and so diligently pursued it was considered that posterity ought to know about him.[147] Yet when, with the completion of the nave porch, the major campaigns on the cathedral church died down,[148] the

---

140 This black-letter inscription, under the west window of the crossing, reads: 'Hoc quod digestum specularis opusque politum Tullii haec/ Ex onere Seabroke abbate jubente.' ('This work that you behold arranged and ornamented, was done out of the labour of Tulley, at Abbot Seabroke's command.'): see London, Courtauld Institute of Art, Conway photographic library, negative no. 412/54. Harvey 1984, p. 302, calls Tulley *magister operum*: reasonable but uncertain.

141 Externally, over the north chancel window, appeared 'Orate pro bono statu dompni Johannis Dunster sacriste de Schirborn qui hoc opus fieri fecit anno Domini' (date lost), while over the east window 'Orate pro bono statu dompni Johannis M. (Meare) abbatis de Schirborn, anno Domini Mᵒccccccxxxiii' occurs. (The former inscription is now incomplete.) There are also shields with 'I.D.' and 'I.M.' with the arms of England and Sherborne abbey. See Luxford 2002(e), figs 190, 191.

142 Harvey 1984, p. 62. This John Clyve is not to be confused with the fifteenth-century sacrist of the same name.

143 For a somewhat similar document, recording the gifts of Thomas Ikham (d.1391), sacrist of St Augustine's abbey at Canterbury, see Cotton 1925. See also the note in CCCC MS 189 commemorating John Derby (d.1404), Ikham's successor: 'decorauit et ornauit ecclesiam predicti monasterii cum xiii fenestris de opere lapideo' (etc.). James 1912, I, p. 450.

144 This latter survives in part: see Barker 1994, fig. 95.

145 Power was perhaps sub-cellarer. There is no indication that Wenlock surrendered his obedience between 1375 and 1377.

146 'ubi post mortem suam iacere disposuit'. For Legh see further BRECP, pp. 835–6.

147 On Alan of Walsingham and John of Wisbech (together with John of Crauden) as patrons, see *Anglia Sacra*, II, pp. 643–9.

148 VCH *Worcester*, IV, p. 396; Engel 2000, p. 189. They did not cease, however: the cloister

Chronologia also comes to an end, and Lyndsey's profile immediately becomes indistinct. He remained sacrist until 1396/7 at least,[149] but none of his *compoti* survive, and while it is known that building on a diminished scale continued at the priory,[150] his activities as a patron are lost from view. There is every reason to suppose that they became, with those of Worcester's other obedientiaries, typical of official patronage once again: ongoing, broad-based, complicated and largely unremarkable.

Unofficial Patronage

Jeffrey Hamburger's 1997 book *Nuns as Artists*, based on a group of twelve coloured drawings of limited artistic merit executed c.1500 by a Franconian Benedictine nun, has received wide acclaim.[151] While the study is not materially wide-ranging, it is highly original, addressing topics that had previously been neglected: the 'spirituality' of late-medieval nuns, the role of images in nuns' devotional practice (first and foremost, the book is a behavioural study), and the production of religious images by nuns (a religious endeavour in itself, it is argued). The role of English monks and nuns as artists during the later middle ages, and the religious dimension of this, are issues that invite attention, but which cannot receive it here.[152] Of great relevance in the current context, however, is another issue to which *Nuns as Artists* draws attention; the procurement and ownership of works of art by individual religious. While nobody would deny outright the proposition that monks and nuns owned works of art, there had been no concerted focus on the topic before Hamburger's study, and the oversight where English monks and nuns are concerned remains.

This state of affairs is not really surprising, for apart from the paucity of documentary evidence and the lack of works which can be definitely ascribed to the unofficial patronage of religious men and women, traditional assumptions concerning encloistered life which serve to obviate examination of the subject linger. One is that monks and nuns were not supposed to own property, another that they had no money with which to buy works, a third that, being enclosed, they had no opportunity of obtaining them. These issues have been dealt with in chapter two, but here it is worth adding that William More's accounts reveal a world of artistic products within easy financial reach of most: a gilt spoon with an image of the Virgin Mary, 4s; a cross and 'other warke' (presumably in latten, but perhaps incised) on a gravestone, 3s 4d;[153] decorative cloth hangings, 8d per yard; a drinking cup, 'byrral grene [in] colour', 2s; a gold ring set with a

---

rebuilding continued into the fifteenth century, and, as noted, the chapter house remodelling went on until c.1392. Harvey 1984, p. 62.

149   *BRECP*, p. 841. In 1391/2 and 1395/6 he was infirmarer, however.

150   *Compoti* of three obedientiaries record sale to Lyndsey and purchase from him of timber and other materials between 1392/3 and 1396/7.

151   Hamburger 1997. Sauerländer 2002, p. 42, offers valid criticisms of Hamburger's method.

152   Coulton attacked the traditional 'monks were artists' assumption: Coulton 1928, pp. 26–72, particularly 32. Cf. *Chapters*, I, p. 74 (1277), where it is recommended that Benedictines in general copy *and* illuminate manuscripts. However, like most, he ignored art of low and mediocre quality such as Hamburger examines. A significant problem here is that much art in the later medieval Benedictine monastery (as generally) *was* of mediocre quality at best. Art was utilitarian, and quality was only occasionally a functional prerequisite: cf. Marks 2004, p. 218.

153   Cf. Saul 2002, p. 173 for the low cost of minor brasses during the late middle ages.

stone, 4s 4d; pictorial stained glass, 6d *quart.* per foot; carved images of saints, 9s a piece (or complete with tabernacles, 13s 4d each); prayer beads of amber, 8d.[154] A further obstacle is the assumption, which has some cogency, that monks and nuns did not need to own personal works of art because they inhabited a realm 'saturated' with images, any number of which might serve private devotion as efficiently as communal. Lydgate's autobiographical *Testament* relates how as a novice at Bury he gained religious conviction through contemplation of a crucifix (and its accompanying text) 'depicte vpon a wall' of the cloister.[155] Such works must often have been set up to facilitate the private prayer recommended by St Benedict.[156] Moreover, burial in the external monastic graveyard (a sort of lawn-cemetery) rather than the church, and subsequent removal therefrom to the charnel house – that ultimate expression of community – took away the need, let alone the opportunity, to commission any sort of sepulchral monument. The conditions for unofficial patronage in the later medieval Benedictine monastery were, it is assumed, unpropitious.

That awareness and cultivation of individuality was perfectly compatible with the corporate awareness that was part and parcel of monastic minds has been demonstrated by Caroline Walker Bynum and others, yet it still requires emphasis if the practice of unofficial patronage is to be given its due.[157] This is because unofficial patronage almost always had to do with the commission and/or purchase of objects for personal use, and personal possessions are, from a psychological standpoint, first and foremost expressions of individuality. If they also express corporate belonging, then it is through emphasis on the individual as a piece in the conventual jigsaw; an integral part of the whole, but retaining his or her own unique 'shape'. Except in a mystical sense, the distinction never completely collapses. Take, for example, the opening page of the *Golden Legend* from Winchester in Cambridge University Library, with its fine miniature of the Last Judgement and inscription commemorating John Drayton, the monk who had it made (Plate 24).[158] It is important here to keep in mind the general belief in the prophetic verity of this Biblico-patristic text, and its terrifying nature: the Judge, it is written, will be 'inexorably severe', 'sentencing irrevocably' to a punishment 'impossible to delay' the multitude deemed unworthy of Heaven.[159] Accordingly, Christ sits glowering at the viewer from within his golden aureole, earth's orb his footrest, exhibiting his punctured hands and side. Attendant angels, also frowning deeply, display the *arma Christi*, while below, others sound the judgement trump to shrouded dead arising from marble coffins. Immediately beneath this occurs the inscription, unabbreviated and in oversized letters: 'Memoriale fratris iohannis de Draytone monachi cuius a anime propicietur deus amen.' Drayton's intent is as unmistakable as it is understandable. He desires of readers *individual* commemoration, which will be of greater benefit to his soul than the collective

---

154 *Jnl.More*, p. 98 (cf. pp. 81, 116, 420), 142, 172, 176, 183, 300, 194.
155 MPLydgate, I, p. 356: 'Myd of a cloister, depicte vpon a wall/ I savgh a crucifyx, whos woundes were not smalle/ With this [word] "vide," wrete there besyde/ "Behold my mekenesse, O child and leve thy pryde." '
156 *RB*, chapter LII; cf. Matthew 6:6.
157 Bynum 1982, pp. 82–109.
158 CUL MS Gg 2 18, fol. 1r. Drayton must have commissioned the manuscript, for the memorial inscription is in the text hand. The manuscript may be slightly pre-1300 rather than post: Ker (MLGB, p. 199) has it 's.xiii/xiv' on paleographic grounds, although *Catalogue CUL*, III, p. 52 has it 'xivth century'.
159 *Golden Legend*, pp. 5–6.

remembrance of the charnel house and the anniversary. To this end he has commissioned the book and had this single illustration inserted by an accomplished artist.[160] The miniature was essential to his purpose. It was both carrot and stick, a summing up for readers of what the potentially salvific good work of prayers for the dead could forestall, and what failure to offer such charity might bring. Its efficacy depended absolutely on the viewer's awareness of his or her individuality, for as everybody knew, there was no safety in numbers on the Last Day. Each would appear before the Judge alone. Yet the image and inscription are perfectly compatible with the sense of *esprit de corps* that Drayton, as a member of a venerable and prestigious institution, must often have felt. In all probability, the manuscript passed from his hands into those of the convent, whence it became the collective property of twelve further generations of monks.[161]

John Drayton's *Golden Legend* highlights a problem with the study of unofficial patronage, namely, that it is often hard to distinguish from official patronage. Although Drayton does not occur in Winchester records as an obedientiary, he may have been one. If he was precentor or succentor, for example, patronage of such a book could have been part of his job. The same conundrum arises concerning the part that Maculinus (no other name is recorded), subprior of Great Malvern, played in the fifteenth-century glazing of Great Malvern priory church. While clearly this was subordinate to the efforts of his prior, Richard Dene,[162] it was apparently significant; his name formerly appeared in four windows of the south nave aisle, as part of the commonplace petition 'orate pro anima Maculini supprioris huius loci'.[163] In the nave clerestory, his name was displayed in another window, this time simply as 'fratris Maculini'; perhaps there had been a promotion between the two campaigns.[164] This is uncertain, and equally so is whether his contribution constituted part of his obedientiary remit, or was made out of private funds, as were the lay contributions to the glazing. In the north transept of Milton there is a further example worth noticing. Here are two purbeck gravestones of monks whose remains were spared the disruption endemic to burial in the monastic cemetery. They are apparently of fifteenth-century date. One has a small brass plate with an inscription: 'Hic jacet Johannes Artur huius loci monachus cuius anime propicietur deus – amen', while the other, on the basis of its indent, once carried similar.[165] No obedientiary status is given, but it is probable that John Arthur and his companion were highly respected officials, for intramural burial was an unusual privilege for a Benedictine below the level of prior/ess. William More's accounts mention that Robert Alchurch, sacrist of Worcester, 'is buryde under a blewe stone before our lady chapell',[166] while another monastic brass (of c.1460) at St Albans inscribed 'Frater Robertus Beauver, quondam huius monasterii monachus' commemorates a monk who was by turns kitchener,

---

[160] This bold insertion implies patronage: cf. the 'ex dono' inscription in TCC MS B 15 1, fol. 1r, in precisely the same position. See James 1900–02, III, p. 408, and James 1912, I, p. 405, for further evidence that Drayton was the patron of this manuscript.

[161] Drayton occurs as a monk of Winchester in 1283, 1305 and 1307: BRECP, p. 686.

[162] For Dene's contribution, see Rushforth 1936, pp. 3, 144, 247, 307. His motto 'Letabor in misericordia' is not a certain indication of patronage wherever it occurs, however.

[163] Rushforth 1936, p. 306. The nave was glazed in the 1480s.

[164] Rushforth 1936, p. 247.

[165] Prideaux 1907, p. 231 (mentioning a third slab, now lost); Stephenson 1926, p. 100; Rogers 1999, pp. 265–6. A John Arthur occurs in a 1417 list of Milton monks: Traskey 1978, p. 138.

[166] Jnl.More, p. 360.

refectorer, infirmarer, and spicerer.[167] A slab with indented inscription and foliated cross of the first half of the fourteenth century, recently unearthed at Coventry, commemorated John Aylmer, a subprior.[168] The rarity and lack of uniformity of such monuments suggests that they were arranged and paid for before death by the individuals they commemorated. Given that a monk or nun could purchase other items of personal property with private means, there is no obvious reason why this might not extend to an inscribed gravestone. However, it is at least possible that monuments such as John Arthur's are manifestations of conventual gratitude for services rendered, in which case they will have been supplied by an obedientiary and entered into a now-vanished *compotus* along with other official expenditure.

In the case of devotional books obviously intended for personal use this particular ambiguity disappears, but another takes its place. The book of hours of *c*.1420 from Gloucester in the Pierpont Morgan Library, New York, illustrates it well.[169] There is no doubt that this manuscript is from St Peter's abbey, for its calendar includes obit dates of various abbots, including Serlo (d.1104), Walter de Lacy (d.1139), John de Felda (d.1263) and Thomas Horton (d.1377) in red, and the first founder, Osric, also rubricated. There are many ornamental borders of featherwork and foliage in red, blue and gold, as well, and three miniatures of professional standard (the third by the so-called 'Oriel Master'):[170] the Virgin Mary enthroned with the Christ child (fol. 7r, Matins of the Virgin); Christ bound and surrounded by tormentors (fol. 58r, Lauds of the Passion) and the Apocalyptic Christ with the dead rising below and a scroll inscribed 'filii [dei] benedicti patris mei' (fol. 92r, Seven Penitential Psalms). But it is not clear whether this manuscript was commissioned by an abbot or prior (in which case, according to the definitions stipulated above, it would not belong to the category of unofficial patronage), or a monk of lower status. The psalters from Evesham of *c*.1310–30 preserved at the almonry museum, with seven historiated initials and copious borderwork, and Romsey/Nunnaminster of *c*.1430, kept in the former abbey church at Romsey and including good illuminated foliate initials, present exactly the same conundrum; they could have been commissioned by any reasonably affluent monk or nun.[171] The ambiguity is less marked in the case of a second, more modest book of hours from Gloucester of *c*.1425–50, for this seems likely to have belonged to a monk of obedientiary or cloisterer status rather than an abbot or prior.[172] It is small, and the decoration, consisting of illuminated foliate borders displaying flowers and fruit so naturalistic that the manuscript is designated a Flemish product, was never completed.[173]

---

167 Prideaux 1907, p. 231; Stephenson 1926, p. 193. On tombs for monks below the status of prior see Rogers 1999, *passim*.
168 Badham 2004, p. 714.
169 Pierpont Morgan MS M 99; see *Catalogue PML*, pp. 145–6 no. 95; *EBK*, II, p. 39.
170 Scott 1996, II, p. 126. Three separate artists were at work here.
171 The Evesham psalter has a local calendar: *MMBL*, II, p. 799. The Romsey psalter's provenance is disputed. It was later held at Nunnaminster: the calendar has obits of eighteen Nunnaminster abbesses. It may, moreover, have belonged to a Franciscan confessor at one or both of the houses. On these issues see Liveing 1906, pp. 288–94; Coldicott 1989, pp. 188–9; *MLGB*, p. 202; Walker 1999, pp. 46, xix appendix 6.
172 I.e. given the dignity of the abbot and prior in question. The manuscript is OBL MS Raw liturg f 1. Its provenance is unproblematic: *Catalogue OBL*, III, pp. 502–3; *EBK*, II, p. 39.
173 A number of borders are incomplete or non-existent. This presents problems for the theory that it is Flemish; for which see Pächt and Alexander 1966–73, I, p. 54. It is not included in Rogers 1984.

What does exist is kindred to that surviving gardener's *compotus* of Glastonbury that records the regular supply of freshly cut flowers to the shrines and chantries throughout the church.[174] Forget-me-nots (fol. 14v), thistles (fol. 15r), red carnations (fol. 17r), red roses in a terracotta pot (fol. 41r), wild strawberries (fol. 53v), yellow daffodils (fol. 72r), and white lilies (fol. 92v), not scattered as in other Flemish work but growing from the bottom margins up through the side borders, capture at once the minutiae, the beauty and the vitality of Creation. Yet still the grounds for a more than suppositional patronage analysis remain insufficient, and the same may be said of most of the other illuminated devotional manuscripts falling within the compass of this study.

Fortunately, the most impressive surviving later medieval manuscript from Glastonbury presents no such problems, and it demonstrates that books of the sort mentioned above were well within the reach (in terms of cost and decorum) of unofficial patrons, at affluent houses at least. This is the large historiographical volume now at The Queen's College, Oxford, again embellished with important miniatures by the Oriel Master, at the charge of brother John Merelynch (Plate 23).[175] A twenty-seven-leaf fragment of the same manuscript, with decoration by the Oriel border artist (fols 1r, 23v), is in the possession of Professor Simon Keynes of Trinity College Cambridge, and is dated 1411,[176] while a copy of Martinus Polonus's *De gestis pontificum et imperatorum* (BL MS Harley 641, fols 117r–206v), and an index belonging to the same (BL MS Harley 651, fols 185r–191v), the former containing another miniature by the Oriel Master (fol. 118r), may also constitute components of it.[177] The manuscript is in one regard a special case, for it was written and contains works by Merelynch himself (a genealogical tree of English kings, and an elaborate index to William of Malmesbury's *Gesta Regum*), but apart from this there is no reason for supposing that books owned privately by other obedientiaries (say, the Bible and two-volume breviary of John of Bromsgrove, later fourteenth-century sacrist of Evesham) would not have matched it in terms of decoration.[178] The evidence of personal possession takes the form of an inscription first found on fol. 48v and repeated on fols 57v, 58r, 66r and 67r (Plate 23): 'liber [*or* libellus] ffratris Johannis Merylynch de perquisito euisdem.'[179] The same inscription occurs in the Harleian manuscripts.[180]

Queen's College MS 304 encapsulates many later medieval Benedictine interests and concerns. Its contents include a number of items by Benedictine and other writers highlighting the primacy and dignity of both Glastonbury and the Benedictine order as a whole.[181] It also emphasizes the spirit of individuality that, it has been argued above, characterizes unofficial patronage. Partially, this is done by the insertion of the patron's own *Tabula linearum regum angliae*, and his index to the *Gesta Regum*. The name

174 Keil 1959, p. 97.
175 OQC MS 304; *Catalogus OQC*, pp. 70–1; *MLGB*, p. 91; Alexander & Temple 1985, p. 43; Scott 1996, II, p. 126.
176 Prof. S.D. Keynes, MS 1. Date at fol. 19v; fol. 20r is wanting. Generally, see Sharpe 2001, p. 283. Whether the Oriel Master and border artist were identical is unclear: Scott 1996, II, p. 127.
177 For the miniature, see Scott 1996, II, p. 126. The artistry, text-hand and size of the leaves here suggest original integrity with OQC MS 304.
178 *Shorter Catalogues*, p. 148.
179 On Merelynch as the owner, see Carley 1996, p. 132; Pantin 1950, p. 196. It is clear that in this case Merelynch was not simply the book's purchaser.
180 BL MSS Harley 641, fol. 206v; Harley 651, fol. 191v.
181 See *Catalogus OQC*, pp. 70–1; Pantin 1950, pp. 189, 196–8, for its contents.

Merelynch thus stands among those of more celebrated authors such as William of Malmesbury, Peter of Ickham, Nicholas Trivet and Adam Murimuth. Mainly, however, it is achieved through the illustrations, which provide a remarkably fresh reflection of the conditions under which the patron must have spent much of his life. If the Oriel Master was a Benedictine – and this is uncertain – then the reflection appears all the more genuine.[182] Here are seven miniatures, of Benedictine and Dominican authors and monks, their sad, earnest, urgent expressions a mark of the world they inhabited, as well as simply artistic idiosyncrasy.[183] In all but one case, a single monk or friar is shown, apparently in the isolation of a private chamber. On fol. 1r, a copyist sits in a large chair with a tester over it, virgin parchment before him and his exemplar open on a stand beside it. The initial on fol. 49r shows a monk sitting on a sumptuous curtained bed, absorbed in a large blue-covered book. On fol. 58r, another monk (his tonsure is represented differently) reaches from his Gothic chair into a small aumbry containing more books. The illustrations on fols 67r, 144v, 151v and 163v similarly show religious either reading or writing. The miniature in BL MS Harley 641 belongs iconographically to this series, and the lost fol. 20r of Keynes MS 1 surely had a similar illustration (which no doubt explains its loss).[184] In their activities these figures represented Merelynch's status as author, scholar, scribe and general bibliophile, while in the comfort and privacy of their surroundings may be perceived the conditions under which he lived and, when not in choir or chapter, worked.

The interior embellishment depicted in these miniatures brings to mind the 'silly ornamental furniture' privately owned by Muchelney's monks in the fourteenth century, and mentioned in chapter two. In terms of status, obedientiaries of medium to large Benedictine houses enjoyed parity with the gentry by the later middle ages,[185] and understandably wished to furnish their checkers and (where they slept apart) chambers to a fitting degree. Partitioning of dormitories, common by 1300, meant that cloister monks and nuns also had personal spaces that could receive decoration. Such embellishment was another product of unofficial patronage. That the few known West Country examples were typical enough is supported by evidence from houses elsewhere in the country. The Dissolution-period inventories of the private chambers of the Benedictine nuns of Minster in Sheppey (Kent), for example, include three instances of personal ownership of devotional panel paintings, and much else beside.[186] Monks, too, bought private devotional works. The surviving Netherlandish panel representing the martyrdom of St Erasmus executed in 1474 for John Holyngborne, monk-obedientiary of Christ Church Canterbury, may be of higher quality than much of what was owned by Benedictines in the west of England, but it reflects the religious and aesthetic bases of that ownership clearly.[187] In 1405/6, John Langreod, Winchester's hordarian, fitted out

---

182 See Scott 1996, II, p. 127. The major surviving work by this artist (the missal now Oxford, Oriel College MS 75) is not of Benedictine use.

183 Such expressions are usual in the Oriel Master's work: Scott 1996, II, p. 126.

184 Folio 20 was the first leaf of the *Gesta Regum*. Three of the other illustrations are found at the beginning of texts, as is that in Harley 641.

185 Harvey 1995, pp. 1–2.

186 *Inv.Kent*, pp. 296–7. 'Dame Anne Clifford's Chamber . . . a table with a crucyfyx of wod payntyd, and an image of our Lady, pay[ntyd] . . . Dame Ursula Gosborne Supprior's Chamber . . . a table of the crucyfyx payntyd' (p. 297).

187 On this panel see Tudor-Craig 1974, *passim*; Marks 2004, pp. 111, 113; *Gothic*, pp. 398–9. For Holyngborne see *BRECP*, pp. 201–2.

his treasury with three linen hangings ('dorsoriis') painted (or perhaps embroidered) with the Five Joys of the Virgin Mary. This purchase, requiring 10s, was entered on his *compotus* under 'emendatio domorum cum necessariis', and thus may conceivably rank as official expenditure; although it was seemingly no more necessary than many of the items that William More purchased for the chambers of his manors.[188] A few decades later, John Temple, monk of Bath, purchased a painted cloth ('pannus intinctus') representing Christ, St John the Evangelist and St Peter on a green background for donation to his *alma mater*, Canterbury College Oxford.[189] An inventory of c.1535 records that the kitchener's oratory at Worcester contained another painted cloth, 'of the goode Lorde [and] ix imagys'.[190] John Avington, sometime *custos operum* and chaplain of Bishop Fox's chantry at Winchester,[191] commissioned in 1526 a devotional triptych representing the Betrayal, Resurrection and Ascension of Christ, with Winchester saints Birinus, Æthelwold and Hedda in grisaille on the exterior, for his own private devotional use.[192] The patronage of this particular work reminds us of Bishop Fox, and his admonition that 'noo mynchyn presume or giue or receyue any thynge' by way of private property, delivered in his 1517 English edition of the Benedictine *Rule*.[193] This was written expressly for the Benedictine nuns of his diocese, and immediately recalls Wykeham's late-fourteenth-century injunctions to Nunnaminster, according to which that house's inmates were forbidden to wear (among other things) 'pins of gold or silver, or silken belts ornamented with gold and silver, and . . . [more than] one ring only'.[194] These orders in turn echoed injunctions made by Henry Woodlock almost a century earlier. With such gifts forthcoming as the girdle with buckle, pendant and six silver studs that William Thornton gave to a nun of this very house (1504),[195] these injunctions, along with the spirit of Fox's *Rule*, seem more than usually optimistic.

This introduces us to the domain of the cloister. Cloister monks and nuns are here taken to include all those fully professed Benedictines who held no obedience other than performance of the *opus Dei*. In smaller houses they might be few: at Romsey in 1502 they numbered only eight in a community of twenty-six, at Sherborne (1504) five in fourteen, and at Muchelney, a decade later, around one third of the total.[196] The division between them and obedientiaries, which Jocelin of Brakelond makes so plain, lost none of its sharpness during the later middle ages, despite the levelling implications of Lateran IV.[197] At Westminster, tables in the frater were arranged 'pro senioribus', 'pro mediocribus' and 'pro inferiores', and the latrines likewise.[198] Larger houses in the west of England will have observed similar customs, although convents the size of Cannington, Pilton and Tywardreath were perforce more egalitarian. The category is

---

188 CRWin., p. 288.
189 BRECP, p. 43.
190 Green 1796, II, p. viii.
191 BRECP, p. 668.
192 The triptych survives, though not on public display, in the private chapel at Knole (Kent). It is illustrated and discussed in Smith 1988(b), pls 58, 59 and pp. 289–91.
193 RBFox, p. 128.
194 Coldicott 1989, p. 86.
195 Coldicott 1989, pp. 86, 206.
196 Power 1922, p. 131 (Romsey); MA, I, p. 335 note g (Sherborne); MA, II, pp. 359–60; VCH *Somerset*, II, p. 105 (Muchelney). Cf. Harvey 2002, pp. xx–xxi.
197 CABury, pp. 23, 88.
198 Pearce 1916, p. 24; Harvey 1995, p. 78.

thus a historical one, and while it does not coincide with the divisions of patronage outlined in this study, it is worth mentioning because it marks the boundary between twilight and almost total darkness where hard evidence for patronage is concerned. Perhaps the alabaster head of John the Baptist unearthed in the foundation of Pershore's conventual buildings belonged to a cloister monk.[199] The same may be true of the iconographic gold rings unearthed at Glastonbury (the Virgin and Child, with the legend *en bon an*) and Cerne (two saints).[200] The objects, and many more like them, are mute. It is the written word that speaks, and cloister monks and nuns, despite their relatively high standard of literacy, hardly documented themselves at all.

Thankfully, Robert Joseph, the self-styled 'prisoner' of Evesham's cloister,[201] found plenty to write about himself.[202] It is in his letter-book that the most candid evidence for patronage on the part of cloister monks and nuns survives. There, examples of patronage on the part of at least four monks are mentioned, all relating to devotional concerns. Joseph had been educated at Oxford and kept in touch with many of the friends he had made there. On 9 April 1530, he wrote to one such friend, lately ill, with his greetings and those of other Evesham monks: 'Acton salutes you and sends you some nutmeg. Stodley sends you a little image ('imagunculum') of St Roch. Malvern sends you these rosary beads . . . Littleton sends you an image ('effigiem') of the Cross. Brodewey, Warwyck, Stafford and many others salute you . . .'[203] The works sent to the convalescent – images which may have taken the form of woodcut prints, and rosary beads – are modest indeed. Where their givers obtained them is uncertain, but does not really matter (unless they made them personally, in which case they would not be classifiable as subjects of patronage). Of prime importance is the window they open onto what may be called the art commerce of the cloister. Art, for the work it could do rather than for its aesthetic value (here surely slight), was the thing that three out of five gift-givers sent.[204] It was thus available, and widely owned. The impression is strengthened by another letter, written precisely two months later, by Joseph to George London, a fellow Evesham monk studying at Oxford. This includes the following request: 'In choosing our Bible, get me one with marginal lines on every leaf, and adorned with little images. There are some which, though of the largest size, yet lack these delineations; if the one you have bought is like that, please get another of the sort we want, instead.'[205] A clearer picture of the ability of cloister monks to procure works of art could not be had. The Bible is evidently to be a ready-made one, and thus either second-hand like the missal that William More gave to Bromsgrove (this seems unlikely), or new, with printed images. The request demonstrates a certain concern with personal possession, but does not make a great deal of the purchase of this work of art. No doubt transactions such as these were as commonplace as Joseph makes them seem, among all ranks of monks and nuns, and throughout the Benedictine cloisters of the west.

199 Hope 1890(a), p. 691.
200 Sherlock 1955–60, pp. 125–6; Blair 1962, pp. 110–11. Cf. the non-Benedictine cloister-nuns' rings discussed in W.A.S. 1952, pp. 235–7.
201 *LBRJ*, p. 75. Cf. the comments of the *Eulogium Historiarum*'s author, a mid to later fourteenth-century cloister monk of Malmesbury (Gransden 1982, p. 103), and the use of the cloister as a place of 'house arrest' recorded in *Linc.Vis.*, I, p. 3; III, p. 312.
202 On Joseph generally, see *LBRJ*, pp. xi-lv; Knowles 1959, pp. 100–7.
203 *LBRJ*, pp. 77–8.
204 A fifth, obedientiary, gift-giver, who sends a piece of cinnamon, is mentioned separately.
205 *LBRJ*, pp. 46–7.

We have another excellent piece of evidence for unofficial patronage generally and that of cloister monks in particular in the 1391 inventory of the Lady chapel at Worcester. Here are a number of artworks ascribed to the generosity of monks, jostling with others given by priors and external patrons. Most of the monastic benefactions are vestments, although we do encounter 'tabula eburnea ex dono cuiusdam monachi de Teukesburie'; perhaps a devotional image of the type (if not the quality) commissioned by John Grandisson, bishop of Exeter (1327–69).[206] The donor may have been an obedientiary, but this is certainly an example of unofficial patronage. It is further recorded that brother John of Gloucester gave a chasuble of red silk with gold embroidery, with a back of blue velvet with imagery. Three monks of this name are recorded at Worcester pre-1391, but the obvious candidate is the monk mentioned as kitchener in 1345/6, who went on to be chamberlain, tertiary prior, almoner and infirmarer, dying in 1380/1.[207] Brother John Leominster, a monk-scholar, public preacher and licensed penitentiary who travelled widely and maintained a private confessor, gave an altar frontal, and Robert Morton (or Merston), subcellarer in 1322/3, donated another. Brother William Mose, listed as one of Worcester's two shrine-keepers in 1313, gave an alb with amice 'preciously gilded, with silken images of the passion of St Catherine', while Roger de Henley, a cloisterer, gave an alb with stole and maniple, the alb with apparels displaying red and green leopards.[208] It is difficult to be sure how the monks concerned came by such items, but in the absence of evidence to the contrary we are entitled to suppose that they purchased the vestments in connection with their priestly duties. Even if they received them as gifts, they were nevertheless personal property to be donated to the convent in acts of unofficial patronage for the good of their respective souls. We know that Robert Morton owned at least one other work of art, for he traded his copy of Guibert de Tournai's *Sermones ad varios status* (now WCL MS F 77) with brother Henry Fouke for a 'jewel' of ivory ('iocali eburneo') valued at 4s 6d (here is further evidence of the 'art commerce of the cloister' mentioned above).[209] The likelihood is that he represented a norm rather than an aberration where Benedictines below the status of prior were concerned.[210] The example of St Albans, where monks gifted decorated manuscripts of their own volition (with abbatial licence), may be cited to support the claim.[211] This was not an institutional idiosyncrasy: Worcester monks also owned, gifted and traded books privately, but no surviving example is decorated.[212]

---

[206] *HMC XIV:viii*, p. 199. Cf. *AoC*, pp. 465–7.

[207] *HMC XIV:viii*, p. 198; *BRECP*, p. 810.

[208] All references at *HMC XIV:viii*, p. 198. See also *BRECP*, pp. 819 (Henley), 836 (Leominster), 851 (Morton), 852 (Mose).

[209] Thomson 2001, p. 50; *BRECP*, pp. 808, 851.

[210] See further John of Thanet (II: d.1319), of Christ Church Canterbury, who owned a red chasuble embroidered with roses and a silver cup: *BRECP*, p. 300. He also owned (or gave) a blue *opus Anglicanum* cope with Christ in Majesty enthroned, done in gold and silver thread. Part of this survives: see Williamson 1996, pp. 192–3.

[211] See for example the *ex dono* inscriptions in BL Royal MSS 2 B VI, 2 F VII, 2 F VIII and 11 D IX, noted in *Catalogue Royal MSS*, I, pp. 41–2, 66–7, 358; cf. *MLGB*, pp. 300–1.

[212] E.g. OBL MS Bodley 442; WCL MSS F 62, 63, 77, 124, 125, 131 etc.: see *MLGB*, pp. 317–19.

Conclusion

The subject of internal patronage below the level of superior does not lend itself to the same treatment as that of superiors' patronage, although in common with it, it is too heterogeneous to permit easy summarization. Not only its convolutions, but also the lack of attention paid to it in previous studies, makes it so. The path trodden here is very fresh, fresher in some places (the patronage of cloister monks and nuns) than in others (the patronage of the priorate), but overall practically undelineated in previous work. It is not that the objects reviewed are unknown (although many of them are scarcely known); it is rather that the concept of patronage being brought to bear on them conflicts to a marked extent with conventional assumptions concerning enclosure, poverty, corporate unity etc. Historians of later medieval monasticism, particularly prosopographers, have in recent years constructed an extremely detailed picture of conventual life, one that has room for as many patronage possibilities as there were monks (nuns are less well understood). The old dichotomy expressed in, and speciously legitimized by, the medieval formula of donation 'to the abbot and convent of . . .' simply does not hold good any longer as an epitome of the later medieval status quo at Benedictine houses. Although *esprit de corps* and collective will played an important role in monastic life, convents were not monolithic in all of their aims, obligations and desires, but varied, complex and miscellaneous in important respects. The challenge for art historians is to place the many surviving artefacts into the detailed landscape that has emerged as accurately as possible, rather than simply slinging them in any which way.

The signal problem is lack of certainty, and this has been dwelt on here not only as a circumstance conditioning the outline of the current study, but also as a caveat to other researchers and an implicit criticism of the carelessness with which attributions have often been made in the past. Monks and nuns below the level of superior documented their unofficial art patronage hardly at all, while the poor survival rate of *compoti* restricts acquaintance with official patronage severely. Patterns have, however, been traced: the autonomy of the priorate, the quotidian nature of the bulk of official patronage, the heights it could reach, and the acclaim that its practitioners might receive as demonstrated by the *Chronologia ædificorum*; the distinct problems inherent in attributing different classes of undocumented artefact to official or unofficial patronage, the individualistic devotional and commemorative concerns that underwrite the claim for the ubiquity of this patronage, and the fact that when it is revealed, as in Robert Joseph's letters, it appears not as an exceptional phenomenon but as part of everyday life. There is reason to hope that, in time, a more substantial picture may emerge.

PART III

AUCTOR PRETIOSA FACIT:
EXTERNAL PATRONAGE

External patronage will be discussed in two chapters, rather than three, for there is no one class of individuals prominent enough to warrant separate treatment of the sort given to superiors. It needs to be acknowledged from the outset that external patronage was rarely crucial to the plan, elevation or decoration of Benedictine buildings during the later middle ages. By and large, monks and nuns did not rely on external patrons to raise, repair and embellish their churches, conventual complexes, granges and other secular buildings for them. They did rely on external agents for maintenance of the prosperity that (largely incidentally) made internal patronage possible: the Dissolution is the ultimate demonstration of this reliance. But such assistance, as suggested in the first part of chapter two, is not what we mean by patronage. All things considered, the patronage of art and architecture was a relatively minor aspect of the secular–monastic exchange.

What the Benedictines sought from influential external agents were reconfirmation of pre-existing rights and privileges, licences to appropriate, to amortize, to initiate or annex markets, fairs and other commercial enterprises, to elect without royal and papal rubber-stamping and to excuse themselves from other forms of authority whose exercise was costly to them, to be exempted from taxes, and various other money saving or generating expedients. Gordon Haigh's study of Winchcombe abbey, which is largely based on monastic, episcopal, royal and papal documents, illustrates the process well.[1] Of the more than one hundred petitions cited by Haigh for the post-1300 period, only one was for direct help with building and embellishment, notwithstanding the fact that the monastery frequently needed work doing.[2] In this, Winchcombe's monks were entirely typical. While it is true that Benedictine pleas to appropriate parish church revenues often cite dilapidation of conventual architecture, the small amounts which successful appeals brought in can have been sufficient for little more than plugging leaks, replacing tiles and sealing holes, if indeed any part of them was applied to such ends. Moreover, citing dilapidation due to poverty may in certain cases be understood as a pre-emptive measure designed to obviate or at least mitigate episcopal criticism such

---

[1] Haigh 1950, pp. 85–185.
[2] Haigh 1950, p. 132 (Papal indulgence granted c.1365 for help with repairs following storms).

as Oliver King's of Bath, John Grandisson's of Tavistock (twice, in 1338 and 1348) and Edmund Lacy's of Cowick (1439).[3]

Even in extraordinary and unpreventable circumstances, for instance the burning of Milton abbey church in 1309, little external assistance that can be classified as patronage was forthcoming. In this case, Bishop Simon of Ghent granted the usual quarantine for those giving succour to the monastery, and Edward II waived some taxes to do with the Scottish wars in the immediate aftermath. But within a decade the king was imposing corrodians again and demanding money on various pretexts (including £40 for a licence to appropriate the church of St Nicholas at Sydling, whose tithes were desperately needed), and by 1320 Pope John XXII was attempting to foist unwanted confraters – corrodians by another name – onto the stricken monks.[4] Rarely if ever was a medium to large-sized Benedictine house covered by this study as badly off as Milton was in the decades after 1 September 1309. By the early 1340s, conventual life was breaking down under the strain. The abbot was in and out of prison, obediences (including that of cellarer) lay vacant, internal dissent, like poverty, was rife, and there was appalling debt, which in 1344 resulted in the disgrace of total bankruptcy and the imposition of royal receivers.[5] That an ancient monastery of royal foundation groaning under such pressure could expect no more by way of contribution towards rebuilding, furnishing and decorating than what episcopal indulgences could bring says something generally about the issue of external patronage during the later middle ages, at least as it relates to higher secular authorities. The Golden Age, evoked afresh by Milton's monks during the later fifteenth century through a panel painting in which King Æthelstan presents a handsome, newly made church to a kneeling abbot (Plate 20), was past. Enter the Age of Iron.

It is important to hold this bigger picture in mind as we turn to some prefatory remarks on chapters five and six. As in part two, the discussion of individual classes of patron will be preceded by a contextual chapter highlighting the main historical conditions necessary for the existence and encouragement of external patronage generally. As the example of Milton suggests, the climate in which patronage subsisted after c.1300 was not propitious for the older religious orders. The later medieval downturn in royal and aristocratic sponsorship of their art and architecture, continuing a slide that for the Benedictines had been occurring since the second half of the twelfth century, was countrywide, and in the west was not marked by the spectacular exceptions provided from time to time by houses in the east of England (particularly, Christ Church Canterbury and Westminster). Tewkesbury, which will naturally receive much attention in coming pages, is a peculiar case and must be treated judiciously, for its rebuilding and embellishment is almost wholly undocumented. Below the level of the nobility, it is now axiomatic that projects in the secular domain, particularly the parish church and private residence, were the main beneficiaries of secular urges to build and embellish. The glorious towers that stud lowland Somerset, many of them belonging to churches with Benedictine rectors (e.g. Isle Abbots, Muchelney, Long Sutton, Weston Zoyland), testify to this. Local people did not lose interest in their monasteries altogether, and monasteries did not lose interest in them. The relationship between the two, which

---

3   Reg.Grandisson, II, pp. 882, 1072 (Tavistock); Clarke 1904–05, pp. 143–4 (Cowick).
4   Traskey 1978, pp. 93–9; CPR 1313–17, p. 159.
5   Traskey 1978, pp. 114–16; VCH Dorset, II, p. 60.

included a great deal by way of commercial, religious and domestic interchange (as a rule, more laypeople worked within the walls of religious houses than monks or nuns, and many also lived therein), was unavoidable, intimate, reciprocal, and mostly positive. This did lead to a certain amount of art and architectural patronage: many examples are forthcoming from the ranks of the sub-nobility. Furthermore (and as suggested in chapter two with reference to Kington St Michael and Glastonbury), the size of such contributions, and the impact they made on the receiver, must be assessed in relative terms if their value is to be properly appreciated. All in all, however, the patronage of the sub-nobility resembled that of society's higher orders in its sporadic nature and the fact that collectively it constituted only a small fraction of a large whole.

The crux of the matter is best understood in terms of competition. It is in such terms that the context and conditions of external patronage are seen to differ (on the whole) from those outlined earlier on for internal patronage. Maintenance of basic prosperity relied, as we have seen, on a raft of largely defensive expedients. Copying and fabricating charters, purchasing books of parliamentary statutes and training or retaining lawyers were defensive measures, their products primarily active in the essentially negative cause of minimizing losses. Even petitions for annexation of parish church revenues and Mortmain licences, and legal action, were basically defensive and passive, insofar as they were based on litanies of loss, distress and degradation. Usually they offered nothing in return beyond the assurance that compliance with a given request would bring the satisfaction of having relieved poverty and consequently affected a good work. They were pleas for non-reciprocal charity; or rather, reciprocity was enforced through the exaction of fees. Competition, however, called for a pro-active, at times aggressive, approach.

What was the nature of this competition? The forces against which the Benedictines were constrained to compete during the later middle ages were manifold. Here they will be discussed under two headings, non-ideological and ideological. Non-ideological competition, which could be called competition for market share but for the fact that it was not purely financial (a good deal of pride and prestige was also at stake), came from many quarters, for a raft of institutions and individuals, both secular and religious, relied for at least part of their substance on lay support. Parish churches, friaries and external pilgrimage sites particularly recommend themselves to our attention, while other monastic and collegiate organizations (especially the secular cathedrals), non-Benedictine hospitals and secular enterprises (parochial and civic, as well as private), and individuals (among whom the self looms largest),[6] also tended to deflect attention from the Benedictines. Maintenance of status, dignity and prosperity (one manifestation of which was art and architectural patronage) depended not only on the successful retention and prudent management of past endowments, but also on the ability of monks and nuns to compete against these factors by promoting their houses as places of (among other things) pilgrimage, display, retirement, burial, and above all commemoration. Ideological competition is another matter. In the period after 1300, monasticism generally came under ideological pressure from malcontents of varying degree and influence, from the popular, through the literary and clerical-heretical, to the orthodox-royal. Cumulatively these pressures were formidable, although they were experienced more acutely in some quarters than others. It was natural that the Benedictines should feel them particularly strongly, and not only because they had the most, in terms of

---

6   Particularly, the 'religious individualism' current among the later medieval gentry and nobility (for the term, see e.g. Fleming 1987, p. 85). Cf. Duffy 1992, pp. 2–3.

material assets, to defend. Their wealth, power and the degree of secular intercourse they maintained meant that they exemplified the vices (real or imagined) that informed many complaints. Some concerns, for example those of Henry V and Cardinal Wolsey noted in chapter two, were aimed specifically at the Benedictine order. Competing against ideological pressure was not a matter of advertising the benefits of Benedictine burial, confraternity or commemoration. It required a counteractive effort aimed at promoting the order's religious integrity, historical precedence and political affiliations. Chapter five outlines the main elements of non-ideological and ideological competition in turn, and also the Benedictine responses to them.

Chapter six classifies external patrons in three groups, coinciding with the arrangement of internal patrons: royalty (the monarch and his immediate family), the nobility (here including external superiors and bishops) and the sub-nobility. Although some such social ranking is usual in modern historical scholarship, it will be admitted that these groups are not completely self-defining in terms of their patronage activities. Indeed, their social definition *per se* is hardly straightforward. As K.B. McFarlane and others have shown,[7] the social status of the laity below the level of royalty and above that of yeoman experienced such upheaval during the fourteenth and fifteenth centuries that what constituted the nobility by 1485 (i.e. between fifty and seventy members – the peerage) was quite different from what it had comprised in 1300 (i.e. some 3000 members). Such issues are bound to result in shades of grey in any study based on lay social hierarchy. The group designated sub-nobility is consequently unstable. It is also, by any definition, large and complex, but to break external patrons down into more than three groups in the context of a relatively short survey such as this would be impractical, and in any case would not obviate the problems of hazy class distinctions. It would, moreover, result in repetition, for some basic motives for patronage were shared by all social classes.

Caveat lector. A flyleaf at the end of a manuscript once belonging to Exeter cathedral contains a fifteenth-century list, born of the same curiosity that drove the ageing William Worcestre (and scribbled in like haste), of verses that hung on boards behind the tables of the guest hall at Launceston, the wealthiest Augustinian house in Cornwall.[8] Here were tables designated 'valettorum' (yeomen), 'clericorum', 'garcionum et operariorum' (grooms and workmen) and 'generosum et armigeriorum' (noblemen and gentlemen): a Chaucerian whole they must have made when the guest-master was busy. Royalty were excluded, for they would not have been obliged to use such facilities, and the poor were acknowledged in a general, moralizing inscription hanging at the end of the hall ('Pauperis in specie Christus cum venerit ad te' etc.). This represents a practical division of external classes according to monastic definition – Benedictine as well as Augustinian, for the same verses circulated at Glastonbury.[9] While chapter six of the present study is not arranged on the basis of such an authentic formula, it is as well to keep in mind the fact that, as the Launceston panels tend to show, monastic conceptions of social hierarchy were apt to be different, and typically more complex, than this study – along with much other recent scholarship – may imply.

---

[7]   McFarlane 1973, pp. 268–9; McFarlane 1981, pp. xxvi–xxvii (introduction by G.L. Harriss); Given-Wilson 1996, pp. 55–8; Carpenter 1986, pp. 36–50. The literature is dense, but McFarlane fundamental.

[8]   OBL MS Bodley 315, fol. 268r (mid-fifteenth century). See Robbins 1963–64, pp. 338–43.

[9]   GM, p. 71.

5

The Historical Context of External Patronage

The Clever Order

During the later middle ages, the Benedictines remained England's privileged monastic order, most richly endowed and longest of pedigree. The Golden Age had taken care of that. For Orderic Vitalis, writing in the first half of the twelfth century, England was 'the land of the Benedictines',[1] and as far as monastic prosperity in general went, it remained so. A popular and profane West Country saying had it that if the abbot of Glastonbury could marry the abbess of Shaftesbury, their heir would own more land than the Crown.[2] When in 1378 the abbot of Westminster explained that St Peter himself had hallowed his church, producing a chronicle to prove it, people took notice, believed, and wrote his words down.[3] In most cases, English kings and their queens continued to be buried and to establish their principal chantries in Benedictine churches. A Benedictine account was still most likely to be called on where crucial historical facts needed clarifying, as in the canonization of St Osmund.[4] This position of privilege is epitomized by the fact that with only two exceptions, all regular parliamentary lords spiritual were from the ranks of the black monks.[5] The surviving roll illustrating the procession of the 1518 parliament is led by a veritable phalanx of Benedictines, beginning with the newly instituted Abbot Beoley of Tewkesbury.[6] By the mid-fifteenth century, the head of any monastic house worth the price of the papal indult could wear the mitre, but only a handful was summoned to parliament.

Yet ever since the introduction of competing orders into England, particularly the very successful Augustinians (c.1095), the Cistercians (1128) and the two main mendicant orders (Dominicans, 1221, Franciscans, 1224),[7] the Benedictine hegemony and reputation in many areas had been under threat. That much of this threat seems to have been perceived or potential, rather than actual, hardly lessens the challenge it represented. To paraphrase a current historian, 'what counts is not a neutral observer's point

1 Quoted in Dickinson 1950, p. 93.
2 VCH Dorset, II, p. 75.
3 English Chronicle, pp. 2, 119–20.
4 Ranulf Higden's Polychronicon (composed between c.1327–60). See Malden 1901, p. 27. Cf. Given-Wilson 2004, pp. 71–2, 73–8. Edward II wrote to Abbot Fromond of Glastonbury in 1312 (or 1322) asking him to search his monastery's chronicles on the matter of foreign exiles: see Stones and Keil 1976 passim; Given-Wilson 2004, pp. 73–4, 229.
5 Regular, that is, after the standardization which occurred under Richard II: see McHardy 1991, pp. 22–3.
6 TCC MS O 3 59, membrane 1; Bettey 2003, p. 68 (ill.).
7 K&H, pp. 114, 214, 222.

of view of whether things were good or bad, but the [monastic] *perception* and *experience* that the times were critical.'[8] By 1300, the pressure described above was being felt everywhere, not only by individual houses, but also by the order as a whole, as appears from the documentation generated by the triennial General Chapters. To maintain dignity and prosperity commensurate with their historical status, it was no longer enough to be the privileged order. The Benedictines had now to become the *clever* order.

To argue this controversial point of view thoroughly would require resort to a historical apparatus for which there is no place in this study. The theory is, admittedly, open to some objections, not least the issue of the extent to which 'Benedictinism' can justifiably be reified. Notwithstanding these, it is raised here as a consideration to be held in mind throughout the following chapter, one that has the potential to contribute to the way in which late Benedictine art, architecture and its patronage (internal and external) is understood and interpreted. It is usual for scholars to represent the Benedictine later middle ages as a period of winding down,[9] of gentrification,[10] religious torpor,[11] and general bending of the *Rule*.[12] This receives some support direct from the horse's mouth – for example, the admissions of Winchcombe's Abbot Kidderminster and the General Chapter of 1520 mentioned above in chapter two.[13] It is as well to remember, however, that their response would have been quite different had the challenge come from other quarters. No doubt they would then have emphasized the sanctity of their order, and its core virtues; or perhaps its wealth and temporal prestige; its great and enduring concern with learning, epitomized by its (putative) foundation of Oxford and Paris universities;[14] or again, its allies, and past challenges successfully met with their help. The superiors, and their convents, knew how to tailor a response.

The point requiring emphasis is that parallel perspectives to the picture of Benedictine decay are available that do not necessarily gainsay received opinion, but rather pick a different set of examples with which to illustrate the post-1300 monastic condition. As Norman Tanner pointed out, circumstances in which one historian sees decline may to another denote growth; an assertion particularly germane to monastic studies.[15] The resourcefulness with which Benedictine houses drew on their past histories (together with the results this attained), the adaptability of convents to local circumstances and competing institutions which stand out in the historical record, the role they assumed in education and religious instruction (through, for example, elementary schooling, preaching and catechesis),[16] the energy and expertise monks and nuns devoted to adver-

---

8   Bostick 1998, p. 8 and note 32. See also Catto 1985, p. 98.
9   E.g. Fleming 1984, p. 48; Owst 1926, p. 49.
10 Cf. Knowles's assessment of William More as 'representative of the age', discussed in chapter four.
11 E.g. Harvey 1995, p. 1; Dobson 1990, p. 170; Harper-Bill 1996(a), pp. 36–43.
12 E.g. Bugslag 1980, p. 58; Dickens 1994, p. 23; Oman 1957, p. 11; Platt 1984, pp. 136–72; VCH *Worcester*, II, p. 343; Youings 1971, pp. 14, 85 (citing Henry VIII) etc. This phenomenon is integral to what F.R.H. Du Boulay called the 'Myth of Decline' concerning the late middle ages (Du Boulay 1970, pp. 11–16), and not simply a facet of 'Fox-Dickensist' Reformation-era history. See also Clark 2002(a), *passim*.
13 Cf. MPLydgate, II, p. 466. The Benedictines are deeply implicated in these satirical remarks. Lydgate's poetry circulated among West Country houses, of course: e.g. GM, pp. 57–60.
14 As trumpeted at St Albans during the fifteenth century: AMSA, II, p. lix. At Winchester itself a publicly displayed tabula claimed that St Swithun had been a don of theology at Cambridge: MMBL, III, p. 358 (referring to Manchester, Cheetham's Library MS 8003).
15 Tanner 1984, p. 54.
16 On catechesis, see Duffy 1992, pp. 2–3; Greatrex 2002, p. 38. However cf. Heale 1994, p. 208.

tising their virtues and attractions and the advantages that these could have for strangers, the alacrity with which they crenellated their houses when threats (real or imagined) arose, and above all the *esprit de corps* to which the documents of the General Chapters (excerpts from which turn up in manuscripts from so many monasteries) and other sources testify, provide firm grounds for emphasizing another point of view.

Perhaps the most obvious objection here is that the Benedictines were no more clever, adaptable, torpid, lax etc. than, say, the Augustinians or the Cistercians. In many respects this is true; the Barlinch schoolbook (early sixteenth century),[17] and the will of John Stourton (d.1439) by which Stavordale priory church was transformed into a family mausoleum,[18] provide glimpses of rural Augustinian convents in Somerset adapting themselves to local circumstances as effectively, in relative terms, as the monks of Winchester and Worcester engaged with their environs. Among West Country houses, Augustinian Cirencester's wealth and Cistercian Hailes's popularity also suggest that whatever the Benedictine convents could do to maintain prosperity, those of other orders could do as well.[19] However, the Benedictines as an order appear particularly able and resourceful in many ways: their closed-ranks approach to and effective disposal of threats from the highest quarters (in spite of the fact that they normally eschewed centralized decision-making); their skilful exploitation – including considerable extension – of a pedigree that no other order in England could come near; the fact that (until 1536–40) they successfully steered a larger ship through increasingly turbid social, religious and political waters to finish the course prosperous, proud and growing etc.[20] If other orders (notably the Brigittines, Carthusians and Friars Observant) were more capable of combining primitive modes of observance with the demands of the world at large, then this was largely because the spiritual microclimates they inhabited were sustained by intensive Crown and aristocratic support.[21] As the superiors told Wolsey in response to his unreasonable demand that the black monks and nuns assimilate the rigour of Sheen and Syon,[22] the Benedictines were different. That they were *perceived* to be different externally, at the highest level at least, is shown here in the fact that Wolsey – like Henry V and reform-minded popes going back to Innocent III – levelled his charges at them alone. Less austere than some, certainly, but not necessarily less disciplined or virtuous, for (as Robert Joseph noticed) there was more to holiness and virtue than fasting and prayer vigils.[23] Away from the rarified environment of Henry V's houses, the very exercise of monastic virtue depended on knowledge of the world and how to survive in it. Thus did the continuator of the Crowland chronicle bemoan the unworldliness of his predecessor, whom he implies failed to provide his readers (a

17 Orme 1984, pp. 55–63.
18 Bates 1904, pp. 97–8.
19 Hailes was a focus for pilgrims throughout England: Vincent 2001, p. 151; Duffy 2003, p. 60; Marks 2004, p. 186.
20 On this growth see, generally, Clark 2002(a), pp. 14–16.
21 See Condon 2003, p. 104; Beckett 1995, *passim*; Rowntree 1981, pp. 286–307. The Brigittines (one house) and Observants (six houses) were both introduced into England by the Crown, and subsidized by it thereafter.
22 Which he presumably did, for the Carthusians and Brigittines, along with the Friars Observant, are named in the Benedictine response: *Chapters*, II, pp. 123–4.
23 LBRJ, pp. 35–6. Strict adherence to the *Rule*, he says, inhibits virtue (including the exercise of Christian charity). See also Heale 1994, p. iii.

Benedictine convent) with the information they needed to survive in a troubled present.[24]

In a letter of deposition sent to Thomas Colyns, prior of Tywardreath, at around the same time as the issue of his reforming injunctions (c.1520), Wolsey had set out a more realistic model of Benedictine conduct. He wrote that the next superior of the modest Cornish house – he had a Tavistock monk, Robert Hamlyn, in mind for the job – should be not simply 'religious' and 'sobre', but 'hable', 'discrete' and 'politique' as well.[25] Which is to say that he had to be capable of surviving in a difficult environment, of combining traditional monastic piety with pragmatism: in a word, to be clever. In Colyns, however, all of these qualities were already combined (along with a healthy measure of stubbornness), and in the event, both he and the order as a whole success-fully resisted the cardinal, retaining the status and conditions to which they were accus-tomed.[26]

From the least to the most, then, the Benedictines proved their resourcefulness in the breach. If their efforts seem hollow in light of the Act of Suppression, then it is as well to remember not simply the pedestrian fact that nothing could stand up to the machinery of Henrician government (Sheen, Syon and the London Charterhouse fell before Evesham, Glastonbury, Gloucester and Tewkesbury),[27] but also that the self-promotional efforts of the Benedictines, a key aspect of the 'cleverness' argued for here, are deeply implicated in England's surviving cultural heritage. What is meant by this is perhaps most clearly illustrated with reference to Gloucester. Henry VIII cited the 'fact' that the abbey church of St Peter contained 'many famous monuments of our renowned ancestors, kings of England' (he had seen the tombs during a visit in the summer of 1535) as a signal reason for having it preserved.[28] We may well ponder this a moment, keeping in mind as we do the fact that there was only ever one king of England buried at St Peter's. The statement places in perspective not only the value for posterity of the part played by the fourteenth-century monks in providing Edward II with a place of burial and a splendid canopy tomb,[29] but also the commission of a new tomb-chest bearing the escutcheons of the Nine Worthies plus the royal arms for the effigy of Robert Curthose (William the Conqueror's eldest son, d.1134) in the late fifteenth century,[30] and, perhaps above all, the sixteenth-century campaign (probably c.1525–30) to provide the monastery's founder, 'King' Osric, with a sumptuous and ostentatious monument immediately to the north of the high altar (Plate 28). The latter, incorpo-rating a crowned and sceptred effigy and a black-letter inscription reading 'Osricus Rex, primus fundator huius monasterii 681' will have been particularly obvious to Henry VIII as he processed to the altar accompanied by Abbot William Malvern,[31] who no doubt

[24] Kingsford 1913, pp. 181–2, cf. p. 260.

[25] Oliver 1846, pp. 45–6.

[26] Colyns may have finally resigned c.1534, although this is not certain: Snell 1967, p. 50. His grave-stone is dated 1534.

[27] By mid-1539, over ninety per cent of England's religious houses had capitulated; yet forty-nine Benedictine institutions stood firm, 'manipulat[ing] the labyrinthine Tudor patronage network for their own survival': Cunich 1997, pp. 158–9.

[28] In the *Charter of Foundation of the Bishopric of Gloucester* (1541): see Rudder 1781, appendix, p. xxxvii.

[29] See chapter six.

[30] Chest dated 'c.1500' in AoC, p. 197. On the armorial embellishment see Anon. 1863, *passim*.

[31] For this occasion, see Fullbrook-Leggatt 1946–48, p. 279.

explained its resonances in the manner most edifying to the monastery. Art installed first and foremost in the cause of self-promotion (as will appear presently, St Peter's was particularly pressed by competitors during the later middle ages) was here deeply implicated in the preservation of the abbey church, its cloister, chapter house, and other conventual buildings. If Benedictine cleverness did not save the order, at least it played a major role in rescuing St Peter at Gloucester, and many other important monuments besides.

Non-ideological Competition

As a lead-in to this subject it is worth remaining at Gloucester, for it provides a paradigm of the non-ideological competition faced by the Benedictines throughout England. During the later middle ages, the town supported eleven parish churches, Carmelite, Dominican, Franciscan and two Augustinian convents, three hospitals and several chapels, all of them competing with St Peter's abbey for public attention.[32] That they were getting it is shown by the great quantity of chantry priests (sixty) serving in the parish churches, and other marks of non-Benedictine prosperity. For example, it was reported in 1538 that 'the Grey Friars is a goodly house, much of it new-builded, especially the church, quire and dorter.'[33] The shell of the nave and the north aisle, of the hall-church type, along with the medieval roof (ex situ) survive as witness to this.[34] Given the institutional poverty of the Franciscans,[35] the money spent on this enterprise had to be solicited from the populace at large (particularly, Maurice, Lord Berkeley, d.1523).[36] To make matters worse, the Holy Blood of Hailes was not far distant, and this was the region's most popular pilgrimage attraction, enthusiastically promoted by the Cistercian monks at this very time (c.1515) through a pamphlet printed in the capital by Richard Pynson, and seemingly also by a printed Missa preciosissimi sanguinis domini nostri iesu Christi, issued subsequently (c.1520) by the same printer.[37] 'I dwell within half a mile of the Fosse Way', wrote Hugh Latimer c.1533, 'and you would wonder to see how they come by flocks out of the West Country to many images but chiefly to the Blood of Hailes; and they believe verily that it was the very blood that was in Christ's body, shed upon the mount of Calvary for our salvation, and that the sight of it with their bodily eye doth certify them . . .'[38] Little wonder, then, that people travelled to Hailes in such numbers. The extensive sixteenth-century heraldic tile pavements excavated on site, the many contemporary sculptural fragments from the cloister and chapter house, and the exceptional illustrated psalter now at Wells, produced in 1514 by Pieter Meghen

---

32 Itinerary, V, p. 158; K&H, pp. 55, 64, 140, 141, 157, 164–5, 214, 216, 222, 225, 233, 235, 520–1; VCH Gloucester, II, pp. 53–61, 84–91, 111–12, 119–22.

33 Suppression Letters, p. 199; Youings 1971, p. 179.

34 Ferris 2001, pp. 99–104.

35 Not that friars owned no real estate: see e.g. Oliver 1846, pp. 68, 151, 334, 424 note *; the cartularies in Davis 1958, pp. 4, 30, 36 etc.

36 Ferris 2001, p. 99.

37 RSTC 12973 (treatise); 16224.5 (mass). On the treatise, entitled A Little Treatise of divers Miracles shown for the Portion of Christs Blood in Hayles, see Oates 1958, pp. 269–77 (dating evidence at 273).

38 Latimer, p. 364; Duffy 1992, p. 193.

(sometime writer of Henry VIII's books) as an aristocratic gift to the convent,[39] survive as sumptuous witness to custom that might otherwise have gone (in part at least) to St Peter at Gloucester.[40] To cap it all, during the later fifteenth and early sixteenth centuries, Gloucester and much of the surrounding country laboured in the grip of economic depression, limiting generally the amount available for spiritual services, let alone the patronage of art and architecture.[41]

Here, in a nutshell, are the most significant elements of non-ideological competition: the parish (and all that went along with it), the chantry, friary, non-Benedictine monastery, hospital, and external pilgrimage cult, with general financial difficulty – a recurring and ubiquitous barrier to patronage – thrown in for good measure. Add to these the fact that Benedictine houses were in competition with one another, as well as external institutions, for public favour, and the picture is further nuanced. The proximity of groups of monasteries like Gloucester, Tewkesbury and Winchcombe, Evesham, Great Malvern, Pershore and Worcester, and also of Abbotsbury, Cerne and Milton, and St Swithun's, Hyde, Nunnaminster, Romsey, and Wherwell, meant that the share of the pie potentially available for each (let alone the smaller houses that subsisted in their shadows) was reduced even more. While it is true that not all houses faced the degree of competition experienced by St Peter at Gloucester, all without exception had numerous rivals.

The parish

The parish church had been an object of lay benefaction for a long time prior to 1300. The late eleventh and early twelfth century witnessed a great deal of parish church rebuilding: while the evidence for this is difficult to interpret, it points unambiguously to widespread, if diffuse, patronage.[42] Each such project accounted for the typically modest art and architectural ambitions of successive generations of parishioners. Thus, the mass-rebuilding of the later fourteenth, fifteenth and earlier sixteenth centuries does not mark a new phase in the history of patronage so much as the augmentation of an existing trend, made possible, desirable and to some extent obligatory by a broad-based rise in prosperity (particularly in wool-rich counties such as Devon, Gloucestershire and Somerset), the increasing accessibility of individual commemoration and intramural burial, and, in many places, the development of the parish as a social unit, membership of which carried responsibilities as well as rights. Eamon Duffy's absorbing study of Morebath parish (Dev.) in the sixteenth century brings home the insularity of lay concerns at the lower end of the social scale. We can no more imagine these men and women paying for the updating of the church of their corporate rector (Barlinch priory) than the rector sponsoring a south aisle at St George's in the village to relieve Sunday congestion.[43] Morebath was more isolated than some, but apparently not atypical for a rural parish at least. Higher up the social ladder, too, there was little incentive for sponsorship of monastic art and architecture.[44] This was because the main occasion for such

---

[39] The colophon names the monastery as the recipient, not an individual.
[40] Eames 1980, I, pp. 257–63; Trapp 1981–82, pp. 30, 35 (ill.); MMBL, IV, pp. 561–2.
[41] Holt 1985, p. 159.
[42] Gem 2001(b), p. 744 et passim.
[43] Duffy 2001, pp. 3, 5, 90 and 1–110 passim.
[44] Evidence from elsewhere in England suggests that the upper ranks of the gentry were slightly more likely to favour old monasticism with benefaction than people lower down the scale: e.g. Fleming 1984, pp. 48–9.

sponsorship – monastic burial – was infrequent among the gentry (i.e. knights, esquires and gentlemen). Where a later medieval person's body was, there, as a rule, was his or her treasure also, and while monasteries offered more opportunities for the burial and commemoration of the sub-nobility after 1300 than they previously had, their services were seldom in demand. Three-quarters of gentry burials in Gloucestershire between 1200 and 1500 were in parish churches.[45] Including members of the nobility, only about five per cent of the laity of the diocese of Salisbury opted for monastic burial between c.1250 and the Dissolution, a figure that would no doubt find correspondences in the other sees covered by this study were the data available.[46] Parish loyalties aside, even those who might have aspired to intramural monastic burial recognized that a monument in a parish church stood out, whereas it would be 'swallowed up among the benefactions of centuries' in a Benedictine one.[47] Winchcombe's Benedictines seem to have lost the privilege of burying the lords of Sudeley for this very reason during the fourteenth century.[48] Given that the single most important function of the sepulchral monument for its patron was the elicitation of intercessory prayer,[49] the gentry preference for burial in parish churches is understandable: for to elicit prayer a monument had to be noticeable, and it was more likely to be so in a (typically) smaller space in which fewer set-piece monuments competed for viewer attention.

There were other factors tending to root lay generosity in parochial soil other than burial and commemoration. Membership of a parish, and of sub-parochial organizations (of which guilds and other groups under religious patronage have received most attention in recent scholarship), called for an ongoing, even life-long commitment that accounted completely for the energies and surplus monies of most. The motives for keeping benefaction local often militated directly against contributions to monastic projects: the desire to increase divine service at a parish level for instance.[50] Such factors obviated broad-based sponsorship of extra-parochial projects of all sorts, of course, and not simply Benedictine ones. The typical lay will (remembering that wills were usually the provenance of the relatively prosperous) of the fifteenth or early sixteenth century leaves a small sum – less than £1, often only a few shillings – to one or more extra-parochial churches (the nearest cathedral benefited particularly from this),[51] but not specifically for building or embellishment.[52] In such an environment, the friars and houses of other orders were apt to fare little better than the Benedictines.

Mendicant rivals

Thus, while in theory a man or woman might choose to support whatever religious institution he or she liked, in practice there was only a limited amount available for religious

---

45 Saul 1980, p. 103.
46 Brown 1995, p. 35 note 48. Between 1500 and 1535, nineteen of 708 testators requested monastic burial (p. 35 note 49: the figure covers all religious orders). Gee 2002, p. 36 note 93, has generated figures showing greater support than this for monasteries amongst aristocratic women during the thirteenth and fourteenth centuries.
47 Quote in Rosenthal 1972, p. 35.
48 Saul 1980, p. 104.
49 Wilson 1995, p. 451; Morganstern 2000, p. 152; Saul 2002, p. 171.
50 See e.g. Burgess 1985, pp. 59–60; Bainbridge 1996, pp. 55–6.
51 E.g. SWE, pp. 75–6, 78.
52 Cf. Brown 1995, p. 30 note 15 with p. 35; Tanner 1984, pp. 119–25 with pp. 126–7.

houses. The mendicant orders, relying as they did on public charity for sustenance and public contact for strength of purpose, probably absorbed a high percentage of this, especially in urban areas.[53] Without doubt, the antipathy said to have characterized relations between friars and Benedictines has been overstated. The notorious ejaculation of John of Worcester's continuator – 'O dolor! O plusquam dolor! O pestis truculenta! Fratres minores venerunt in angliam'[54] – should not be taken to reflect the status quo post-1400. There are, however, cases in which mendicant ability to attract lay sympathy seriously disadvantaged both black monks and nuns, in terms of art and architectural patronage as well as honour. This is suggested generally by that fact that after 1272, at least 108 houses of friars were founded in England, against one Benedictine priory.[55] More specifically, the phenomenon dubbed 'burial-hunting' by Coulton proved a particular bone of contention.[56] The most celebrated later medieval case tending to Benedictine disadvantage comes from Westminster, where, in John of Reading's words, the Franciscans of Newgate 'seduced' Edward II's queen Isabella into bequeathing her body to them at the expense of the abbey (1358).[57] Locally, Gloucester was at loggerheads with the Grey Friars over burial rights,[58] the Dominicans of Exeter were attracting illustrious burials at the expense not only of Cowick, Polsloe and St Nicholas's priory but also the dean and chapter of the cathedral,[59] while at Worcester during the thirteenth and fourteenth centuries, great acrimony resulted from a switch in allegiance by the Beauchamp earls of Warwick from the cathedral chapter to the Franciscans. William Beauchamp was interred in the mendicant church in 1298, fuelling a protracted dispute over burial rights which occupied diocesans, chroniclers and of course lawyers.[60] The Worcester chronicler describes the ostentation with which the earl's body was processed to the Franciscan church in a way that manifests his concern over the potential that such 'advertisement' had to further damage Benedictine prospects.[61] This concern was well-grounded, for in 1347, William Beauchamp, lord of Emley, founded a Dominican house in the city (entailing building and embellishment),[62] a circumstance still provoking Benedictine angst in the 1530s, when it was recorded afresh among the cathedral priory's muniments.[63]

---

[53] Cf. the Norwich evidence in Tanner 1984, pp. 119–21.

[54] Sheppard 1912, p. 246.

[55] Tanner 1787, pp. vi–viii. The interest in founding, as opposed to supporting, mendicant houses, had dwindled by 1377, however.

[56] Coulton 1936, p. 50.

[57] CJR, pp. 128–9; Gransden 1982, p. 106; cf. Binski 1995, p. 178. A splendid alabaster tomb costing £106 18s 11d, which along with the other grand tombs there presumably attracted many visitors, was erected in the friary: see Harvey 1984, p. 244.

[58] Ferris 2001, p. 98.

[59] Death and Memory, pp. 7–13; Orme 2004, pp. 19–20; Oliver 1846, p. 335. Ultimately, episcopal restrictions might be imposed on mendicant 'burial-hunting': e.g. Oliver 1846, p. 152.

[60] VCH Worcester, II, p. 171; Cart.Beau., p. xvi.

[61] Annales, IV, p. 537.

[62] VCH Worcester, II, pp. 167–8; K&H, p. 219.

[63] WCL MS A xii, fol. 113v (where the erroneous date 'circa millesimo ccccxlviij' is given).

Other institutions

As suggested above, similar comments may be made about other sorts of extra-parochial institution. Secular colleges, founded (or re-founded) by the dozen in later medieval England, were a particular target of aristocratic and gentry benefaction.[64] The collections of tombs they contained were often extensive: the now-lost monuments of the Hatch branch of the Beauchamps at Stoke-sub-Hamdon (Som.), a college founded in 1303, might otherwise have graced a local monastic church.[65] Moreover, the substance of Benedictine houses was in some cases reduced in favour of colleges: Romsey and Shaftesbury both suffered in this regard,[66] while the revenues of many small houses were applied by Henry VI to Eton. Of the numerous secular colleges founded in the west of England after 1300, the most inconvenient from a Benedictine point of view was that at Westbury-on-Trym (Gloucs.), initiated by Bishop Walter de Cantilupe of Worcester (1237–66) on the site of an ancient black-monk house close to the Severn.[67] In the late thirteenth century, Bishop Giffard had proposed raising Westbury to joint-cathedral status with Worcester: like his counterpart at Bath and Wells, he would then control a Benedictine and a secular chapter, and (what is more) have an influential foothold in the *banlieue* of lucrative Bristol. The plan, which never bore fruit, was revived on a less ambitious but still substantial scale by Bishop John Carpenter (1444–76), who is styled Westbury's 'alter fundator' by Leland.[68] Carpenter had the college rebuilt, enlarged and unofficially raised to cathedral status, and began to style himself 'bishop of Worcester and Westbury'. (That he was also provost of Oriel College and chancellor of Oxford University during a busy period of collegiate foundation there helps to explain his enthusiasm.) He had his tomb erected within – the *transi* still exists, albeit mutilated, encased in a Victorian monument – and a statue of himself placed in a niche over the west door. The project was – needless to say – highly unpopular with Worcester's monks, who foresaw in it a substantial diminution of their dignity. Carpenter's attempt to divide his see was not pursued by his successors, but Westbury remained a prosperous independent foundation, with a value of £232 at its dissolution in 1544.

Hospitals (e.g. Warland at Totnes, subsequently a Trinitarian friary),[69] educational colleges, chantries, even anchorites (to whom wealthy benefactors might refer possessively – 'my anchorite' – as they once had monks and nuns),[70] all represented better value for money than sponsorship of Benedictine projects, and consequently posed a challenge to Benedictine prosperity.[71] Primarily, it *was* a case of value for money. There is no strong evidence to suggest that non-Benedictine patrons generally avoided

---

64 See K&H, pp. 411–46; Cook 1959, pp. 106–218; Jeffery 2004, *passim*.
65 *Itinerary*, I, pp. 158–9.
66 *Itinerary*, II, pp. 23–4.
67 K&H, p. 443; *VCH Gloucester*, II, pp. 106–8; Thompson 1917, pp. 163–6; Pevsner 1958(a), pp. 473–5; Cook 1959, pp. 71–4; Jeffery 2004, pp. 175–8.
68 *Itinerary*, V, p. 227.
69 Orme 1987–91(b), pp. 41–2. The influence that hospital foundation had on the later medieval 'devotional landscape' is notoriously uncertain (Heath 1990, p. 658; Saul 1980, p. 103), although the sheer number of them (for which see K&H, pp. 310–410 *passim*) speaks for itself. Over and above their foundation, they could attract important burials: e.g. *Itinerary*, II, p. 59 (St Bartholomew's hospital, Gloucester).
70 E.g. (Devonshire, of 1419) in Davies 1908–09, p. 104.
71 Cf. Orme 1987–91(b), p. 43.

Benedictine houses for ideological reasons, or because the religious integrity of black monks was considered in some sense deficient (the charterhouses at Hinton and Witham in Somerset were hardly flooded with benefactions during the fourteenth and fifteenth centuries).[72] The ideological factors to be mentioned below do not, on the whole, appear to have been matters of broad public concern: the threat they presented to Benedictine interests was largely latent, a potential cause of harm rather than an active one. Had monasteries offered the same scope for effective display and commemoration as the institutions just mentioned, then most of those wealthier patrons with a surplus to commit to the health of their souls would have paid greater attention to them than they did. Further, the fact that they were already well established, in material as well as liturgical terms, meant that those willing and able to glorify God (in whatever manner) through benefaction also tended to look elsewhere. These factors were disadvantageous for old monasticism generally, and those not adequately endowed, for example Augustinian St Oswald's at Gloucester and Cistercian Abbey Dore (Herefords.), endured a precarious final two centuries.

Non-Benedictine pilgrimage sites

Pilgrimage is another matter, for here the Benedictines could expect to hold their own. Their collective status as custodian of the greatest quality and quantity of holy relics was beyond challenge, and in any case, the social as well as religious functions of pilgrimage during the later middle ages ensured the ongoing popularity of established cults.[73] Additionally, the 'many images' mentioned by Latimer will have included a good few in Benedictine houses: the silver Virgin of Worcester for example (which he particularly hated).[74] Yet in this reference to cultic images, a challenge to Benedictine hegemonies more wide-reaching than the Blood of Hailes is adumbrated. The crowds plying the Fosse Way were indicative of a broad shift in devotional focus that might have occupied art historians more than it has, namely, a common predilection for images over relics.[75] A miraculous (and perhaps indulgenced) painted or sculpted representation of a saint, subject of meditation (e.g. the Five Wounds of Christ, Five Joys of the Virgin Mary) or object with holy associations (e.g. the *arma Christi*, the Holy Cross alone,[76] the Veronica) might now prove as great an attraction as a miraculous relic, and this lead to both a proliferation of pilgrimage sites and a localization of pilgrimage (which is not to say that people ceased to travel to major shrines further afield), for while few churches possessed important relics, all had multiple images.[77] Relics did not lose their pulling power, but they had to compete for attention with imagocentric cults. In any case, relics also proliferated in the later medieval countryside. The annotated *Cathalogus sanctorum pausantium in Anglia* in Lambeth Palace Library MS 99 (fols 187r–196r), of c.1380–1400, while nothing like plenary, contains a roll-call of saints and saint-like persons

---

[72] Rowntree 1981, pp. 286–355, discusses all the surviving evidence for benefactions to English charterhouses, including Hinton and Witham.

[73] Duffy 1992, pp. 190–2; Carley 1996, pp. 129–30.

[74] Nilson 1998, p. 165; *Latimer*, p. 403.

[75] Marks 2004, pp. 186–227 makes an important contribution.

[76] As early as 1318 Cistercian Abbey Dore (Herefords.) was attracting large numbers of pilgrims to the cross in the conventual church: Harper-Bill 1980, p. 105.

[77] Duffy 1992, pp. 166–7; cf. Marks 2004, pp. 186–90.

bewildering in length and complexity, including many non-Benedictine West Country examples.[78] It is clear that, even setting aside important cults such as those based in Hailes, Hereford and Salisbury, the Benedictines did not have a monopoly on the pilgrimage trade in the region and period under scrutiny.

Responses to Non-ideological Competition

Assimilation

It needs to be acknowledged that the Benedictines, as individuals if not as an order, did not always function in opposition to these potentially prestige and income-sapping phenomena. As men and women of their time they participated in the trends of the age, to the degree permitted by relatively generous prevailing standards of decorum. Just as many superiors kept hunting dogs, and monks and nuns often dressed in irregular clothes and owned personal property, so did they involve themselves in parish life, cooperate with mendicants, go on pilgrimages and take part in many other quotidian affairs. Manifestly, the degree to which they assimilated themselves stood them in good stead concerning the successful promotion of the virtues and advantages of their own order and its individual houses (i.e. know thy opposition). However, by and large this interchange should not be regarded as a strategic exercise so much as a further manifestation of the progressive enlargement of the monastic landscape particularly evident after the turn of the fourteenth century.[79]

Bristol, Cannington, Dunster, Leominster, Little Malvern, Romsey, Sherborne, Tewkesbury, Totnes: at these and other Benedictine houses, parish and monastic communities worshipped under the one roof, while, elsewhere, parish churches (sometimes more than one, e.g. Evesham) stood within monastic precincts. Parochial-monastic relations were, as suggested previously, largely sympathetic and cooperative, and under such conditions interchange was natural.[80] Thus we find the magnificent chantry chapel of Clement Lichfield, prior and (from 1513) abbot of Evesham, annexed to the nave of All Saints, Evesham.[81] Such interchange was not restricted to intra-claustral parish churches, as the graves of John Muddisley and Thomas Wason, monks of Glastonbury, in the forinsec church of St John the Baptist suggest.[82] Other Glastonbury monks were buried in St Mary's at Meare.[83] Clearly, these men no more desired the obscurity which burial in their respective abbey churches or cemeteries would have brought than did the local gentry interred alongside them.[84] The 'payer of vestymenttes of Rede Velvett of

---

78 BL MS Harley 3776, fols 118r–127v is a fifteenth-century copy (with some variant readings). James and Jenkins 1930–32, pp. 163–5, print some of the list's odder characters.

79 Greatrex 2002, p. 39.

80 Heale 2001, pp. 185–225, deals with this issue where Benedictine cells are concerned. See further Heale 2003, pp. 1–11; Heale 2004, pp. 208–18, 301–3.

81 Built before 1513: Cox 1980, p. 23.

82 Daniel 1902, p. 20. Both were buried in 1498. Wason had been prior.

83 Collinson 1791, II, p. 275.

84 Collinson 1791, I, p. 72, claims burial of a prior of Bath in the local parish church of St James. Egelina, abbess of Shaftesbury 1394–97, willed burial in an Essex parish church: Anon. 1924–6, pp. 94–5. For examples of monastic burials in parish churches outside the West Country see Rogers 1999, pp. 266–7.

the bequest of my lord of Glastynbery' mentioned in the churchwardens' account of 1507 for the Somerset parish of Pilton (whose tithes were impropriate not to the abbey but to Wells cathedral) shows a superior of the highest rank seeking parochial involvement.[85] The prioresses of Kington St Michael who had themselves represented in the chancel windows of their local parish church (Christina Nye, d.1474 and Cecily Bodenham, elected abbess of Wilton, 1534), accompanied by supplicatory inscriptions ('Ihu xpe fili [dei] miserere mei' and 'orate pro anima vel bono statu domine Cecile Bodenham prioressa qui hanc fenestram [fieri fecit]' respectively), exhibit the same tendency.[86] Nor (rectorial matters aside) was commemoration the only motive for monastic participation in parochial affairs. For many years (1385/6–1470/1, at least) the sacrist of Tavistock made an annual oblation at the rood of St Eustache's parish church, as the churchwardens' accounts show, and it seems fair to say that this is an example of what will have been a rule rather than an exception.[87]

Constructive interchange with mendicant communities was also a feature of late medieval Benedictinism. The Sherborne missal, written by a black monk (John Whas) and decorated by a black friar (John Siferwas) and his assistants, is a robust evidence of this, and an illustration in the Evesham psalter showing a Benedictine and a Franciscan singing together from the same service book (fol. 94v) also demonstrates the point. Some Benedictines even became friars; William More was made a Franciscan tertiary,[88] while it appears that one John Brinston, monk of Winchester, obtained a licence to become a mendicant during the 1520s.[89] Prior More hired Franciscans and Dominicans to celebrate the obsequies at the funerals of his parents and superiors, while other priors invited members of both orders to say masses for the souls of deceased Worcester monks, sour grapes over the Beauchamp affair notwithstanding.[90] By his 'will' of c.1322, Geoffrey Fromond, abbot of Glastonbury, paid for mendicants to commemorate dead monks of his house.[91] Friars also preached general sermons in Benedictine monastery churches: a particularly well-known example, of 1536, comes from Glastonbury (clearly there was a long-standing connection here).[92] At Polsloe, Romsey, Wherwell and other Benedictine nunneries, the sisters employed mendicant confessors,[93] homiletic and devotional material penned by friars was popular in Benedictine houses generally,[94] and the monks of Bath even owned 'unum pannum de auro cum ymaginibus fratrum minorum'.[95] Such interchange extended to non-mendicant houses. Examples of forinsec Benedictine chantry priests will be mentioned presently, and, in 1511, a monk of Evesham is found working alongside a Cistercian of Bordesley in the dwindling secular college of Wingham in far-off Kent.[96]

---

[85] CWA Somerset, p. 53.
[86] Aubrey, pp. 88–92. The inscriptions are lost. The second was incomplete when Aubrey visited.
[87] CWA Tavistock, pp. 3–12.
[88] Jnl.More, p. 281: 'to the grey fryurs for my brotherhood . . . 12d.' Cf. Knowles 1959, p. 120.
[89] Winch.Anth., p. 10 (order not suggested).
[90] Jnl.More, pp. 127, 133, 140; BRECP, pp. 859, 876, 891, 896.
[91] CGA(C), pp. 256–7.
[92] LPHVIII, X, pp. 121–2; Owst 1926, pp. 51, 156.
[93] Oliver 1846, p. 163 (Dominicans, Franciscans); Liveing 1906, p. 292 (Carmelites, Franciscans); Coldicott 1989, p. 62 (Carmelites, Franciscans).
[94] Greatrex 1998, pp. 271–2; Winch.Anth., pp. 39–40.
[95] Cart.Bath., p. 158.
[96] K&H, p. 444.

Benedictine pilgrimage to external sites was also common, and as he or she blended with the crowds riding, walking or sailing to shrines near and far the black monk or nun achieved the greatest possible degree of assimilation with Everyman. Chaucer's caricatures are overworked:[97] let us rather imagine William More trotting off to Cistercian Hailes to prostrate himself before the Holy Blood (1530),[98] John Whitington, monk of Worcester, losing himself among the antiquities and wonders of the Eternal City (1441),[99] or, more poignantly still, the aging Abbot Boys of Evesham supplicating the *Beau Dieu* of Amiens, kneeling besides Nicholas of Verdun's shrine of the Three Kings at Cologne, gaping up at the opalescent frescoes in the nave at Assisi, and toiling over the Somport on the road to Compostella (1366–67).[100] He was not the only West Country Benedictine to take St James's way during the later middle ages.[101] In the matter of pilgrimage, as in their commerce with local parishes, with the mendicant communities that formed an unavoidable part of their *milieux*, and at many other points, Benedictines demonstrated a marked ability to blend into the socio-religious landscape that surrounded them. If the concept of the Benedictine order was in important regards monolithic, then the predilections of individual monks and nuns were not. 'The tonsure does not make the monk, nor the rough garment/ But [rather] a virtuous soul and constant activity'.[102] If these lines, jotted on the flyleaf of a chronicle by a ruminant Malmesbury monk, be accepted, then the individual Benedictine was in essence as indistinguishable ideologically from many of his contemporaries in the world as he was in his own cloister.

Display

The point regarding assimilation is an important one, but it should not be allowed to obscure Benedictine efforts to counteract the potentially damaging factors aforementioned. The strategies adopted for maintaining standards of living and prestige differed according to the size, administrative structure, location and wealth of a house. Common to all, however, was an emphasis on sanctity and hospitality. Display also played an important role, for then as now, the big, colourful and marvellous drew people in. The abbots and convents of Evesham, Glastonbury and Gloucester, though they thought in terms of what is now called Decorated and Perpendicular Gothic, were nevertheless at one with their contemporary Leon Battista Alberti, whose apology for architecture as the most effective vehicle for self-promotion, as well as commemoration and beautification, would have struck a chord had *De re aedificatoria* been available to them. 'There is hardly any man so melancholy or stupid', Alberti wrote, 'but pursues those things which are most adorned, and rejects the unadorned and neglected'.[103] Robert Aske, a leader of

---

97 See Knowles 1955, pp. 365–6, on whether or not Chaucer's monk was Benedictine. Chaucer's nun certainly was.
98 'Expenses ryding to Hayles from Cropthorn in pilgrymage, 2s 4d.' *Jnl.More*, p. 314.
99 *BRECP*, pp. 892–3.
100 Boys was licenced in 1366 to go on pilgrimage to Amiens, Cologne, Assisi and Santiago: *HRH*, p. 42.
101 E.g. *BRECP*, p. 787 (John de Cleve). See further Trevelyan 1838, pp. 64, 75.
102 'Non tonsura facit monachum, nec horrida uestis/ Sed uirtus animi perpetuusque uigor.' TCC MS R 7 10, fol. 162v (thirteenth century). See James 1900–02, II, p. 225.
103 *Doc. History of Art*, pp. 221–2, 229.

the Pilgrimage of Grace, testified to this in his own apology (1537), stating that England's monastic houses constituted 'one of the beauties of the realm to all men and strangers passing through.'[104] Certainly, they had astonished another Italian at the close of the fifteenth century – and he was from Venice.[105] Beautifying a house was not only a matter of decorum, pride and paying God his due, but a means of attracting external support as well. Gloucester's crossing tower, like the Tower of London, soon became proverbial, lodged in the popular imagination just as Abbot Seabroke and Robert Tulley would have wished.[106]

Sale of 'spiritual services', corrodies and confraternity

Increasing the number of monks in priestly orders was another expedient adopted to buttress unstable fortunes. Without papal dispensation, no priest could legally say more than one mass a day,[107] and thus, extra ordinations advertised a house's capacity to accept more in the way of commemorative duties. Extra ordination also augmented the reputation of an institution in a general sense. As one historian has it, 'the more priests, the more altars, the more services; the greater the prestige of the house, and the greater the chance of attracting more endowments.'[108] Since 1311, it had been theoretically compulsory for monks aged twenty-five and over to accept priestly orders at their superior's request.[109] Monk-priests need not serve in their own church. At Tavistock and Tywardreath, for example, Benedictines staffed chantries in the parish church, at High Ham (Som.) they served the cure of souls, while at Hereford they were employed in the cathedral, further demonstrations of the versatility on which later medieval prosperity so often relied.[110] Nunneries marketed themselves as sites of commemoration and burial by increasing facilities for mass-priests. During the fifteenth century, Wilton abbey church was served by sixteen male religious, the majority presumably chantry priests. Shaftesbury, too, had at least eight perpetual chantries at this time,[111] a sense of whose richness lingers in the fragments of Perpendicular screenage displayed in the abbey museum, the cartulary of the chantry of St Catherine with its elaborate form of ordination (1415),[112] and the mid fifteenth-century alabaster panel of that saint's dormition, retaining traces of gilt and leaden fixing plugs, and thought to have formed part of the reredos of the same chantry's altar.[113]

Benedictine popularity and, in the short to medium term, prosperity, were further

104   LPHVIII, XII:i, p. 901.
105   Relation, p. 29. The Venetian ambassador's visit probably occurred in 1496 or 1497.
106   'John Gowere, who built Campden church and Glo'ster towre': Harvey 1984, p. 123. Cf. Itinerary, II, p. 61: 'This tower is a pharos to all partes about from the hilles.' The many copies of its openwork parapet, from Cardiff to Llandaff and Taunton to Great Malvern, amply attest its fame in the west. Cf. Durham Univeristy Library MS C III 22 (incidentally, a Benedictine book): 'A foole had rather have a bable than the tower of London.' MMBL, II, p. 490: sixteenth century.
107   Wood-Legh 1965, p. 291 (Christmas day excepted).
108   Rosenthal 1972, p. 41.
109   Coulton 1936, pp. 69–70.
110   Oliver 1846, pp. 41, 91; Schaell's Memoir, p. 115; Swanson and Lepine 2000, p. 69.
111   Mayo 1894, p. 42.
112   Davis 1958, p. 100 (no. 886: BL MS Egerton 3135, where the form of ordination is at fols 100v–103v).
113   Cheetham 2003, p. 36 and fig. 29. For discussion see Eeles 1927–29, pp. 113–14; Long 1928(a), pp. 108–11.

augmented through the advertisement and sale of corrodies and grants of spiritual confraternity. The letters of confraternity that survive from Westminster and other Benedictine houses remind us what a popular phenomenon the latter was.[114] Benedictine houses had long provided such services, but in the aftermath of Mortmain and the epidemics of the fourteenth century most came to regard them as a primary source of income.[115] The expedient was controversial, for it burdened posterity. Under Prior John of Dunster (1461–81), the convent of Bath raised £666 for the construction of a new frater substantially through the sale of corrodies:[116] with the church a 'soden ruyn', one is tempted to call this robbing Peter to pay Paul. The monks of Glastonbury sold many full corrodies 'for the relief of the debts of the church', effectively pre-empting the same charge.[117] Corrodians and confraters, who might be men or women (e.g. John and Johanna Baker at Kington St Michael), typically received burial and commemoration, as well as mundane benefits such as clothing, food and drink, and a place to sleep, read, worship etc. They might even be professed as monks or nuns on their deathbeds, and buried in the black Benedictine habit.[118] At the least, their names would be entered alongside those of benefactors and other associates in their house's *Liber vitæ* (what William More called an 'annual', John Baker a 'mortilage', the parishioners of Morebath simply 'church boke'),[119] which reposed on the high altar during mass so that those listed within might share in the salvific benefits of the eucharist.[120] Some compelling examples of such books survive: Hyde's, begun c.1031 and still in use during the later middle ages, is the most noteworthy from a house covered by this study.[121] At the other end of the scale lies the Kington St Michael obit book. Evesham's *Liber vitæ*, destroyed in 1731, compartmentalized confraters in a typically tidy – and business-like – fashion (Plate 38).[122] As revealing as the layout is the fact that a particularly important confrater might transcend his category if the monks considered it politically or financially expedient. Thus, William Beauchamp, earl of Warwick (who, we recall, was ultimately buried by Franciscans), is listed not among the *laici* but rather with the *monachi et sacerdotes istius loci*: and in rubric to boot (Plate 38).[123] This recalls the fact that the Benedictines sought confraters for more than pecuniary reasons. Every individual had his or her allies, and when confraternity was granted these also became associated with a monastery in a potentially constructive way.

---

114 For lists of Benedictine letters of confraternity see Clark-Maxwell 1924–25, p. 52; Clark-Maxwell 1929, pp. 206–7. See also Welander 1991, ill. at p. 332.
115 Knowles 1950, pp. 475–9 (for confraternity to 1216).
116 Manco 1993, p. 89.
117 *Collectanea*, pp. 22–3; *Star Chamber*, I, p. 22.
118 See generally *Benedictines in Britain*, p. 56.
119 *Shorter Catalogues*, p. 664; CUL MS Dd 8 2 , fol. 11v; Duffy 2001, p. 99.
120 Cf. Morganstern 2000, p. 4.
121 Recently re-edited by Professor Simon Keynes (Copenhagen 1996). For a useful short notice see Backhouse 1999, p. 37.
122 Formerly BL MS Cotton Vitellius E xii, fols 73–83r. A cognate volume, also destroyed, was Vitellius E xvii. Sections of both survive in an eighteenth-century transcript, BL MS Lansdowne 427, fols 1r–196r.
123 BL MS Lansdowne 427, fol. 10v. See further *Cart.Winch.*, p. 67; *Reg.Bransford*, p. 172.

Relic and image promotion

Summarizing the relic and image promotion that played such an important role in Benedictine self-advertisement during the later middle ages is particularly difficult, for the order never seems less monolithic than in the relic lists and imagery of its constituent houses. Islwyn Thomas, in a brilliant thesis regrettably never published, shows how a house's relic list expressed at once its unity, continuity, power, wealth and corporate identity.[124] By and large, the same may be said of the imagery that a monastery contained. Let us return to Gloucester for an example of what is meant here, setting aside the iconography of the windows and concentrating on the sculpture. The luminous effigy of Edward II (Plate 9), encased in its bristling, shrine-like tomb, had been the focus of a short, sharp cult during the thirty or so years after 1327 that had, the Gloucester chronicler claims, generated enough money to fund completely the reconstruction of the south transept, presbytery vault and choir stalls.[125] (If true – and the matter will be scrutinized in due course – then this was probably the single most remunerative Benedictine cult relevant to this study.) Two centuries later, the magnificent new founder's monument was inserted to the east of this (Plate 28), while still further east, the great reredos of the Lady chapel, likely to have been installed during the 1460s or 1470s,[126] received a complement of thirty-nine images. The identities of many of these are known through graffiti carved (presumably by a monk) into the backs of the niches to guide the image-setters. To say the least, the programme was highly idiosyncratic, a medley of saints and saint-like individuals whose importance for the convent is attested by calendar evidence,[127] but who in many cases would scarcely have been recognized beyond the abbey's jurisdiction: St Arilda (a local virgin martyr),[128] St Odulf (a ninth-century Frisian missionary whose relics were at Evesham),[129] St Kineburga (first abbess of St Peter's, from c.681),[130] Lucius (putative first Christian ruler of Britain, thought buried at Gloucester in the second century),[131] Harold (a boy supposedly slain by Gloucester's Jewry in 1168),[132] and St Aldate (a putative fifth-century British bishop of Gloucester)[133] stood cheek by jowl with the Virgin Mary, the archangels Gabriel and Michael, Sts Catherine, Margaret, Stephen, John the Evangelist, and James Major.[134] Lest it be thought that this stone congregation was solely for internal consumption, it may be pointed out that Abbot Malvern's poem, written in the vernacular and publicly

---

124 Thomas 1974, pp. 319–40.
125 *HMGlouc.*, I, pp. 46, 47; cf. below, pp. 157–62.
126 The Lady chapel was built *c*.1457–83: Harvey 1978, p. 217.
127 The twelfth-century calendar of Oxford, Jesus College MS 10 (fols 1r–6v: *EBK*, II, pp. 44–56), and the thirteenth-century marginalia in LPL MS 179, fol. 15v, are particularly interesting as showing the continuity of interest in such characters as Sts Aldate, Arilda and Kineburga across the centuries.
128 Date unknown. See *Itinerary*, II, p. 60; Lindley 1951, pp. 152–3; Cottle 1988, pp. 8–9.
129 In the 1390s, Evesham gave Odulf's feast parity with that of the Holy Trinity: *CAEve.*, p. 308.
130 *HMGlouc.*, I, p. 4. Also culted by the Benedictines of Peterborough.
131 See *HRB*, p. 47. Winchester's monks also claimed him, and even established a 'retrospective' monument set with a brass: *Short Survey*, pp. 47–8.
132 *HMGlouc.*, I, pp. 20–1.
133 Farmer 1987, p. 11; cf. *EBK*, II, pp. 40, 45 (where Aldate is added in a fourteenth-century hand); LPL MS 179, fol. 15v.
134 On the ensemble see Short 1946–48, pp. 21–36; Cottle 1988, p. 9; Welander 1991, pp. 563–6.

displayed on a *tabula* in the north nave aisle, mentions many of these figures, including Osric, Kineburga, Arilda and Edward II.[135] Others, the boy Harold for instance, were also clearly intended to attract public notice.

The vital signs of St Peter's at Gloucester were thus strikingly healthy on the eve of the Dissolution. Far from descending into a condition of self-satisfied bourgeoisification, the monks, ever sensitive to their environment, looked to take the initiative wherever possible. How many people were attracted by the tombs, inscriptions, new Lady chapel with its reredos, and the collection of relics corresponding to the imagery described is unknown, but it is clear that the convent was doing its best to capture the external imagination under difficult circumstances. All over the West Country the same process was in motion. That many of those being promoted now seem as obscure as (say) St Arilda, and that their cults were probably no more remunerative, does not diminish the intensity of the effort. The convent at Malmesbury, for example, had relics and an image of St John the Sage, 'that translatid Dionysius out of Greek into Latine.'[136] During the later fourteenth or early fifteenth century they also commissioned a retrospective tomb for King Æthelstan (d.939), at which time they were successfully promoting him as a saint.[137] Leominster had St Cuthfleda and Romsey St Merewenna, both virgins and quondam abbesses; Hyde possessed the relics of Sts Cachita and Iwig to go with the somewhat more mainstream Judoc, Grimbald, and the tomb of the saintly Alfred the Great; Winchcombe defended the merits of Sts Coenwulf and Kenelm against the odds (for Hailes was only a mile away); and Shaftesbury made its name among pilgrims with King Edward the Martyr (d.979), whose cult, if the evidence of the Spreyton inscription given in chapter four is any indication, was widespread in the west during the late middle ages.[138] Important and fashionable cults throve alongside local ones. The monks of Abbotsbury had a stone-vaulted chapel dedicated to St Catherine built on the hill above their monastery during the later fourteenth century, celebrated her feast in copes, and spangled the pages of their surviving breviary (early fifteenth century) with Catherine wheels (Plate 39): clear indications of an active cult.[139] As noticed in chapters one and three, pilgrims to St Swithun's had a new shrine to marvel at by the end of the fifteenth century, while those at Worcester could view a 'monstrans wᵗ þᵉ brayns of Seint Thomas of Canterbury', and powdered flesh of the same saint, on their way to venerating the cultic image of the Virgin Mary.[140] The latter alone was garnering close to £60 annually in cash and wax during the early sixteenth century.[141] At the same time,

---

135 *MP*, pp. 148–9, 153.

136 *Itinerary*, I, pp. 131–2.

137 LPL MS 99, fol. 194r: 'Apud Malmesbiry requiescit *sanctus* Johannes qui dicitur sapiens ibidem et iacet *sanctus* Æthelstanus quondam Rex Anglorum.' The list is not local, for elsewhere (fol. 189v) Malmesbury is located in Dorset. Æthelstan's reputation for sanctity had travelled by *c.*1380, then – hence the term 'successful'.

138 LPL MS 99, fols 188v (Shaftesbury), 191v (Winchcombe), 194r (Hyde, Leominster, Romsey).

139 RCHM Dorset 1952, pp. 3–4 (chapel); LPL MS 4513, fols 27v, 81v, 99r, 140r, 144v, 148v, 152v, 161v, 203r, 206r, 238r, 240v, 243r, 245r, 251v, 272v, 275r, 278v, 282v, 293r, 296r. (Fols 208r, 225r and 265v have crowned 'M's instead, because the text at these points honours the Virgin Mary.) Cf. *EBK*, I, p. 12 (*c.*1300). St Catherine also occurs, with her wheel, on the seal of Abbot Walter de Stokes (1348–54): Birch 1887, p. 422 (no. 2540). Kathleen Scott (pers. comm.) suggests an early fifteenth-century date for the borders. Cf. e.g. Scott 1996, I, pls 1, 18, 109–10.

140 Green 1796, II, p. v; *Inv.Worc.Lib.*, p. 163 ('de puluere carnis [beati Thomæ]').

141 Nilson 1998, p. 165.

such flocks of pilgrims were pouring into Glastonbury to venerate St Dunstan that Abbot Beere was obliged to relocate the feretory in order to obviate theft of gold and silver from it.[142] Capitalizing on this attention, he (and no doubt his convent) began a great chapel east of the retrochoir dedicated to the canonized King Edgar (d.975), the centrepiece of which was a magnificent copper-gilt tomb (here is the aforementioned concept of beautification in the service of self-promotion in action).[143] As pointed out in chapter three, he also championed Joseph of Arimathea's cult,[144] apparently commissioning Pynson to print a verse *Lyfe of Joseph of Armathia* in 1520.[145] This was a complement to the monumental sculpted Deposition group (here was St Joseph in action) set up in 1382 under Abbot Chinnock's auspices in the cemetery chapel of St Michael.[146] There was plenty more besides – Glastonbury's relic lists extend to 286 names.[147] Individuals such as St Walter of Cowick who crop up throughout these remind us that houses with only a handful of monks such as Cowick also sought the advantages accruing from pilgrimage: there is definite evidence that the priory on the Exe contained a shrine of St Walter at the end of the middle ages.[148] From the first to the last, the promotion of relics, images and their holy associations was vigorously fostered by West Country Benedictines in an attempt to garner and maintain public interest. The above represent only a handful of examples: the list goes on, it is practically endless.

Hospitality and other expedients

Of the infrastructure put in place by the Benedictine houses as a further encouragement to visitors (particularly those 'middle-class pilgrims' or 'strangers of quality' who might not stay with the abbot but still required decorous lodgings),[149] only a mere acknowledgement can be made here. Inns were a particular object of conventual patronage, and were often built to a high standard.[150] The half-timbered New Inn at Gloucester, raised, we are told, by the obedientiary John Twyning *c.*1455 in Upper Northgate, complemented a pre-existing Benedictine inn (later known as the Fleece) in the parish of St Mary de Grace.[151] Sherborne also had a 'new Yn', ascribed by Leland to the patronage of Abbot Peter Ramsam (1475–1504).[152] The stone Pilgrims' Inn at Glastonbury (now

---

[142] *Mem.Dunstan*, pp. 426, 433, 434; Luxford 2002(a), pp. 119–20 note 26.

[143] *Itinerary*, I, p. 289; MA, I, p. 8. The nuns of Romsey apparently also claimed Edgar: *Short Survey*, p. 59.

[144] Lagorio 2001, pp. 78–9; Carley 1996, pp. 69–70.

[145] RSTC 14807; *Jos.Lyfe*, pp. 35–52. Around 1511, Wynkyn de Worde produced a prose *Lyfe*: RSTC 14806; printed in *Jos.Lyfe*, pp. 25–32. Direct contact between Glastonbury and these printers is unproven, but surely unquestionable, at least where Pynson is concerned.

[146] *Mag.Tab.*, p. 521. While St Joseph's primary relics were never discovered, an epitaph stating 'hic jacet excultus Joseph pater ille sepultus . . .' etc. circulated at Glastonbury during the fifteenth century (GM, pp. 61, 117), along with a prayer petitioning Christ to reveal the bones: see *Itinerary Worcestre*, pp. 296–7; Carley 2001, *passim*; Vincent 2001, pp. 152–3.

[147] GR, pp. 606–14.

[148] For Walter, a twelfth-century Benedictine monk, see GR, p. 594; *Itinerary Worcestre*, pp. 124–5. For his shrine and cult at Cowick in the later fifteenth-century see Orme 1990, pp. 390–1. For the shrine and 'Saint Walter's gate' at Cowick see Yeo 1987, pp. 13, 23.

[149] Carley 1996, p. 64; *Linc.Vis.*, I, p. 110 note 2.

[150] Pantin and Rouse 1955, pp. 46–7; Baskerville 1937, p. 28; Snape 1926, p. 112.

[151] Welander 1991, p. 238.

[152] *Itinerary*, I, p. 295; Fowler 1951, p. 267.

called the George), erected at the expense of Abbot John Selwood some time between 1456 and 1473, did justice to the abbey's public image.[153] It had, among other things, a most appropriate stained-glass programme, and we can only imagine that similar displays were common enough in such places, where the monks had (so to speak) a captive audience. Along with the abbatial arms were represented figures of the three theological virtues (Charity suckling her two daughters), a reminder to guests of what they were receiving and at whose behest.[154] Ultimately, the abbot and convent of Evesham could refer to their monastery per se as a mighty inn for the receiving of noble visitors.[155] Nor can other expedients devised to attract custom be discussed at length: the surviving *tabulæ* from Glastonbury, with their extravagant claims concerning (for example) the salvific efficacy of Avalonian soil (not one in a thousand buried therein would go to hell, no matter how evil – such was the testimony of a Saracen!), and the almost innumerable indulgences offered to generous visitors by prelates past,[156] are vivid reminders of what is likely to have been established practice at many Benedictine houses. Each topic justifies a study in its own right, and must receive it if the vitality and strength of purpose of later medieval Benedictinism is to be fully understood and appreciated. The aim here has simply been its recognition.

Ideological Competition

Antonia Gransden identifies the catalysts for later medieval monastic chronicle writing thus:

> The monks wrote to defend their order and their houses against enemies and critics . . .
> They found critics among their rivals, the regular and secular canons and the mendicants. Criticism was particularly virulent in the late fourteenth century, when a new enemy emerged, the Lollards. Individually each monastery had enemies, actual or potential: the diocesan, royal and papal agents (especially tax collectors), and neighbouring landlords . . . The monks wrote to strengthen their position.[157]

This summary establishes an outline of the ideological competition faced by the Benedictines (and, as implied here, old monasticism generally) that may be more firmly drawn by adding the criticisms of Henry V and Wolsey mentioned previously, and in certain cases (the psychological importance of which overshadows the degree of the actual threat) a militant attitude in the laity. Ideology worked harder still against the alien houses. Tainted with Frenchness, these usually poverty-stricken outposts experienced little peace in the lead-up to the 1414 Act of Suppression. 'Woe is me! that ever I came to England, for troubles assail me on all sides', wrote the prior of Otterton to his superior (the abbot of Mont St-Michel in Normandy) early in the fourteenth century,[158] a cry that must have echoed around the west, from Loders to Monk Sherborne,

---

153 *Gothic*, p. 257; Dunning 2003, p. 398.
154 Bond 1915, pp. 138–9 and 139 note 1.
155 Baskerville 1937, p. 27.
156 *Mag.Tab.*, pp. 522–5.
157 Gransden 1982, p. 343; cf. Coates 1999, pp. 70–1.
158 S.F. 1968–70, p. 5.

Stogursey to St Michael's Mount. Edward III remarked that alien priories did more harm to England than all the Jews and Saracens in the world – clearly, the auspices were not good for some time before 1414.[159]

The threat of disendowment

Not that the shadow of dispossession hung over the alien priories alone during the early fifteenth century. The slashing of monastic representation in parliament by Edward III was an important act of disenfranchisement in its own right. While attendance among the lords was certainly an irksome prospect for most superiors, and one which resulted in the widespread employment of proctors, the principle involved was an important one.[160] Root and branch disendowment of all bishoprics and religious houses had been proposed in a strikingly succinct, businesslike manner (the calculations of ecclesiastical wealth and what might otherwise be achieved with them, whether accurate or not, are remarkable) in a bill presented to parliament, probably in 1410,[161] and if the matter was not subject to majority support, the fact that the Commons entertained it at all (and the St Albans chronicler wrote the matter down) tends to suggest that it represented a considerable potential threat. Its intent had, moreover, been adumbrated in an earlier bill (1404), and was supported by a later one (1415), dampened down by Archbishops Arundel and Chichele respectively.[162] Taken together, these proposals constitute an interesting context in which to read the criticisms of Henry V (1421), and the Benedictine response to them. Those in favour of disendowment argued that depriving the enclosed orders of their lands and buildings would constitute an act of charity: to force monasticism back into its primitive condition would benefit both the religious themselves and society as a whole.[163] While this proposition may have influenced the king, there can be little doubt that the prospect of material gain was on the minds of many influential supporters of reform.

Heresy

While principally a financial proposition, the bill of c.1410 was manifestly influenced by Lollard ideas and sympathies. For the Benedictines, the rot of proto-Protestant representation at the highest secular level had set in substantially before this, however. In 1378, during the parliament held at St Peter's, Gloucester, no less an individual than John of Gaunt sponsored the personal attendance and apologetics (in the matter of clerical taxation) of John Wyclif (c.1324–84), a circumstance the effect of which, while deliberately ignored by the abbey's historian, is hinted at by a marginal annotator of the surviving *Polychronicon* belonging to the house. The names and events singled out beside the text for their special significance read thus: 'De Rege Arthuro' (fol. 90v), 'S. Petri ecclesia' (fol. 94r), '*Sancta Kyneburga*' (fol. 94v), 'Oswaldus' (fol. 97r), 'Oswy' (fol.

---

159 Clarke 1904–05, p. 139. Cf. Graham 1929, pp. 111–17. Indeed the alien houses were targeted by Edward I: CFR, I, pp. 362–4.

160 Knowles 1955, pp. 303–4. On proctors see McHardy 1991, pp. 22–7.

161 Youings 1971, p. 135; Harper-Bill 1996(a), p. 80, labelling this the 'Lollard disendowment bill'.

162 Tanner 1787, p. vii; Knowles 1955, pp. 107–8, mentioning a further, abortive petition of 1394. This threat, as Benedictines realized, was not unprecedented: cf. e.g. CGA(C), pp. 128–9.

163 Scase 1989, pp. 109–13.

finem pfectū tribuat nobis oīpotens pius ꝫ misericors dūs. Amen. Tres ſūt qui teſtimonī dant ī cœlo pater et filius ꝫ ſps ſcōs et hij tres vnū ſūt. Tu a̅.

Ad cōpletor pſal. Qui ū vinocare. Dnū hȳtat. Hāc.

Hesū redemptor ſecli uerbū patris altiſſime lux luciſ iuiſibiliſ cuſtos tuorū pringil. Tu fabricator oīū diſcretor atꝗ tempoꝝ feſſa laboꝛe corpoꝛa noctis quiete recrea. Te de precamur ſupplices ut uos ab hoſte liberes. ne ualeat ſeducere tuo redemptos ſanguine. Ut dū graui ī corpoꝛe breui manem̄ tēpoꝛe ſic caro nīa dormiat ut mens ī xpō uigilet. Preſta pater omīpotens ꝑ xpm iḷīm xpm dīīm qui tecū imperpetuū regnat cū ſancto ſpū. Amen. v̄. Cuſtodi nos dīīc. Kyriel. xpel. Kyriel.

Iſte liber ꝑtinet dominē Aliciæ Champnys nouiali moneſterij Shaſton quæ dicit̄ Alicia emit ꝓ quinꝗ decem ſolidos ꝫ de dominio Richardo maiſhall Rectore eccliē pochiali ſancti Trinitatis de Shaſtinꝫ ꝓdicā

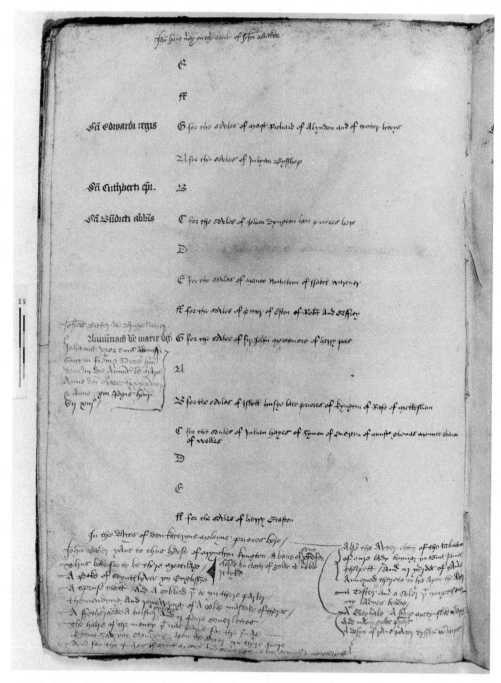

2. A page of the Kington St Michael obit book, including a memorandum of gifts to the priory by John Baker (CUL MS Dd 8 2, fol. 11v): 1490s or early sixteenth century.

3. Decorated choir stall canopies, Winchester cathedral: first quarter of the fourteenth century.

4. The Beauchamp (*alias* Warwick) (R.) and Fitzhamon (*alias* Founder's) (L.) chantry chapels at Tewkesbury abbey: 1420s and 1390s respectively.

5. The chantry chapel of Arthur, Prince of Wales, at Worcester cathedral:
first quarter of the sixteenth century.

6. Bishop Richard Mitford of Salisbury (L.) and Abbot Robert Brunyng of Sherborne (R.) from the Sherborne missal (detail of BL MS Additional 74236, p. 36): between 1399 and 1407.

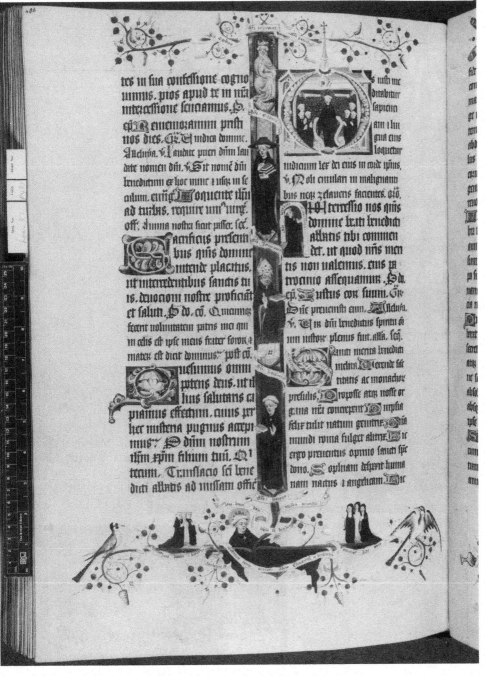

7. 'Tree' of the Benedictine order from the Sherborne missal
(BL MS Additional 74236, p. 488): between 1399 and 1407.

8. 'Magnificat' window in the north transept façade of Great Malvern Priory church: c.1501–02.

9. Detail of the effigy of King Edward II at Gloucester cathedral: c.1330.

10. Choir and presbytery of Gloucester cathedral, looking east: between 1337 and 1377.

11. Nave elevation of Winchester cathedral (north side):
late fourteenth and early fifteenth centuries.

12. West front of Bath abbey church: probably commenced in 1499 or 1500.

13. North walk of the cloister at Gloucester cathedral, looking east: last quarter of the fourteenth century or (perhaps) first decade of the fifteenth.

14. Perpendicular bell tower, formerly part of the precinctual wall of Evesham abbey: 1520s and early 1530s.

15. Tomb of Hugh III Despenser and Elizabeth Montacute at Tewkesbury abbey, from the east: 1350s.

16. Misericord bracket of a recumbent king, Gloucester cathedral: mid fourteenth century.

17. Statue of Christ holding the Charter of Human Redemption, from the north aisle window of the west front of Bath abbey (the arms are those of Bishop King – *on a chevron, three escallops* – impaling those of the see of Bath and Wells): early sixteenth century.

18. Fragment of a sculpted figure of
Thomas Despenser: 1420s.

19. Supplicating figure of Prior John
Cantlow of Bath, from the east
window of St Catherine's church,
St Catherine: c.1500.

20. Panel painting of King Æthelstan bestowing a votive 'model' church
representing Milton abbey church on a Benedictine abbot:
late fifteenth or early sixteenth century (with modern repainting).

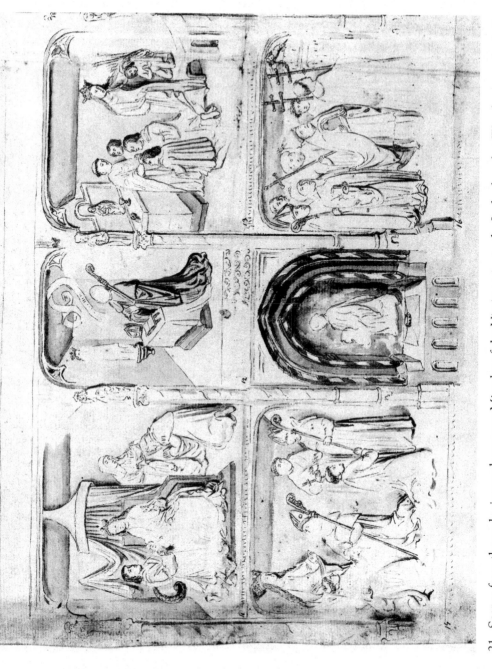

21. Scenes from the early sixteenth-century Miracles of the Virgin series in the Lady chapel at Winchester cathedral (detail of BL MS Additional 29943, fol. 20r): from a watercolour by John Carter (1748–1817).

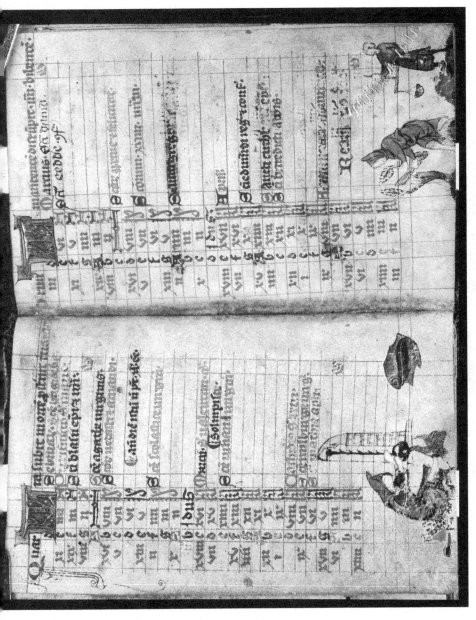

22. Calendar pages (February and March) from a psalter formerly belonging to Joan Stretford, nun of Wherwell (BL MS Additional 27866, fols. 6v–7r): first quarter of the fourteenth century, with fifteenth-century additions.

23. Illuminated initial and ownership inscription in an historical compendium formerly belonging to John Merelynch, monk of Glastonbury (detail of OQC MS 304, fol. 67r): early fifteenth century.

natali dñi usqz ad septuagesimam: partim cõtinet est tempe recõciliacõis qd est temps leticie. s. a natali: usqz ad octauas epiphie. partim est tempore pegnacõms: s. ab octaua epiphie usqz ad septuagesimam. Et potest accipi hec quadruplex tempoz uaria cõ. Primo: penes quatuoz tempoz distinctiones. vt hiemps referat ad pimũ. ver ad scdm. Estas ad terciũ. Auctupñs ad qrtũ. t pa ad appricatõms: satis pat; Scdo: penes quatuoz diei partes. ut nox referat

octaua pentecostes: usqz ad aduentũ dñi

Memoriale fratris iohannis de Draytone monachi. cuius aíe anime propicietur deus Amen.

24. Illustration of the Last Judgement and memorial inscription to John Drayton, monk of Winchester, in a *Golden Legend* formerly held at Winchester (detail of CUL MS Gg 2 18, fol. 1r): *c*.1300.

25. Impression of the reverse of the common seal of Evesham abbey, engraved in the second half of the thirteenth century and in use throughout the post-1300 period: from an antiquarian engraving published in 1851.

26. Impression of the reverse of the common seal of Pilton priory: die engraved c.1450.

27. Oddo and Doddo, from the Founders' Book of Tewkesbury abbey
(OBL MS Top Glouc d 2, fol. 8v): c.1500–10.

28. Monument to 'King' Osric at Gloucester cathedral, from the south-west: probably c.1525–35.

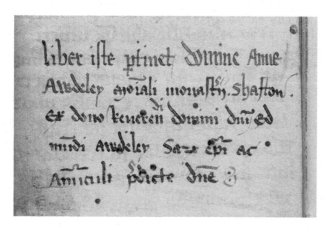

29. Inscription of donation and ownership in an illustrated psalter formerly belonging to Anne Audley, nun of Shaftesbury (detail of LPL MS 3285, fol. 191): first quarter of the sixteenth century.

30. Memorial image of Abbot John Islip of Westminster, from the Islip Roll: 1532.

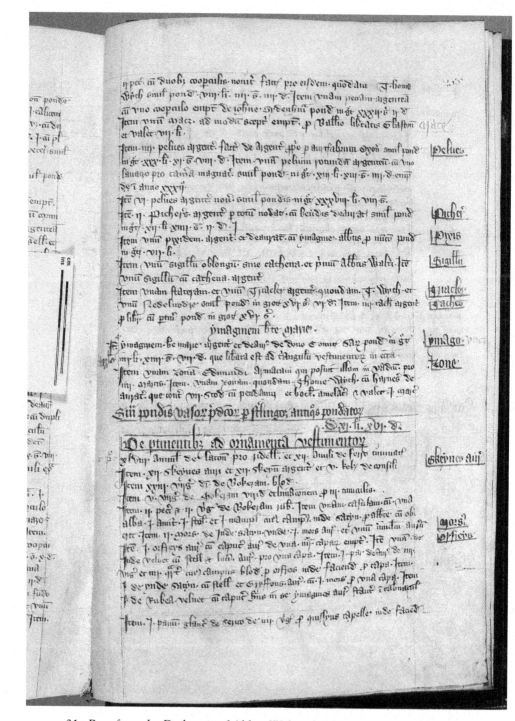

31. Page from the *Declaracio* of Abbot Walter de Monington of Glastonbury (TCC MS R 5 16, p. 255): c.1375–90.

32. Detail of the alabaster effigy of William Malvern, last abbot of Gloucester,
at Gloucester cathedral: 1530s.

33. Marginal image of the feretory of St
Dunstan at Glastonbury abbey (detail of
TCC MS R 5 16, p. 211). The inscription
reads Iohannes de Braynton perfecit ut
patet ('[Abbot] John of Breynton
completed it as it appears'): c.1508.

34. Decoration of the opening page of Prior William More of Worcester's register for 1518, by the monk-artist Thomas Blockeley (WCL MS Avi(ii), fol. 111r): 1518.

35. Compotus of the receiver of Cowick priory for 1484/5, detailing, among other things, expenditure on art and architecture (detail of DRO muniment W1258M/G4/53/2): 1485.

Presta quesumus omnipotens deus: ut beati petri
martyris tui fidem congru-
a deuocone sectemur qui
pro eiusdem fidei dilataci-
one martyrij palmam me-
ruit optinere.
Preces quas tibi domine
offerimus interce-
dente beato petro martyre
tuo clementer intende: et
pugiles fidei sub tua pro-
tectione custodi.
Fideles tuos domine cus-
todiant sacramen-
ta que sumpsimus. et
intercedente beato petro
martyre tuo: contra om-
nes aduersos tueantur
aduersus.

... me.

Suscepit pastor bonus
qui posuit animam suam pro ou-
ibus suis et pro suo grege mo-
ri dignatus est.

Notandum quod
venerabilis in
christo pater dominus
Willelmus More prior
ecclesie cathedralis
beate marie wigor-
nie hoc missale
ecclesie de Bromsgroue
dedit. Anno domini
M cccc l xxj.

Be it knowne
That the Vene-
rable father
in Christ Lord
Willm More
Prior of the
Cathedrall Ch-
urch of Blessed
Marie in Worc-
ester gaue mee
this Missale to
the Church of
Bramsgraue.
In the yeare of
our Lord 1521

36. Donor inscription from a fourteenth-century missal given second-hand to
Bromsgrove parish church by Prior William More of Worcester
(CUL MS Additional 6688, fol. 372v): donor inscription between 1518 and 1536.

37. *Chronologia ædificorum*, recording the patronage of John Lyndsey, sacrist of Worcester (WCL MS A xii, fol. 77v): probably 1530s.

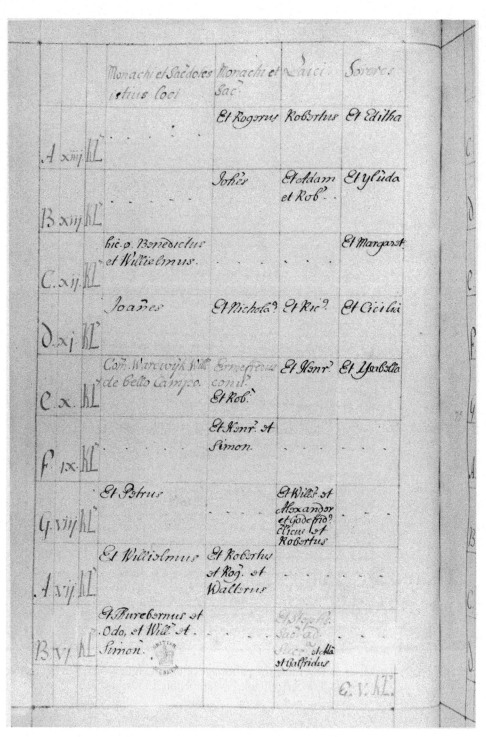

	Monachi et Sacdotes istius loci	Monachi et Sac?	Laici	Sorores
		Et Rogerus	Robertus	Et Editha
A xiiij KL				
		Johes	Et Adam et Rob?	Et ylüda
B xiij KL				
	hic. ø. Benedictus et Willielmus.			Et Margaret
C.xij.KL				
	Joañes	Et Nichola?	Et Ric?	Et Cicilia
D.xj KL				
C.x. KL	Com. Warewijk Will de bello Campo.	Ermefreius cond? Et Rob?	Et Henr?	Et Ysabella
f. ix. KL		Et Henr? et Simon.		
G.viij KL	Et Petrus			Et Willi? et Alexander et godefrid? Elicus et Robertus
A.vij.KL	Et Willielmus	Et Robertus et Rog. et Walterus		
B.vj KL	Et Purebernus et Odo, et Will? et Simon.		et Stephs Sac? ad Sacr? et Galfridus	
G.v.KL				

38. Page from an eighteenth-century transcript of the *Liber vitæ* of Evesham abbey, demonstrating the compartmentalization of those commemorated (BL MS Lansdowne 427, fol. 10v).

39. Page from the surviving breviary of Abbotsbury abbey showing border-work and distinctive Catherine wheel motif (MS LPL 4513, fol. 144v): early fifteenth century.

auro, quorum primus cuius campus albus
est continet dracones cum alis expansis flores i
ore gerentib: Secundus cuius campus indie
est continet dracones et lilia. Tercius cuius camp
rubeus est continet dracones cum arboribz auro
intextis. Quartus de serico cuius campus indie
cum arboribz uiridibz intextis. Item unam yma
ginem uirginis gloriose argenteam z deaurata
ponderis quatuor librar. quatuordecim solidor de
cem denarior. Duo thuribula argentea z dean
rata quorum primum cum cathenis deauratis spra
se compositum ponderis. Et solidorum. Secun
dum argenteum et deauratum ponderis. vi. librar.
cum uno nauetto ad modum nauis formato et
uno cocleari argenteo simul ponderantibz quin
ginta tres solidos. Et plenis omnibz saluo custo
diend dedit unum triangulum satis forte cum una
cista deputata et breue serata ac alia minore infra
candem inclusa. Item dedit altari sci iohis bap
tiste unum calicem argenteum deauratum ponderis
quinquaginta unius solidi. Item capelle be
uirginis unum par aueez ex auro puro quod sibi
domina Philippa regina Anglie quondam dedit una
casulam duas tunicas tres albis cum duabz sto
lis et tribz manipulis de uiridi serico cum rosis albis
intextis. Item unam casulam. unam album stolam
et manipulum duas tunicas primum et frontel
lum pro altari de uelueto uiridis indicis uiridibz

41. Page of a copy of the *Historia monasterii Sancti Petri Gloucestriæ*, recording works done at St Peter's abbey during the fourteenth century (BL MS Cotton Domitian A viii, fol. 140r): first half of the fifteenth century.

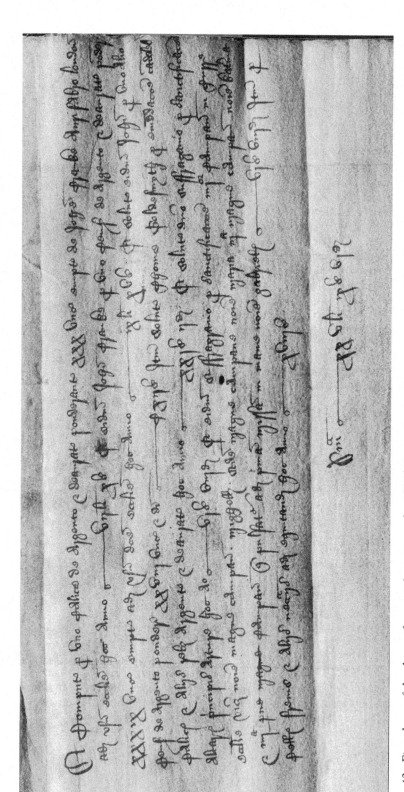

42. First sheet of the dorse of a sacrist's *compotus* for 1516/17 mentioning the consecration of the altar of Prince Arthur's chantry chapel at Worcester cathedral (detail of WCL muniment C 429): 1517.

43. Figure of Edward Despenser from the Trinity chapel at Tewkesbury abbey: probably between 1390 and 1410 (tabernacle a nineteenth-century restoration).

44. Edward Despenser holding a seven-branched candlestick, from the Founders' Book of Tewkesbury abbey (OBL MS Top Glouc d 2, fol. 24r): c.1500–10.

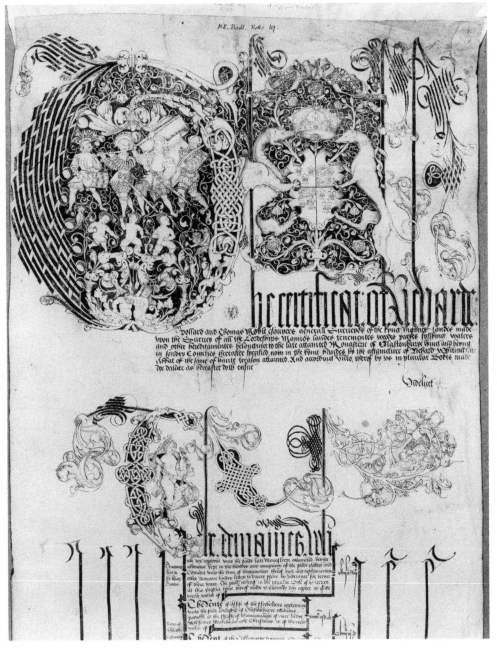

45. Pen-and-ink drawings of the survey roll of Glastonbury abbey's lands, drawn up
for Richard Pollard and Thomas Moyle in September 1539
(detail of OBL MS Bodley Rolls 19, membrane 2): probably 1540.

99r), the abbey's foundation (fol. 100r), the birth of St Dunstan (fol. 110r), Edward the Martyr's death (fol. 113r), 'De glastonie' (fol. 124v), the foundation of the New Forest (fol. 125r), 'Robertus Cowrthose' (fol. 129r), 'Hugo de sancto victore' (fol. 131v), 'pestilencia magna' (fol. 138r), the translation of St Thomas Cantilupe (fol. 148v), the accession of Richard II (fol. 158r), and finally, 'Wycliff' (fol. 162r).[164] This list provides an unusually immediate impression of the cloud that Wyclif and his adherents represented in the monastic mind: they stood out with the celebrities. As with the Dissolution, the real substance of this cloud can only be appreciated if we dispense with hindsight and attempt to stand in monastic buskins. The account given by Thomas Walsingham (St Albans) in his *Chronica maiora*, which describes Wyclif as 'organum diabolicum' and includes much breast-beating over the Gloucester parliament, is a better starting point than any West Country source,[165] although there are plenty of manifestations in manuscripts from the region.[166] Wyclif attacked the property-based economies of old monasticism with great vigour and (as also deplored by Walsingham) powerful backing.[167] Such treatises as his *De Civili Domino* (1375–76, i.e. before the Gloucester parliament) are replete with criticisms of Benedictine conduct, and all the more damaging for their espousal of the virtues of mendicancy (Franciscan in particular).[168] The threats here were thus oblique as well as direct, for a treatise implying support for the mendicants worked against the Benedictines as surely as a proposal for disendowment.[169] Further, he collectively designated monks (along with other male regulars – nuns are excused) 'Magog', chief accomplice of the Antichrist (i.e. the Pope), and a particular menace in what may well be the last days.[170] Many of Wyclif's views gained wide and enduring currency,[171] and while the West Country in general was apparently not as deeply affected by Lollardy as other quarters (e.g. Coventry, London, Oxford),[172] Gloucestershire certainly experienced its share, and the monks of St James at Bristol will have been acutely aware of their position in a city with a reputation as a hotbed of heresy.[173]

---

164 OCCC MS 89. The margins of fol. 143r have been cut off, and with them any reference to Edward II.

165 *Chron. St Albans*, pp. 75–85 (quote at 85).

166 E.g. BL MS Cotton Nero D.iii, fol. 222r (from Evesham): 'Papa Urbanus vi. dampnavit xxiiij conclusiones erronias quas Johannes Wyclyf doctor in theologium tenuit.' (1382) Wyclif is also called 'hereticus'.

167 Cf. Walsingham's treatise *Defensio de praerogatiuis et dignitatibus ordinem monasticum concernentibus*, cited in Sharpe 2001, p. 689; Pantin 1950, pp. 214–15, under the title *Inveccio contra ordinem monasticum detrahentes et loca eorum destruents vel permutantes*.

168 *De Civili Domino*, pp. 37, 94–5, 126–7, 252–3, 369.

169 This was an ideal: the enmity between Wyclif during his later career and the mendicants is notorious. See e.g. Bostick 1998, pp. 97–100; Scase 1989, p. 114.

170 Bostick 1998, pp. 67–9; see also Scase 1989, pp. 113–14.

171 Although Duffy 1992, p. 6, questions Lollardy's popularity and influence as presented in much of the scholarship cited in Heath 1990, pp. 666–7.

172 Davies 1991, p. 200. Duffy 2001, p. 87, mentions Devonshire's lack of Lollardy. The same may be noted of Cornwall.

173 Davies 1991, p. 200; Saul 1980, p. 101; Powell 1973, pp. 98–100. The amorphous nature of 'Lollardy' is here taken for granted. 'If Wyclifitism was what you knew, Lollardy was whom you knew' (Davies 1991, p. 212): this encapsulates the concept's breadth.

Orthodox criticism: mendicant

According to John Capgrave (d.1464), Wyclif's attitude to the religious orders was expressed in the opinion that the 'reules mad be Augustin, Benet and Fraunceys adde no more perfeccion ouyr þe gospel þan doth lym-whiting onto a wal.'[174] This art and architectural metaphor suggests a monolithic value system, but in reality, of course, there was much actual and perceived ideological difference between the orders. For their part, the mendicants might be as ready to impugn Benedictine wealth (along with that of other landed orders) as was Wyclif, and earlier into the breach. At the Council of Vienne in 1311, representatives of the Dominican order had openly attacked the Benedictines for failing to live according to the Rule they professed: this was the basis of most mendicant complaints about monasticism until the Dissolution.[175] In the years after 1360, the academic friars in particular singled out monastic possessioning for special condemnation.[176] They even supported early proposals for some form of dispossession of the property-owning orders.[177] Their potential influence as preachers enhanced the threat they represented. For their part, the Benedictines responded by attempting to tar the Friars with the heretical brush. Chronicle sources for the west are wanting, but the Westminster monk John of Reading's statement (under 1354) that the 'order of Mendicants' (i.e. the Franciscans) entire should be burned, 'as their sermons and disputations have always been laced with heretical opinions against holy religion and the Church', frames the matter for us.[178] That Thomas Northfelde, Franciscan of Worcester, was arraigned for sorcery (in 1432) probably came as no surprise to the Benedictines of the cathedral priory.[179] An inscription in a religious and literary miscellany owned by John Buriton, sacrist of Winchester during the 1530s, suggests that despite the positive intra-order relations mentioned above, Benedictines continued to consider certain mendicant opinions heretical: 'Iohannes Buryton monachus sancti Swithuuni. Y bowthe hym [i.e. the book] of brynstane coste me 3s. 4d. Erytike otherwyse callyd whythere postata I pray God he may repent and recant.' The words 'Brynstane' and 'Erytike', which occur one above the other, have a box drawn around them to emphasize the point. John Brinston was a monk of Winchester who apparently became a friar some time during the 1520s or 1530s, after which his vows, along with certain sentiments expressed in the book (e.g. 'the church of Winchester quoth he/ hathe a fayre grace . . . Were neuer better prestys then haue ben there professyde'), presumably made the prospect of keeping it unpalatable.[180]

---

[174] I.e. they obfuscated the truth. *Abbreuiacion*, p. 181.

[175] *Chapters*, I, pp. 173–4; cf. e.g. Gransden 1974, pp. 497–8.

[176] To such attack, as Knowles notes, rich houses such as Glastonbury were especially vulnerable: Knowles 1955, pp. 64–5.

[177] Knowles 1955, p. 50.

[178] *CJR*, p. 119. The language is perhaps unusually polemical. Cf. *Chron. St Albans*, p. 878.

[179] Sheppard 1912, p. 246.

[180] Quotes at *Winch.Anth.*, fols 23r, 226r (cf. pp. 9–10); see also *MLGB Supp.*, p. 112; *BRECP*, p. 678. It is not absolutely certain that this John Brinston and the friar of that (uncommon) name who preached at Glastonbury in 1536 were identical, however.

Orthodox criticism: secular

Ideological attacks on the property-owning necessary to Benedictinism issued from the orthodox secular clergy as well. The seculars' main enemies were, notoriously, the mendicant orders that constituted their main competition for lay goodwill, but they also wrote against monks and canons. John Trevisa (d.1402), vicar of Berkeley (Gloucs.), when translating Higden's *Polychronicon* into English, interpolated the text with opinions of his own including the aforementioned notion that monastic disendowment would be charitable ('almesse' as he put it). He cited St Jerome as an authority and the demise of the Templars as an exemplar.[181] William Langland (c.1332–c.1400) is another example, well-worn but serviceable here, for he was probably educated by the Benedictines of Great or Little Malvern,[182] and wrote a broadly popular (sixty-one manuscripts survive) vernacular text voicing the need for ecclesiastical reform – *Piers Plowman* – that quickly found its way into monastic libraries.[183] Glastonbury, for one, had a copy,[184] and extracts from the work in BL MS Additional 60577 suggest that Winchester did too.[185] Herein is found not only the complaint of John Gower noticed in chapter four, i.e. that a monk or nun has no business getting about outside the monastic precinct, but also the familiar objection that religious do not honour their duties, that they are rich enough as it is (Langland had clearly never experienced what Knowles called the 'muddy existence' of many rural Benedictine priories), and therefore that people waste their substance, impoverish their heirs, and imperil their souls by supporting them.[186] The Benedictines in particular are implicated via disparaging remarks concerning 'the abbot of Abingdon and all his progeny', Abingdon here understood as the wellspring of English monasticism.[187] We also find the notion that regular clergy in general are Antichrist's agents, noted above with reference to Wyclif.[188] To a marked extent this is ideology in the service of pecuniary interests, for a barely disguised theme evident throughout is the issue of (non-ideological) competition for lay benefaction. Despite the rhetoric, *Piers Plowman*, along with Trevisa's interpolations, Gower's *Mirour de l'omme* and other products of the secular clergy (and non-clerical rectors with an interest in the prosperity of their holdings),[189] wears its true purpose upon its sleeve.

---

181 Scase 1989, pp. 110, 111. On Trevisa's translation see Taylor 1966, pp. 134–40.

182 Langland, IV:i, pp. xxvi–xxvii.

183 Matheson 1998, p. 9. The A-text was begun c.1365, and constantly revised to c.1390.

184 CUL MS Dd 1 17, article III, fols 1r–31r (B-text, prologue – *passus* 20); after 1381, possibly early fifteenth century. The provenance of this manuscript, since the mid-sixteenth century attributed to Glastonbury, was clouded by Ker's rejection (*MLGB*, p. 91), which was followed by Benson & Blanchfield 1997, p. 33. Andrew Watson, however, reinstates it to 'Glastonbury ?' (*MLGB Supp.*, p. 38), as does Crick 1989, pp. 67, 70. Dr Ian Doyle believes it was perhaps made elsewhere but 'moved' to Glastonbury during the fifteenth century: Benson & Blanchfield 1997, p. 33. Tellingly, the first editor of the text of article II, fols 83r–93v (Gildas, *De excidio Britanniæ*) wrote in 1568 that the manuscript was formerly Glastonbury's: *Catalogue CUL*, I, pp. 23–4. He may reasonably be assumed to have had access to information not now existing.

185 *Winch.Anth.*, p. 35, fol. 212r.

186 See e.g. Langland, II, pp. 158–9, 271–3; also Knowles 1955, p. 136.

187 Langland, II, p. 159.

188 McGinn 2000, pp. 189–91 (discussed at some length).

189 E.g. Gower (c.1330–1408) himself, a non-clerical rector.

Local hostility

The final type of ideological competition to be noted is that brought by the secular laity, occasionally (as at Winchcombe in 1398) under the influence of a spirited, articulate parish priest.[190] The issues arousing lay ire were usually location-specific, and directed towards individual houses rather than the order as a whole. Outbreaks of discontent were sporadic, although houses such as Gloucester found themselves under pressure relatively often. Particularly vicious assaults were made on the abbey by townspeople in 1363, 1449, 1463, 1513 and 1518;[191] in the first of these a servant of the monks was murdered and his head impaled over the west portal of the abbey church.[192] And indeed, the widespread insurrection of the mid-fifteenth century put the fear of Jack Cade and his 'capitaneos' into everyone. Sherborne, for one, suffered here. The abbey church had already been largely incinerated (in 1437) as the result of a disagreement with the parish over the location of its font,[193] and a recrudescence of this dispute in 1450 is explicitly linked by the house's chronicler to Cade's rebellion.[194] Small wonder that around this time Abbot Frome ordered the construction of a 'great embattled wall' around the sixty acre precinct at Glastonbury.[195] In terms of length and embellishment – it was set with 'many rich and stately pictures cut in stone' – this was more than a match for that raised by his rival Thomas Bekynton at Wells (who also feared the influence of Cade).[196] The fourteenth century, too, had witnessed plenty of Benedictine crenellation: Evesham (twice, in 1332 and 1336), Shaftesbury (1367, for the church and belfry specifically), Worcester (1369) and Winchcombe (1373) all applied for the requisite licences.[197] While the desire to belong to the 'crenellated club' defined by Charles Coulson may have been an influential factor, security was undoubtedly more important.[198] Shaftesbury, for example, applied to crenellate following an incident of lay aggression that cost not only money but the lives of some of its employees.[199]

There were other displays of anti-monastic sentiment on the part of the laity: serious later medieval episodes at Dunster (various, culminating in those of 1498 and 1512), Evesham (1376), Exeter St Nicholas (fourteenth century), Malmesbury (c.1500), Stogursey (c.1442), Tewkesbury (1367), and Totnes (1459–60)[200] find later medieval parallels throughout the east (e.g. Abingdon, Bury St Edmunds, Peterborough, St Albans, St Benet-at-Holm, Wymondham). Although these cases do not demonstrate or

---

[190] Haigh 1950, pp. 144–5.
[191] See Kingsford 1913, pp. 355–6; GCL Register C (ii), fols 61v–65r; VCH Gloucester, IV, pp. 60–1.
[192] Kingsford 1913, p. 356.
[193] Itinerary, I, pp. 152–3; Monckton 2000, pp. 93, 112 note 59.
[194] Kingsford 1913, pp. 347–9; TCC MS R 7 13, fols 108r–11r. CLC, p. 195, provides independent evidence of the insurrection of 1450.
[195] CGA(H), I, p. 280.
[196] Monkton 1999, pp. 84–5; cf. Harvey 1978, pp. 197–9; Carley 1996, p. 59 (suggesting rivalry with Bekynton); Clayton 1927–29, p. 81; Short Survey, p. 79 (images).
[197] Coulson 1982, p. 94.
[198] Coulson 1982, pp. 70–3 et passim.
[199] VCH Dorset, II, p. 75.
[200] Maxwell-Lyte 1909, II, pp. 399–403; French 1997, pp. 222–38 (Dunster); MA, II, p. 7 note a (Evesham); Brakspear and Parry 1960, p. 13 (Exeter); Luce 1979, pp. 50–1 (Malmesbury); Ballard 1992, p. 14 (Stogursey); VCH Gloucester, VIII, p. 116 (Tewkesbury); Watkin 1914–17, II, p. 958 (Totnes).

even suggest widespread and enduring anti-monastic sentiment, their psychological impact, particularly when taken along with incidents involving the houses of other orders – e.g. the murder of the abbot of Premonstratensian Torre (Dev.) in 1351[201] – should be reckoned far more significant that the actual harm done. The monks of Gloucester personally owned daggers and crossbows, and small wonder following the debacle of 1367.[202] Glastonbury, too, had an armoury full of guns, swords and ammunition in the time of Henry VIII: for defence of the realm, true, but also for personal preservation.[203] The monks there were reminded by John of Glastonbury of the days when their unarmed forebears had been constrained to fight for their lives with works of art, swinging silver crucifixes and candlesticks about for want of swords.[204] Lay antipathy did not always involve violent confrontation. The 'Order of Brothelyngham', a mock-religious order begotten in Exeter in 1348 with the aim of ridiculing regular clergy, is an example of secular ill-feeling no less than the attacks to which Gloucester was subjected. The members of the 'order, or rather error' (as Bishop Grandisson put it) placed themselves under the leadership of a lunatic raver called the 'abbot', whom they carried about on a throne and pretended to worship as an idol, and went through the town detaining people and extorting money from them. The beliefs about monasticism that their behaviour exhibited are revealing – monks and nuns blindly followed leaders, were idolatrous, avaricious, even luxurious (thus 'Brothelyngham'). In fulminating an excommunication against them, Grandisson called them 'a threat to religion, the king and the church' – not least to the monks of Cowick and St Nicholas's, and the nuns of Polsloe.[205]

Responses to Ideological Competition

At many social levels, then, the Benedictines faced ideological competition that interfered, or had the potential to interfere, with their ability to attract external patrons for their art and architecture. Crenellation and armaments could only keep aggressors out; they would not bring custom in.[206] In fact, it was demonstration of pedigree, of the legitimacy and virtues of the monastic condition, and of the order's illustrious associations that formed the central planks of the Benedictine response. This in turn lent legitimacy to a possession-based economy, by representing it as time-honoured practice, instituted, sanctioned and encouraged by saints and princes alike. None of this was new, for monks and to a lesser extent nuns had always sought to prove these things. However, the urgency of the manner in which they promoted themselves and the manifestations this

---

[201] Oliver 1846, p. 171.
[202] *HMGlouc.*, III, p. lviii. Admittedly, the daggers doubled as status symbols.
[203] Archbold 1892, p. 275. Cf. *BRECP*, p. 491, under Dan John de Carleton (who bought arms and armour for the defence of the Norwich Benedictines in 1384/5); *Linc.Vis.*, III, pp. 284 note 1, 290 (Peterborough, 1440s).
[204] CGA(C), pp. 158–9 (late eleventh century).
[205] *Reg.Grandisson*, II, pp. 1055–6; Chope 1920–21, pp. 62–4. In 1421 just such a threat was brought to bear on the prior and monks of Cowick: see Yeo 1987, p. 19.
[206] Although a monastery might thus be chosen by an influential external interest as a 'bank': see e.g. Gransden 1982, p. 411; Oman 1957, pp. 35–6; *Cart.Beau.*, p. xii.

took show that the need for self-assertion, if not new, was at least perceived in a different way.[207]

Education and sermonizing

Some time during the later fourteenth century the Franciscan Richard Trevytlam wrote a poem, De laude Universitatis Oxonie, which criticized monks for leaving their cloisters for the purposes of study, and also for attacking friars. In particular, three Benedictines are singled out, one of them from Glastonbury.[208] So what do we encounter in a Worcester monk-student's notebook of the fifteenth century, but an outline of a disputatio on the question whether or not it be right for a monk to leave his cloister in search of a university degree.[209] The conclusion is not hard to guess: what is instructive is the pragmatism, the immediacy with which the challenge was met.[210] This is a typical Benedictine response to ideological pressure, from social equals at least (kings and their agents might, as we have seen, receive a more passive reply). The question, recognized as potentially problematic, is not ignored or fudged, but tackled head-on. Indeed, the sermon, along with the academic dispute, became a significant method of self-advertisement as well as defence. Although St Benedict makes no reference to preaching or any other form of public discourse, the silence he recommended was clearly counterproductive under later medieval conditions, and corporate Benedictinism recognized this fully. 'Monks' it was proclaimed at the General Chapter of c.1363 'should study the art of presenting the word of God before others (i.e. in public) in order to become more efficient and well qualified in disputation and in preaching.'[211] Accordingly, all monk-scholars at university were required to preach in public four times annually – in the vernacular as well as Latin.[212] The utilitarian intent of this is obvious. Adam Easton (d.1397), a particularly skilful Benedictine preacher, was even pressed to remain at Oxford beyond his time to defend his order against the friars.[213] His works migrated west – to Worcester,[214] for example, from which an outstanding thirty-eight volumes of monastic sermon literature survive.[215] In the library there they rubbed covers with Durandus's Rationale divinorum officiorum, whose first book states that towers symbolize preachers (and prelates), the bulwarks and defences of the church militant: for those who read or heard the Rationale, the great red sandstone church above the Severn will have represented a mighty preacher in its own right, thanks to the patronage of John Lyndsey and others.[216] Much of the Worcester sermon literature is either

---

[207] Cf. Pantin 1950, p. 210.

[208] Sharpe 2001, p. 516; CGA(C), p. xxix.

[209] Greatrex 2002, p. 40.

[210] For another illustrative example see Heale 1997, p. 137.

[211] Chapters, II, pp. 64 ('probably 1363'), 75; Greatrex 1998, pp. 260–1.

[212] Chapters, II, p. 214.

[213] Chapters, III, pp. 28–9; Greatrex 1998, p. 261. Easton, later appointed a cardinal, was a monk of Norwich. Durham's Uthred of Boldon (d.1397), on whom see Knowles 1955, pp. 48–54, and Sharpe 2001, pp. 699–702, was perhaps the greatest Benedictine polemicist of the period.

[214] Sharpe 2001, p. 13.

[215] Thomson 2001, pp. xix, xxix; Greatrex 1998, pp. 258–60. Some of this literature is pre-1300.

[216] WCL MS F 129, fol. 4r: 'Turres ecclesie predicatores sunt et prelati ecclesie qui sunt minimie et defensio eius'. Cf. Durandus, p. 19. Thomson 2001, p. 92, has the manuscript 'at Worcester soon after its manufacture' (in xiv[in.]). For John Lyndsey see above, chapter four.

mendicant or mendicant influenced – further evidence of the ability of Benedictines to adapt themselves to circumstances. What they could usefully borrow from the friars they would. The surviving West Country Benedictine pulpits of the fifteenth and early sixteenth centuries (e.g. Cranborne, Milton, St Benignus at Glastonbury, Meare, Long Sutton, St Catherine, Totnes), are mute reminders of this fact.[217]

Demonstration of antiquity

Another significant aspect of Benedictine strategy was the demonstration of antique associations, in particular, ancient origins. That this was a matter of great practical and symbolic importance at many levels of society during the later middle ages scarcely requires emphasis: antiquity sanctioned authority, no less in 1500 than it had for Suger of St-Denis and Gervase of Canterbury. Precedence, for example, was frequently determined according to seniority. Glastonbury's John Chinnock was awarded primacy at a national synod on the basis of his claim to represent England's oldest religious house (believed founded in 63 A.D. by Joseph of Arimathea and his disciples), and the same claim was exploited at foreign ecclesiastical councils, as well.[218] The monks assiduously collected and invented evidences of their house's putative status, in an effort to see off rival claims as well as at self-aggrandizement.[219] They even pressed a fourteenth-century foundational list from impecunious, Premonstratensian Leiston on the Suffolk coast into service, no doubt valuing the evidence of countrywide and pan-denominational acceptance of their claims that it carried.[220] Ultimately, the demonstration of age might serve as a weapon in the fight for survival. The monks of Winchester thrust a copy of their house's early history (from 604) upon Thomas Cromwell as justification of the convent's right to remain alive,[221] an act that, though unsuccessful, highlights the faith that Benedictine houses placed in the utilitarian efficacy of their antiquity.

The efforts made to this end were not to the advantage of individual houses alone. The whole order benefited when a constituent monastery or nunnery successfully promoted an ancient, illustrious pedigree, because this brought a general legitimacy to match general threats such as those levelled by Henry V, Wolsey, and the class of bishops who, increasingly from the mid-fifteenth century, fell out of sympathy with monasticism and began to judge it again as St Bernard had judged Abbots Suger and William of St-Thierry: according to the letter of the *Rule*.[222] To the end of corporate self-justification, a remarkable series of treatises (all variations on the same theme) purporting to demonstrate the antiquity, dignity and sanctity of the monastic condition

---

217 Long 1922(b), p. 24 (Cranborne), pp. 25–6 (Milton, now at Winterbourne Witchurch (Dor.)); Dobson 1950, pp. 71, 76, 78 (Glastonbury, Meare); Pevsner and Cherry 1989, p. 869 (Totnes). The Long Sutton pulpit is embellished with the initials of Abbot John Petherton of Athelney (1424–58). Athelney abbey was the church's corporate rector.

218 CGA(C), p. lx; Lagorio 2001, pp. 68–72.

219 Many of these were publicly displayed on the so-called 'magna tabula', an expedient also adopted (as seen) at Gloucester and Winchester. *Mag.Tab.*, pp. 437–42, lists many other recorded examples.

220 TCC MS R 5 33, fol. 20v. This list and another from St John's abbey at Colchester are printed and analyzed in Luxford 2003(b), p. 279 (ill.) *et passim*.

221 *VCH Hampshire & I.W.*, II, p. 109; Gransden 1982, p. 494 note 1.

222 See Knowles 1959, p. 76. We apprehend something of this in Henry V's speaking of 'de pristina religione monachorum' (*Chapters*, II, p. 99). See also *RCR*, pp. 340–1.

were penned during the fourteenth and fifteenth centuries, and widely disseminated.[223] 'Monasticism' here equals 'Benedictinism': the treatises are quick to point out the relatively late foundational dates of all other orders, canons regular included. A number are actually headed 'Tractatus de prima institutione monachorum nigrorum'.[224] They argued, among other things, that the monastic life had its primitive origins before the time of King David (Samuel was a foundational figure),[225] that the Essenes, St John the Baptist and the disciples of Christ (after the Ascension) had been monks, and that Christ himself had been the true author of the (perfect) monastic life. (Cf. Matthew 19:21; Luke 9:23.) Benedictine authors, missionaries and saints (up to 210 in number) are listed,[226] and there are occasionally digressions condemning Wyclif, the friars or both.[227] The original version seems to have issued from Bury St Edmunds – a copy of this is found in John Merelynch's miscellaneous volume discussed in chapter four.[228] Further copies particularly relevant here existed at Evesham, and (in all likelihood) Winchester and Worcester.[229]

These texts had their iconographic equivalents, the greatest known being the remarkable assemblage of 148 canonized monks of the Benedictine order painted on the parclose screenwork of the altar of Sts Jerome and Benedict in Durham cathedral (to which house ten surviving treatises on the origins and status of monasticsm belonged).[230] Here were popes (eight), emperors and kings (fifteen), archbishops (thirty-four), bishops (forty-one), abbots (thirty-two) and *doctores* (eighteen), each with name and vocation inscribed (often at length) beneath.[231] In the 'Tree' of St Benedict, an image based on the visual *topos* of the Jesse Tree often borrowed to illustrate both ecclesiastical and secular pedigrees, the treatises find a simpler but no less representative iconographic counterpart.[232] Here the root springs not from David's father but from St Benedict – and from heart, not loins. There is a wonderful example in the sanctorale of the Sherborne missal, at that most intrinsically Benedictine of feasts, the Translation of St Benedict (Plate 7).[233] That St Jerome (d.420), who was styled first 'modern' founder of the black monks (to head off Augustinian claims to precedence),[234] stands on a limb

---

[223] Pantin 1950, *passim*; Dobson 1973, pp. 379–82, 85–6; MA, I, pp. xix–xxv. An interesting redaction of 1493 (on *tabulæ*) combining the text with images of Benedictine monks and nuns exists at Augsburg's Staats- und Stadtbibliothek: *Catalogue Augsburg*, pp. 286–7. At least one of the English treatises was displayed on *tabulæ*: Pantin 1950, p. 207. Perhaps some English copies of the treatise were also illustrated.

[224] E.g. Pantin 1950, p. 201.

[225] This gave monasticism a pedigree of roughly the same length as the kings of England (Brutus ruled Britain c.1115–1092 B.C. according to Galfridian estimates).

[226] Pantin 1950, p. 192.

[227] E.g. Pantin 1950, pp. 194, 205, 212–15.

[228] Pantin 1950, pp. 194, 197–8; QCO MS 304, fols 58–66v.

[229] *Shorter Catalogues*, p. 144; Pantin 1950, pp. 208–9.

[230] RD, pp. 105–17; Dobson 1973, p. 381; Piper 1998, p. 308; cf. Sharpe 2001, pp. 342–3.

[231] Rowntree 1990, p. 40, prints an early sixteenth-century Carthusian text in which these numbers are much exaggerated, indicating the successful distribution of such Benedictine 'propaganda'.

[232] See in general Batselier 1981, pp. 79–80. For further Benedictine use of the Jesse Tree topos see CGA(C), pp. 128–9.

[233] Page 488. The image is not a perfect counterpart to the treatises, for it includes monks and nuns of the three main orders using the Benedictine *Rule* – Benedictine, Cistercian and Cluniac – to left and right of St Benedict. A purely Benedictine example exists in Chantilly, Musée Condé MS 1401, fol. 126r (Jean de Stavelot's *Vita beati Benedicti*).

[234] This is made explicit in the missal (p. 368): Herbert 1920, p. 24.

above St Benedict (d. *c*.550) does not matter. It is the spirit that gives life here, not the letter.

As the Durham screens and the Tree of St Benedict suggest, art and architecture played an important role in demonstrating length and quality of pedigree. When a Benedictine house 'marshalled its antiquity',[235] it did not rely solely on the written word: art and architecture, indeed, might stand as arguments in their own right. Houses incorporating Saxon or Romanesque architecture (e.g. Bath, Bristol, Deerhurst, Gloucester, Great Malvern, Malmesbury, Pershore, Romsey, Shaftesbury, Tewkesbury, Winchester) were at an obvious advantage here, for ancient buildings, as Glastonbury's promotion of its *Ealdechirche* as a relic demonstrates,[236] were an indisputable proof of age.[237] Realizing this, the monks of Gloucester (like their counterparts at Winchester) retained most of their ancient chapter house, originally built *c*.1075–80, and with it its painted memorials to illustrious associates. They also had their founder Osric represented holding a model donor church of deliberately anachronistic form (Plate 28).[238] In addition they had the ancient nunnery that Osric had founded represented in a window of their cloister.[239] Elsewhere, as previously noted, Sherborne advertised its status as an ancient bishopric with paintings of its bishops on the chapter house vault:[240] these may well have included St Osmund, whom the monks claimed as a former ruler of the see at the very time of his canonization (1456).[241] Robert Fitzhamon (d.1107) received his stone-cage chantry chapel, complete with purbeck tomb and brass (now lost) to the north of the high altar of Tewkesbury abbey church, lest anyone suspect that the Decorated Gothic of the east end denote discontinuity in the foundation, while Oddo and Doddo (early eighth century) had a page to themselves at the beginning of the Founders' Book (Plate 27), lest anyone suspect that Fitzhamon had started it all. The same manuscript has an illustration of Robert the Consul, first earl of Gloucester (d.1147) and bastard son of Henry I, who was also represented in sculpture: the base of an image inscribed 'Robertus Consull filius Regis' survives.[242] It was for the Consul that Geoffrey of Monmouth wrote the *Historia Regum Britanniæ*, and we need not doubt that Tewkesbury's monks were aware and proud of this link with British antiquity.[243] The same earl founded the priory of St James at Bristol, and the convent there also sought to

---

235 Cf. Crick 1991, p. 217.

236 E.g. CGA(C), pp. 8–9; Goodall 2001, pp. 185–92.

237 On this issue of deliberate retention see Gem 2001(a), p. 265. Dr Gem discusses such retention during the pre-Conquest period, but it is also apparent in the later middle ages.

238 Payne and Payne 1994, pp. 87–104 (names and shields in the chapter house, dating 'anywhere between 1200 and 1350' (92)). The east end of the chapter house was modernized during the later fifteenth century, however. See Luxford 2002(d), pp. 180–1, on Osric's 'donor' church.

239 MA, I, p. 564.

240 *Itinerary*, I, p. 153. See also the Sherborne missal's twenty-five episcopal 'portraits' (Aldhelm-Hereman), from p. 363, and further afield, the surviving fifteenth-century panel paintings in the choir and south transept at Augustinian Hexham (Northumberland), a bishopric until 821. Cf. Robert Mannyng of Bourne's analogy of the incorrupt bishop disinterred by monks 'as fresshë as he were depeynte': *Handlyng Synne*, p. 343. These were 'living' portraits alright.

241 TCC MS R 7 13, fol. 36r (*c*.1460) has 'Hoc tempore floruit Sanctus Osmundus Episcopus Shirbornensis et postea Sarum'. The claim is apparently unique to this source. See Luxford 2002(c), pp. 287, 292 note 18.

242 OBL Top Glouc d 2, fol. 15r. For the base see Morris with Luxford 2002, pp. 86–7, no. 18; Luxford 2004(a), p. 7.

243 HRB, p. 1.

advertise its illustrious roots in a difficult climate through identification with him. Leland describes the Consul's tomb before the high altar: 'a sepulchre of gray Marble ['ex viridi Jaspide', the Founders' Book says] set up apon 6. pillers of small hethe'.[244]

Conventual common seals, the images of which were designed to convey an epitome of a monastery's spiritual (and often temporal) authority to outsiders, frequently carried indications of antiquity. Evesham's seal, discussed in chapter two, is one such example (Plate 25). Another is that of Malmesbury's proud little cell at Pilton (die engraved c.1450; in use 1534), the reverse of which represents King Æthelstan, the putative founder (Plate 26).[245] The claim by the corporation of Barnstaple, and by extension that of Pilton, to have been granted foundational powers and liberties by Æthelstan had been debunked by a royal inquiry during Edward III's reign, but this did not stop the monks from restating it each time they sealed a document.[246] More effective still as a proof of antiquity was the use of an ancient seal. Thus, the nuns of later medieval Wilton employed a late tenth-century seal representing St Edith (d.984), blessing with her right hand and holding what is apparently a book in her left: it was used in 1372, and again at the end, in 1539.[247] Finally, Benedictine convents were aware of the value of the attributive armorials specified in rolls, and many embellished their buildings with them. The great *tabulæ* displaying Conquest-period armorials on show at some monasteries (that at Battle abbey, with 364 shields, was appropriately the most extensive) are not recorded for the West: the convents there were concerned with earlier origins.[248] Each of the surviving examples in glass – e.g. Milton (Æthelstan), Muchelney (Æthelstan, plus another king, unidentified)[249] and Prinknash (Osric) – and stone – Gloucester, remains of south gate (Osric), Milton, abbot's hall (Æthelstan) – retains its immediacy, if not its credibility, as a cipher of antiquity and authority.

Demonstration of authority

The works representing Robert the Consul at Tewkesbury and Bristol, the seals of Evesham and Pilton, and the attributive armorials mentioned here remind us that authority as well as age was what the Benedictines sought to demonstrate. A vast quantity of art, not to mention text, was produced with the aim of proving illustrious associations. In particular, it is royal links that receive emphasis, often at the expense (as suggested at the beginning of chapter two) of actual founders. As the issue is closely related to that of the stress laid on antiquity, and as many of the works illustrative of it have been mentioned in previous pages, it does not require extended treatment here. It is worth noting, however, that any house, from Pilton with its seal to Glastonbury with

[244] *Itinerary*, V, p. 88 (hethe = height); OBL Top Glouc d 2, fol. 15v. The tomb now identified as Robert Consul's (south aisle, east end: Gardner 1951, p. 138 note 1, 141 ill. 265), is nothing of the sort.

[245] Birch 1887, pp. 702–3 (no. 3841); Williams 1993–98, II, p. 35.

[246] HMC IX:i, pp. 204 col. a, 212, col. a. The traditional claims of Pilton and Barnstaple remained current, as Leland and John Speed subscribed to them: *Itinerary*, I, p. 300; K&H, p. 73. Heale 2004, p. 29, reasonably suggests twelfth-century foundation for Pilton.

[247] Heslop 1980, p. 4; Birch 1887, p. 808 (no. 4335); cf. Williams 1993–98, II, p. 37.

[248] The Battle abbey roll is printed in *Brut*, II, pp. 535–7.

[249] Now in the parish church's east window: see Woodforde 1946, p. 120; BL MS Additional 17463, fol. 177v.

its tombs of Edward the Elder, Arthur and Guinevere and Edmund Ironside,[250] images of kings on its nave vaults and names of others inscribed on its pavements, might exploit royal associations in an effort not only to enhance its status generally, but also to advertise the quality and quantity of divine service offered (where a king lay, there was bound to be perpetual commemoration) and the back-up that could, theoretically at least, be called on if the convent was threatened in any way. They also functioned to elicit patronage. The author of the *Rites of Durham* explains that the thirty-four images of kings and queens on the pulpitum of that house were instituted 'to incite and provoke theire posteritie to the like religious endeavours' – a pragmatic rationale for this type of imagery if ever there was one.[251] The houses of the west were no less pragmatic in their approach. The enormous, crenellated, 'Great' (or 'Abbot's') gate at Evesham, built between 1316 and 1332, with stone images of the Virgin Mary, St Ecgwine and 'regum fundatorum nostrorum', is a particularly clear statement of this.[252] Sub-royal aristocratic associations were harnessed to the same ends, of course, but of royal associations, especially ancient royal associations, the Benedictines could legitimately boast louder than any other order. The quantity of surviving retrospective royal iconography is thus greatest among Benedictine remains (set pieces such as York Minster's pulpitum and the later fourteenth-century statuary of Westminster Hall notwithstanding), and it need not be doubted that this faithfully reflects later medieval proportions generally.

Conclusion

A refrain poem translated from the French by John Lydgate (c.1370–c.1451) intended to highlight the corruption of the mid-fifteenth century by inverted description of the status quo begins thus: 'Þis worlde is ful of stabulnesse/ Þere is þer inne no varyaunce/ But trouthe, feyth, and gentyl[n]esse/ Secre[t]ness, and assuraunce'. Each verse ends 'So as þe crabbe goþe forward.'[253] Crabs, of course, go sideways, not backwards – the supposedly inverse analogy is thus as ambiguous as the times must often have seemed, not only to Benedictines like Lydgate but to people of all degrees.[254] Uncertainty generated a tendency to perceive threats that may be dismissed with hindsight, but that nevertheless seemed real enough to those who experienced them, and that elicited written, painted, sculpted and built responses that allow particularly immediate access to minds conditioned to think in competitive, strategic terms. Benedictine material and textual culture of the period is thus, functionally and semantically, especially rich; for as outlined here with reference to the main general challenges facing the order, the extent and complexity of problems confronting Benedictines were matched by the resources

---

250 Arthur's tomb had a crucifix at the east end, a cross on the slab, and an image of Arthur at the west, the whole being supported by crouching lions: *Itinerary*, I, p. 288; cf. Eton College MS 96, fol. 24r: *MMBL*, II, pp. 707–8. Bond 1915, pp. 133–4, thought he might have excavated part of Arthur's (purbeck) effigy.

251 *RD*, p. 17. See also Piper 1998, pp. 307–8.

252 *CAEve.*, p. 292.

253 *MPLydgate*, II, pp. 464–5 (French original), 465–7 (Lydgate's translation). See also *GM*, p. 58; *Manual*, VI, pp. 1895–6.

254 The poem is one of a class of satires and complaints concerning the general evils of the age, on which see *Manual*, V, pp. 1432–42, 1667–71.

available to meet them. For every condition working against the goodwill on which external patronage of art and architecture relied, there was a specific palliative. In these remedies may be perceived the particular genius (i.e. 'cleverness') of the order. Benedictine convents may no longer have been at the forefront of liturgical innovation, but the ingenuity and integrity of black monks and nuns was not thereby extinguished: notoriously, religious observance was only one of a number of conditions necessary for the justification of a monastery by 1300. If the external patronage to which it is time to turn seems rather slight, and not demonstrative of profound secular interest in the black monks and nuns, then it is as well to remember that this is due to the competitiveness of the environment, to changing fashions and beliefs, and to the instability engendered by the mutability of the times, rather than to want of self-promotion, strategic thinking and ingenuity on the part of the Benedictines themselves.

6

External Patronage

Royal Patronage

The nature of royal patronage: expectation and reality

Royalty has been a recurring theme throughout this study. In chapter one, the detritus to which Benedictine records, art and architecture have been reduced by royal decree was surveyed. Over every surviving artefact stretches the long shadow of Henry VIII. At various points, chapters two and three each discussed the prestige value for the Benedictines of demonstrating the involvement of monarchs – past or present – in their affairs. Conversely, chapter two also pointed out the problems that a cash-strapped or zealous monarch might pose for the monks and nuns under his protection. The introduction to section three adumbrated the subject of royal intervention (or the lack of it) in monastic building, embellishment, and prosperity in general, while chapter five considered the use of royal iconography in Benedictine art. The monarch, whether in person or as an 'idea', has been the most influential non-Benedictine personality to emerge.

This is understandable in light of the status of the king generally in later medieval life (i.e. both public and private affairs, and public and private psychology), and especially in those areas such as conventual monastic life that came directly under royal control. The king was most things to most Benedictine houses at various stages during their later medieval existence: tutelary patron, judge, protector, critic, receiver, debtor, guest, grantor, taxator, and at last even supreme temporal religious authority. He had a claim on all collective monastic prayers and, potentially, a share in every mark entering the conventual coffers.[1] Instinctively, embattled regular clergy laid their troubles before the king.[2] And, as all monks and nuns will have been aware, he might exercise his 'power fundatorie' whenever he considered it necessary.[3] The bracket of a fourteenth-century misericord at Gloucester is supported by a sleeping king, emblematic of the fundamental, usually dormant royal support on which monks and nuns rested (Plate 16). Overall, the relationship was dense, reciprocal and organic. It grew – often, as we have seen, visibly – through the warp and weft of Benedictine life. To hive off a component of it such as the patronage of art and architecture has the potential to diminish it if the broader perspective is not maintained. Yet for the broader perspective there is little space here. This caveat, and the repeated reference to monarchs past and contemporary

---

[1] On royal rights to monastic prayer see Wood 1955, p. 134.
[2] Youings 1971, p. 21.
[3] As Henry VIII threatened to do at Gloucester in 1510: see GCL Register C(ii), fol. 36r–v.

made in preceding chapters, must therefore stand as evidence of a relationship the importance of which transcends the current focus.

As suggested previously with reference to Milton, the degree of immediate royal intervention in Benedictine campaigns of building and embellishment was slight. However, it should be acknowledged that past historians have often posited Crown involvement in projects for which documentation and other reliable sources are lacking. Milton itself provides one example, Bath, Dunster, Great Malvern and Gloucester (the latter will be discussed further below) others.[4] In such cases, the grounds of the speculation (if any) must be examined for what they will yield. Often this turns out to be very little. Where Milton is concerned, the direct architectural patronage of Edward III and Philippa of Hainault (whose interest in architectural patronage has recently been characterized as 'clearly not extensive')[5] has been argued for because a chantry was established for the benefit of their souls at the abbey in 1329.[6] In fact, were one to enumerate possible catalysts for such a foundation, direct involvement in building patronage would come some way down the list. While unambiguous documentation is not necessary for discussing Benedictine projects in the context of royal (or for that matter sub-royal lay) patronage, a certain minimum standard of cogency is.

The reputation that pre-Plantagenet monarchs have as founders – usually, if erroneously, taken to mean builders as well – of Benedictine monasteries and nunneries, the interest shown by the Crown in particular black-monk houses after 1300, the remarkable largesse of the usually parsimonious Henry V in the construction of Sheen and Syon (a third house, for French Celestines, was substantially raised but never completed),[7] and the king's role as overlord of all monasteries holding *in capite*, may lead one to expect that later medieval kings had a substantial role in the patronage of English conventual art and architecture. Such an expectation, no doubt, elicits the unsubstantiated attributions mentioned above. It is, however, misguided: there is no clear reason why monarchs of the period should have spent their money on Benedictine projects. Indeed, there are a number of straightforward reasons why they should not have done so. Most obviously of all, the reigning monarch and his family were no more beholden to contribute to Benedictine projects than to those of their lay vassals. A charter of royal foundation, regardless of reconfirmations, did not entail an obligation to maintain a fabric. The king's relationship in this regard was not analogous to that of a rector to his parish church. Religious houses were independently endowed, and independently responsible for their own maintenance.

Where we do encounter royal involvement in the construction and embellishment of monasteries, it is almost always connected to the monarch's commemorative aspirations, or else to the augmentation of the political, religious and historical profile of his dynasty. Thus, the church in which a monarch and his family chose to be buried benefited in particular. Later medieval Benedictines were acutely aware of this, as the regnal

---

4   Collinson 1791, II, p. 18, attributed Dunster church entire to Henry VII.
5   Sekules 2000, p. 157.
6   Oswald 1966, p. 1650.
7   The Celestines boasted that 'thei kepe Seint Benet reule *ad litteram*' (*Abbreuiacion*, p. 242), which presumably appealed to Henry. For Henry's patronage see *HKW*, I, p. 266 and note 9; K&H, p. 109. The construction of these three houses, as an *amende honorable* imposed on Henry IV by Pope Gregory XII, was anyway a special case.

lists including place of interment found among their manuscripts tend to show.[8] It is Westminster Abbey and Christ Church, Canterbury (the latter housed the tombs of the Black Prince, and Henry IV and Joan of Navarre) that are listed most frequently after 1300, of course. These two institutions can be viewed either as anomalous, in that they were Benedictine houses that continued to attract major royal contributions long after the black monks had fallen from favour generally among patrons, or as typical, insofar as the contributions they received were contingent on their function as royal sepulchres and centres of dynastic display. The latter perspective is clearly the constructive one to take. There is no straightforward evidence that the Benedictine status of Westminster and Canterbury was, of itself, a determining factor in the matter of royal largesse post-1300.

Henry V's request for burial at Westminster helps to substantiate this point. What Henry desired, according to his will, was not association with Benedictines (whom, as we have seen, he regarded as spiritually corrupt), but membership of the 'royal fellow-ship of death' established by Henry III, and especially, association with particular, speci-fied saints.[9] It is noteworthy that he made his will in 1415, the same year in which he laid the foundation stone of the house of St Bridget at Syon.[10] The point is further supported by the fact that the only two examples proper[11] of royal burial in West Country Benedictine houses after 1300, Edward II at Gloucester (1327) and Arthur, Prince of Wales at Worcester (1502), correspond to the two most important apparent (for neither is reliably documented) examples of royal patronage to be surveyed below.

A further reason for lack of royal contributions to West Country Benedictine projects during the later middle ages was the increasingly sedentary nature of the royal court, and the resulting lack of immediate contact between monarchs and convents. The appear-ance and 'personalities' of the larger houses, and probably a number of the smaller ones as well, must have been far more distinct to Henry II than to Henry VI or VII. Although, as pointed out in chapter two, sporadic royal visits to the West continued, the peripatetic court of the Norman and early Plantagenet era, which had ensured annual and sustained royal presence in the region (for example, St Peter's at Gloucester and St Swithun's, Winchester, with Westminster Abbey, had been England's three so-called 'crown-wearing' centres),[12] was a thing of the past by the fourteenth century. As late as 1216, King John had been buried at Worcester and Henry III crowned at Gloucester, but subsequent monarchs – the murdered Edward II is a peculiar case – favoured London, Canterbury or Windsor. The general reduction in the political impor-tance of Benedictine superiors, evident in the thirteenth-century decline in monastic promotions to the episcopacy,[13] and the reformation of the lords spiritual during the 1320s, which drastically reduced the numbers of regular heads coming before the king at parliament,[14] were factors that decreased contact between the Crown and the houses

---

8 Post-1300 West Country examples include *Cart.Much.&Ath.*, pp. 188–90 (Athelney); CUL Dd 8 2, fols 3–4 (Kington St Michael); BL MS Additional 43405, fol. xxvii verso (Muchelney); WCL MS A xii, fol. 103v (Worcester).
9 See *Foedera*, IV:ii, pp. 138–40, for Henry V's will.
10 *HKW*, I, p. 265.
11 As noted below, Henry VI's son was buried at Tewkesbury in 1471.
12 On Gloucester as a centre of royal ceremonial, see Hare 1997, pp. 41–78, especially 53–7.
13 Gibbs and Lang 1962, pp. 5, 7; Knowles 1948, pp. 321–2; Knowles 1955, pp. 369–70.
14 Knowles 1955, pp. 302–4; Tanner 1787, p. xvi.

covered by this study still further. 'Out of sight, out of mind' is not quite the appropriate term, for respective kings and queens maintained a healthy regard for particular institutions and their superiors. The admiration of Edward III and Philippa of Hainault for Glastonbury, which will receive more attention below, is one example, and Henry V's choice of John of Fordham, prior of Worcester, to attend the Council of Constance (1414–17) another.[15] Moreover, the Crown certainly remembered its far-flung monastic vassals when it came to requesting payments – which might include works of art – from them.[16] If nothing else, however, the reduction in contact between the king and his West Country Benedictine vassals curbed opportunities for patronage substantially. Insofar as they bear reliable witness, royal wills back up the idea that later medieval monarchs did not identify strongly with religious houses beyond the outskirts of London.[17]

Not that England's monarchs failed to spend money on building and embellishment in the West after 1300. On the contrary, they spent a great deal on military and domestic architecture, and this further limited whatever potential may have existed for Crown patronage of Benedictine projects. Edward II spent £224 on Exeter Castle between 1321 and 1325, and the Black Prince continued to support the works thereafter. Hereford castle, in the outer bailey of which stood the ancient church of the Benedictine priory of St Guthlac, cost the king's administrators substantial sums during the fourteenth and early fifteenth centuries. The castles of Bristol, Salisbury and Winchester, too, made constant, heavy demands on the royal purse, while the hunting lodge on Woolmer manor and certain of the New Forest lodges in Hampshire received costly repairs and additions during the fourteenth and fifteenth centuries.[18] At Bath, the king's lodgings within the monastic precinct incurred ongoing royal expenditure, although it seems that the prior sometimes financed the work.[19] The Crown also owned, and was presumably responsible for, buildings within the precinct at Worcester.[20] The greatest sums, however, disappeared into that perennial money-pit, Gloucester castle. Between 1304 and 1308, the Crown authorized £150 to be spent on it, and another £322 was outlaid between May 1308 and February 1310. In the four years following 1331, the tottering structure consumed £675 more. For two decades after 1336, the royal accounts contain many instances of further expenditure. All of this was simply palliative, and Richard II was constrained to spend another £330 on repairs in the 1380s, Henry IV £71 in 1406, Henry VI £200 in 1428 and again in 1438, with more to follow later in his reign. Edward IV, too, spent money on the edifice. It took the shrewd, avaricious Henry VII to finally write the castle off.[21] While debate over the degree of royal involvement in the remodelling of the abbey church will continue, there is no doubt

---

15 *Abbreuiacion*, p. 242; BRECP, p. 806. Clearly, Henry V's disgust with the Benedictines can be overstated.

16 E.g. MA, II, p. 448 (Hyde, 1338: including 'unam crucem auri cum diversis petris'.).

17 *Royal Wills, passim*; Jordan 1959, p. 303. Nothing is left to a West Country Benedictine house post-1300 in any royal will.

18 HKW, II, pp. 580–1 (Bristol), 648–9 (Exeter), 676–7 (Hereford), 827–8 (Salisbury), 862–4 (Winchester), 983–6 (New Forest lodges), 1017–18 (Woolmer).

19 HKW, II, p. 898. All recorded expenditure at Bath is thirteenth century.

20 See HKW, II, pp. 888–9 for buildings associated with Worcester castle, originally royal but in Beauchamp hands until regained by Henry VII in 1487. Despite later medieval renovations (Guy 1991, p. 4), they were apparently ruinous by the Dissolution: *Itinerary*, II, p. 90.

21 HKW, II, pp. 654–6. On Henry's avarice, see Lockyer 1991, pp. 84–5.

that successive monarchs were spending enough to rebuild much of the abbey church on the adjacent castle. Whatever their disposition towards St Peter's, this must have limited their enthusiasm for and ability to contribute to a project that was not formally their responsibility.

The impression of minimal expenditure on Benedictine art and architecture that royal accounts and wills give is backed up by the testimony of monastic chroniclers, who are all but silent on a subject about which they would fain have boasted, tending as it would have done to exult their respective institutions. The fuss that Thomas Walsingham makes over Edward II's gift of 100 marks towards the building of the choir stalls at St Albans is indicative of this.[22] It is true that the Benedictine attitude to the authority of their royal overlords was ambivalent. A document written at Evesham around the time that the monks were having statues of royal founders placed on their great gate speaks of the need to excommunicate the officers of the king should they seek to meddle in conventual affairs. 'It will be expedient', it continues, 'to admit no-one who claims an official right.'[23] Glastonbury, too, obtained a royal guarantee in 1331 that no minister of the Crown would thenceforth 'in any way enter within the monastery's gates for any purpose' other than the collection of feudal dues,[24] while the abbots of Athelney and Muchelney went so far as to actively assist the rebel faction during the West Country uprising of 1497.[25] However, the king's personal presence carried a prestige that domestic chroniclers were on the whole expert at emphasizing, and resentment of royal authority does not tend to manifest itself in their work. Indeed, the tokens yielded by the gift-giving rituals integral to royal visits (the main regular occasion for Crown patronage of Benedictine art in the West after 1300) are made by the chroniclers of Glastonbury and Gloucester to sound like treasures.

Examples of royal patronage

Glastonbury

Examples of these 'token' benefactions and the circumstances of their bestowal will put the issue in clearer perspective, while also introducing some of the few documented cases of royal art and architectural patronage available to this study. In Glastonbury's general cartulary there is an eyewitness description of the four-day visit to the monastery by Edward III and Queen Philippa in December 1331.[26] The eighteen-year-old king was somewhat in awe of the ancient abbey, and was no doubt excited by the prospect of a visit that, it has been argued, was the catalyst for his subsequent Arthurian enthusiasm.[27] Calendared among the Fine Rolls is proof of his respect: the king dictates his belief not only that Glastonbury is the tomb of saints, 'consecrated by the Lord himself', but also that '[his] progenitors, catholic kings, on account of the sanctity of the place . . .

---

22 GA, II, p. 124.
23 Tindal 1794, p. 191.
24 CGA(C), pp. 262–3 (cf. the incident recorded at pp. 242–3). See also CCR, Edward III 1327–30, p. 332.
25 BL MS Royal B vii (roll), first membrane. The abbots were fined 100 marks and £60 respectively. The abbot of Athelney, who heads the list, was fined more heavily than any other religious individual or institution on a roll of over 3000 names.
26 Cart.Glaston., I, pp. lxxxiv–lxxxv, 194–5.
27 Lagorio 2001, pp. 64–5; CGA(C), p. xxvii.

enriched [it] abundantly'. He mentions former kings buried in its holy earth, and also speaks, albeit in formulaic terms, of his 'special affection [for] the person of Adam of Sodbury, abbot'.[28] Yet his enthusiasm and respect, and that of his queen, received only the slightest artistic expression. Philippa, who arrived at the abbey before the king, presented the convent with a piece of silk sewn with gold drops. This, the writer reports, was subsequently made into a chasuble, which is interesting for a number of reasons, above all for its demonstration of the monastic desire to maximize the symbolic and perhaps also the pragmatic value of a royal gift, regardless of its monetary value.[29] The present given by the king was a piece of cloth of gold the length of the high altar, which recalls the 'pannum auro textum' that Edward I sent to the high altar of Worcester in 1303.[30] (In 1293 the same king had given two cloths of gold, in 1295 two 'pannos nobiles', and in 1300 a cover ('baudekinus'), all to the same altar; i.e. to the convent.)[31] We are not informed whether this, too, was made into vestments, though it is a distinct possibility. John of Glastonbury tells us that Edward III also presented Abbot Sodbury with 'a very noble cup, with a beautifully enamelled ewer', though whether on this occasion or another is not specified.[32]

In the *Ostensa* of Abbot Walter de Monington, which as we have seen lists his art, architectural and bibliographic benefactions to his convent, there is a further indication of the importance carried by royal, as opposed to other, gifts. Among the remarkable catalogue of vestments listed at the beginning of the document, we find the following: 'Also to the Lady chapel a set of prayer beads [made] out of pure gold that was given to him by Philippa, former queen of England.'[33] (Plate 40, lines 21–3.) Philippa and Monington shared a good relationship – good enough for the abbot to be able to write personally to the queen (in 1357) seeking her help in regaining Edward III's pleasure after a dispute over the imposition of royal corrodians[34] – and it is thus not surprising to discover that she had bestowed such a gift as a sign of her favour. Nor is it surprising to find them distinguished on the basis of their royal provenance from the other sumptuous items mentioned in the document. They are the only items listed in the *Ostensa* to carry the name of their previous donor, though it is highly likely that a proportion of the others had also been given to Monington by external associates. Here, as with the earlier gifts of Philippa and Edward, it was the giver that made the gift precious.[35]

---

28 *CFR*, IV, pp. 123–4.
29 While the relative value of such cloth will have been high, the quantity given (as with Edward's cloth of gold) was not great.
30 *Annales*, IV, p. 556.
31 *Annales*, IV, pp. 514, 521, 544. *Baudekinus* can denote a copper coin, but this seems an inappropriate gift for a king. Cf. BL MS Cotton Galba E iv, fol. 121v (of 1315), where it is used in the sense proposed here. In 1294, 1295 and 1300 he gave a brooch (two of these at least were of gold) to the shrine of St Wulfstan: *Annales*, IV, pp. 516–17, 521, 544.
32 *CGA(C)*, pp. 262–3: 'vnam cuppam cum aquario subtilius emalata, que sibi contulit Edwardus tercius post conquestum'.
33 'Item capelle *beate* virginis unum par aueez ex auro puro quod sibi domina Philippa regina anglie quondam dedit.' TCC MS R 5 16, p. 218. This was probably written c.1380. For 'aueez' as prayer beads cf. *The Middle English Dictionary*, under 'ave'.
34 Keil 1964(b), p. 344; Carley 1996, p. 50.
35 We recall here Robert Burnell's gift to Bath of vestments from the private chapel of Eleanor of Castille, mentioned in chapter two.

Gloucester

And so to Gloucester. The chronicler's first mention of a royal visit post-1300 (Edward II's, in the 1320s) is a piece of artistry, which sets up the putative circumstances of the royal interment at the abbey in 1327 in a manner designed to place Abbot Thoky in the best possible light.[36] Not surprisingly, there are no benefactions mentioned at this point, for they would have interfered with the narrative drive. Subsequently, however, gifts bestowed by Edward III, the Black Prince and the queens of England and Scotland are listed.[37] The king, it is reported, gave a model ship of gold in fulfilment of a vow made when 'troubled by grave misfortune at sea' (a storm off the coast of Brittany in 1341,[38] or perhaps relating to his successful naval campaign at Sluys, 1340).[39] He had been 'freed' by the intercession of his own father,[40] whom he had presumably supplicated (otherwise, short of an epiphany of which the reader is not told, the chronicler, or whoever else originally generated the story, would have had no knowledge of the identity of the saint that succoured the king). The golden ship, which is implicitly valued at £100 (we are informed that he redeemed a second such ship for that amount in cash at the abbot and convent's request), in fact cost Edward £53 5s 8d *ob*.[41] An impression of its appearance is perhaps preserved on the obverse of the gold nobles and half-nobles minted for the first time during the 1340s.[42] The Prince of Wales gave jewels with which to embellish the ship, and also a sumptuous gold reliquary-cross containing a fragment of the True Cross. Philippa donated gold ex-votos in the shapes of a heart and an ear, also to embellish the ship, while Joanna, queen of Scotland (Edward III's sister), gave a necklace set with a ruby. With a single exception,[43] these are the only external gifts of art mentioned individually in the latter part of the chronicle, although there were definitely others, for the writer tells us that at the tomb of Edward II 'various other gifts, both of silver and gilded, were given by a variety of lords and ladies'.[44] Clearly, it was the status of the works as royal benefactions that made them worth mentioning in what is on the whole a strongly abbot-centred context.

This leads directly into perhaps the most vexed patronage issue covered by this study, the degree of royal involvement in the remodelling of Gloucester's transepts and presbytery, the tomb of Edward II and the choir stalls, in the decades following 1327.[45] The Gloucester chronicler studiously avoids mentioning any royal assistance with or even interest in the programme. Rather, he attributes the patronage to the abbot and convent, with the aid of oblations made at the royal tomb by the 'faithful' (admittedly, these may be thought to include Edward III and his family). The south transept, remodelled under

---

[36] *HMGlouc.*, I, pp. 44–5.

[37] *HMGlouc.*, I, pp. 47–8.

[38] Coulton 1928, p. 18 note 3.

[39] Ormrod 1989, p. 860. The gift was bestowed in 1343.

[40] *HMGlouc.*, I, p. 47.

[41] Ormrod 1989, p. 860. Five ships were made, and sent to four different religious houses. If St Peter's did receive two, then this shows a particular regard for it on the king's part.

[42] Cf. *AoC*, pp. 490–2.

[43] *HMGlouc.*, I, p. 57. Even this (the pontifical ornaments given to Walter Froucester and his convent by the duke of Gloucester) was an act of royal patronage, for the duke was Thomas of Woodstock, Edward III's youngest son.

[44] *HMGlouc.*, I, p. 48. Many of these were presumably cash oblations, but not all (some were gilded).

[45] The remodelling is misleadingly presented in many sources as a straightforward case of royal patronage: e.g. Pearsall 1995, p. 51.

Abbot Wigmore c.1330–36 (a pulpitum was also erected),[46] and the crossing (i.e. choir) vault and stalls on the northern side of the choir, erected during Adam de Staunton's abbacy (1337–51), are explicitly stated to have been paid for by offerings. The presbytery, high altar and the choir stalls on the south side, which he dates to Thomas Horton's abbacy (1351–77), are not attributed to any particular patron(s), while the north transept, remodelled 1368–74, he ascribes to a process of abbatial and conventual cooperation that has been mentioned above in chapter three.[47] The golden ship and other royal gifts, as thank-offerings for Edward II's intercession, are associated by the chronicler with the royal cult (the model ship occupied the bracket that still protrudes from the north side of the tomb-chest),[48] but not with the fabric of the abbey church.

On the basis of what has been suggested previously, concerning the eagerness of chroniclers to exaggerate royal attention, this silence apparently indicates a lack of royal participation. However, there can be no doubt that Edward III was interested in the abbey for the fact that his father was buried in it. As early as December 1328 he reconfirmed the charters of the borough of Gloucester 'in honour of the body of our father, which lies buried at Gloucester'.[49] In line with official decorum and filial loyalty, he attended his father's funeral at the abbey, and, it is supposed, actively fostered the cult, seeing in it an opportunity both to emulate the Capetian dynasty's success with Louis IX and to override the cult of Thomas, earl of Lancaster, executed in 1322 on Edward II's orders.[50] That this illicit cult was popular in the west, and consequently in need of competition, is shown by a note in the cartulary of St Guthlac's priory, Hereford (a cell of St Peter's), mentioning a publicly displayed image of the earl that earned the monks there 8s 4d in oblations.[51] Thus, despite the fact that not a shred of royal documentation concerning the project survives (in striking contrast to the well-documented, contemporaneous work at Gloucester castle), successive scholars have supposed significant royal involvement in the creation not only of Edward II's tomb, but also in the Perpendicularization of its architectural setting.[52]

The fabric itself, including the tomb, its effigy, and the choir stalls, backs this assumption up (Plate 10). In fact, it is the most reliable document we have in this case. That the tomb, the earliest part of the programme completed (c.1330–31),[53] incorporates an

---

[46] Its statuary and tabernacles came later: HMGlouc., I, p. 50.

[47] The three campaigns are sketched out in HMGlouc., I, pp. 46, 47 and 50 respectively.

[48] Wilson 1980, p. 119; AoC, p. 416.

[49] HMC XII:ix, pp. 402–3 ('ob honorem corpis patris nostri, quod apud Gloucestriam requiescit humatum'); VCH Gloucester, IV, p. 21.

[50] Tout 1921, p. 95; Crossley 1987, pp. 72–3; Stone 1972, pp. 160–1. However, Ormrod 1989, p. 870, denies official Crown participation in the cult.

[51] Manifesting a singular irony, i.e. that while the mother house was enriching itself through Edward II's cult, its daughter was benefiting by Thomas of Lancaster's. The reference is OBC MS 271, fol. 124v. The image was in St Peter's church, Hereford. The entry concerning it is a miscellaneous insertion no later than c.1330–40.

[52] E.g. Stone 1972, p. 160–2; Harvey 1978, pp. 79–80; Wilson 1980, pp. 113–26; Tracy 1987, p. 44; Wilson 1990, pp. 204–7; Morganstern 2000, pp. 82–91. Ormrod 1989, pp. 870–1 and note 123 accepts Thomas of Canterbury's participation in the tomb's manufacture but suggests that the monks commissioned and paid for it. He appears to neglect the effigy, however.

[53] Morganstern 2000, p. 83, supposes 1327 or 1328, misrepresenting her source (Wilson 1980, p. 117). She thus styles Isabella, Edward II's widow, the controlling patron, rather than Edward III. Wilson 1980, p. 150, actually supposes that work on tomb and south transept overlapped. See also AoC, p. 416.

alabaster effigy (Plate 9), suggests knowledge of and a desire to follow a trend set by the Capetian kings of France, who had previously commissioned *gisants* of white marble for dynastic and retrospective memorials.[54] The use of purbeck for the tomb-chest follows a tradition existing among royal monuments at Westminster.[55] Moreover, the effigy holds an orb as well as a sceptre (the first English sepulchral effigy to do so), and the face is modelled on an established pictorial type of Christ (and God the Father), evincing a concern with sanctity from the outset.[56] All three characteristics suggest a controlling royal interest (though whether on the part of Edward III or his mother is unclear): apart from anything else, such artistic conventions are most unlikely to have been familiar to the convent of St Peter's. Indeed, it is usual to ascribe the effigy to London court artists.[57] The canopy, too, in the mouldings of its shafts, its tabernacles of complex plan and cinquefoil ogee arches with closely set cusps, was clearly the product of a designer conversant with the late Decorated architecture of London and Kent (notably, that of St Stephen's chapel, Westminster, and the Benedictine houses of Canterbury).[58] It has been attributed to Thomas of Canterbury (d.1336), Edward III's master mason at St Stephen's chapel.[59] That it was made out of limestone from Painswick, some four miles south-east of Gloucester, shows only that it was carved locally.[60]

Due to the use of metropolitan and Kentish forms in its window tracery, Christopher Wilson attributes the design of the south transept to Thomas of Canterbury as well. In support of this, he also indicates internal features demonstrating French influence; for example, the distinctively Rayonnant graduation of the tracery and the prominence of the vault responds.[61] John Harvey had previously supposed William III Ramsey (d.1349) partially responsible; but this view is no longer tenable.[62] The two scholars agree, however, on the main point at issue here; that a royal mason played a leading role in the earlier phases of the remodelling at least, in the process introducing the Perpendicular style to a region whose architectural character it would soon come to dominate. The design of the presbytery and north transept, though in important respects different to that of the south transept (the presbytery vault, in particular, has strong West Country Decorated resonances), may also have benefited from the expertise of royal masons.[63]

54 Erlande-Brandenburg 1975, pp. 75–86, 158–72 and pls XXXV–XLV; AoC, p. 417; Williamson 1995, pp. 171–2.
55 Wilson 1980, p. 117.
56 Morganstern 2000, p. 83–7; cf. Stone 1972, p. 161.
57 Stone 1972, pp. 160–1, is widely cited.
58 Wilson 1980, pp. 118–19, notes similarities with London-made choir furnishings at Exeter cathedral.
59 Wilson 1980, p. 121; AoC, p. 416.
60 Richardson 1951, *passim*; Wilson 1980, p. 117.
61 Wilson 1980, pp. 139–40, 151, 154–6; Wilson 1990, p. 205; Morris 2003(c), p. 12. Thomas of Canterbury would have had access, Professor Wilson suggests, to thirteenth-century French architectural drawings at Westminster. On French (specifically Norman) influence at Gloucester see Morris 2003(c), pp. 11–12.
62 Harvey 1984, pp. 244–5 (unrevised from the 1954 edition of *English Medieval Architects*, pp. 217–18); Harvey 1978, p. 77. Harvey, in a noticeably forced argument, stated that Ramsey 'provided small-scale drawings on which the general ordinance of [the works at Gloucester] was based', but admitted ignorance of the master responsible for the detailed design work. On this question see Wilson 1980, pp. 159–60, 225–6.
63 See Harvey 1984, p. 245; Wilson 1980, pp. 168, 374–7 note 1; Wilson 1990, pp. 207–8. The architect of the presbytery and north transept remodelling may have been a West Country man,

Additionally, the miniature lierne vaults, tracery with reticulations and split cusping, and the continuous band of squared quatrefoils of the cresting have lead to an attribution of the design of the choir stalls to either William Hurley (d.1354) or Hugh Herland (d.1405), both royal carpenters.[64] At Bath 150 years later we find royal masons, the Vertues, contracted to build a surpassing fan vault not, it seems, through the offices of Henry VII, but rather at the behest of Sir Reginald Bray and Oliver King. This reminds us that the employment of leading royal artisans on an important project need not involve the Crown directly.[65] In the case of Gloucester, however, Edward III's concern with dynastic image, when taken together with the involvement of his leading masons and carpenters, argues persuasively for direct royal patronage.

The amount contributed to the project by the Crown is impossible to estimate. The fact that the chronicler cites domestic fabric rolls as evidence of the total cost of the third phase of building suggests that the abbot and convent did bear this charge themselves,[66] coming as it did forty years after the heyday of the cult (unless they were provided by the king with a cash grant that was then channelled through the relevant obediences, to appear on their *compoti* as usual). The sums specified at this point – £781 0s 2d and £444 0s 2d – are precise, demonstrating an enduring (given that the chronicle was written c.1400) interest in a 'heroic' programme of works, further evidence of which is found in the margins of the finest surviving manuscript of the chronicle, BL MS Cotton Domitian A viii, fols 126v–161v. A fifteenth-century reader has noted the most important elements of the remodelling in an anglicana formata hand that contrasts markedly with the cursive anglicana text-hand. On fol. 139v we find 'Nota de ala australi' (the south nave aisle, built under Abbot Thoky before 1327), on fol. 140r 'Nota de ala *sancte* andrie [sic]' (the south transept: Plate 41), on fol. 140v 'Nota de magna volta chori', and on fol. 141v 'Nota de ala *sancti* pauli' (the north transept). Other building works are also noted – an example appears in the lower margin of Plate 41 – demonstrating something evident when the text of the chronicle is taken as a whole, namely, that the remodelling of their church was only the most important among a string of thirteenth- and fourteenth-century building works in which the monks and their superiors were engaged (and that had made St Peter's the great and beautiful monastery that it was at the time of writing). The only non-architectural information privileged by prominent marginal annotation is the headings giving the names of successive abbots; and these are in the text hand. The enduring interest that the remodelling held for Gloucester's monks may reasonably be supposed incentive enough for the chronicler's scrutiny of the fabric rolls concerning the first and second phases of the works as well as the third. That we are told nothing of the cost of these campaigns may suggest that the works were taken in hand (partially or wholly) by the Crown, as they were at Westminster in the thirteenth century and Sheen and Syon in the fifteenth, and thus that no expenditure worthy of citation appeared in the monastic accounts. However, this is the most that can be said, and the complete absence of Crown docu-

---

although the fact that Kentish mouldings exist in the former (Morris 2003(c), p. 15) complicates the picture. The simplification of mouldings in the elevations after construction of the south transept may reflect economies rather than a change of architect(s).

[64] Tracy 1987, pp. 47–8. The stalls were locally made, however.

[65] *Correspondence*, p. 4.

[66] *HMGlouc.*, I, p. 50.

mentation about a project that spanned more than four decades remains disconcerting.[67] The obvious caveat that the loan of royal artisans does not demonstrate an injection of royal funds should be kept in mind.[68]

Thus, we are apparently faced with a Benedictine historiographer who sought to disguise royal patronage rather than emphasizing it. Why he did so is problematic, but his occasional unreliability as a witness is not in doubt. It has been proven conclusively, for example, that his testimony to the heroism of Abbot Thoky's expedition to fetch Edward II's body to Gloucester from Berkeley castle is a fabrication.[69] In fact, the Crown paid for the procession to St Peter's, and for the accompanying paraphernalia. Of this there was a great deal, including a carriage embellished by master John de Eastwick with four golden lions, sculpted figures of the four Evangelists, eight censing angels and two large, gilded lions rampant, a wooden effigy of the king embellished with a copper-gilt crown (cost 47s 3d), and a hearse at Gloucester whose decoration required 800 gold leaves. Furthermore, royal ministers rather than Thoky selected Gloucester as the resting place of the murdered king: it was an obvious choice given its proximity to Berkeley, and its immemorial function as a seat of royal ceremonial.[70] A wish to demonstrate conventual self-sufficiency in the remodelling of the church may be supposed to have conditioned the chronicler's testimony,[71] although it should be noted that in his account of the Gloucester parliament of 1378, his claim that Edward I had declared Abbot John de Gammages 'the most reverend ['venerabilis'] man in my kingdom',[72] and at other points, he shows a typical Benedictine interest in advertising positive royal contact with his house.

Another possibility is that the Gloucester chronicler wished to exaggerate the success of Edward II's cult, by emphasizing the fact that the church could, as he has it, 'easily have been completely rebuilt' with oblations,[73] and that this necessitated playing down substantial royal involvement. The fact that the statements and implications concerning the cult receive no strong support from any independent source suggests that they may be artful products of a cult-less house seeking to enrich its sacred history, and perhaps to attract attention thereby.[74] The chronicler's claims bear comparison with

---

67 An oaken parclose with locks to protect Edward II's tomb, cost 8s 9d, is recorded among royal expenses: Moore 1887, p. 226.

68 Ultimately, of course, the possibility exists that these artisans were working freelance.

69 HMGlouc., I, pp. 44–5.

70 Moore 1887, p. 221; Tout 1921, pp. 92–3; Wilson 1980, p. 114. The Crown also granted the monks custody of the convent and retention of the abbatial mensa during voidances in recognition of expenses incurred by them in burying Edward II. On the same occasion it licensed the abbot and convent to appropriate three parish churches, without fining them for the privilege: CPR 1327–30, p. 243.

71 Wilson 1980, p. 115.

72 HMGlouc., I, p. 41.

73 HMGlouc., I, p. 47. To add weight to the claim, and perhaps also to avoid perjuring himself, the chronicler attributes it to popular opinion: 'ut opinio vulgi dicit, quod si omnes oblationes ibidem [i.e. Edward II's tomb] collatæ super ecclesiam expedirentur potuisset, facillime de novo reparari'.

74 This lack of supporting evidence is the more remarkable because the focus of the cult was a king. Ranuph Higden, writing within living memory of Edward's death, reports Edward's popular reputation for sanctity ('De cujus [i.e. Edward's] meritis, an inter sanctos annumerandus sit, frequens in vulgo'): Polychronicon, VIII, p. 324. In 1396 a concerted attempt was made to canonize Edward: Wylie 1894, p. 202. Further, Edward II is designated a saint in some early sixteenth-century sources: MP, p. 153 (v. 15); Cambridge, Corpus Christi College MS 177, fol. 214r (but drawn from Higden:

similar ones found in the first part of the Lanercost chronicle, probably written around 1300.[75] Here, *sub anno* 1272, it is recorded that John, an astrologer of saintly life, was buried in the middle of the choir of St Peter's at Howden, the collegiate church in the East Riding of Yorkshire of which he was a prebendary. He had personally commenced the reconstruction of the choir: after his death a tomb-centred cult ignited such that 'out of the oblations of the crowds of visitors we see not only the choir but also the broad nave of the church being completed'.[76] However, architectural historians have tacitly dismissed this claim, and not without reason. Nicola Coldstream ignores it in her detailed analysis of Howden's architecture and patronage, cogently promoting the bishops of Durham as sponsors of the work.[77] (To the bishops we may reasonably add the canons of Howden.) Sir Alfred Clapham, who also tacitly dismissed the Lanercost chronicler's account, had earlier pointed out the substantial contributions of Walter Skirlaw, bishop of Durham from 1388 to 1406, to the later stages of building.[78] While the Lanercost chronicler did not have the same stake in Howden's reputation as the Gloucester historian had in that of his abbey, his evident desire to promote the reputation of a reputedly saintly individual and his *locus* of burial by exaggerating the part which popular devotion played in the construction of a monumental and sumptuous church (St Peter's Howden was certainly this) constitutes a suggestive analogy here.

Questions can thus legitimately be raised about the accuracy of the patronage information contained in the Gloucester chronicle. They cannot, however, bring us closer to the actual nature or degree of royal involvement in the mid-fourteenth-century remodelling. Nor can they interfere with the fact that the chronicler's account became the accepted version of events, both within and outside the abbey. In 1524, Abbot Malvern repeated the assertion that through pilgrims' oblations 'the south isle of this church/ Edyfyed was and build, and also the queere', in his poem on the foundation of the monastery that hung on public view in the north nave aisle.[79] By this time, what was probably the most important act of royal art and architectural patronage relevant to this study had been forgotten.

Worcester

The patronage circumstances of Prince Arthur's stone-cage chantry chapel (Plate 5) at Worcester are even less distinct, although in the absence of documentary evidence to the contrary the monument may reasonably be assumed a royal responsibility. While the tombs of royalty past were often maintained at monastic expense – at Worcester for example, sacrist Robert Alchurch (d.1532) paid for the tomb-chest on which King

---

see James 1912, I, p. 412); London, Society of Antiquaries MS 476, p. 216 (paginated ms.) (where he occurs as 'Sanct Edward de gloucestre' in a heraldic context). However, this is not strong backing for the chronicler's claims about the remodelling of his church.

[75] The precise date depends on whether one considers this first section to extend to 1297 (Gransden 1974, pp. 495–6) or to 1312: *PJH*, p. xi and note 4.

[76] 'Nam sepultus solemni mausoleo in medio ipsius chori [i.e. John of Howden] habetur pro sancto, et ex oblationibus frequentantium populorum non tantum chorum sed navem ecclesiæ latam videmus compleri et operosam'. *Chron.Lanercost*, p. 93; cf. *PJH*, p. xii note 1. In fact John of Howden died in 1275.

[77] Coldstream 1989, pp. 117–18 *et passim*. Bony 1979, pp. 16, 59–60 – in any case little concerned with patronage – also ignored it.

[78] Clapham 1934, p. 399.

[79] *MP*, p. 153; cf. *Itinerary*, II, pp. 59–60.

John's effigy now rests[80] – those of royalty present were, typically, the obligation of the incumbent monarch or his progeny. Moreover, the enclosure of Arthur's tomb resonates with the only other example of a 'cage'-type royal funerary monument, the bronze chantry chapel of Henry VII and Elizabeth of York at Westminster.[81] Conversely, Arthur's stone-cage chapel strikes one as an intrinsically unlikely product of monastic initiative, and bears no apparent relation to other early sixteenth-century screening or fittings at Worcester in design terms. However, the architecture of the chapel, incorporating openwork crenellations, latticed transoms and three-light windows with two-centred arches displaying unusual foiled reticulations in the heads, is not obviously metropolitan, at least in surface detail. It does not resemble the work of contemporary London designers as seen in, for example, Henry VII's chapel at Westminster,[82] the chapel of King's College, Cambridge, the retrochoir of Peterborough abbey church, the cathedral-priory church at Bath, Prior William Birde's monument in the same building, and the chantry chapels built for Clement Lichfield at All Saints and St Lawrence, Evesham.[83] This lack of resemblance sounds a note of caution, for if the chapel was locally designed, as it was made,[84] then it is conceivable that the Worcester convent did play some part in its patronage. The simplicity of Prince Arthur's tomb-chest may also give pause: it may be a London product, but it is insufficiently distinguished to be attributable to royal patronage on stylistic or qualitative grounds.[85]

It has recently been pointed out that the chapel's vault is close in design to the vaulted oriel of the former abbot's house at Tewkesbury, built during the reign of Abbot Henry Beoley (1509–34).[86] If this similarity indicates a common designer, then the vault at least of the chapel may be ascribable to a West Country mason. However, that it was designed at or near Worcester is very unlikely, because both the monument and the arcade bay which it occupies have been mutilated to ensure a fit, indicating a miscalculation in height and length improbable on site. It remains a reasonable assumption that at least some elements of the chapel were designed in London (or at any rate by London craftsmen), and thus that its patronage was largely if not exclusively royal.[87] Its non-architectural embellishment lends weight to this. A number of its sculpted

---

80 *Itinerary*, V, p. 230: 'Johannes rex, cujus sepulchrum Alchirch sacrista nuper renovavit'. A poem preserved by John Bale (d.1563) dates this to 1529: Engel 2000, pp. 214–15. This chest is evidently modelled on Prince Arthur's.

81 Not counting the iron railings of the Canterbury tombs of Edward the Black Prince and Henry IV and Joan of Navarre, or the screen of Edward II's tomb at Gloucester, which was, it seems, conceived primarily as an extension of the choir screen. Cf. Wilson 2003(a), p. 177.

82 Dow 1992, p. 75, notices a close connection between the chapel and the bronze enclosure surrounding Henry VII's tomb: cf. Duffy, M. 2003, p. 270. Wilson 2003(a) and Tatton-Brown 2003 ignore Arthur's chapel as a comparandum.

83 Cf. Harvey 1984, pp. 307–9. Lichfield's chapels were almost certainly designed by Robert Vertue junior (fl.1506–55: Harvey 1984, p. 307).

84 According to McClure it is built of Painswick (or Bath) limestone: McClure 1912, p. 564. However, more than one type of stone seems to have been used.

85 On Arthur's tomb-chest see Duffy, M. 2003, pp. 268–9.

86 Morris 2003(a), p. 157.

87 The arms of Sir William Uvedale, controller of Prince Arthur's household, may indicate some patronage involvement on his part: Duffy, M. 2003, p. 267. A forthcoming study of the chapel's architecture by Dr Linda Monckton will discuss the possibility that elements of the heraldry indicate non-royal lay patronage. Cf. the discussion of the patronage of the Magnificat window at Great Malvern below, p. 186.

figures are formally too close to sculptures existing in Henry VII's chapel for coincidence.[88] Lawrence Stone thus confidently declared the whole chapel a London product, its sculptures by the same workshop as those of the Westminster Lady chapel.[89] The chapel's heraldry, including the portcullis, the roses of Lancaster and York, the double Tudor rose, the sheaf of arrows (a personal motif of Catherine of Aragon, Arthur's consort), the badge of the Order of the Garter, the open fetterlock with falcon ensconced (also found at Westminster), and the royal arms, and its many statuettes of royal figures (both canonized and otherwise), also smacks of Crown involvement. The five defaced statues of the reredos, which include two unidentified kings (Sts Edward the Confessor and Edmund of East Anglia or Edward the Martyr are the most likely candidates) flanking a Man of Sorrows supported by angels, with Sts George and Antony the Hermit occupying the outer niches, reflect royal iconographical concerns: two royal figures and St George also appear on the reredos of Henry V's chapel at Westminster, and Sts Edward, Edmund of East Anglia, George and Antony are represented among the sculptures of Henry VII's chapel in the same church.[90] For these reasons, and in spite of the total lack of relevant documentation, it seems acceptable to suppose the monument a product of royal patronage.

Prince Arthur died in April 1502, and his chapel is usually said to have been erected in or around 1504.[91] However, a sacrist's *compotus* in the Worcester cathedral archive records the consecration of the chapel's altar by an unidentified suffragan bishop in 1516/17: 'Item *soluti dominus* suffraganis *pro sanctificacione altaris principis Arture* hoc anno vj s. viij d.'[92] (Plate 42, lines 5–6.) If this was a first consecration, as opposed to a reconsecration, then it could be argued that the chapel's patronage rested with Henry VIII and (possibly) Catherine of Aragon rather than Henry VII. However, for a number of reasons this seems unlikely. The time lag is one, the heraldry another, the design seemingly a third: one baulks at dating the screens of the elevation later than 1510. At most, we can entertain the possibility that the components of the chapel were manufactured within a few years of the funeral, but that its erection was delayed for some reason.[93] The chapel was, in fact, never completed.[94] The monument as it stands recalls the melancholy excess of the funeral described in the account preserved by John

88 McClure 1912, pp. 564–5 and interleaved pls; Dow 1992, p. 73.
89 Stone 1972, pp. 227–8. Lindley 2003(a) does not directly contradict this, but cf. pp. 287–8, 291–2
90 Hope 1914, pp. 168–70 and pl. XVIII; Gardner 1951, p. 241 ills 467–9. Gardner 1951, p. 261, believed the reredos of Arthur's chapel a 'reproduction on a smaller scale' of that of Henry V's (which has lost its central image). For the sculptures of Henry VII's chapel see Lindley 2003(a), pp. 266, 281, 286, 287–8, 290, 291; Gardner 1951, pp. 248–9, 253 and ills 478, 483, 493.
91 Mc Clure 1912, pp. 540, 544, 564. See also Green 1796, I, p. 98; Engel 2000, pp. 188, 209, 216. Stone 1972, p. 227, has 'probably . . . about 1504–06', while Duffy, M. 2003, p. 267, tentatively suggests pre-1509. Morris 2003(a), p. 157, is prudent: 'c.1502–16'. These are estimates: as the late Phillip Barker noted, 'the early history of the chantry . . . remains . . . an enigma': Barker 1997, p. 28.
92 WCL Muniment C 429, first sheet, dorse (a paper roll).
93 Phillip Barker thought that the chapel originally stood elsewhere in the cathedral: Barker 1997, pp. 27–8. If true, its relocation could explain the need for reconsecration. However, it is hard to agree with him, for there is no arcade bay of sufficient width to accommodate the chapel beside those of the other angles of the crossing; and clearly it never occupied one of these. Cf. the mutilation of the arcade voussoirs at Gloucester, necessary for the insertion of Osric's monument, mentioned and ill. in Luxford 2002(d), pp. 179–81.
94 McClure 1912, p. 565. MacKenzie 1997, p. 27, considers that the chapel is an assemblage of mostly

Leland.[95] It is a description of which Johan Huizinga would have been proud: a great, colourful, rain-and-mud-drenched, grief-stricken and very public progress from Ludlow castle (where Arthur died) to Worcester, characterized by wailing and floods of tears, the tolling of bells, the dispensation of gold nobles, the glow of countless torches, and the clothing in heraldic escutcheons of every object with which the cortege came into contact. The hearse prepared to receive Arthur's coffin in the cathedral church, forerunner of the chapel itself, was the 'goodliest and best wrought and garnished' that the account's author – presumably a herald with experience of many important funerals – had ever seen: a visual point of reference exists in Abbot Islip of Westminster's hearse (1532) as represented in his obituary roll.[96] The chapel was almost certainly planned under the same impetus as the lavish and mournful funeral. For fear of the plague, Henry VII did not attend the latter, but he certainly paid for it (in total, £566 16s),[97] and may perhaps have seen and approved the plans for the chapel before its erection at Worcester.[98]

Prince Arthur's chantry chapel qualifies as Benedictine art and architecture, and thus as an object of royal patronage, because while it remained Crown property, it became a structural element of the monastic church, part of its ground plan, and a major part of the monks' 'topography'. A superior's tomb, that of Bishop Giffard, was dismantled to accommodate it, and Giffard's effigy encased in its undercroft along with that of Matilda Clifford (d.1301).[99] The chapel thus incorporates an important part of the monastery's collective heritage. It was administered and cared for by monks, and those who attended choir were confronted by it at least eight times a day. However, the art and architectural accoutrements of royal ceremonial as used in Benedictine contexts did not always remain Benedictine in this way. When Prince Arthur was baptized at Winchester in 1486, the cathedral church was bedecked with astonishing richness. An account of the ceremony, given in Leland's *Collectanea*, is preceded by a set of 'ordinances . . . as to what preparation is to be made . . . for the christening of the [royal] child'.[100] The account itself makes it clear that these were observed to the letter. It is demanded that:

> The whole church where the child shall be christened must be hanged with rich Arras or cloth of gold in the best manner, and in like sort shall the altar be arrayed, also, and well carpeted throughout the whole chancel underfoot . . . the porch [of the church] must be hanged and ceiled with rich cloth of gold of Arras work . . . the font must be hanged about with cloth of gold. Over the font must be hanged a great and large canopy of damask, satin or Reynes[101] the underside of cloth of gold, or well embroidered . . . [etc.][102]

Here, however, it may be presumed that apart from the dispensation of a few gifts of the sort mentioned above with reference to Glastonbury, all of this paraphernalia was taken

pre-Tudor elements from more than one source, but this view, tentatively advanced, is discounted here.
95 *Collectanea Leland*, V, pp. 373–81.
96 *Collectanea Leland*, V, p. 378; Duffy, M. 2003, p. 266; Hope 1906, pl. XX.
97 McClure 1912, p. 564.
98 Cf. McClure 1912, p. 564.
99 Strange 1904, p. 69.
100 *Collectanea Leland*, IV, pp. 179–84 (ordinances), pp. 204–15 (baptism).
101 I.e. cloth from Rennes in Brittany: *Linc.Vis.*, II, p. 4 note 1.
102 *Collectanea Leland*, IV, pp. 180–1, cf. pp. 204–6. See also TCC MS 0 2 53, fols 49–53.

away again afterwards. Indeed, the ceremony is said to have cost the host convent a good deal,[103] as must the funeral at Worcester. As noted in chapter two, even the four-day visit of Edward III and Philippa of Hainault to Glastonbury in 1331 cost the monks and their abbot £800, i.e. more than the remodelling of the north transept at Gloucester.[104] While such expenditure was usually a sound investment for the respective convents and their superiors, the benefits did not manifest themselves in terms of art and architectural patronage.

The Patronage of the Nobility

The significance of noble patronage for Benedictines

Royal visitation and burial have emerged as the two main motives for Crown patronage of Benedictine art and architecture. Whatever kings, queens and princes gave on these occasions, they deigned to give, and such gifts were accepted with the gratitude and humility befitting a vassal of the highest secular authority. With the nobility, however, Benedictine monks and nuns were on a more equal social footing, and the decorum governing acts of patronage was correspondingly different. Reciprocity – overwhelmingly in connection with commemoration – now emerges as the defining principle of a relationship that produced a good deal more in terms of building and embellishment than royal associations did, but that also seems to the modern observer to lack the open-handedness on the part of patrons celebrated by Benedictine chroniclers past. William Malvern, in his poem on the foundation of St Peter's at Gloucester, looked back on a lost age of noble munificence with almost tangible nostalgia. 'Whilome Religion in earth was moch loved/ Greatly glorified of many worthy lord', he wrote, reeling off a string of noble associates who had formerly granted to his abbey lands, services and even themselves, as monks.[105] The implication here is self-evident: once upon a time ('whilome') monasticism was esteemed by the nobility, but now it is not.

The issue of declining support has arisen at a number of points previously, and does not require further emphasis. It relates, however, to one of the main reasons that Benedictines had for encouraging noble patronage of their art and architecture during the later middle ages, and this deserves some recognition. This can be given with reference to the art and architectural patronage of Malvern and his convent. The monks of Gloucester were as aware as any of the positive connotations carried by visual proofs of aristocratic favour, and the negative potential of inability to display the same. The most demonstrative of these proofs to which houses with royal rather than noble overlords might aspire was an aristocratic tomb or chantry chapel. Such monuments effectively constituted large-scale, three-dimensional advertisements of the religious integrity, honesty and loyalty of the institution in which they were located, for they declared a conviction that the place of burial would not be interfered with, allowing its incumbent to rise from the spot that he/she had chosen on the Last Day (an issue of particular importance),[106] and that the commemoration necessary to expedite the soul's release

---

[103] Greatrex 1993, p. 158.
[104] CGA(C), pp. 262–3.
[105] MP, p. 153.
[106] Cf. Coulton 1928, pp. 433–5.

from purgatory would be performed as stipulated in the chantry ordinances. Each consti-tuted a resounding vote of confidence of great potential value in an age when competi-tion for external support was strong, and questioning of Benedictine *mores* frequent.

With this in mind, Abbot Malvern and his convent must have cast an emulative eye over the presbytery of nearby Tewkesbury, the Berkeley mausoleum at St Augustine's, Bristol, and those of other monasteries further afield (Westminster being the ultimate referent), cluttered as they were with the monuments of illustrious dead. Some of these monuments – Robert Fitzhamon's, for example – had even been updated to meet con-temporary standards of ostentation. That Tewkesbury and a number of other monas-teries (e.g. Hailes) were under the tutelary patronage of noble families, and were thus at an advantage in attracting noble burials, will not have diminished the ambitions of the monks of St Peter's. It seems that they too desired an east end distinguished by fashion-able monuments, not simply to flaunt their high status and honour past benefactors, but also to advertise the integrity, honesty and loyalty mentioned above. To this end (largely if not solely) they renovated their own presbytery furniture, around the same time that the abbot penned his poem (1524).[107] In addition to the erection of Malvern's own chapel and tomb, the campaign included the installation of Osric's cenotaph, and, quite possibly, the relocation and elevation of Abbot Serlo's retrospective effigy.[108] In the style of its screening, Malvern's chantry chapel was designed to correspond to the parclose surrounding Edward II's tomb, and the choir screens on the south side of the presbytery. The recently renovated tomb of Robert Curthose before the high altar – Gloucester's answer to that of Arthur and Guinevere at Glastonbury, Kenelm at Winchcombe and John at Worcester – must be reckoned integral to the whole. When complete, the ensemble compared with those of Tewkesbury, Hailes, Winchcombe and other noble mausolea, with a space that could have received a further monument left conspicuously vacant opposite the tomb of Edward II for any important benefactor who might wish to negotiate the construction of his own memorial there.[109]

This apparent attempt by the abbot and convent at Gloucester to imitate the displays of aristocratic approbation existing at Tewkesbury and elsewhere complemented less wholehearted efforts on the part of their predecessors, one example of which is the renewal c.1500 of the Curthose tomb-chest, another the installation of the armorials of 'many truly noble men, of the most ancient Gloucestershire families, indeed Clifford, Whittington, Throckmorton, Pauncefoot and many others . . . munificent benefactors ['mæcenates'] in the construction and embellishment of the monastery's buildings' in two rows in the Lady chapel's east window and Abbot Butler's chapel on the north side

---

107 The stylistic and structural consistencies of the work prove it a single project. Malvern's tomb-chest has the pomegranate motif with a 'K' superimposed (for Katherine of Aragon), familiar from Abbot Ramryge's chapel at St Albans and demonstrating a date pre-1530. Yet the abbatial effigy (unless added later) represents a *senex* (Plate 32), whereas Malvern was not yet thirty when elected in 1514. All this argues for a date in the 1520s.

108 The bracket on which Serlo's effigy is set is clearly a later insertion: the jointing of the stonework demonstrates this. While it may have been added before Malvern's abbacy, its position opposite his chantry chapel – a locus of symbolic importance given the veneration afforded Serlo at Glou-cester – suggests that it was added under his auspices. If earlier, one may expect it to have been built one bay further east. Stylistically the bracket does not correspond to any other component of the presbytery furniture.

109 There is apparently no record of a pre-existing monument in this location.

of the ambulatory.[110] That these individuals did contribute to the fabric is questionable (the account quoted from here is dated 1608, and errs in a number of particulars),[111] and the motive for installing their armorials is more profitably sought in the desire to demonstrate noble endorsement to visitors to the two recently built chapels.[112] A grander demonstration of the same desire appeared in the fourteenth-century glazing of the presbytery, Lady chapel, west cloister walk, and vestry at Worcester, which illustrated literally dozens of noble, clerical and royal benefactors, with accompanying inscriptions specifying the donations of each.[113] The majority of these windows were not, as it happens, noble gifts, but they did seek to persuade members of the nobility to render service to and seek burial in the cathedral,[114] which at most would result in the erection of further important monuments, and at least provide the monks with a mandate for augmenting this artistic advertisement of aristocratic support and trust. The value of this glass, and of the tombs and armorial roundels at Gloucester, as advertisements pitched at noble patrons (whose gifts would carry prestige as well as the less edifying pecuniary advantage brought by the benefactions of the sub-nobility) should not be underestimated.

The aim of garnering additional, prestigious sepulchral monuments for the message they sent about conventual virtue and reliability was only one reason that monks and their superiors possessed for seeking noble patronage. Others have been alluded to in previous pages, and need not be dwelt on at length here. Beautification for its own sake and to the glory of God was one: a king, no less, had set the example here with the words 'Lord I have loved the beauty of thy house'.[115] Another was the demonstration of powerful allies in an age fraught with potential difficulties. When, during the early fourteenth century, the abbot of Glastonbury celebrated mass in a red chasuble emblazoned with the Lancastrian arms, he was making an explicitly political statement concerning the support on which he might draw, as well as contributing to the good estate of the earl, vicariously represented in the charges on his back.[116] Handsome mortuary fees and gifts provided monks with a further incentive to seek the burials that constituted the chief occasion for noble patronage. The monks of Tewkesbury, for example, received by the will of Isabella of Warwick (1439) the money from her fillets of peach coloured rubies (which she ordered sold at 'vtmest pryse') that they might 'groche noʒt wᵗ my lyenge'.[117] Far from complaining, they were apparently most willing to receive her tomb.[118] In some cases, such gifts took the form of art and architectural patronage directly. In 1422, Sir Humphrey Stafford willed to the high altar of Abbotsbury a blue velvet cope with gold panels and a chasuble with apparels of blue velvet, each with two

---

110 MA, I, p. 564.

111 OBL MS Wood B 1, fol. 1r. This manuscript tract, the *Memoriale Ecclesiæ Cathedralis Gloucesteriæ Compendarium*, is widely and erroneously said to be lost. However, see Hare 1992, pp. 30–1; Luxford 2002(d), p. 198 note 18. The incomplete edition of it in MA, I, pp. 563–4, is undated.

112 While the superstructure of Abbot Butler's (1437–50) chapel was not new, its fittings were.

113 Thomas 1736, pp. 11–18, 31–2.

114 Cf. Marks 1993, p. 89. Obviously, this display had more than a utilitarian significance for the monks. Its continuation into the vestry is particularly revealing of this.

115 Psalm 26:8: 'Domine dilexi decorem domus tuae'.

116 CGA(C), pp. 250–1; cf. Michael 1997, pp. 55–6 *et passim*.

117 *Earliest English Wills*, p. 116.

118 Cf. Lindley 2003(b), p. 178, where possible reasons for complaint are suggested.

tunicles;[119] while a member of the Carey family left the same convent £40 as a mortuary towards the construction of a new dorter.[120]

This financial motive was particularly important for impecunious houses. At Barrow Gurney during the second half of the fourteenth century, a burial occupying the entire floor of the little chapel connecting the nun's church to the priory was authorized.[121] The location was desirable for the patroness, Lady Joan d'Acton (or her executors), because it was walked over by the nuns and their priest eight times a day. In lieu of a three-dimensional tomb, impossible due to the chapel's function as a passageway, the vault was sealed with a flat monument displaying a large Latin cross and colourful blocks of encaustic tiles. Many of these were heraldic, while others carried the letters 'MR' for 'Mary Regina', to whom the priory was dedicated. A band of tiles running around the edge of the monument bore a variant of a common petition: '+ Dame : Joa+ne : Dactone : Gyst : + Icy : Dieu : de : + Sa Alme en : Eyt : Mercy'. That Berkeley arms appear on the tomb may suggest, as it has been supposed, that Joan had Berkeley connections,[122] but seems more likely to allude to this family's status as patrons of the priory. Such a burial would presumably have been subject to their approval. However, the main advantage probably accrued to the nuns, for whom even a contribution of a few pounds for burial and commemoration would have represented a substantial augmentation of their annual income, estimated c.1535 at approximately £24.[123]

Depending on the pedigree, status and manner of death of the incumbent, a noble-man's monument might also possess value as a pilgrimage site, and this provided Benedictine convents with an additional reason for seeking them. The image of Thomas of Lancaster administered by the monks of St Guthlac's priory at Hereford highlights the remunerative value of association with such a cult. At Evesham, the popularity of Simon de Montfort's cult brought the monks both prestige and money. Indeed, the works of Abbot Brokehampton's time are said by one authority to have benefited from the 'daily' oblations of pilgrims at the earl's (empty) tomb before the high altar.[124] At Tavistock, and indeed up and down England, the Righteous Earl was styled 'sanctus' in liturgical calendars,[125] and the monks of Evesham added 'the killing of Simon de Montfort and his companions' (the latter also reputed thaumaturges) to their *Liber vitæ* under 4 August.[126] While the popularity of the cult was waning by 1300, the monks continued to encourage it: they copied the surviving collection of the earl's 135-odd posthumous miracles after 1323.[127] A century and a half on, Tewkesbury's convent (or perhaps the Tudor regime) found an opportunity to turn another crude killing into the basis of a cult. Henry VI's son Edward fell at the Battle of Tewkesbury in 1471, and was buried at the entrance of the monastic choir, under a slab set with a monumental brass.[128] A contemporary Tewkesbury chronicler called him one 'for whom god

---

119 *Reg.Chichele*, II, p. 621.
120 Hutchins *Dorset*, II, p. 720.
121 The date is uncertain: see Scarth 1883, p. 117; Were 1911, *passim*.
122 Scarth 1883, p. 117.
123 See below, appendix 1.
124 Cox 1988, pp. 21–2, 25. The royal dictum of Kenilworth and papal censure led to disinterment in 1266 or 1267.
125 *Itinerary Worcestre*, pp. 112–13 (Tavistock); Cox 1988, p. 21, for veneration of Simon elsewhere.
126 BL MS Lansdowne 427, fol. 13r; Cox 1988, p. 21.
127 Cox 1988, p. 39 note 137.
128 Rogers 1983, pp. 187–9.

works',[129] and evidence of pilgrimage to the site survives in early sixteenth-century documents, including a handsome oblation of 5s offered by Henry VII's queen, Elizabeth of York.[130] At Glastonbury during the first half of the fourteenth century (and no doubt thereafter), numerous 'secular relics' were displayed on an abbatial tomb immediately to the north of the high altar, along with the remains of major saints. These included 'Carodocus dux Cornubie', 'Elnotus dux' 'Alpharus dux', 'Ethelstanus dux', 'Elwynus dux', and 'Iderus filius Nuti', a number of whom shared King Arthur's tenuous Galfridian pedigree.[131] These examples, only some of those available for the west of England, testify not only to the ongoing and widespread nature of a well-recognized devotional phenomenon, but also to the readiness with which Benedictine convents exploited it when the opportunity knocked.

The significance of noble patronage for the nobility

In turning to the reasons that the nobility had for sponsoring Benedictine art and architecture we are required to acknowledge a distinction suggested above with reference to Prince Arthur's chantry chapel. It is simply this: is a line to be drawn between art and architecture legally belonging to Benedictines, and that located in a Benedictine context but remaining the legal property of lay administrators? It is usually impossible to tell whether an external patron having a monument raised in a Benedictine house considered him or herself to be giving anything by way of art or architecture to that house thereby. It is possible to regard the construction of a chantry chapel or tomb with adjoining altar as essentially a relocation of a private domestic chapel to the site of burial, a point of view somewhat endorsed by the common practice of simply transferring ornaments – liturgical vestments, books, plate, altar-linen and statuary – from one to the other.[132] Gifts in cash and kind would naturally be paid to the monastic hosts for accepting a space-annexing monument into their midst, but the monument itself remained the property of its patron and his or her heirs. A chantry chapel, particularly one in a nunnery church, might even be staffed by a secular rather than a Benedictine priest, who would lock its door after use.[133] As stated above, such monuments and their appurtenances constitute the bulk of our examples of aristocratic patronage; yet can they meaningfully be considered Benedictine?

For the reasons given in connection with Prince Arthur's chapel it is here asserted that they can. Once installed, the monument became part of an artistic whole that was greater than the sum of its parts, one component of a vast *Gesamtkunstwerk* which, as we have seen, increased a house's prestige and the ability of its inhabitants to attract attention and revenues to themselves, as well as serving other functions counting to conventual advantage. A lucid (and distinctly proprietorial) statement of the pride that the sum total of a Benedictine monastery's paintings, sculpture, altars, and sepulchral monuments might engender exists in the tracts *De picturis et imaginibus* etc. and *De altaribus, monumentis, et locis sepulcorum* etc. written by an unknown monk of St Albans

---

[129] Kingsford 1913, p. 377. For the chronicler as a monk see Rushforth 1925, pp. 132–3.
[130] Rogers 1983, p. 188; Marks 2004, p. 186.
[131] GR, pp. 596–7; cf. e.g. HRB, pp. 52–4, 57 (Caradocus), 120 (Iderus).
[132] Oman 1957, p. 11; Rosenthal 1972, p. 86. Many examples are found in medieval wills.
[133] E.g. Reg.Chichele, II, p. 621. Here, however, the key remained with the monks.

in or around 1428.[134] These remarkable documents are not unlike modern guidebooks; the reader is walked around the abbey church, chapter house and cloister, and has various things pointed out to him en route. These things are not only those contributing to the monastery's beauty, but also those that render it essentially unique, that make it St Albans, as opposed to any other ecclesiastical institution. De altaribus contains descriptions of many monuments of noble men and women,[135] woven together with its description of monastic tombs (in which St Albans was apparently exceptionally rich). The picture that emerges from this survey is not one of isolated 'islands' of private property on one hand and monastic sepulchres, altars, images etc. on the other, but rather of an integrated and powerfully Benedictine whole, a monastic environment drawing its prestige, beauty and religious identity from its physical as well as its metaphysical unity.

In any case, Henry VIII's commissioners recognized no distinctions. Claims to private ownership, whether by tutelary patrons or those holding property within monastic houses, were brushed aside at the Dissolution,[136] and monuments of the nobility (and sub-nobility) wrecked or sold along with other objects of internal and external patronage.[137] 'A noble man caullid Philip Fitz Payne was buried and his wife with hym under an arch on the north side of the presbyterie', Leland noted on his post-Dissolution trip to Sherborne, '[but] this tumbe was of late defacid.'[138] This example shows that even where a church was preserved, its lay monuments might be attacked or sold off as part of its monastic trappings. Any objection to the 'utter ruinous suppression' on the grounds of defraud of property was condemned as contrary to a greater good: 'the will and deed of every private man for a common weal may be altered by the supreme authority in every country', the Henrician apologist Thomas Starkey wrote, with reference to this very subject.[139] The royal sale of Tewkesbury abbey church to parishioners in 1543 included not only the superstructure and internal screenage but 'all manner of images, tomb-stones and gravestones'.[140] This example is hardly unique: Reading abbey and the secular college of Stoke-by-Clare provide parallels for the sale of monuments, and in fact a lengthy list could be compiled.[141] To all practical extents, then, monuments were considered part and parcel of the institution that housed them; in destruction as well as construction. Sir Giles Strangeways did manage to retain the Lady chapel at Abbotsbury – usually one of the first elements of a monastic complex to go – as a family mausoleum (it was subsequently destroyed in the Civil Wars),[142] but this was exceptional, and the pathetic submissions of Lord Thomas de la Warr to Cromwell concerning the 'powre chapell' (poor indeed!) that he had lately erected at Benedictine Boxgrove (West Suss.) must have found many echoes in the West Country as Evesham, Glastonbury, Winchcombe and others began to totter.[143]

---

134 AMSA, I, pp. 418–50; Lloyd 1873 passim. For another 'tomb guide', from Augustinian Worksop, see MA, VI, pp. 122–4.
135 E.g. AMSA, I, pp. 435, 437–44.
136 Cf. Youings 1971, pp. 155–9.
137 Lindley (forthcoming) deals with the issue of the destruction of English monuments during the 1530s to 1550s.
138 Itinerary, I, p. 153.
139 See Youings 1971, pp. 168–9, for the quotes.
140 Bennett 1830, appendix 15 (pp. 356–9), at 357.
141 See Preston 1935, pp. 119–21 (Reading); VCH Suffolk, II, pp. 149 and note 6.
142 Long 1931, p. 29.
143 Knowles 1959, p. 293.

The distinction matters for two reasons, the first being that of basic definition. This study is concerned with Benedictine art and architecture, as opposed to that of external associates stored in Benedictine contexts. If physical context be the only criterion for labelling a work 'Benedictine', then the items of plate and other *jocalia* stored by the nobility for safe keeping in monasteries might be considered here too. Second, it conditions our understanding of the nobility's reasons for privileging Benedictine houses with their sepulchres, and gifts such as liturgical vestments and books. The assumption that the nobility thought of their monuments as chattels, exclusive of their context and removable at will, has the potential to alter significantly our conception of a patron's devotional motives, and the bond that obtained between him/her and the convent of choice. The two parties seem less essential to one another's well-being thereby, less intimately bound up in that deeply rooted 'cult of living friends in the service of dead ones' so well described by John Bossy.[144] In fact, patrons did not expect their monuments ever to leave the settings in which they had them built. A nobleman's tomb or chantry chapel was his *post mortem* castle, to remain where it was until the end of the world.

The motives that the nobility had for contributing to Benedictine projects can for the most part be explained in relatively straightforward terms. Tradition, the desire to demonstrate *esprit de corps* and familial unity in death as in life, the prestige attaching to association with and burial in a personal church (even if this was effectively only an aisle or chapel), and the guarantee of the perpetual and profuse commemoration usually forthcoming in such locations were the main considerations for members of the nobility seeking burial in a house traditionally favoured by their forebears. The outstanding example available to this study is Tewkesbury, the chosen sepulchre of Clare, Despenser and Beauchamp earls of Hertford and Gloucester, Gloucester, and Warwick. Other examples are the priory church of Dunster, in which successive generations of the Mohun and Luttrell families were interred, and that of Cowick, which served the Courtenay earls of Devon in the same way for a period during the thirteenth and fourteenth centuries.[145] In these cases, the houses came under the tutelary patronage of those buried within them.[146] Tutelary patronage was not, however, necessary for a Benedictine church or part thereof to serve such a function. The Staffords and Strangeways treated the east end of Abbotsbury abbey church, and the lords of Sudeley a now uncertain part of the east end at Winchcombe,[147] as family mausolea for various periods during the later middle ages.

Along with these motives, it is commonly asserted that such mausolea were initiated and maintained as displays of dynastic power, in the manner of private collegiate churches such as Holy Trinity at Arundel (East Suss.) and St Mary and All Saints at Fotheringhay (Northants). Tewkesbury, for example, has been described as above all 'a monument to the power of a private family . . . a symbol of their temporal might as much as their piety'.[148] Yet this concept requires qualification if it is to make good historical sense. With whom did the power actually lie in these places? The assumption that a

---

[144] Bossy 1983 *passim*, especially pp. 37–42 (quote at 42).

[145] After which they appear to have favoured Exeter cathedral. Forde abbey was traditionally their favoured religious house.

[146] For Cowick as a Courtenay house, see Oliver 1846, p. 153.

[147] Saul 1980, p. 104. In 1364 the lordship of Sudeley passed to the Botelers who apparently favoured the parish church. However, as we will see, Henry Boteler was later buried in the abbey church.

[148] Buchanan 1995, pp. 83–4. Note that in fact, more than one family was involved.

collection of tombs and other dynastic paraphernalia (at Tewkesbury, which may serve as our example here, this extended to stained glass, non-sepulchral micro-architecture, small-scale sculpture, wall painting, manuscripts, tiles, metalwork and weaponry)[149] attested the strength of an individual and his or her family, and that this was a motive for his or her augmentation of it through further acts of patronage, raises more questions than it answers. The power of the earls and their wives – almost all of the external patronage at Tewkesbury seems to have been exercised by the latter – can have been manifested in the following ways. First, the art and architecture they commissioned, as a form of conspicuous consumption, was proof of their wealth. Second – and this also relates to the matter of conspicuous consumption – it demonstrated the ability of the patrons to shorten the dread but necessary purgatorial process. Third, the objects of patronage demonstrated the power to visually dominate a large monastic institution, perhaps (falsely) implying power over monastic affairs in general. The panoply was also a display of dynastic integrity, and of illustrious pedigree, even if (as must have been well known) the power base of the dynasty had diminished substantially between c.1230, when the mausoleum was initiated, and 1439, when Isabella Despenser ordered her tomb, and the pedigree had suffered frequent and occasionally disgraceful interruptions.[150]

However, the monuments huddled around the high altar at Tewkesbury can also be interpreted as the products of patronage motivated by insecurity and dependence. The beseeching female supplicant in the east window (c.1340),[151] and the pleading figures of Edward Despenser atop his chantry chapel (Plate 43), the same knight and his wife Elizabeth within the chapel (below a Throne of Grace Trinity three times their size, c.1390),[152] and Isabella Despenser in the Founders' Book (early sixteenth century),[153] register the humility that anxiety about their *post mortem* fates must have imposed on them. This anxiety was stated with greater clarity in the design of Isabella's tomb, a cadaver tended by free-standing figures of Mary Magdalene, St John the Evangelist and St Antony the Hermit, with 'all a-bowt [the tomb-chest] . . . pore men and wemen In theire pore Array with their bedys In theire handes'.[154] It comes through most powerfully in the minutiæ of the chantry ordinances described in the Founders' Book, and elsewhere. For example, Guy de Brien (d.1390), patron of the ostentatious Perpendicular canopy tomb in the north presbytery aisle, requests masses of seven different dedications each week, plus numerous prayers and doles to be said by and given to numerous individuals on his anniversary;[155] Elizabeth Despenser, wife of Edward (d.1409), provides for seven priests to sing daily mass until her first anniversary, as well as 1000 masses immediately;[156] Sir Hugh Mortimer (d.1416), apparently requesting burial in the Fitzhamon

149 Richard de Clare's (d.1262) tomb was adorned as a shrine by his wife, with precious metals and stones, his sword and his spurs. See OBL Top Glouc d 2, fol. 19r; Luxford 2003(c), p. 59.

150 E.g. the attainder and execution for treason of Hugh II Despenser (1326) and Thomas Despenser (1400).

151 Probably Eleanor de Clare (d.1337) or Elizabeth Montacute (d.1359). The figure may be *ex situ*: see Brown 2003, pp. 187–8.

152 Tristram 1955, p. 256; *Tewkesbury Abbey*, colour pl. 12.

153 OBL MS Top Glouc d 2, fol. 27r. See *Tewkesbury Abbey*, colour pl. 6.

154 *Earliest English Wills*, pp. 116–17. Martindale 1995, p. 170, questions whether the tomb was ever made. For another monument incorporating free-standing statuary see *Gaignières Drawings*, II, p. 56 (no. 1408).

155 OBL Top Glouc d 2, fol. 23r–v.

156 Bennett 1830, p. 175 note †.

chapel, asks for 2000 masses straight away;[157] while Isabella Despenser (d.1439) desires no less than four masses daily, each of different dedication, and funds places at the monastery for extra monks for the purpose.[158] The matter of insecurity must not be over-played here where it appears strongest, for it can be reasonably related to all objects of artistic patronage concerning death and commemoration during the later middle ages; nevertheless, it is worth pointing out as a valid parallel perspective to that usually taken by scholars dealing with Tewkesbury.

Dependence is another matter. The typical historical analysis of Tewkesbury abbey church follows the visual suggestion of the mausoleum and all but ignores the convent. The lack of monastic buildings, and of data concerning them (the site never having been systematically excavated), facilitates this.[159] However, it must be admitted that whatever power the dead earls, their relicts and associates possessed was mediated and to some extent conditioned by the monks who worked, walked and worshipped in a body thirty to forty strong in the self same environment. The presbytery was in fact a very busy place, full of black habits; and no wonder, with so many perpetual chantries concentrated under the one vault. Moreover, the monks actively contributed to the visual splendour of the mausoleum. *They* built the Fitzhamon chapel, after all (1397),[160] produced the Founders' Book with its characterful chivalric imagery,[161] and probably also the crenellated choir and chapel screens with their *cruces ansatæ* like miniature arrowslits. The power on display was as much theirs as it was the nobles', and given that they possessed, according to the *Valor Ecclesiasticus*, the largest annual income of any house covered by this study bar one (£1598), they had both means and licence for a good deal of display. That the earls and their families understood their art and architec-tural patronage in this rarefied, Benedictine context differently to their secular displays of power and prestige (e.g. the castles of Bristol,[162] Caerphilly, Holm Hill, Warwick etc.) is to some extent epitomized by the praying sculpture of Edward Despenser atop the Trinity chapel (Plate 43). This figure is not unique, as has been claimed, but it is rather unusual; at least in the context of English sculpture.[163] Like that of Thomas Erpingham on his eponymous gate at Norwich cathedral priory (1420), and the never made royal effigy that Henry VII ordered placed atop Edward the Confessor's shrine at Westmin-ster,[164] the patron is here unambiguously subservient to a higher power. He renders his

---

[157] *Reg.Chichele*, II, p. 287.

[158] OBL Top Glouc d 2, fols 30v–31v.

[159] Morris 2003(a), *passim*, says what can currently be said on the precinctual buildings.

[160] OBL Top Glouc d 2, fol. 14r.

[161] Luxford 2003(c), pp. 61–4.

[162] For Bristol castle as a temporary Beauchamp seat during Edward II's reign, see *HKW*, II, p. 580.

[163] Pepin 1980, p. 183 claims it is unique. The continental comparanda are more numerous; e.g. the figure of Hans Ehinger (d.1383) by the sacrament house tabernacle in Ulm cathedral, and the now lost sepulchral examples recorded for Roger de Gaignières: see *Gaignières Drawings*, I, pp. 110 (no. 596), 150 (no. 831), 160 (no. 891), 189 (no. 1064); II, pp. 10 (no. 1128), 13 (no. 1149), 15 (1160), 29 (no. 1243), 32 (no. 1259), 45 (1344: royal), 54 (no. 1398), 61 (no. 1442: royal), 70 (no. 1492), 81 (no. 1553), 87 (no. 1588). Lindley 2003(b), p. 171, notices that the figure's taber-nacle is a restoration. For an impression of the original see Kendrick 1950, pl. X (a).

[164] Woodman 1996, pp. 185–6; *Gothic*, p. 359 (Erpingham); Condon 2003, p. 133 (Henry VII's request). Also Stone 1972, pp. 182–4; Martindale 1995, pp. 169–70 note 53. There are many further parallels in contemporary English painting: e.g. Gransden 1982, pl. III; Binski 1995, p. 182 ill. 260; TCC MS B 2 16, fol. 107r; TCC MS B 11 7, fol. 20r (Scott 1996, I, colour pl. 9) etc. Numerous English examples in sculpture may have fallen victim to iconoclasm.

soul, as he does his chapel and its appurtenances, to a God he could hope to reach only through Benedictine agency. The Founders' Book shows Edward somewhat differently, presenting a magnificent seven-branched candelabrum to the (monastic) reader (Plate 44).[165] It is an act of exchange, a jewel of great price for the masses needed to shorten the pains of purgatory. The sword held in Edward's left hand is now redundant, for the transaction requires humility, trust and submission on his part, not a display of temporal power. The principle of reciprocity comes to the fore, and the monk comes into his own.

It is relevant here to remember Isabella Despenser's payment to obviate monastic complaints concerning the erection of her tomb. As stated above, the monks are unlikely to have complained in any case, but Isabella's conviction that they might suggests that they had stood up to their tutelary patrons before, and would do so again if given cause. Tewkesbury's Benedictines were not simply spiritual liverymen, then, but an independent, self-determining and powerful corporation, as their historiography, surviving cartulary, and their abbot's status (admittedly only from 1514) as a spiritual peer, demonstrate as amply as their income. Each act of noble patronage within their church did contribute to an overall expression of the earldom of Gloucester's, and later Warwick's, historical integrity, financial capability, piety and influence over monastic affairs, and was almost certainly conditioned by a desire to do so.[166] The famous representations of past earls in the clerestory windows of the presbytery, which manifest a typical chivalric willingness to serve God militarily,[167] demonstrate all of these things. There may also have been a desire to rival the architectural display of Hailes and Westminster.[168] However, the driving motivation behind this patronage was that of speeding the progress of souls, in some cases unshriven ones, through purgatory, a task contingent on monastic mediation. There was a concomitant desire to honour and please God through the embellishment of his house (indeed, the Founders' Book stresses the beauty of the monuments, not their status as symbols of power), the multiplication of divine service, and the support of the monks his servants, in whose hands the care of their souls rested. These motives underlie most acts of noble and sub-noble patronage, and may be reasonably considered a determining factor in the construction and choice of location of even those tombs in West Country Benedictine churches erected by unknown patrons. The latter include the 'sunken' chantry chapel on the south side of the presbytery at Great Malvern,[169] the fragmentary 'weeper' tomb of c.1370–1400 at Little Malvern (part of what was in the seventeenth century one of Worcestershire's greatest surviving collections of medieval monuments),[170] and the magnificent ogee-arched mural recess in the south transept at Romsey, which must date c.1300–30 on stylistic grounds,[171] and is the finest tomb surviving from any nuns' church covered by this study.

Acts of noble patronage could also be determined by the decorum of gift-giving

---

165 OBL MS Top Glouc d 2, fol. 24r. The implicit comparison is with Judas Maccabaeus, one of the Nine Worthies (Edward was a renowned warrior: see Froissart, pp. 107–9). Cf. I Maccabees 4:49; Strauss 1959, p. 6; Luxford 2003(c), p. 63.

166 Although not all noble patrons of Tewkesbury were earls or their wives (e.g. Guy de Brien, Lord Welwyn).

167 In this they closely resemble the sword-grasping effigies of so many tombs.

168 Morris 1974, p. 144.

169 Luxford 2002(e), fig. 231.

170 Habington, II, p. 190; Downing 2002, pp. 170–2, cf. pp. 193–4.

171 Luxford 2002(e), fig. 87. The monument itself will not have belonged to an abbess, whose sepulchres were typically very modest.

discussed with reference to royalty. Works of art were commonly given as tokens of respect and perhaps affection between equals. Wills and other documents often mention items passed on or assigned to a particular purpose by an owner who had himself received them as a gift. Edward Despenser, lord of Tewkesbury, bequeathed to Nicholas Lytlyngton, abbot of Westminster (1362–86), a drinking vessel (*hanaper*) given to him by the abbot of Glastonbury, presumably Walter de Monington: this example is particularly suggestive of the equality in terms of dignity and social status that obtained between the country's lay and monastic elite.[172] Again, in Monington's *Declaracio*, which demonstrates an interest in provenancing aristocratic gifts, it is stated that he had given his convent 'a silver-gilt image of the Virgin Mary weighing in all four pounds thirteen shillings and seven pennyweights, gift of the earl of Salisbury.'[173] (Plate 31, lines 20–2.) Exactly what motivated William or John de Montague (whose earldoms coincided with Monington's abbacy) to give the statue to the abbot is not known, but the fact that it is acknowledged as a gift to Monington alone suggests that it was a private offering made at a personal level, and not by way of restitution.[174] Perhaps the dedication of Glastonbury conditioned the iconography in this case, for in the will of Bishop Cobham (1317–27) of Worcester, whose cathedral priory was also dedicated to the Virgin Mary, we find another silver statue of the mother of God, 'gift of the abbot of St Augustine's, Bristol', assigned to the episcopal chantry altar.[175] Humphrey Stafford (d.1442 or 1443), buried at Abbotsbury, left a similar image to Salisbury cathedral, which shared this dedication.[176]

Political associations and the prestige attaching to them will also have stimulated noble gift-giving. Bishop John Alcock of Worcester had the royal family of Edward IV represented in the east window of Little Malvern priory as a statement of support for a king whom he served as Chancellor of England. Much of the glass, attributable to the wide-ranging workshop of Richard Twygge and Thomas Wodshawe, is gone; but figures representing Prince, later King, Edward V and his sisters survive to register the strength of Alcock's feeling, and perhaps the depth of his strategy.[177] The gift of pontifical ornaments to the abbot and convent of Gloucester by the duke of Gloucester, although here counted as a royal benefaction (for as noted above the duke was Edward III's youngest son), suggests a phenomenon about which we would know more if previous donors were named in inventories and catalogues of abbatial largesse. The duke had supported the petitions to Rome for a grant of *pontificalia* by John Boyfield (1377–81), and those that he gave to Walter Froucester were, according to the domestic chronicle, the first worn by an abbot of Gloucester.[178] They were thus highly symbolic, for the duke as well as the monks, whose influence with the convent and prestige in general were enhanced by having effectively mitred one of the most powerful ecclesiastics in a region under his

---

[172] *ELW*, p. 44.

[173] TCC MS R 5 16, p. 255: 'ymaginem be*atie* marie argent*eam* et deaur*atam* de dono com*itis* sar*um* pond*eris* in grocis iiij li. xiiij s. vij d.' For some reason a later hand has crossed out the weight and written 'vacat' in the margin.

[174] It would have been an unorthodox form of payment for prayers. Normally cash or plate was given, and to the abbot and convent. It may be noted that at TCC MS R 5 16, p. 253, we find 'unum par de bedes puri auri de dono comitisse sar*um*' recorded as a gift.

[175] Thomas 1736, p. 150.

[176] *Reg.Chichele*, II, p. 620.

[177] Marks 1993, p. 42; *Gothic*, p. 176 and pl. 19.

[178] *HMGlouc.*, I, pp. 56–7.

auspices. Henry Boteler, lord of Sudeley, roofed in lead the entire abbey church of Winchcombe (c.1460–70), and was later interred in St Nicholas's chapel behind the high altar, by the side of St Coenwulf (d.821).[179] While the motive in this case was probably a commemorative one primarily, the symbolic connotations of roofing such a venerable portion of God's estate and negotiating a sepulchre next to its founder (a canonized Mercian king) must have garnered the patron a good deal of local prestige. That it won him influence with Winchcombe's other lord, the abbot, is implied by the location of his tomb.

Ecclesiastical lords occasionally contributed to Benedictine art and architecture out of a sense of pastoral duty. Thus Cardinal Beaufort willed £200 towards the fabric of the dilapidated Hyde abbey.[180] Earlier, William of Wykeham had assigned £40 to Romsey for work on the nuns' church and cloister, as well as contributions to other, non-Benedictine, conventual fabrics.[181] Thomas Polton, bishop of Worcester (d.1443), was less expansive, willing 40s to the nuns of Cannington 'for the repair of their priory', but his gift will still have been welcomed at a house whose annual income c.1535 was about £39.[182] Walter de Stapledon, bishop of Exeter (1308–26), bequeathed £4 towards the tower of Athelney abbey church, which was being rebuilt at the time.[183] In these and many further cases, we cannot be certain that the money was used for the stipulated task,[184] but the patrons certainly regarded themselves as builders.

These are only the most obvious motives that the nobility had for patronizing Benedictine art and architecture. There were, demonstrably, many others: the spirit of emulation, for example, created a powerful impulse. When in 1375 Hugh de Courtenay (d.1377), ninth earl of Devon, had a stone-cage chantry chapel raised for himself and Margaret de Bohun (d.1391), his wife, in the nave of Exeter cathedral, he established a precedent apparently followed by Elizabeth Despenser, patron of the Trinity chapel at Tewkesbury.[185] On surviving evidence, these are the two earliest examples of this ultra-prestigious class of monument built for lay patrons. Ultimately, as with royal patrons, the Benedictine status of a convent is unlikely to have been all that influential in the matter of gift-giving. Many members of the West Country nobility had extensive 'spiritual portfolios', the individual elements of which they considered revenue and prestige-generating property first and foremost. Their choice of sepulchre was conditioned by a mixture of pragmatism and idiosyncrasy that rarely seems to have taken account of the precise colour and calling of the monks and other ecclesiastics beholden to them. In the event, Hugh de Courtenay chose burial in Exeter cathedral,[186] yet he was tutelary patron of Benedictine Cowick, the Cluniac priory of St James at Exeter, and the Cistercian abbeys of Buckland and Forde, too, and in theory might have chosen any of them for his interment.[187] Certainly, his loyalties lay no more with the Benedictines than with their reformed colleagues, the Cluniacs and Cistercians. Some patrons may

179 Itinerary, II, p. 54; Landboc, II, p. xliv.
180 VCH Hampshire & I.W., II, p. 119.
181 Test.Vet., p. 770.
182 Reg.Chichele, II, p. 488; K&H, p. 253.
183 Hugo 1897, p. 125.
184 Cf. Smith 1951, p. 218.
185 Cook 1947, p. 104; Orme 1986(a), p. 25. The chapel (but not the tomb, for which see Death and Memory, pl. 9) was destroyed during the early nineteenth century.
186 He was steward to the bishop of Exeter: Prideaux 1934–35, p. 120.
187 For the diversity of Hugh de Courtenay's spiritual revenues see Prideaux 1934–35, pp. 164–5.

have opted for burial in a black monk or nun house due to the order's age and strength, for age and strength stood tall in the historical and devotional imagination of the later medieval nobility. However, if this was the case then we have no record of it, and it seems more likely that the historical interests of patrons such as Henry Boteler of Sudeley focused on the pedigree and associations of particular houses rather than the Benedictine order *per se*. From a historical point of view, Winchcombe was attractive to him because it was demonstrably a Mercian royal mausoleum and tomb of saints: that it was a limb of the oldest, richest and strongest monastic order was presumably of less importance.

Examples of noble patronage

It goes without saying that a patronage study is as much about human psychology and behaviour as it is about art and architecture. Thus the subject of motives – Benedictine motives for seeking noble patronage and the nobility's motives for sponsoring Benedictine art and architecture – has been dealt with at some length. However, a fuller description of some of the examples glanced at in the foregoing discussion, plus a few not yet mentioned, is required to bring the profile of noble patronage into a relief that will satisfy the art historian as well as the historian. The panoply at Tewkesbury deserves to come first and occupy most attention, for when those elements recorded but now lost are taken into consideration, it will be seen to have constituted one of the most important noble mausolea in the country.

Tewkesbury

Excluding the hapless Prince Edward and the five nobles buried in the abbey after the massacre of 1471,[188] at least twenty-four noble men and women were buried at Tewkesbury between the Conquest and the Dissolution.[189] Nineteen of these interments occurred after 1300, and most were originally crowned by important monuments. Between c.1315 and the 1360s much of the church was remodelled and extended through the addition of a five-bay Lady chapel, related architecturally to the very beautiful Decorated work of Pershore abbey's crossing tower.[190] It was reglazed, retiled and refurnished during the same period: all of this work was of notably high quality. In the second quarter of the fifteenth century, an important, iconographically secular sculptural programme representing nobility associated with the abbey was produced, which became a source for the illustrations of the Founders' Book, the surviving pre-Dissolution copy of which belongs, as noted in chapter one, to the period c.1500–10. The text and heraldry of this book derive from a short chronicle occupying the dorse of an armorial roll (the recto has a standard pedigree of Henry VI, with fifty-three minor illustrations),[191] made c.1476 and representing the descent of the founders and tutelary

Forde and the collegiate church of Tiverton both contained Courtenay tombs: Oliver 1846, pp. 317, 338.

[188] Kingsford 1913, pp. 377–8; Rushforth 1925, *passim*. Fifteen knights were buried in or around the church on the same occasion.

[189] See the table in Blunt 1898, pp. 129–30. One heart burial, of Isabella Mareschall (d.1240), is also recorded.

[190] Morris with Thurlby 2003, pp. 119–20.

[191] OBL Lat misc b 2, roll: see *Catalogue OBL*, V pt. 2, p. 835; Pächt & Alexander 1966–73, III, p. 78. Almost all the illustrations are 'portraits' of kings.

patrons of Tewkesbury abbey.[192] The presence of certain charges otherwise unique to the 'Warwick' rolls of John Rous (c.1411–91), and the exceptional use of an armorial 'key' to the identity of the arms in the schemes of quarterings given in the roll, indicate that Rous himself may have been involved in this work.[193] The original text, however, is certainly a Benedictine product, for the writer uses the first person plural when speaking of the convent. The matter is important from the point of view of patronage, as Rous was in the employ of the earls of Warwick,[194] sometime tutelary patrons of Tewkesbury. If he did work on the roll then it would suggest not only their sponsorship of this comparatively minor enterprise but also their interest in the history of the abbey and their place in it, as heirs of Oddo and Doddo, legendary dukes of Mercia. Such an interest would in turn inform our understanding of the objects patronized by them.

The only documented elements of this display that survive are those mentioned in the Founders' Book. Tombs and chantry chapels, along with some ephemera given by the lords of Tewkesbury and their associates (chiefly vestments and metalwork), are recorded therein as abbatial monuments and bequests are in the domestic chronicles of Evesham, Glastonbury and Gloucester. There is no reason whatsoever to doubt that these were products of noble patronage. Of the Clare tombs only fragments survive, saving the gravestone and casement of the elaborate brass of Maud de Burgh (d.1315) in the presbytery.[195] The patronage of the Despensers is represented by the Trinity chapel with its *priant* figure of Lord Edward (Plate 43), the fragmentary tomb of Hugh II (d.1326) in the ambulatory,[196] and the complex Perpendicular canopy tomb of Hugh III and Elizabeth Montacute, presumably built around the time of the former's death in 1349 when the remodelling of the presbytery was complete, and referring in its canopy to Edward II's tomb at Gloucester (Plate 15). In elevation the canopy is just as complex as its royal equivalent, and arguably as successful. It depends less on the ogee, relying instead for its formal and spatial dynamic on a subtle alternation of planes in the second and third registers, the two intermediate bays of the second being set marginally further back, and rising higher, than the main three. The third register follows the arrangement of a central bay flanked by narrower and lower lateral bays (here recessed) seen in English funerary monuments from Crouchback's (d.1296) at Westminster to William of Waynflete's (d.1486) at Winchester, with a further canopy rising higher yet: the monument thus increases to a crescendo, unlike Edward II's, which terminates in three pinnacles of uniform height. (Both canopies are to some extent conditioned by their architectural contexts.) The airiness and delicateness of the whole are never compromised (unlike the canopy of Guy de Brien's monument opposite, which incorporates the screen into which it is built), and the whole appears to float over its alabaster incumbents and the embattled chest they lie upon. This is the patronage of the West Country nobility at its most aesthetically refined.

The Beauchamp (or Warwick) chantry chapel two bays west of the Despenser tomb on the presbytery's north side is another remarkable example of the aesthetic ambitions

---

192 The chronicle is continued in a later hand to c.1480.

193 Information from Mr John A. Goodall, who is currently editing the roll. The roll's devisor had ecclesiastical connections and a special knowledge of the earldom of Warwick's heraldry. It is far-fetched to suppose that two such men existed. See *Tewkesbury Abbey*, colour pl. 5.

194 For Rous's career see Gransden 1982, pp. 309–27.

195 Countess Maud was wife of Gilbert III de Clare, last of the Clare earls (d.1314).

196 On this important but little-discussed monument see Lindley 2003(b), pp. 163–5.

of noble patrons (Plate 4). It was built over the sepulchre of Richard Beauchamp by Isabella Despenser, his wife: the Founders' Book records its consecration in 1423, the year after his death.[197] An unmistakable desire to outshine the presbytery's pre-existing monuments caused an unusual and precocious design, incorporating a hybrid lierne-fan vault with proto-pendants, an upper storey over the western part of the chapel apparently designed for no utilitarian purpose,[198] and three monumental image niches in the west wall.[199] Two of these may have contained praying images of the patron and her husband facing east.[200] Alternatively, the niches may have housed images of the chapel's three patron saints, Mary Magdalene, Barbara and Leonard. Heraldry clothes the dado and quatrefoil roundels above the doors, and there are twelve image niches, now damaged, on the blind panels of the lateral elevation at either end of the chapel. The bays are of uneven length, which coupled with the experimental vault design give the whole a less symmetrical appearance than the canopy tombs and other, boxier stone-cage monuments in the presbytery. It is by virtue of this deliberate imbalance as well as its size and refinement that it stands out.

The secular sculptural programme mentioned above belonged to this chapel, and with its context can be safely assigned to the patronage of Isabella Despenser (Plate 18).[201] It comprised twelve statues, each approximately 70 cm in height, which occupied the niches at either end of the chapel's lateral elevations: they were thus arranged vertically in trines. This series is likely to have begun with Robert Fitzhamon (d.1107), the Norman lord promoted in the abbey's institutional histories as its re-founder, and to have included the following tutelary patrons down to Isabella Despenser's lifetime: Robert the Consul, first earl of Gloucester (d.1147); William Fitzcount, the second earl (d.1183); Gilbert I de Clare (d.1230); Richard II de Clare (d.1262); Gilbert II de Clare (d.1295); Gilbert III de Clare (d.1314); Hugh II Despenser; Hugh III Despenser; Edward Despenser (d.1375); Thomas Despenser (d.1400); Richard Despenser (d.1414). It is possible that Richard Despenser, who is not illustrated in the Founders' Book, was not part of the series, and that either Prince (later King) John (d.1216) or Richard I de Clare (d.1217), both of whom do appear, was included instead.[202] As such, the monument represented a grand example of the so-called 'kinship' class recently elaborated by Anne McGee Morganstern.[203] Like the armorial roll with its Rous associations, the production of these statues suggests a particularly close identification with the historical associations of Tewkesbury on the part of their patron, because it demonstrates her interest in setting herself and her dead husband at the head of an illustrious series of tutelary patrons. Although they do not appear to have been represented among the external sculptures (the suggested programme was deliberately retrospective), Isabella and Richard Beauchamp may, as noted, have been embodied by images in the niches in

---

[197] OBL Top Glouc d 2, fol. 28r. In fact the year 1433 is given, but this is clearly a mistake: see Luxford 2003(c), pp. 60, 294 note 52.

[198] Hudson 1910, p. 66, thought it supported a wooden statue.

[199] On the chapel's design and stylistic associations see Monckton 2004, pp. 38–40; Morris with Thurlby 2003, pp. 129–30.

[200] Lindley 2003(b), p. 174.

[201] On these sculptures and their relation to the chapel see Luxford 2004(a), pp. 8–9 et passim (including ills of all identifiable fragments); Lindley 2003(b), p. 175; Morris with Luxford 2002, passim; Hudson 1910, pp. 64–5.

[202] See Luxford 2004(a), p. 9; Morris with Luxford 2002, p. 88.

[203] Morganstern 2000, pp. 3–9 et passim.

the west end of the chapel's upper stage; and in any case were represented via patronage, burial and inscription.[204]

The figures were smashed during the sixteenth or seventeenth century, but enough pieces of them were recovered during the nineteenth to permit reconstruction of the iconographic scheme. Comparison of them with the Founders' Book shows that they were a model followed by the manuscript's monastic illustrator.[205] They were not his only source. In four cases, he included the wives of early earls seated alongside them: the sculptor represented only single standing figures. Fragments exist for at least nine secular figures, eight of which can be identified with confidence (two via inscriptions).[206] The Founders' Book has twenty-three single figures and couples, plus the representation of Isabella Despenser on her deathbed noticed in chapter one. It is possible that other sculpted or painted imagery within the abbey provided models for the Founders' Book's artist and that this, too, was the product of noble patronage. At least one image of a tutelary patron – presumably a sculpted one – is recorded above a choir stall, identified by an inscription in gold letters.[207]

If the patronage of these sculptures and monuments is unproblematic, then that of the architecture is not. The work is now utterly undocumented, although, as will be noted, there can be no reasonable doubt that at least some of it was paid for by the tutelary patrons. Beginning in the second decade of the fourteenth century, the abbey church was extensively remodelled in four overlapping phases, recently defined and analyzed by Richard Morris.[208] Phase I (c.1315–28) included the construction of the chevet and Lady chapel, plus vaulting and the erection of arcade arches in the presbytery aisles and eastern chapels of the north transept. Phase II (c.1322–37) saw the demolition of the Romanesque presbytery (excepting the six sanctuary piers, which were retained but shortened) and its rebuilding in a West Country Decorated idiom, including a complicated lierne vault. Phase III (c.1335–49) incorporated the revaulting of the nave and nave aisles with lierne vaults, and their decoration with a major series of historiated bosses.[209] It also included the construction of the great west window, whose original design was probably influenced by the early Perpendicular window of Gloucester's south transept, and the glazing and furnishing of the east end. Finally, Phase IV (1350s and 1360s) embraced vaulting of the crossing, revaulting of the transept arms, and other relatively minor works necessary for the stylistic integrity of the new work. Building is likely to have continued into the last quarter of the fourteenth century, and extended to the monastic precinct. Outstandingly, a sumptuous new cloister was begun late in the fourteenth century or early in the fifteenth.[210] This was evidently based on Gloucester's, for the remaining blind tracery replicates that of the windows of the south,

204 A later inscription on the chapel records Isabella's patronage, and the place and date of her death: Lindley 2003(b), pp. 173–4.
205 On the manuscript's illustrator see Luxford 2003(c), p. 62; Luxford 2004(a), p. 11.
206 One of these eight fragments is now missing. Happily, it was published immediately after discovery: see Georgius 1824, pp. 308–9 (with ill.).
207 See Blunt 1898, p. 62.
208 Morris with Thurlby 2003, pp. 117–27. See also Bony 1979, pp. 51–2, 87 notes 23, 25.
209 See Cave 1929, *passim* and Morris and Kendrick 1999, pp. 3–16 for the bosses.
210 A minor lay bequest towards completion of the 'cloister at Tewkesbury' is recorded c.1503: Leedy 1980, p. 207; Morris 2003(a), p. 149. However, as the cloister was dilapidated at this time (Betty 2003, p. 67), this would seem to relate to repair, not construction.

west and north walks at St Peter's, and the remnants of conical springers panelled with mouchettes, indicating a fan vault, are also identical.[211]

To date, art and architectural historians have been content to ascribe the patronage of this work wholesale to the tutelary patrons. In doing so, they have mostly followed a seminal article published by Richard Morris in 1974, which established a chronology for the works that was tied to the careers of the tutelary patrons and their wives.[212] According to this, Hugh II Despenser conceived the remodelling in a spirit of emula-tion, intending to match the splendour of Hailes and Westminster; for was he not on a social par with the earl of Cornwall and a financial one with the king? A lag perforce followed his attainder and execution, but another campaign was begun during the early 1330s, funded by Eleanor de Clare, her second husband William de la Zouche, and subsequently her son Hugh III Despenser. The vaults of the transept were erected after Hugh's death, and, later still, Guy de Brien built that over the crossing, as the existence of his arms in the vaulting witnesses.[213] The monks are to be credited with nothing whatsoever.[214]

In a recent study, Dr Morris has revised both his chronology and his views on the architecture's patronage. He now posits significant involvement on the part of the convent, and tentatively ascribes a commissioning role to superiors such as Thomas Kempsey (1282–?c.1328).[215] In the current author's view this is entirely reasonable. It is overwhelmingly likely that the rich and self-important monastic chapter at Tewkesbury made a crucial contribution to the project's patronage. There is little point in appor-tioning responsibility where there can be no certainty either way, although it is worth pointing out that the Founders' Book, which makes much of other benefactions by the tutelary patrons to the monks, is completely silent on the subject of the remodelling. As its writer's agenda is to lionize founders rather than abbots, this omission cannot be accounted for in the manner that the Gloucester chronicler's silence may be. With this said, it will be admitted that to posit total monastic patronage of the architecture on such slight, negative evidence would be radical. Although the abbot and convent may well have funded the cloister and the choir furniture themselves, the Despensers and their successors are very likely to have played an important role in bringing the plan and elevation of Tewkesbury abbey church into line with that of Hailes, Westminster, and ultimately Gloucester.[216] It is worth noting (as does Dr Morris) that the tomb of Hugh III Despenser occupies the position immediately to the north of the high altar in the remodelled presbytery. This suggests that he may have considered himself (or else been considered by others) a 'second founder', worthy of interment beside the first founder, Robert Fitzhamon.[217] If this was the case, then it is indicative of an important role in the abbey's architectural patronage.

---

[211] Morris 2003(a), pp. 148–9.

[212] Morris 1974; cf. e.g. Bony 1979, p. 37; Crossley 1987, p. 71; AoC, p. 416; Buchanan 1995, pp. 83–4.

[213] Morris 1974, pp. 142–6.

[214] Indeed, they are only mentioned once in Morris 1974, at p. 144 note 9.

[215] Morris with Thurlby 2003, pp. 117–27: for patronage see 125–6. No terminus for Kempsey's abbacy is known: HRH, p. 74.

[216] Gloucester's nave already had a Gothic vault, of course, completed in 1242 '[per] virtute monachorum': HMGlouc., I, p. 29.

[217] Morris with Thurlby 2003, p. 125. The current author has reached this conclusion independently.

Other examples

The case of Tewkesbury highlights many of the problems with discussing patronage where monuments and architecture are plentiful but documentation is lacking. Experience of such problems is a rare luxury, however: for the most part, jejune documentation informs us about glories lost. The existing information on the mausolea at Abbotsbury and Cowick is relatively unambiguous where patronage is concerned, but one is hard put to envisage the works described by it, particularly because the churches themselves have vanished. At Abbotsbury, where the convent's annual income was less than a quarter of Tewkesbury's,[218] the monuments of noble men and women clearly contributed significantly to the artistic whole. The large, early fourteenth-century, double gravestone of Thomas and Eleanor de Luda (now divided between the parish churches of Askerswell and Whitchurch Canonicorum) was originally inset with elaborate Decorated canopies, foliate crosses, and Lombardic inscriptions in latten. Given the rare prominence afforded to the couple's obits in the calendar of the abbey's breviary (both graded *in albis*), we are entitled to suppose that it occupied a position of prominence, perhaps close to the high altar and the tomb(s) of the abbey's Anglo-Saxon founders, Orcus and Tola (whose obits are graded *in cappis*).[219] On surviving evidence, the chapels and monuments of the Stafford and Strangeways peers and their wives were more ostentatious than this. Humphrey Stafford's will (1442) informs us that he had recently paid for the construction of a chapel dedicated to St Anne ('nuper edificate per me') in the east end of the conventual church, in which he desired burial.[220] This chapel adjoined another, of St Andrew, which already housed the tombs of his parents, first wife and some of his children. By the mid-fifteenth century, then, the number of noble monuments at Abbotsbury was already considerable. The list of ornaments left by Sir Humphrey for his chantry is long and revealing of the patron's concerns: a rich complement of silver-gilt liturgical plate, a large crucifix with images of Mary and John, an image of St Agnes, 'two parti-coloured damask cerecloths, red and blue, called reredos and frontal . . . to be placed over the altar',[221] a missal and a breviary following the Use of Sarum, and a number of fine mass vestments. If all of the chantries at Abbotsbury were so richly appointed – and that of Sir Humphrey Stafford the elder (d.1413), at least, is bound to have been[222] – then the east end of the church must have preserved something of the atmosphere of Tewkesbury.

Cowick, as an alien priory standing on the flood-prone river Exe, suffered much disruption during the later middle ages, and its Courtenay tombs must have provided one of the main rallying points in its struggle for survival. When Hugh, Lord Courtenay, died at Colyton (Dev.) in 1291, he was taken to Cowick for burial despite the fact that three of his children were interred in Colyton parish church. His widow Eleanor died in London in 1328, and she too was taken to Cowick. Their daughter-in-law Agnes

---

218 Approximately £390 annually *c.*1535 (see below, appendix 1).

219 Blair 1987, p. 147 (fig. 150: slab); LPL MS 4513, fols 3r (obits of Thomas and Eleanor de Luda), 3v, 6r (obits of Tola and Orcus). Only two further obits appear in the calendar, of which one is abbatial (fol. 5v: probably Roger de Brideton (d.1258), *in albis*), the other lay (fol. 5r: Alice Russell, *in albis*).

220 *Reg.Chichele*, II, pp. 620–3.

221 'Duos pannos cericos bipertitos rubeos et blodios de damaske vocatos reredos et frontell' . . . ad ponendam super altare': *Reg.Chichele*, II, p. 621.

222 Though his will is uninformative: SMW(c), pp. 312–13.

(d.1340), wife of Hugh de Courtenay, eighth earl of Devon, was buried 'with great honours' close to them, while the earl himself, grief-stricken, lingered only a few months and was also received by the prior and monks. The account of his funeral in Bishop Grandisson's register provides an immediate picture of the importance of such burials for small houses.[223] The earl's body was processed from Tiverton to Exeter cathedral with great pomp, and from there to little, impecunious Cowick, accompanied by a great many lay and ecclesiastical dignitaries including the bishops of Exeter and Salisbury, and the abbots of Cistercian Buckland, Premonstratensian Torre, and Benedictine Milton and Sherborne. The earl's will, with its declaration of favouritism for the priory, was publicly exhibited, and the body laid in a tomb whose appearance is unknown, but which is reasonably thought to have been magnificent.[224] Cowick's chancel must have been cluttered: the nave is unlikely to have been used for such burials.[225] All that remains of this, one of the West Country's greatest collective acts of noble patronage, is a selection of encaustic tiles decorated with images of vested priests and the Courtenay arms.[226] An imposing granite coffin with a foliate cross on its lid, unearthed from a collapsed vault on the site of the priory church's chancel, has been connected with Courtenay patronage, but may equally have been intended for a prior.[227]

Dunster has fared better, although much has still been lost. On the south side of the chancel is a mural tomb with elaborate ogee canopy over, containing the sandstone effigy of a woman, probably Ada, wife of Sir John III de Mohun (d. c.1324).[228] The soffit of the cinquefoil arch is moulded in three orders, and each of the four foils of the open cusping carries a staring, sculpted head: apparently a variant of the 'weeper' idea.[229] There is a trefoil in the main spandrel, the extrados is richly crocketed, and the whole framed by two small, panelled piers with crocket and finials. To the immediate north of the high altar stands the handsome tomb of Sir Hugh I Luttrell (d.1428), a typical Perpendicular monument, its horizontal canopy richly brattished, the many foils of its cusped and sub-cusped arch carrying foliage and angels bearing escutcheons.[230] The quatrefoil-panelled tomb-chest also has shields, four each side, all of them blank. This tomb now houses two effigies: that to the south, a high quality but badly damaged knight in alabaster, represents its incumbent.[231] These monuments strike the aristocratic notes in an otherwise decidedly parochial interior. In the south chancel aisle is an *ex situ* gravestone of coarse local alabaster, displaying a coarse, probably locally engraved effigy and marginal black-letter inscription.[232] This belongs to Elizabeth Courtenay (d.1493), wife of Sir James Luttrell (d.1461), and while of considerable intrinsic interest, it represents an undisguised economy when compared to its precursors by the high altar.[233] By nature and by date it recalls the 'once upon a time' of Abbot Malvern, and it is note-

---

223 *Reg.Grandisson*, II, pp. 939–40.
224 Oliver 1846, p. 55.
225 Yeo 1986, p. 323; Ralegh-Radford 1986, pp. 383–4.
226 Yeo 1986, pp. 324–5; Yeo 1987, p. 4.
227 Yeo 1986, p. 326; cf. Ralegh-Radford 1986, p. 384. Radford's argument is flawed, but his conclusion may be sound. The coffin is now displayed at St Nicholas's priory, Exeter.
228 Fryer 1917, pp. 16–17.
229 The heads have been re-cut: Pevsner 1958 (b), p. 155.
230 Luxford 2002(e), fig. 85.
231 See Fryer 1922, p. 48; Fryer 1924, pp. 73–4; Gardner 1940, p. 98.
232 Fryer 1925, pp. 52–3; Pevsner 1958 (b), p. 155.
233 It may, however, have been part of a more elaborate monument.

worthy that, within a few years, her son Sir Hugh II Luttrell (d.1521) extensively renewed his private chapel in Dunster castle.[234] His charity in the matter of church building and embellishment apparently ended where it began, at home.

The collections of noble monuments at Abbotsbury, Cowick and Dunster will probably not have matched those of larger Benedictine churches such as Glastonbury and Worcester. These, as Leland, Habington and other antiquaries noted, contained large numbers of noble, gentry, superiors' and priors' tombs mixed together. There is no point in cataloguing the known examples here, for the foregoing comments concerning patronal motives and the descriptions of noble mausolea have sufficed to underscore the overwhelmingly commemorative nature of noble patronage during the later middle ages, along with all else that a noble man or woman's memorial implied. If there were documented cases of noble participation in other types of Benedictine project – reconstruction of churches, precinctual or forinsec buildings in particular – then these would attract our notice immediately as interesting variations on a strongly sepulchre-oriented theme; but the fact is that there are not. With the exception of the aforementioned episcopal examples, the most that we encounter are small sums of cash bequeathed to 'fabrics': Jasper, duke of Bedford (d.1495), £10 to Winchcombe; Thomas, Lord Berkeley (in 1417), 40s to Gloucester; Humphrey Stafford, earl of Devon, 20s to Glastonbury (in 1463) etc.[235] The era that plastered its churches with benefactors' names, often transforming its sacred buildings into virtual obit rolls,[236] has left precious little by way of noble names chiselled on its stones. It is likely that heraldry does denote involvement in art and architectural patronage in many cases, but unsupported its evidential value is usually low, as noted in chapter one. For instance, the arms of the earl of Warwick, which formerly occupied a place of honour over the apex of the east window at Great Malvern, may denote assistance with the extensive rebuilding of the priory church c.1430–60.[237] The Beauchamp earls had a long history of positive contact with the priory, which is all the more notable for their apparent stinginess in the matter of religious support generally.[238] With an annual income c.1535 of some £308,[239] and no assistance forthcoming from the parent house of Westminster (from which the Worcestershire cell enjoyed effective independence), the monks were hardly in a position to erect a new east end, transept and sumptuous Gloucester-style tower unaided. Yet if the earls did contribute – and it is quite an 'if' – then we are still left with no idea of how much; a conundrum that has become one of the leitmotifs of this study. It deserves notice that the projected vault of the east end was never built,[240] suggesting major economies that do not sit happily with the notion of significant noble patronage.

Many lost inscriptions existed in glass, of course. That these might denote acts of patronage transcending the window itself is demonstrated by an inscription formerly in the east window at Little Malvern. This trumpeted the patronage of John Alcock, bishop of Worcester (1476–86), of the extensive remodelling of the priory church

---

234 Dodd 1999, p. 55.
235 *Reg.Chichele*, II, p. 123; SMW(a), pp. 196, 328.
236 See Richmond 1996, p. 186.
237 Nott 1896, p. 6 (arms, 'taken from thence in one of the early restorations'); Harvey 1978, p. 195 (build dates).
238 *Cart.Beau.*, pp. xvi, 39 (charter 61), 40 (charters 62, 63).
239 K&H, p. 54.
240 Pevsner 1968, p. 160.

during his period as a royal minister under Edward IV: Alcock was here functioning in his capacity as titular head of house.[241] Other examples from St Catherine and Evesham have been noted elsewhere in this study. Yet there are no such inscriptions concerning the nobility at Great Malvern, and if such existed elsewhere then they have now vanished. Fortunately, a number of windows sponsored by members of the nobility are recorded at Benedictine houses, and it is with these vulnerable works, which against the odds have often proven more durable than stone, that we will conclude our précis of noble patronage. Semantically, whatever their iconography, these differ little from tombs and chantry chapels. The *Magnificat* window in the north transept at Great Malvern (1501 or 1502) – another product of the Twygge and Wodshawe workshop – helps to illustrate this (Plate 8).[242] Besides the devotional subject matter, Henry VII, Queen Elizabeth, Prince Arthur, Sir Reginald Bray, Sir John Savage, and Sir Thomas Lovell appear in the glass. Rushforth was thus content to ascribe it to Henry VII's patronage, but more recent scholarship has emphasized the obvious point that while the three noblemen represented had a vested interest in being shown with their royal over-lords, the reverse was not the case, and that the patronage is thus more likely to rest with them.[243] Bray, for one, is supposed to have paid for a window representing Great Malvern priory church in his parish church of St John in Bedwardine, Worcester, demonstrating a striking degree of identification with the house.[244] What the composi-tion as a whole, with its supplicating figures kneeling at prie-dieux below the scenes from the career of the Virgin Mary, and its *orate pro bono statu* inscriptions, demonstrates is not only patronal desire to curry favour with the king but also with the higher power on whom ultimate prosperity depended. In terms of subject matter and meaning it is effectively an extension of tomb and chantry.

A number of lost windows at Worcester given by noble donors, mixed like the tombs of the nave and east end with others commemorating ecclesiastics and gentry, exhibited the same tendencies. Along the east walk of the cloister were windows with numerous escutcheons and such inscriptions as 'orate pro anima Domini Johannis Pheilpes, Baronis de Donyton, qui hanc fenestram fieri fecit', 'Orate pro bono statu Richardi Cornwall Domini et baronis de Burford . . .' etc.[245] The west window of the cathedral, not part of the 'glass cartulary' described previously, contained below the transom a series of kneeling noblemen clad in armour, and above, their identifying armorials: Mortimer, Beauchamp, Despenser, Botefort, Wendham, Beauchamp of Powick, and the royal arms.[246] The identity of the patron(s) is less than clear, but the intention, to garner recognition for temporal status as an adjunct to commemoration for spiritual well-being, is easily recognizable.

241 Habington, II, pp. 190–1; Marks 1993, p. 17; *Gothic*, p. 176.
242 Marks 1993, p. 42.
243 See Rushforth 1936, pp. 369–76; Marks 1974, pp. 200–1.
244 Habington, II, p. 130; Marks 1974, p. 201.
245 Thomas 1736, pp. 27–8.
246 Thomas 1736, pp. 21–2.

The Patronage of the Sub-nobility

Motives and meanings: Benedictine

That the possessions of the later medieval gentry were of similar constitution to those of the nobility, the substantive differences lying in quality and quantity, has been pointed out in numerous surveys, most recently by Christopher Dyer.[247] Much the same may be said of the objects of patronage: tombs, windows, vestments, plate, and modest contributions to building projects account for the bulk of what the gentry gave to Benedictine houses, and at sub-gentry level a similar picture emerges. The reasons for this are as simple and as complex as human nature. The desire to imitate, within bounds defined by means, opportunity and sumptuary laws, the consumption of a higher social class, had an important effect; a familiar result of which is the population of mechanical and slightly lopsided Tudor mural tombs in purbeck and freestone that haunts the corners of our parish churches. Armorials, of course, are another manifestation of the tendency: only charges and tinctures distinguish noble from sub-noble benefactions in the windows of Great Malvern and antiquarian descriptions of the lost lights of Worcester. Imitation alone does not account for such correspondences, of course. The universal desire for spiritual salvation, for recognition among one's peers, to provide altruistic support for religious observance, and to conform to contemporary fashions all help to blur the boundaries for the modern observer between an object of noble patronage and one paid for by a member of the sub-nobility. Moreover, a noble man or woman might give a gift of small value, which any relatively well-off merchant or gentleman could match. As noted previously, the very social distinction as posited here is itself often cloudy.

The picture is further complicated by the rise of an affluent and broad-based merchant class, whose members were often willing to spend large amounts on art and architecture. The term 'sub-noble' should thus not be taken to imply a lack of potential patronage power during this period. One wonders what the Benedictines of St Nicholas's priory, Exeter, thought from their Romanesque environs when in the three years following 1526, John Lane, merchant of the Staple, constructed his fan-vaulted chantry-aisle on the south side of St Andrew's at Cullompton, whose revenues constituted a mainstay of their income, from which village their prior (William Cullompton, 1522–36) hailed, and to which they had a long-standing historical connection.[248] It may have struck them as ironic that while Lane's tithes entered their own shallow coffers, most of his God-given surplus went into raising an edifice more magnificent than they could have dreamed of erecting for themselves, on the very site where their forebears had once settled. By comparison, the only gift of architecture the monks can be shown to have received during the period under consideration was a 'small house on the west side of the hall of Walter Joy', courtesy of one Roger Tanner and his wife Matilda.[249] 'No false modesty amongst the rich men of the late Middle Ages', wrote Nikolaus Pevsner of

247 Dyer 1998, p. 76.
248 On the historical connection see Rose-Troup 1936–37, p. 140. On the aisle and its sculpture see Carus-Wilson 1957, *passim*.
249 *Cart.StN.Exon*, p. 383: 'parvum domum in *occidentalis* parte aulæ Galfridi Joye'. The charter is undated, but immediately precedes two others dated 1311.

the Lane aisle.[250] No indeed, and it is clear that the lack of mercantile concern for Benedictine projects was perfectly compatible with artistic and architectural advertisements of their virtue and solvency. As we have seen, by the fifteenth century there were plenty of other options, and even the priory of St James, which in Bristol might have expected more, apparently fared no better than St Nicholas at Exeter.

In spite of all the factors tending to monastic disadvantage, however, a quantity of sub-noble contributions did accrue to the Benedictines. This, we may say, was practically unavoidable, given the size of the 'catchment area' commanded by each house. In theory each monastery had a large pool of potential sub-noble donors: those who lived, worked and worshipped within its walls; its tenants; the kith and kin of its monks or nuns; the townspeople who relied on its custom; any who came to venerate its relics or partake of its hospitality; those who lived in monastic boroughs (Cerne, Evesham, Glastonbury, Leominster, Malmesbury, Milton, Pershore, Tavistock, Weymouth, and Winchcombe), where the presence of the Benedictine overlord was particularly strong;[251] the gentry who served or did business with it in various ways; the agricultural workers who farmed its estates; the parishioners of impropriate churches who paid it tithes and other dues; and all those dependent on or under the influence of the above. The concept of a catchment area requires qualification, of course, for it is not synonymous with the sum total of a given monastery's social capital. The more populous a house's environs, the more competing institutions it was likely to support. In effect, the catchment area was not that of one (or more, at Exeter and Winchester) Benedictine house, but rather that of many religious institutions: just how many has been examined with reference to Gloucester, and the smaller houses of Exeter were yet more challenged. Sheer weight of numbers, however, plus the fact that testators usually advantaged multiple religious institutions in their wills (the order of preference in later medieval Somerset being parish church – friary – cathedral – monastic house), distilled a sum total of patronage that, if relatively small, was in total substantial.

Just as the products of sub-noble patronage were, in type and frequently in quality, materially indistinct from those of the nobility, so the motives generating that patronage were in many respects similar. For their part, the Benedictines recognized similar advantages in sub-noble patronage as in noble, although understandably the gifts of a duke or an earl were more prestigious than those of a gentleman or merchant. It follows that the latter were less likely to attract the notice of chroniclers, as a broad survey of English Benedictine history writing of the later middle ages shows. However, the status of financial incentive did not alter with social position. A pound was a pound no matter from whose purse it issued, and even an ancient and self-important convent, if cash-strapped, might concede to a wealthy sub-noble patron that which its forebears would not have granted a noble one. The will of one Henry Burnell esq., proved in 1490, requests burial at Sherborne, St Ealdhelm of Malmesbury's ancient cathedral and resting place to two Anglo-Saxon kings, thus:

> In such place that the Mynisters of god may stond upon my body in tyme of Redyng of the gospellis [i.e. in the monks' choir], or els my body to be buried in the myddys of the high aulter so that my body may ligh part underneth the same auter so that the

---

[250] Pevsner and Cherry 1989, p. 303.

[251] For these monastic boroughs see Trenholme 1927, p. 95. This, the only substantial work on the subject, says nothing of art and architectural patronage. See also Knowles 1955, pp. 263–9.

Mynesters of Crist that shall sey masses ther may stond upon my body whiles they shall mynester the blyssed sacrament of our Lordes body.[252]

The final decision, he says, lies with the abbot, but he may confidently be assumed to have come to a previous arrangement with the latter, for not to have done so would have been to risk rejection and imperil his soul. In this case, it is not clear what, if any, art or architectural dimension attached to the transaction. Sub-noble burials did, however, tend to have such dimensions, at least when they were intramural. For accepting a corpse plus an incised gravestone, or one set with a brass, or a commemorative window positioned close to the sepulchre, a Benedictine convent could expect a mortuary of anything between 10s and £20. It also gave the convent an opportunity to provide remunerative spiritual services, and more simply, relief from the charge of paving and glazing that gifts of this sort obviated. How much the mortuary brought in differed with individual circumstances. Burnell paid £5 to the abbot of Sherborne, which was to cover a mass with placebo and dirge at his funeral as well as his interment, while each monk got £1 for prayers. However, the prior of Bath had received only £1 for accepting John Sparhawke into a grave before the altar of Majesty in 1467. Sixty-seven years later, his successor was paid £4 for a similar service at the hour of the convent's greatest need. The testator in this case was one Isabella Chancellor, who wished to lie in the north transept 'under a stone there all redy by me prepared': the work of art, such as it was, had been produced before death, as must have often occurred. At Cannington in 1498, the prioress got 6s 8d, the sub-prioress 3s 4d and each nun 12d for burying and praying for Joan Sydenham.[253] Richard Alldyngton of Evesham paid 20s – 10s to the abbot and 10s for a mortuary – for burial 'before the Image of owr ladye on the north side of the [abbey] church' in 1533.[254] The list goes on, with much minor variation.

Where the financial motive for seeking sub-noble burials is concerned, art was by and large an epiphenomenon. The money bequeathed by a testator was first and foremost for burial and commemoration: the gift of minor works of art was not understood by any party to constitute the main reason for seeking and accepting interment in a Benedictine house. However, such works were important to monks and nuns. A floor set with gravestones, windows strung together with bidding prayers and armorials, and shrines hung with rosaries and other gifts, bespoke the popularity and external faith in conventual integrity mentioned above with reference to Benedictine motives for seeking noble patronage. It was an edifying and potentially valuable form of advertisement. It cannot be demonstrated that any convent manufactured sub-noble memorials in order to augment its apparent popularity in the way that Gloucester manufactured and updated royal and abbatial ones, but it would not be altogether surprising to find that one or more had done so: just as, unsolicited, they paved their churches with tiles bearing noble arms. The visible evidence of interment bespoke social capital, and that galvanized social capital might stand a vulnerable house in good stead was suggested when, in 1537, the women of St Nicholas's ward, Exeter, violently assaulted two 'Breton carvers' detailed to the defacement of the priory church's rood loft with its images of saints.[255] The action came too late – St Nicholas's had been dissolved earlier in the year

---

252 SMW(a), p. 290. Cf. the request of William Ryder (d.1432) of Totnes: Oliver 1846, p. 239.
253 SMW(a), pp. 214, 363; SMW(b), pp. 24–5.
254 Evesham Wills, p. 51.
255 Youings 1971, pp. 164–5; Duffy 1992, p. 403.

– but the point, that works of art demonstrated an integrity to which local people might respond positively, is not thus less forcefully made. Any augmentation of a house's embellishment by external patrons could strengthen the bonds between laypeople and monks or nuns, by increasing the convent's local reputation for sanctity (and augmentation of local regard was all that most could hope to achieve), and by involving the relatives of the giver in a nexus of common interest.

That one tomb might attract others, or at least further cash bequests, was as obvious to Benedictines as to anyone else. Thus, for the financial and demonstrative reasons mentioned above, as well as for the motives that may be taken for granted without risking the completeness of our survey (such as the aesthetic desire for additional embellishment, the sense of *esprit de corps* that signs of public popularity must have helped to foster, and the augmentation of holiness resulting from sanctified gifts such as altarcloths, plate and vestments that often accompanied the reception of a tomb), monuments were solicited by most Benedictine convents. In particular, members of one family sought burial with their relations, wives with husbands, sons with fathers. If they did not, they might still make financial bequests to the house where a relation was buried. Sir John Byconnil decided on burial at Glastonbury, and built a private chapel there, amortizing lands to the convent for maintenance of a chantry.[256] Naturally enough, when his wife Elizabeth came to be buried (1504), she wished to lie beside her husband. The result for the convent was an extra £10 for prayers, £10 to employ a 'sadde preest w^t oute cure' for one year (a handsome wage indeed), £10 towards maintenance and ornamentation of the chapel, and £20 towards the 'building' of the abbey Lady chapel.[257] When Agnes Green died in 1423 she willed burial before the altar of St Christopher at Muchelney, bequeathing a silver basin thereunto. Her husband, William Green, died four years later, also willing interment at Muchelney and leaving two vestments and a chalice as well as the usual fees.[258] William Knoyell was buried at Sherborne, where he had requested burial in his will of 1501: in 1508, Peter Knoyell (whose precise relation to William is unknown) left 6s 8d to the same house, even though he opted for burial elsewhere.[259]

Motives and meanings: patronal

The issue of family ties brings us to the reasons that sub-noble external patrons had for contributing to the physical upkeep and embellishment of Benedictine houses. These were manifold, of course, and most of the broadly held ones are familiar enough. Devotion, the emulative urge, local affiliations, and the wish to display one's piety and connections in a venerable setting can all be represented as influential catalysts. A handful of motives that do not appear to have attracted close scholarly attention particularly recommend themselves for discussion. The desire to advertise blood relations with Benedictine monks or nuns through works of art, and to seek burial and/or commemoration in the convent they served, is a subject about which a considerable quantity of data could be assembled. The evidence can be ambiguous, as it is not always clear whether

---

256 Cf. *Itinerary*, I, p. 289.
257 SMW(c), pp. 72–4.
258 SMW(a), pp. 109, 122–4.
259 SMW(c), pp. 19, 120.

the stimulus for such advertisement and burial came from the religious in question or his/her relations. At Glastonbury, Abbot Sodbury (d.1334) had his tomb not in the abbatial mausoleum at the east end but in the nave, with his mother buried at his left hand and his father at his right.[260] Hugh, brother of Abbot Monington, was interred under a 'plain gret stone' in the south transept.[261] A tomb apparently belonging to a knightly relative of Abbot John de Gammages and his wife existed in a chapel in the nave of Gloucester abbey.[262] These non-monastic burials, parallels for which are available from other parts of England, and from non-Benedictine contexts as well as Benedictine ones, probably constitute the initiatives of superiors rather than those of the external agents who benefited by them. However, in the case of John de Staunton, half-brother to Adam de Staunton, abbot of Gloucester, there is no such ambiguity. John, it seems, wished to lie in the house ruled by his relative (the potential advantages of this in terms of commemoration do not need spelling out), and as part of the agreement funded the erection of an altar dedicated to St Thomas Becket, which must have been embellished with the necessary accoutrements: reredos or retable, frontal, vestments, plate, linen, and liturgical books. He was buried 'extra clausuram ejusdem altaris', from which it appears that his patronage extended to parclose screens, and his brother the abbot – *privilegium clericatus* – within.[263]

There are further indications of the same tendency. In the west window of the south aisle at Deerhurst, for instance, are two small panels of fifteenth-century glass left over from a larger memorial window. They have been brought from elsewhere in the church,[264] and whether they were originally set up in the monastic division or the parochial nave is uncertain. Represented are three sons and three daughters, the eldest of the sons habited and shorn as a Benedictine.[265] In another example, the will (1507) of one Joan Benet, requesting burial in the churchyard at Glastonbury, assigns a girdle of blue, partly gilt, to the Lady chapel, a gold ring to the abbot, and a silver cup, two salt cellars (both gilded), and six silver spoons to her son John Benet, monk of the abbey. The west transept window at Great Malvern, c.1501, once contained representations of two monks (one a prior) with their respective relations behind them, kneeling and participating in the bidding prayer they offer. Only fragments of these figures remain.[266] The desire to advertise Benedictine relations was also expressed in works outside the monastic context. A brass of 1504 in the parish church of Bramley in Hampshire carries an inscription commemorating Gwen More, wife of John Shelford and 'Modyr to dame Elizabeth Shelforde abbes of the monastery of Shaftysbury', along with Elizabeth's arms.[267] In the parish church at Minchinhampton, Gloucestershire, is a shroud brass of c.1510 showing John Hampton and his wife Helen in their winding sheets, six sons and

---

[260] *Itinerary*, I, p. 289. Henderson 1937, plan, puts the Sodburys in the monk's choir, but apparently without hard evidence for doing so. Cf. Prior William Molassh of Christ Church Canterbury (d.1438), buried in the crypt with his parents: *BRECP*, p. 236.

[261] *Itinerary*, I, p. 287.

[262] *Itinerary*, II, p. 61.

[263] *HMGlouc.*, I, p. 48.

[264] Butterworth 1890, p. 113.

[265] Given the iconographic formula and lack of sacerdotal accoutrements (e.g. a prayer book) it seems unlikely that the monk is a chantry priest rather than the eldest son. See Luxford 2002(e), figs 246, 247.

[266] Rushforth 1936, pp. 408–9.

[267] Stephenson 1926, p. 158; Cave 1904–09, pp. 260–2 (including ill.).

three daughters praying at their feet. The eldest son is a monk, apparently a Benedictine, and the eldest daughter – 'Dame Alice' – a (Brigittine) nun.[268] The church of Sts Peter and Paul at Combe Florey (Som.) has a niche in the north nave wall which formerly contained a heart burial of one Maud de Meriete, nun of Cannington. A beautiful inscription in Lombardics above the niche advertises Maud's vocation in a manner which the Merietes of Hestercombe, the local landowning family responsible for the inscription, must have found suitably edifying: 'Le: Quer: Dame: Maud: de: Merriet: Nonayne: de Cannyhtune:'.[269] While such forinsec examples do not say anything about the patronage of Benedictine art and architecture *per se*, they relate closely to a largely vanished class of works whose existence is confirmed by the examples noticed in monastic contexts. This class of works is testimony to an important but unexplored motive underlying the patronage of Benedictine art by sub-noble benefactors.

Others patronized Benedictine art not because they wished to advertise links with Benedictine relatives, but because they wanted to become Benedictines themselves, by obtaining a grant of confraternity. We have already seen this phenomenon at work in the case of John Baker and his gifts to Kington St Michael, and in chapter two with Robert Pedder, his wife and John Nyvett, who gave works to Tywardreath in the fifteenth century. These examples give reason for thinking that the practice was an established one, and perhaps widespread. After all, to give gifts rather than cash on acceptance into confraternity avoided any whiff of simony that might otherwise have arisen, and also ensured that some material evidence of the transaction remained before the convent's eyes, thus increasing the opportunities for commemoration. As inventories and donor inscriptions indicate, the giver of an item of plate, a book or a vestment might be remembered, whereas money became invisible all too quickly.

John Baker's case is particularly interesting. He was an armiger, as the escutcheon appearing along with his alias John Elys inside the first leaf of the Kington obit book shows,[270] and this suggests that he possessed at least some means. That he chose to pay the nuns of Kington St Michael with a miscellany of art (some of it second hand), chattels and relics is therefore noteworthy, for it suggests this very point – a desire to make a mark on the visual culture of the convent so that his soul might the more readily be prayed for. This is confirmed throughout the obit book, where 'pray for the sowle of John Baker' occurs *passim*, a constant exhortation to the priest(s) and nuns who read the entries, and is stated most clearly in the incongruous inscription on fol. 11v, describing his gifts in detail (Plate 2). It also refers back to an important reason for Benedictine desire for sub-noble patronage, i.e. that it saved money. A work donated was one that did not then need to be bought. It is rather poignant to find Baker paying for *half* of an image of St Saviour. We are here entitled to suppose a process of negotiation, careful financial calculation on the part of the impecunious nuns, and a subsequent agreement concerning Baker's share in the commission.[271] Probably, the image of Christ, as a component of the high altar, was more expensive than those of Sts Catherine and James that Baker paid for in full. In any case, this will not have been John Baker's main consideration when assessing his chattels and deciding what best to give to the nuns. His own

---

268 Playne 1915, p. 69 and facing pl.
269 *Sic*. Illustrated in Luxford 2002(e), fig. 249. Cf. Gittos 2002, p. 160, where a late thirteenth-century date is suggested for this inscription.
270 CUL MS Dd 8 2, fol. 1v. For Elys as Baker's alias see BBA, p. 33 (nos 958, 959).
271 Or perhaps the convent insisted on paying for half of this, its most important image.

redemption was manifestly more important to him – 'humanum est cadere' reads the acknowledgement beneath his arms on fol. 1v. The quality of illustration in the early fourteenth-century service book he gave,[272] which he had bound together with the new obit calendar (indeed, the size of the latter is apparently conditioned by that of the older book), was thus employed to the end of patronal commemoration. We do John Baker's ingenuity and urge for spiritual self-preservation an injustice if we overlook his recognition of the fact that anyone coming to the obit book would be tempted to turn and linger over the gorgeous miniatures contained within the same cover. The temptation was no doubt familiar to him personally.

Others patronized art not from a desire to express family ties or pay their way into confraternity but to advertise their status as employees of Benedictine convents. As with the advertisement of familial relations, a number of examples of this practice also occur in non-monastic contexts. One thinks of the inscription on Winchcombe's fourteenth-century barn at Enstone, commemorating Robert the Mason, bailiff of the manor; the brass of John Brook (d.1522), steward of Glastonbury abbey, at St Mary Redcliff, Bristol; and the sumptuous tomb of John Camell (d.1487), sometime bursar of the abbot of Glastonbury, in the parish church of St John the Baptist.[273] In the latter case, the purse of office is ostentatiously displayed on the right hip, and the inscription, which was illegible by the later eighteenth century,[274] no doubt declared his professional capacity. Such offices were prestigious as well as lucrative. These examples in secular contexts suggest the motive; evidence from Shaftesbury is our best collective proof of it. The secular servants of the abbey seem to have been eager to advertise their status as such, a prime example being the inscription by which Alexander Cater and Christopher Twynho, respectively lay sacrist and steward of the abbey, are declared instigators of the major surviving calendar of its muniments (BL MS Egerton 3098) in a preface to the manuscript. This was begun in 1500 for Abbess Margery Twynho (Christopher's sister) and finally completed in 1505.[275] The undecorated manuscript is not classifiable as art, but Alexander Cater's freestone tomb did qualify as such. In the abbey museum at Shaftesbury a fragment of it is displayed, sporting a scroll incised with part of a memorial inscription ('Dormit Alexander Cater hoc sub marmore . . .' etc.). The same museum houses another fragment of a sixteenth-century tomb, of a priest who had served the monastery, Thomas Scales. There is a metrical 'Epitaphium Thome Scalis' beautifully cut into the fragment in black letter, along with the date of death, 1532. In the parish church of St Peter is a third evidence, a small brass set into a large purbeck gravestone commemorating Stephen Payne, 'quondam seneschali hujus monasterii', who died in 1508.[276] The 'hujus' suggests either that the brass and slab have been relocated from the abbey to the parish church or else that the latter, annexed as it was to the former, was considered part of the conventual complex. The monument may in any case be considered a Benedictine work of art in the sense understood here. Such works, evidence of a significant stimulus to sub-noble external patronage, were not unique to Shaftesbury. To

---

272 See Sandler 1986, I, pls 61–3.
273 *Star Chamber*, II, p. 253 note 32; Stephenson 1926, p. 146 (Brook); Fryer 1922, pp. 49–50; Gardner 1940, p. 98; Dunning 2001, p. 101 (Camel: tomb originally in the south transept). See Stephenson 1926, p. 565 for an example pertaining to St Mary's abbey, York.
274 Cf. Collinson 1791, II, p. 264.
275 Bell 1933–4, pp. 18–22, especially 20.
276 DNHAFC 1903, p. liii. See Luxford 2002(e), figs 251 (Cater), 252 (Scalis), 253 (Payne).

cite perhaps the grandest example, William Frost, member of the Hampshire gentry and a long-time steward of Richard Fox, joined with the titular abbot and prior (Henry Broke, 1524–36) in patronizing the construction of the Caen stone choir screens of 1525 in the cathedral.[277]

A desire to contribute to a major new programme of work seems to have elicited many benefactions. The evidence is clear: when a new church, major building or significant part thereof went up, so did sub-noble interest in contributing towards art and architecture. The windows at Great Malvern, installed between c.1440 and 1501 as part of the project of renovation, are evidence of this. At Worcester, the now lost cloister windows glazed during the late fourteenth and early fifteenth centuries provide further testimony. Examples from both will be mentioned below. The monks of Bath received £10 towards reconstruction from John Compton in 1503, and a new window in 1524 courtesy of Thomas Chapman.[278] The repetitive application of Edmund Compton's rebus in the east window of the Gloucester Lady chapel has led one scholar to consider him the patron of the work,[279] although it is much more likely that he simply contributed to the glazing, and perhaps also to the fabric. If Worcester and Great Malvern give any indication, then Compton will not have been alone in his patronage. Great Malvern's architecture must have been the object of numerous bequests: the 100s bequeathed by William Harris (d.1428) 'for the work of his church' is presumed to refer to the early stages of the remodelling there.[280] At Evesham, the ostentatious detached bell tower (Plate 14) erected under the auspices of Clement Lichfield was an object of local testators' generosity; surviving wills of 1530 and 1531 contain donations towards its completion.[281] It is claimed that such donations, and all that was invested in them, helped to save the tower from destruction at the Dissolution,[282] which if true would suppose many more such individual acts of patronage.

Novelty *per se* does not recommend itself as a primary motive. Neither, in particular, does the wish to advertise family ties or employer status. Even the desire for acceptance into confraternity seems a secondary reason for patronizing Benedictine art and architecture. The major underlying motive was the desire for commemoration to the end of spiritual succour. This subject has occurred at many points throughout this study, and scarcely needs re-emphasis. It is important to affirm its status as the most important motive, however, lest it be thought that a portion of the sub-nobility maintained some specific affection for the Benedictine order. This is not to deny that the people of Evesham contributed to Abbot Lichfield's tower because it enhanced the beauty of their surroundings and functioned as a symbol of collective piety and pride in which they, as well as the abbot and convent, partook. Those of Bath and Great Malvern are likely to have supported their local Benedictine projects for the honour that such buildings and their fittings did to God and the saints. The apparent bequest of Thomas Lyttleton (d.1481: or perhaps his son, William) of a window-light representing St Christopher at the latter church is cited more than once in the literature as an example of a devo-

---

277 Cf. Smith 1988(b), p. 282. Here, Frost's heraldry, motto and initials are convincing evidence of his patronage, for no other motive can be reasonably suggested for their inclusion.
278 SMW(c), pp. 47, 231.
279 Rushforth 1921, p. 205; Welander 1991, p. 265 (ill.).
280 Rushforth 1936, p. 315.
281 BGAS 1884–5, p. 9.
282 Cf. Willis 1718, I, p. 197; VCH *Worcester*, II, p. 126; Bugslag 1980, pp. 73–4.

tion-generated act of patronage.[283] However, in most cases it would be wrong to place devotional considerations unrelated to death and commemoration before a given patron's concern for his or her own soul, and those of relatives and friends. It will be noted that Lyttleton, if indeed he was the patron, presented his window around the time of his death, and that all other evidence connecting him to St Christopher relates to commemoration as well.[284] To seek burial in a Benedictine church on the basis of a familial or professional tie was to stand one's soul in excellent stead. To give works of art in exchange for confraternity was, as discussed, a method of perpetuating one's presence and thus the prayers said for one. A new building project constituted a rare opportunity to display one's tomb, 'portrait', armorials and bidding prayer before the large audience that would certainly be attracted to it, as well as its resident religious. Practically all of our written evidence for patronage at sub-noble level, be it in wills, inscriptions or elsewhere (e.g. the Kington obit book) expresses some measure of anxiety about the afterlife. Donors, it is fair to say, were also supplicants.[285]

Sub-noble patronage was, on surviving evidence, usually mediated by an executor, or at least accomplished close to death: hence its commemorative associations. Even when this was not the case, however, a desire for spiritual succour usually emerges as the main underlying motive. Gifts contributed by visitors to shrines are an obvious example, although a slightly ambiguous one, for the intended beneficiaries of such offerings were God and his saints, rather than Benedictine monks or nuns. The Worcester fabric confraternity provides a clearer illustration. The confraternity, initiated during the thirteenth century and revived in 1302 when the sacrist's income proved insufficient for work in hand,[286] was in more or less constant operation thereafter throughout the later middle ages: it realized £24 7s in 1423/4, and 8s 6d in 1521/2.[287] Members gave what they could manage to the fabric fund, in return for a series of spiritual benefits (provided, of course, that their gifts were given after confession and with a contrite heart). The third part of all penances placed on them was remitted, 1028 days of plenary indulgence granted, and a perpetual share in the benefits accruing from all conventual prayers assured. The bodies of the dead, no matter how they had died, might also be buried in the consecrated ground of the priory cemetery, so long as their names were enrolled in the book of confraternity. Presumably, then, living relatives could enroll dead ones; a great advantage for those who had died unshriven. Significantly, these assurances were given not by a consecrated bishop but by the prior, John de Wyke (1301–17), in his capacity as acting diocesan during a period *sede vacante*.[288] They concern spiritual succour, and prosperity during life, exclusively: Wyke and his convent knew what the public at large wanted most from a Benedictine monastery. Although they may have played a part in encouraging people to join, other advantages that might have motivated people to enroll in the confraternity (e.g. a sense of corporate belonging, an altruistic desire to honour God and his saints) are not emphasized in Wyke's letters at all.

---

283 Rushforth 1936, pp. 216–17; Marks 1993, p. 63: hard evidence of Lyttleton patronage is lacking, however.
284 *Test.Vet.*, pp. 362–3.
285 Cf. Kauffmann 2001, p. 270.
286 *Annales*, IV, p. 417. Durham had a similar system: Smith 1951, p. 256. See also *Lib.Albus*, pp. 28–30.
287 *CRWor.*, p. 63; *Acc.Wor.*, pp. 36–7.
288 *Lib.Albus*, pp. 28–9.

Examples of sub-noble patronage

This topic need not detain us long, as there is no sub-noble 'Tewkesbury' that demands attention. The only project that may be regarded as its equivalent is the rebuilding of Totnes, mentioned in passing in chapter four. Totnes was an alien priory granted denizen status c.1415, and thereafter not annexed to any greater house.[289] It never seems to have exploited the potentially prestige-enhancing and remunerative opportunity handed to it by Geoffrey of Monmouth, according to whom Totnes was the place at which Brutus, first king of Britain, landed after his heroic journey from Greece c.1115 B.C.,[290] and the *Valor Ecclesiasticus* estimated its annual income at only £124. This was evidently not enough to assist with the complete reconstruction of the conventual church that occurred between the 1430s and the 1450s, and the parish, to whom the nave pertained, agreed to pay for the conventual chancel as long as the convent maintained it thereafter.[291] In collective terms, the chief motive here was apparently the prosperous parishioners' desire for an up-to-date, prestigious church, rather than the inharmonious imbalance that characterized so many churches by the early fifteenth century. Their ambition is reflected in their shortlist of potential models for the tower – Callington (Corn.), Buckland, Tavistock and Ashburton (all Dev.), their eventual choice of the finest – Ashburton – for their prototype, and in Leland's testimony that Totnes had 'the greatest belles in al those quarters'.[292]

The patronage of Totnes was unusual, the product of unusual circumstances. Individual bequests towards fabric-maintenance, and occasionally to specific projects, were more the norm where sub-noble patrons were concerned. Although these might be large, such as the eighty marks that William Wenard left (1441) to the construction of the nuns' bell tower at Polsloe, they were usually small: the 2s left by Henry Popham to the fabric of Winchester in 1418 cannot have paid for much.[293] John Hempstone left 40d to the fabric of Totnes church in 1393, apparently to the monastic division.[294] The fabric of St Nicholas's priory at Exeter received 3s by the will of Henry de Berbilond, vicar choral of the cathedral, in 1296 and 5s by that of Peter Soth, layman, in 1327.[295] Another Benedictine fabric, Bath cathedral priory church, received 3s 4d from William Starke in 1417, and £10 from Ralph Hunt, citizen, in 1432.[296] William Knoyell left 20s to the 'reparacion' of Sherborne abbey church in 1501.[297] These, along with the examples mentioned previously, were all one-off cash payments, to be delivered by executors who were also charged with distributing similar amounts to non-Benedictine institutions. Lest it be thought that William Wenard had a surpassing regard for Exeter's black nuns, mention of the 100 marks that he left to the city's Franciscans towards a new cloister should be made.[298] In 1394, Richard and Joan Chideock assigned rents in perpe-

---

[289] K&H, p. 78: priors were appointed from Christ Church Canterbury, 1416–36.
[290] *HRB*, p. 13.
[291] Watkin 1914–17, II, p. 967; Pevsner and Cherry 1989, p. 868. The prior gave £10 in 1449: Watkin 1914–17, I, p. 407; II, p. 956.
[292] Salzman 1997, p. 24; Pevsner and Cherry 1989, pp. 131, 868; *Itinerary*, I, p. 218.
[293] *SMW*(a), p. 148; *Reg.Chichele*, II, p. 123.
[294] It comes after a bequest to the prior in his will: W.S.W. 1851, p. 307.
[295] *Death and Memory*, pp. 151, 159.
[296] *SMW*(a), p. 80; *SMW*(c), p. 334; *Reg.Chichele*, II, p. 464.
[297] *SMW*(c), p. 19.
[298] *SMW*(a), p. 80.

tuity to the fabric of Cerne abbey,[299] but their preference for a Benedictine convent alone and the manner of their bequest were unusual.

Vestments, altar-linen and other textiles appear to have been relatively common bequests to Benedictine houses. Ecclesiastics might leave a proportion of their decorated liturgical vestments, just as the monks of Worcester did to the Lady chapel of their own monastery. Thus John Ganvill, canon of Wells (d.1407), left his second best amice and surplice to the abbot of Muchelney.[300] Liturgical vestments were also gifted by the laity: John Mompesson left (1500) a pair of vestments of Bruges satin with his arms impaling those of his wife, represented in the cross on the back, to the convents of Shaftesbury and Wilton (he left the same to Fontevrauldine Amesbury); Robert Warre, esq., bequeathed to the abbot and convent of Athelney a piece of cloth of gold out of which a vestment was to be made in which his soul might be prayed for (1465); and during the fourteenth century the monks of Worcester received two pairs of vestments (one of silk with silver flowers embroidered into it) from one W. Goldsmith, and a chasuble of red silk with rams and flowers embroidered in gold from one John of Gloucester (not a monk).[301] Altar linen was given to Worcester by Goldsmith and his wife Isabella (two towels – hardly works of art) and Cecilie Stockton ('one good altar-cloth not yet sanctified'), while John Ganvill gave a quantity of towels, napkins etc. to Muchelney. He also gave all of the stained hangings adorning his private oratory at Wells, a gift paralleled in kind if not quantity by Joan Mudeford's bequest of 'one entire best cloth of colour' to the monks of Athelney in 1484.[302]

Plate and other *jocalia* were even more commonly given. Of course, such bequests could double as cash – even the bishop of Exeter might pay his steward in plate rather than coin[303] – but inasmuch as they qualified as works of art, so do they represent acts of patronage. The examples listed here have been selected in order to provide an impression of the sorts of articles most commonly donated. Martin Lerchedeken, a canon of Exeter cathedral, willed his personal silver pyx to the nuns of Polsloe in 1430. A silver cup was left to the prioress of Polsloe for her personal use by Henry Brokelond (d.1403), also a canon of the cathedral. John Ganvill, above-mentioned, gave a gilded silver water vessel to Muchelney. In 1424, William Milton, dean of Chichester, bequeathed to the abbot and convent of Gloucester a gilded silver cup with the figure of a serpent stamped into it. John Rugge, vicar of St Thomas at Exeter, left the nuns of Polsloe 'a jewel' in 1536.[304] Such gifts were not the exclusive preserve of churchmen. In 1486 John Kelly left a standing silver cup with gilded cover 'made in the form of a bell', plus a spoon with 'K' on the handle (conveniently symbolizing Katherine, the priory's patron saint, as well as the giver's surname). Glastonbury received two gilded silver salt cellars (to the abbot), a silver bowl and a silver cup (to the convent) of John Dyer (d.1495), while Joan Sydenham gave the nuns of Cannington a miscellany of plate. Elsewhere it appears that Cecilie Stockton had given Worcester a 'precious belt' with gold letters worked into

---

299   VCH Dorset, II, p. 55.
300   SMW(c), pp. 306–7.
301   SMW(c), p. 11; SMW(a), p. 208; HMC XIV:viii, p. 198.
302   HMC XIV:viii, pp. 198–9; SMW(a), pp. 208, 251.
303   Prideaux 1934–35, p. 120.
304   See respectively Reg.Chichele, II, p. 477; Oliver 1846, p. 164; SMW(c), pp. 306–7; Reg.Chichele, II, p. 287; Oliver 1846, p. 164.

it.[305] The monks of Bath received of one Sybil Pochon (in 1403–04) a pair of jet and silver rosary beads. This was detailed to the image of the Holy Trinity within the church. A materially similar bequest was made by Margery de Crioll (d.1319) to Elizabeth de Pavenham, nun of Shaftesbury: 'my pater noster of coral and white pearls, which the Countess of Penbrok gave me'. Further in this vein, Thomas Austell left to Richard Beere, abbot of Glastonbury, 'a payer of beedys of x stonys sylver and gilt that was Byshop Lacys' (Edmund Lacy, of Exeter, 1420–55) in 1509.[306] A string of ten beads does not make the Langdale rosary, but as a personal devotional item of a man widely reputed to be a saint,[307] this was nevertheless a valuable and prestigious gift.

Windows are the final item of sub-noble patronage requiring attention. Memorial stained glass windows must once have been almost inestimably numerous. It is often supposed that they constituted a relatively expensive form of commemoration,[308] but in fact the early sixteenth-century accounts of William More discussed above have revealed pictorial stained glass at approximately 6d per foot, heraldic glass at 8d.[309] It must also be remembered that many individuals left money for the glazing of a single light rather than a whole window. The will of William Wenard (of 1441), which we have already encountered, allots 8s 4d to every parish church in Cornwall and Devon on condition that his name be written on a glass window (or some other public place) so that it may be seen by all men, 'as well friends as enemies, that when they chance to see my name publicly written they perchance will be induced to pray more quickly for my soul'. The Benedictine churches of St Swithun at Winchester and Tavistock also received the sum, and were enjoined to perform the same service.[310] This amusingly ambitious request[311] – one cannot believe that Wenard knew how many churches were involved – suggests how effective a form of commemoration windows were perceived to be, the fact that such commemoration need not cost much (admittedly these were not pictorial windows and he did not even necessarily give the glass), and that Benedictine churches could be enlisted in the service of such a commonplace commemorative function as readily as parish churches. The convent at Bath was apparently as apt to lend itself to such usage as Tavistock and Winchester. There, Thomas Chapman, a business associate of the convent's, felt confident in willing 'the glasing of a wyndowe as well as my wyfe shall ordre hit'.[312] The glass of Great Malvern and what we know of that at Worcester confirms the impression that windows in Benedictine contexts were available, relatively inexpensive and popular.

The glazing of Great Malvern was a collective enterprise, accomplished over roughly sixty years by individuals of all ranks discussed in this study except royalty. It manifests a sort of patronal egalitarianism, in that it allowed individuals of sub-noble status with means and inclination to advertise their names, connections and virtues in the same space as those of bishops, abbots and the secular nobility. The great windows – east, north and west – were admittedly the domain of patrons of high social standing, but

---

[305]   See respectively Oliver 1846, p. 164; SMW(a), pp. 382, 363; HMC XIV:viii, p. 198.
[306]   See respectively Bath Deeds, p. 90; ELW, p. 5; SMW(c), p. 134.
[307]   Cf. Itinerary Worcestre, pp. 116–17; Orme 1986(b), pp. 416–18.
[308]   E.g. Marks 1993, p. 6.
[309]   Jnl.More, pp. 194, 219.
[310]   SMW(a), p. 148.
[311]   But not unique: see e.g. Richmond 1991, p. 129.
[312]   SMW(c), p. 231.

elsewhere the barriers dissolve, and images of laymen such as Thomas Carter, Richard Osney and Richard Matthew were found (they are now largely destroyed) in mid-century lights of the presbytery clerestory, as well as in the nave. These individuals occupied the central window on the north side, the next window west being the founders' window, with its figures of Sts Werstan and Edward the Confessor, the latter donating a sealed charter to a kneeling ecclesiastic.[313] Founders and latter-day sub-noble donors occupy the same space, which would not have occurred at Tewkesbury, but nevertheless might where a convent needed financial support. In fact, what is known of Great Malvern's glass permits a glimpse of what must once have been a common arrangement in other Benedictine houses (and which is familiar from many parish churches). Its implications are more significant than in the case of socially broad-based contribution to building, to monastic sacristies and to libraries, for here the act of patronage is commemorated pictorially, or at least in publicly displayed writing. Great Malvern resembled an obit-book in which names of all degrees existed under one cover. The idea that the church constituted a microcosm of the celestial Jerusalem sanctioned, if it did not cause, the mingling of all social ranks in this way.

We rely for the examples of which we know as much on antiquarian description as on what remains. Their iconography is as varied as the conditions and personalities of their patrons, and replete with interesting features and juxtapositions. Two windows in the south choir aisle, glazed c.1450, catch the attention in particular, the first for its curiousness, the second for its ability to illustrate important issues. Walter and Joan Corbet were represented with an 'orate pro animabus' inscription in glass of c.1450 in the south choir aisle, with no fewer than eighteen children – eight daughters, ten sons – around them.[314] With such a brood they might have expected more commemoration than most, yet still thought it worthwhile to commission this concrete representation. The window to the west of this contained kneeling figures of William Walwin and Jane his wife supplicating Sts Lawrence and Nicholas, with a Malvern monk (prior from 1449), John Benet, and another layman supplicating Sts Stephen and Giles. Husband and wife shared one prayer ('Christ help us/ through the merits of Laurence and Nicholas'), while Benet and the unidentified layman shared another ('God be merciful unto us/ Stephen and Giles pray for [us]'). The whole was underwritten by a longer inscription, the end of which the antiquaries did not record: 'All you who will pass by this little window pray for our souls and ask God . . .'[315] This is more than an illustrative example of individual patrons sponsoring individual lights as opposed to entire windows, it is a case of shared patronage to a common end among social equals who nevertheless occupied quite different social niches. The priory church's east end, for all its numerous non-monastic visitors, remained the domain of John Benet and his colleagues. Its Benedictinism relied on this, as well as the chapter house and cloister, for whatever spatial and (along with the habit, Rule and opus Dei) ideological self-definition it retained by the mid-fifteenth century. In the idealized, vitrified church of the windows however, the monk might mingle with laity, share prayers with them, define and represent his hopes according to a common goal and by common means in which they also shared. The temporal barriers have disappeared, and the four kneel as one. Such observations help to demonstrate the

---

313 Rushforth 1936, fig. 54.
314 Rushforth 1936, p. 352.
315 Rushforth 1936, pp. 354–6 (underlining added).

particular advantages that the patronage of Benedictine windows had over that of other types of art, and thus why they were comparatively popular with the sub-nobility.

The hierarchy at Worcester was different. There, the east end contained an extensive series of benefactors, mostly retrospective representations, and probably glazed at monastic expense. There was still scope for sub-noble lay representation, however. The east window of the Lady chapel did not belong to the larger scheme, and contained a number of gentry couples, along with pairings of nobles, monks and superiors. All were apparently represented in the same way, kneeling in prayer, one behind the other, with their names written above them. The west window of the north nave aisle contained representations of two gentry couples (one John Powell and his wife, the other unidentifiable) praying face to face, here with their names inscribed underneath them. In the east and north walks of the cloister were windows carrying gentry names and armorials, though apparently without figures.[316] Here, as in the Lady chapel lights, was a blend of internally and externally patronized glass. The monastic iconography included the window commemorating John Lyndsey mentioned in chapter four and a number showing priors and sub-priors. The later medieval Benedictine monastery accommodated the patronage aspirations of all, and as Prince Arthur's chantry chapel went up in Worcester's choir, so the sub-noble population of the diocese commissioned the windows through which it was lit, or contributed what they could to the fabric fund via the confraternity established to accommodate that most medieval of predilections, the urge to give. 'Let your giving match your means; if you have little do not be ashamed to give the little you can afford; you will be laying up a sound insurance against the day of adversity.'[317] This biblical principle, the bedrock of Worcester's fabric confraternity, was the basis on which degrees of individual generosity often appear to have been calculated. By such standards, a relatively poor man could feel himself as magnanimous a patron of Benedictine art and architecture as a superior, or even a king.[318]

[316] Thomas 1736, pp. 11, 22, 28–32.
[317] Tobit 4:8–9.
[318] For a late medieval English formulation of this concept, and its application, see Hope 1925, pp. 80–1.

Conclusion

Five Things We Would Like to Know

Art and architectural patronage, like the appreciation and study of art and architecture, is a relatively minor division of human endeavour mediated by social, economic, psychological, religious, and other factors scarcely less complex and liable to flux.[1] Its objects can of course be analyzed in formalistic, iconographic and material terms, but insofar as they communicate facts about patronage, these art historical considerations are subordinated to their value as documents. In the context of a study such as this, a lost, documented object of patronage – Godfrey Giffard's tomb, for example, or any one of the copes acquired by Walter de Monington for Glastonbury – can be more important than a surviving one for which no convincing evidence of patronage exists. This only seems odd if we lose sight of the fact that we have been engaged in a behavioural study, art historical in a fundamental sense (for most acts of later medieval artistic creation were founded on patronal demand), but not in the style-composition-iconography sense. To study human behaviour is to study idiosyncrasy and caprice as well as tidy-mindedness and lives regulated by the compact environs of the *claustrum*, town, castle, parish, or court. We deal with intellects as singular our own, and all the more impenetrable for the intervening centuries. We are not entitled to ask the impossible of such dealings: to expect them to yield a smooth, homogenized set of conclusions would be to ask the witness if not the wrong, then extremely unfair, questions.

Nevertheless, the foregoing chapters have important implications over and above the broad findings that have been summarized in the concluding sections of the chapters. These we must try to spell out, notwithstanding the imperfections of the available evidence. The five questions which follow encapsulate the most significant of these implications. They are not arranged in any particular order, although the first perhaps recommends itself most immediately for attention.

(1) How does the patronage of Benedictine art and architecture in the west of England change over the period 1300–1540?

In answering this question, it is particularly important to keep in mind the undulating nature of the written evidence at our disposal. The dawn of this period coincides with the twilight of domestic Benedictine chronicle writing: a major reason for the bias of art historically orientated monastic studies in favour of the early and high middle ages.[2] Given the dearth of relevant *compoti* and wills we have no consistent and continuous set of profitable written sources for our region and period. If we did, then the parameters of this study might have been narrowed accordingly.

---

[1] Cf. the observations in Baxandall 1972, pp. 1–3.

[2] The most significant manifestation of this affecting art historical studies is Otto Lehmann-Brockhaus's catalogue of printed Latin sources, which ends c.1307.

On the basis of what we know, it may be concluded that relatively little overall change occurred during the period. The pre-1300 relish for major programmes of conventual church-building did not diminish, and although it is apparently more marked in the fourteenth century than thereafter (e.g. Glastonbury presbytery, Gloucester presbytery and transepts, Milton, Pershore crossing tower, transept vault and Lady chapel, Tewkesbury, Worcester), many important programmes initiated before 1400 continued into the fifteenth and even the sixteenth: Evesham (presbytery remodelled from 1395), Gloucester (west front, western bays of nave, central tower, Lady chapel), Glastonbury (crossing vault, Edgar's chapel), Milton (crossing vault, transept), Muchelney (presbytery remodelling), Sherborne (remodelling of the presbytery and nave), Winchester (nave, presbytery aisles and vault, pulpitum).[3] Bath, of course, was entirely rebuilt from the end of the fifteenth century, work ceasing only with the Dissolution. In many places the degree and vigour of such projects is disguised by near-total losses, poor or non-existent documentation, and insubstantial archaeological data: Athelney abbey church's apparent reconstruction during the early fourteenth century is a representative case.[4] In passing, we may note that the Black Death and related epidemics, though they may have nipped nascent projects in the bud, and otherwise retarded patronage in the short term,[5] do not in general appear to have had a lasting influence on patronage at the larger houses.

Beyond the monastic church, other projects also went ahead unabated. Many major convents (Athelney, Evesham, Glastonbury, Gloucester, Malmesbury, Milton, Muchelney, Pershore, Sherborne, Tavistock, Tewkesbury, Winchcombe, and Worcester at least) received new or at least completely remodelled main cloisters post-1300, although some, e.g. Winchester, ostentatiously retained their ancient ones. Many others received new dorters, fraters, almonry buildings etc. At smaller conventual churches circumstances were different. Rebuilding was, as at the larger churches, piecemeal, but apparently less frequent and ambitious. Some, such as Dunster and Totnes, were rebuilt, but largely or wholly at the expense of the parochial interests that had a stake in them. This is consistent with the fact that most were either poor, or cells of larger houses, and thus not priority targets for renewal. The churches of nuns were less vigorously rebuilt, but not ignored. If Wykeham's will is adequate testimony, Romsey was rebuilding or renovating its cloister during the early fifteenth century, while the nuns of Shaftesbury built themselves a grand south presbytery aisle during the fourteenth century, probably a Lady chapel, and a new pulpitum. The Perpendicular fragments in the abbey museum show that the church also received extensive internal embellishment.

Such major programmes are a good gauge of the health and continuity of patronage generally, for they indicate both relative prosperity and an implicit degree of confidence in its continuity, even if undertaking them did entail debt. Where undocumented or unreliably documented, they do not say a great deal about the continuity of patronage by the various classes studied here, but this is not as significant as it may seem; first because they may be reliably assumed to have been largely internal initiatives (they were internal responsibilities, after all), and second because they imply strongly a certain amount of external contribution, even if this cannot actually be demonstrated.

[3]   For the existence of a Perpendicular pulpitum at Winchester see Lindley 1986, p. 613.
[4]   This is *pace* Morris 1979, p. 180, who charts a later medieval slump in such projects. His premises are significantly flawed, however.
[5]   See Lindley 1996, pp. 141–3.

A new project, as noted in chapter six, gave external patrons an opportunity for potentially salvific (and otherwise edifying) good works, and in any case, an episcopal and/or papal indulgence was often proposed as a carrot for eliciting contributions. There is no strong indication that patronage of Benedictine embellishments dropped off during the period after 1300, either. Indeed, this is to be expected, because renewal of wall paintings, glass, vestments, plate, books etc. was necessitated by wear and tear, changing fashions, and reconfiguration of their architectural settings.

We are on less certain ground where changes in the patronage exercised by individual classes of patron are concerned. On the basis of what has been said above, it appears that superiors' and convents' patronage of major projects remained more or less constant throughout the period, and while it fell away at particular houses after 1400 (e.g. Athelney, Hyde, Pershore, Shaftesbury, Worcester), it experienced an upsurge at others towards the end of our period (e.g. Bath, Evesham, Glastonbury, Muchelney, Great and Little Malvern, Tavistock).[6] On balance, then, internal patronage remained healthy, the patrons committed to a cause that was at any rate integral to the monastic calling. It is impossible to divide responsibility for internal patronage in an attempt to discern whether or not the contributions of superior and convent remained constant or fluctuated between 1300 and 1540. The evidence simply does not reliably attest relative degrees of responsibility. It may be that close scrutiny of estate records (themselves patchy in terms of survival) pertaining to superiors' and convents' incomes would generate some informative data. Robert Dunning noticed systematic exploitation of the estates of Muchelney abbey during the later fifteenth century consistent with the requirement to fund some large initiative such as the rebuilding that the monks were then engaged in.[7] If the divisions of this estate and degrees of exploitation could be broken down then this could at least indicate (though it would not prove) how relative degrees of responsibility should be apportioned. Due to the patchiness of documentary survivals and the idiosyncrasies obtaining among the various monasteries, however, such an analysis would only be viable on a house by house basis.

For external patrons the indications are as follows. The most that can be said of royal patronage in general is that it was not significant, and progressively less so after 1400; but this progression is not amenable to concise definition. Where the nobility was concerned, patronage of Benedictine art and architecture was at its post-1300 height during the fourteenth century, falling away progressively thereafter as the extent, solvency and confidence in tenure of the nobility declined, competition for the provision of religious services increased, and the type of 'spiritual services' requested changed.[8] In the case of the sub-nobility, whose lesser financial position meant that acts of patronage were on existing evidence confined to deathbed bequests, support for Benedictine art and architectural patronage seems to have remained strong throughout our period. It can even be said to have risen towards the end of the middle ages, and while this may partially have to do with the larger quantity of fifteenth- and early sixteenth-century wills surviving, it apparently reflects the growth in size and prosperity

6   Tavistock's cloister was 'new' in 1478: *Itinerary Worcestre*, pp. 114–15.
7   *VCH Somerset*, III, p. 44.
8   E.g. the perpetual chantry, the obvious location for which was a 'perpetual' institution such as a monastery or cathedral, became less important, with shorter, often more intense bursts of commemoration becoming fashionable.

of the sub-nobility in the west of England during the period, as well as their desire to support multiple institutions for the perceived good of their souls.

(2) What does the patronage of Benedictine art and architecture during the later middle ages reveal about the nature of Benedictine art and architecture?

Identifying the phenomena intrinsic to a work of art or architecture is a controversial business. As this is not the place for philosophical speculation, 'intrinsicality' is broadly construed here without apology. The key concepts to be touched on are not presented in any particular order (obviously there is no one correct order). While this study has not been greatly concerned with the intrinsic nature of art and architecture, an answer to the question as posed is desirable, because it indicates the relationship of art and architectural patronage to other concepts and phenomena central to art historical inquiry (retrospection, symmetry, quality, colour, innovation etc). In doing so it also implies the limits of a patronage study within a broader spectrum of aesthetic and ideological concerns central to both medieval and modern ideas about architecture and art.

Renewal and continuity of construction were clearly important in their own right to patrons: to express contemporary aesthetic and social fashions, for devotional reasons, and for maintenance of *esprit de corps*. Stylistic consistency, an aspect of the symmetry we may expect of regulated minds, mattered. At Glastonbury, the architect working during Walter de Monington's abbacy replicated aspects of the early Gothic style of the choir when designing the ambulatory and presbytery aisle extensions executed during the 1360s and early 1370s,[9] and those responsible for the remodelling of the east ends of Gloucester and Tewkesbury clearly aimed at visual integrity. However, such consistency was infrequently of overriding importance, and the ancient and the modern were often juxtaposed to great effect: we see examples of this in the nave at Tewkesbury, the presbytery aisles at Gloucester and the chapter house at Worcester, and it existed at Romsey and Shaftesbury, too, before they were violated. Retrospection was also important, but was often accomplished by not patronizing new projects (e.g. Glastonbury Lady chapel, the chapter houses of Gloucester, Sherborne, and Winchester). Size and splendour were as significant to Benedictines as to their secular counterparts, lay and ecclesiastical. Colour, gaudiness even, counted for a great deal, especially in the component elements of liturgy and hagiolatry. Accordingly, precious metals were considered to be of primary aesthetic and utilitarian importance, although imitation precious materials (e.g. gilded copper, pseudo-pearls and gems) were acceptable in all contexts apart from those obviated by canon law. Formal, chromatic and iconographic variety was inevitable and considered desirable. The expression of this variety was dense and ubiquitous; some of its most striking formal products were the polygonal chapter houses of Evesham, Tavistock and (externally) Worcester, and the lavatorium at Sherborne; but it is equally apparent in the Sherborne missal, and was so when Glastonbury and Winchester's cope chests were full. Innovation, if not as important to patrons as to modern scholars, is nevertheless a feature of much Benedictine art and architecture, as noticed in chapter one. Commemoration, often expressed in the intended location as well as the constitution of works patronized (e.g. tombs of patrons positioned by or in objects of their patronage; inscribed books and liturgical plate such as William More's Bromsgrove

---

[9]   Wilson 1980, p. 319.

missal and Roger Yatton of Evesham's chalices), infused much Benedictine art and architecture of the period. Apparently of less importance was the expression of 'Benedictineness' by Benedictine patrons. The Tree of St Benedict and the sculptural programme of the west front of Bath abbey provide recognizable examples of this,[10] but in general, the property (if we may call it that) is to be sought in other phenomena not specifically Benedictine, most outstandingly in retrospection. The chapels and tombs of external patrons exhibit a powerful concern for public display and demonstration, in particular the proof of kinship ties, secular status and devotional affiliations (expressed by their locations as well as their iconography). To borrow an observation of the late Andrew Martindale's,[11] the Despenser and Beauchamp monuments at Tewkesbury declare what the objective social status of their incumbents was as much as who they were personally; although the extent to which this is so is substantially due – here as elsewhere – to the loss of accompanying inscriptions.[12]

These observations are not revolutionary: one or two may even sound trite. Admittedly, moreover, some of them relate only tangentially to the topic of patronage. They tend to confirm that there was little intrinsically 'Benedictine' that patrons sought to express in the order's art and architecture during the later middle ages, although the two works cited here, along with such evidences as the description of the Benedictine saints represented at Durham, do express the concept to such a developed degree that it must be thought to have constituted an important consideration, at some if not at all houses. The iconography of Sts Benedict, Scholastica, Maur, Dunstan, and others of the order, of which lamentably few examples survive, would be an obvious starting point for a study of what might be called the 'Benedictiness of Benedictine art', although such representations were not, of course, peculiar to the black monks and their reformed counterparts, and in any case, the unquantifiable extent of losses in all contexts would make conclusions tenuous.[13] Certainly, the data has been too thin to admit incorporation of the topic into this study.

Quality is another matter about which patronage *per se* is relatively uninformative. The Sherborne missal and Gloucester's cloister do not represent a mean: both houses possessed works of considerably lower quality. Available finances and the intended status of an object were of course influential factors in determining the quality sought by patrons, but when they conflicted, one might just as easily triumph as the other, resulting either in debt or relatively low-quality art in prestigious contexts. In the case of the latter (e.g. the Romsey retable, the monumental figures of Sts Margaret and Antony on the back of the choir stalls at Gloucester, and the panel paintings left over from Milton), we cannot always be sure that the patrons would have recognized the works they sponsored to be of relatively low quality. Decorum was clearly more important, and so long as this was not compromised, quality as we tend to estimate it was not always a consideration.[14]

---

10 On this example, not discussed above, see Luxford 2000, pp. 325–9.
11 Martindale 1995, p. 155.
12 For lost external inscriptions on Tewkesbury's chantry chapels see OBL MSS Wood C 11, fol. 55r; Wood D 11, fol. 62v. There were others on the thirteenth-century Clare tombs.
13 On the imagery of Sts Benedict and Dunstan see respectively Batselier 1981, *passim*; Ramsay and Sparks 1988 (the latter illustrating non-Benedictine examples).
14 This is not to suppose that a medieval person's ability to discriminate degrees of quality in a work of art or architecture was substantially different from our own.

To sum up: the size, wealth and popularity of the houses covered by this study differed so greatly that little consistency can be identified in the nature of the art and architecture commissioned by and given to them during the later middle ages. Any blanket statements made concerning it are likely to fall foul of counter-examples, or else be applicable to English art and architecture of the period in general (e.g. the comments above concerning variety and quality). Unless Benedictine custodianship, which is the only characteristic that all of the works covered by this study have in common, be accounted an intrinsic property – and to do so would seem odd – then we will admit that there is nothing Benedictine by nature about Benedictine art in general.

(3) What does the patronage of Benedictine art and architecture reveal about the Benedictine order during the 240 years leading up to the Dissolution?

It has already been suggested that the expensive and ongoing programmes of construction and embellishment pursued by Benedictine convents across the west of England after 1300 express a measure of confidence in the maintenance of prosperity. Indeed, they may be interpreted as an expression of more than simply financial confidence. The size and beauty of Benedictine buildings, on estates as well as within the monastic precinct, are an excellent gauge of the overall strength and pride of the order, as well as its relative solvency. They powerfully evoke the recognition and affirmation by monks, nuns and their superiors of the core virtues and privileges of English Benedictinism. This is not unjustifiable reification. That there was a strong vocational self-identification and consciousness among Benedictines has been attested more than once to this point.

That intraclaustral projects were seen by their patrons as expressions of faith in divine providence and judgement, oblations to God and public manifestations of his power, seems fairly obvious given the religious climate of the age, and of the monastic orientation in particular. The matter deserves emphasis, however, as it is certainly the first reason that any contemporary internal patron would have given for the initiation and sustenance of these projects. The old clichés about creation of beautiful works in out-of-the-way places for the 'eyes' of God – the exquisite angels of Gloucester's presbytery vaults, for example, or the inscriptions skied away in Great Malvern's clerestory[15] – have more than a ring of truth, no matter how unsatisfying they may seem to secular historians.[16] Past commentators have cast aspersions (by implication as often as direct accusation) on the religious integrity of late English monasticism in particular, and it is common to find examples culled from episcopal visitation reports and the myriad surviving documents of the Dissolution era cited in support of the view.[17] This is not the place to argue for the convictions of the later medieval Benedictines, but it may be affirmed that there is every indication of deep, widespread and self-conscious pious commitment among black monks and nuns throughout the period covered by this study.[18] It follows that their patronage of art and architecture, in both action and

---

[15] Cf. Habington, II, p. 188: 'I will passe now to the north side of the church, where the windows are of that height that noe man can discover the writeing'.

[16] On the supposed deficiencies of secular (or 'modernist') history see Bennett 2000, pp. 199–200.

[17] Greatrex 2002, passim.

[18] See e.g. Heale 1994, esp. pp. 94–9, 190–235 (a study with order-encompassing implications). See further Chapters, III, pp. 98–9, for a devotional work authored by a Worcester monk which was sent to Bury c.1417–19: a local but probably not rare circumstance.

product, reflects this. That of external patrons, as stressed in chapter six, stands as an independent witness to lay belief in the holiness of individual convents, if not the order as a whole.

Not all that glitters is gold, however. Among the items belonging to the Worcester Lady chapel in 1391 was a burse embroidered with the wheel of fortune.[19] The patronage of this item is a small but telling indication of awareness of the inconstancy of human existence, and by extension the instabilities facing an established and independently endowed institution competing for maintenance of prosperity and dignity with other powerful interests, heavily reliant on external goodwill and support, and subservient to a secular authority in constant need of financial assistance. The contents of the priory's *Liber albus* and its continuations state the same case in greater detail.[20] Viewed retrospectively, the iconography of the burse epitomizes a dominant characteristic of later medieval English Benedictinism that the registers of the priors reveal only at length. This was the spirit of doubt; the implicit, inevitable reverse side of the confidence discussed above. It did not directly contradict that confidence, but rather stood alongside it, informing it occasionally to the point of overstatement. The strongest expression of the coexistence of Benedictine confidence and doubt covered by this study is not to be found in the patronage of a work of art or architecture, but rather the text of a domestic history that relies heavily on such patronage to disguise doubts that nevertheless frequently bubble to the surface. It is John of Glastonbury's chronicle.

This doubt did not manifest itself as self-doubt. As argued in chapter five, the Benedictines generally seem to have considered their place in the world and their claims to sanctity, antiquity, property etc. thoroughly justified. It was rather doubt about the political, financial and moral support they might expect from the external agents with whom they were constrained to interact, and on whom their prosperity ultimately depended. Such doubt led the English Benedictines generally to support and develop the concept of triennial provincial chapters instituted according to canon twelve of the Fourth Lateran Council (1215), and to sustain and elaborate the system of internal visitation also decreed therein. (This canon was widely ignored on the Continent.)[21] It also motivated them to other expressions of co-operation and solidarity, a number of which were collected together in the treatises on the origins of Benedictine monasticism that have been discussed in chapter five. Here, the tacit aspects of public affirmations of confidence must be recognized for what they are. Positive pronouncements about the world and one's place in it, at least as they flowed from the lips and pens of the proprietors of later medieval institutions, also implied degrees of anxiety and mistrust.[22] It may seem unreasonable to say that because they express pride, solidarity and confidence, the crossing towers of Worcester and Gloucester, or the great Perpendicular gate tower at Evesham (for example), also convey doubt and anxiety. However, as there in ample evidence to demonstrate the doubts under which their patrons laboured, the notion deserves impartial consideration. For external patrons, this concept has been examined in relation to Tewkesbury in chapter six.

The order, then, was confident in the strength and defensibility of its core values,

---

19 *HMC XIV:viii*, p. 198: 'Item alius [casus corporalis] de rota fortune.' No donor's name is recorded and it may be assumed a product of monastic patronage.
20 WCL MSS A v, A vi(i), A vi(ii), A vi(iii); priors' registers covering 1301–1540.
21 Bennett 2000, p. 205.
22 Cf. Douglas 1987, p. 1.

deeply and traditionally religious, and given to doubts concerning the reliability of those external powers with which it had to interact. One other core concept expressed in terms of art and architectural patronage, that they were 'clever' negotiators of the world and their place in it, has already been discussed, and we need not recapitulate it here. Further important concepts also recommend themselves. Later medieval Benedictines had a manifest concern for display, particularly where the performance of the liturgy and the 'progresses' and other public appearances of heads of houses were concerned.[23] Their art and architectural patronage bears vivid witness to this. It goes without saying that they also had highly developed aesthetic sensibilities, something evident in the use of aesthetic terminology found in their writings, in the objects recorded as commissioned internally, those calendared in inventories, and of course those which survive. To argue for the existence of a collective aesthetic sensibility would be to overstate the case; but it is clear that the black cowl which came to symbolize monasticism generally for many after the Dissolution[24] was in fact inconsistent with the typical Benedictine's love of the intricate forms, bright tinctures, metals and gems, and rich textures that characterized the products of the order's patronage. The matter takes shape more fully when the later medieval Benedictine predilection for polyphonic music (an object of much expenditure from Glastonbury and Winchester to Tywardreath after c.1480), poetry, and literature is considered.[25]

(4) What does the patronage of Benedictine art and architecture reveal about lay attitudes to the Benedictines during the period 1300–1540?

This study has not looked in detail at external patronage of non-Benedictine art and architecture, but has indicated a number of the other targets for this patronage: parish, college, non-Benedictine monastic house, hospital etc. It has been noticed that Benedictine houses received a small proportion of what was available for patronage relative to the amount that flowed to other institutions (and relative to their collective size). On this inauspicious basis, and if patronage be taken as a reliable gauge of goodwill broadly, it may be concluded that lay attitudes generally to the Benedictines were cool. Yet it has also been pointed out that the lay patronage which did flow to Benedictine houses registers belief in the holiness, honesty and continuity of those institutions. It seems reasonable to suppose that individuals, families and corporations who did place their faith in Benedictines were not radically out of step with the majority. Indeed, there is every indication that their attitude represents a broadly based lay belief in the holiness, honesty and continuity of the houses covered by this study. Although no English nobleman went about as the Münch family of Basel did, with a black monk emblazoned on his coat of arms,[26] the faith that the Beauchamps, Coutenays, Despensers, Mohuns, Luttrells, and Staffords (not to mention the kings and queens of England) had in the

---

23 E.g. those fairs under Benedictine control, at which a monastic presence was inevitable. See for instance the richly appointed prior's fairground chamber (fourteenth century) mentioned in CRWin., p. 10.

24 Cf. Duffy 2001, p. 120.

25 For Tywardreath's music see Orme 1987–91(a). On Winchester's Lady chapel music during the fifteenth and early sixteenth centuries, see Bowers 1999, pp. 210–37.

26 See Goodall 1990, p. 82. Numerous memorials incorporating this escutcheon survive in Basel cathedral.

resident clergy of the houses in which they were buried is nevertheless self-evident. That more noblemen did not seek burial and commemoration in Benedictine churches, chapter houses and cloisters does not indicate a low opinion of the order generally or its houses individually; but rather that other types of religious institution also enjoyed healthy reputations. The same, by and large, may be affirmed of the sub-noble laity. The incidences of civil unrest mentioned in chapter five, along with other oft-mentioned factors such as the occasional complaints of disgruntled parishioners who considered their religious needs inadequately served by Benedictine rectors, must not be allowed to colour the whole picture disproportionately.[27]

On the basis of art and architectural patronage specifically, it is difficult to say more than this. It should be pointed out, however, that it would be wrong to exaggerate the intrinsic importance of Benedictinism to the laity. Indeed, chapter six suggested that the Benedictine status *per se* of a house was on the whole not influential in eliciting an external patron's generosity. Rather, it was the characteristics of a particular house that appealed to them; its sanctity, antiquity (and the reliability this implied), the fact that their ancestors were interred there, the fact that it was engaged in a programme of new works etc. With this in mind it seems potentially hazardous to posit widely held lay attitudes to the order generally. Despite the fact that by the later fifteenth century the *Rule of St Benedict* was available in print and translation to laypeople,[28] we discover disappointingly few indications of lay attitudes to Benedictinism. Official documents (the surviving records of the Court of Chivalry for example) often define houses according to the rule they professed, and the late medieval antiquaries, William Worcestre and John Leland, had a developed ability to discriminate between houses of different orders that may be supposed to have extended to the bulk of the lay populace. But Worcestre and Leland do not comment on the virtues and vices of the order as they perceived them. The former's attack on the monks of St Benet-at-Holm, while noting the order to which they belonged, is local and issue-specific, not general and all-embracing like the complaints of Henry V and Wolsey.[29]

Lay attitudes to the Benedictines, then, are properly sought in the attention shown to individual houses, or conversely, in attitudes to monasticism generally. The former issue does not require exposition in view of what has already been said. For a grasp of the latter, it will be helpful to cite a few illustrations of the lay tendency to generalize about monasticism. Robert Aske's apology defended monasteries in general; in 1536 Henry VIII discriminated between 'the little and small abbeys, priories and other religious houses of monks, canons and nuns' and the 'great solemn monasteries' without reference to orders;[30] when the supporters of traditional religion in the Western Rebellion (1549) demanded the re-establishment of two religious houses in each county, they said nothing of orders or rules;[31] the Trenchards of Wolfeton Hall (Charminster, Dor.),

---

27 Youings 1971, e.g. pp. 14–15, 139–41, is particularly guilty of this, but hardly stands alone.
28 See *Manual*, II, pp. 460–2; also *Itinerary Worcestre*, pp. 250–1; *Benedictines and the Book*, nos 4–6 (unpaginated); *RBFox*, p. 19.
29 *Itinerary Worcestre*, pp. 2–3. A personal grudge probably also generated the sardonic macronic verse in LPL MS 633, fol. 85v: 'Gracia nulla perit nisi gratia Blakmonachorum / Est et semper erit litill thank in fine laborum.' James and Jenkins 1930–32, p. 781.
30 Youings 1971, p. 155.
31 Rose-Troup 1913, p. 221: 'Item we wyll that the halfe parte of the abbey landes and Chauntrye landes, in euerye mans possessions . . . be geuen again to two places, where two of the chief Abbeis was with in euery Countye'.

along with other families, displayed the arms of Benedictine and non-Benedictine houses in the stained glass heraldry of their manor house without any apparent distinction on the basis of order;[32] the wills of the laity do not tend to mention the order of the houses they privilege.[33] These and many other indications suggest that monasticism was in practical terms a monolithic concept to laypeople across the social spectrum. Thus, while the Benedictine status of a house will have been obvious to patrons of its art and architecture, the same house is likely to have been thought 'monastic' in a less precise sense as well, i.e. as opposed to 'mendicant' or 'secular'. On this account, the attitudes of the laity towards monasticism generally can be understood to a significant degree as synonymous with their attitudes to Benedictinism. This conclusion receives some support from the fact that throughout the west, Benedictine houses dominated the monastic landscape. There were alternatives, and testators sought them out (for size and popularity were not always contiguous), but the 'great, solemn monasteries wherein . . . religion [was] right well kept and preserved' were overwhelmingly those of black monks and nuns.

Thus, though the patronage of Benedictine art and architecture by a proportion of the laity may be taken to indicate broadly positive attitudes to individual houses of the order, it would be unwise to suggest that it reflects anything substantial about attitudes to the order as a whole, or demonstrates a developed conception of Benedictinism as a distinct entity within the broader spectrum of monasticism. Members of the laity may have had such a conception, of course, as secular and regular ecclesiastics did. However, available evidence does not provide a reliable gauge of it, and it is thus safer to confine conclusions about what patronage reveals of lay attitudes to the Benedictines to particular houses of the order.

(5) What, if anything, does the patronage of Benedictine art and architecture reveal about the Dissolution of 1536–40?

This question would seem to require an answer. The study so far has avoided undue reference to the Dissolution because the author considers that it has little bearing on the subject at hand. This has not been a study of the art of decline, because monastic decline, like so many aspects of history, is a phenomenon of hindsight. As a common-sense position, this does not need to be argued for at length. It is meaningless to invoke historical determinism, for even if the Dissolution was inevitable, there is no concrete suggestion that anybody knew it. The Dissolution was to English monasticism what the eruption of Vesuvius in A.D. 79 was to Pompeii and Herculaneum. If, in the last days, some indications of catastrophe hovered over the mountain, then the people could not or would not recognize them for what they were. They went on leading their time- and habit-conditioned lives, building their spacious houses, covering their walls with wonderful paintings, and trusting that affairs would continue as usual.

Yet the Dissolution came, totally dismantling every convent covered by this study, and destroying or transferring the ownership of practically every work mentioned in it. There it is, alive for us today in the astonishing pen-and-ink illustrations of the survey roll of Glastonbury's lands drawn up under the auspices of Richard Pollard and Thomas

---

[32] Hutchins Dorset, II, pp. 547–51.
[33] Except in the case of mendicant houses.

Moyle in September 1539, immediately after Abbot Whiting's attainder (Plate 45).[34] The naked figure of 'Veritas' and the profile representation of 'Solymon Turkischar' savour of truth's victory over corruption and superstition, while the drummer, piper, standard-bearer and musketeer of the main initial march symbolically over the lands of the ancient abbey, laid out at their feet on no fewer than fourteen closely written membranes.[35] The royal achievement, crowned with the phylactery thrice inscribed 'Vivat Rex', stands alongside, guarantor of the dispossession, and its chief beneficiary. The tenor is one of unalloyed triumph: 'veritas vincet tandem' reads the inscription accompanying naked Truth. Mission accomplished.

Considered at length, with all that the abbey of Glastonbury was, owned and meant in mind, these illustrations inspire a sort of horror. They also insist that the act of general dispossession they symbolize, which has had such a fundamental impact on the course of monastic studies in this country, be addressed at some level here. So we must say what can be said; and that is simply that the patronage of Benedictine art and architecture tells us nothing about the Dissolution. Or, put another way, it tells us that neither internal nor external patrons had any inkling of it. It is possible that at a minute to midnight, Benedictines and their supporters became suspicious, but this is not apparent in the art and architectural record. Nikolaus Pevsner, considering Clement Lichfield's sixteenth-century bell-tower at Evesham (Plate 14), wrote that 'it is astonishing how unaware England's abbots were of the gathering storm. If they had not been, how could they indulge [sic] in such conspicuous display?'[36] His astonishment was misplaced. For Lichfield, as for the local laity who contributed to the project around 1530, there was no intelligible indication of the storm's approach. Even Gloucester's prophetic abbots could not have foreseen it. They did not, they kept building. The evidence that certain monastic interests sold off or 'panic-leased' property during the 1530s in preparation for the end[37] must be matched alongside the building boom of which Evesham's tower is one manifestation. It must be reckoned against the sacrist of Glastonbury who recorded payments for plate, stained glass and other items in his *compotus* for 1539, the same house's appointment of an organist 'yn syngyng and playng upon the organs yn the high quier . . . [for the] terme of his lyfe' in 1534, and the conviction of Thomas Style, who willed burial with the monks of Bath in 1536.[38] It must negotiate the well-known fact that on 18 December 1537 Henry VIII personally refounded the former Augustinian priory of Bisham in Berkshire for a Benedictine abbot and thirteen monks.[39] He who seeks will find as many indications and more that monks, nuns and the laity they interacted with had no notion of the Dissolution (or at very least, and after 1535, no firm conviction that it would happen to them)[40] as he will that they detected their fate beforehand and stripped assets to mitigate its impact on their lives. Arguably the most telling of these indications reside in acts of art and architectural patronage.

---

34 OBL MS Bodley Rolls 19. Illustrations occur on the first, thirteenth and fourteenth membranes. Cf. Whalley 1969, p. xiii and pls 1–4, and the illustrations of the first membrane of BL Egerton MS 2164 (roll of property formerly belonging to the Benedictine abbey of St John, Colchester).
35 Each membrane is approximately 30cm high by 45cm wide.
36 Pevsner 1968, pp. 145–6.
37 See e.g. *Suppression Letters*, pp. 193–4 (Gloucester); Youings 1971, pp. 136–8 (Bath).
38 Watkin 1948, p. 77; SMW(b), p. 30.
39 LPHVIII, XII:ii, pp. 94, 168; K&H, pp. 59–60, 148; Knowles 1959, pp. 302, 318.
40 Cf. Cunich 1997, p. 156.

Epilogue: Coming full Circle

At the end of the 1530s, throughout the 1540s and into the early 1550s, a great trade in second-hand monastic art and architecture sprang up in western England. The commissioners sent plate and significant vestments off to the Tower of London, retaining some items of lesser value as perquisites, which they sold locally.[41] Many books disappeared abroad; others went into private libraries, not least that of Henry VIII.[42] Anything that could be salvaged was: monastic buildings and fittings were cannibalized to construct and restore secular ones. The modern perambulator of Shaftesbury, Cerne, Tewkesbury and many other West Country towns and villages passes chunks of Benedictine structures built into more recent ones with greater or lesser congruity. These later buildings are of all degrees: it will be remembered that much of the superb sculpture of Winchester's great reredos was sawn flush and buried for the sake of garden walls.[43] Oaken Perpendicular doors bearing Abbot Richard Kidderminster's initials were hung on a house in Winchcombe, while the abbey's bells were dispersed as far as Stoneleigh in Warwickshire.[44] Seven loads of timber from the chapter house at Glastonbury made their way to Wells, at a cost to Richard Brampton, the cathedral's *custos operum*, of £2 2s; and 6½ cwt of lead from the ruined monastery cost him £2 3s 4d.[45] (Perhaps some of the more historically minded canons saw the irony in this.) The parish church of St Mary at Sherborne became a clearing house for ex-monastic goods. Much material from Cerne abbey found its way there: 'Item rec' off Ric' Corser ffor iiij statues þᵗ came from Cerne, xijs' and 'Item rec' of John Morrante for v images that came from Serne ijs viijd' etc. the churchwardens' accounts for 1549–50 record.[46] Why Richard Corser, John Morrant and many others like them wanted these images, particularly at such a late date is unknown. (Parliamentary injunctions of 1547 had banned devotional images from public places of worship, so they were not destined for parish churches.)[47] Many must have found their way into private homes, as aides to meditation, decoration, souvenirs, remembrancers.[48]

In some cases, substantial components of Benedictine buildings, or even buildings entire, moved. Parts of Milton's cloister went to make the south nave aisle at Hilton, while the churchwardens of St Mary's, Cerne, secured for their church a new east window. In neither case is there a perfect fit, but the parochial interests were understandably unwilling to look a gift horse in the mouth: here was Perpendicular glory on the cheap. The hexagonal lavatorium at Sherborne was transposed to the town centre, where Leland saw it in the early 1540s, and where it still stands, with its central boss of

---

[41] Archbold 1892, pp. 176–7.

[42] Indeed, monastic books had been 'pouring' into the royal library since the early 1530s: *Lib.Hen.VIII*, p. xxiii.

[43] Atkinson 1935, pp. 159–60; cf. *Gothic*, p. 461.

[44] See chapter one. The doors are ill. in Luxford 2002(e), fig. 255.

[45] *HMC Wells*, II, p. 271: *compotus* of 1549/50.

[46] *CWA Sherborne*, pp. 123, 170. These are unlikely to have been ex-parochial images, for also on sale from Cerne were large quantities of building materials that cannot have come from the parish church.

[47] Duffy 2001, pp. 177–9.

[48] In January 1550 private ownership of images was comprehensively prohibited by an act of parliament: Marks 2004, p. 264; see also Duffy 1992, p. 568.

the abbey's arms proudly displayed by reverential angels. The magnificent mid-fourteenth-century cloister, however, was torn down for a pittance, and its stone deployed around the town.[49] Glastonbury soon became known as 'the quarry', and Shaftesbury's abbey church, though the last in Dorset to be surrendered to the commissioners, was razed to the ground by the mid-1540s.[50] As monasteries became mythologized as sites of alchemy, prophecy, mournful ghosts and buried treasure,[51] the novelty value of former Benedictine works came to outweigh their utilitarian significance. At Haselby in Wiltshire, John Aubrey (d.1697) heard Sir Hugh Speke boast that 'he hath the abbot of Glastonbury's carpet here, in the midst whereof is his coat of arms, richly embroidered'.[52] In 1759 Horace Walpole bought 'a monk's chair full of psalms' from the same abbey, which was sold at his death for seventy guineas.[53] Successive proprietors of Old Wardour castle (Wilts.) placed a premium on a wooden *poculum caritatis* standing on three feet and carved about with the Twelve Apostles, which they had obtained after the great abbey fell.[54]

Thus the objects of patronage, like their dispossessed owners, endured a diaspora. The proportion not actually destroyed was scattered across the social spectrum, from the king downwards. Even ex-Benedictines owned them, and in exceptional cases, they were retained by their original patrons. William More, for example, held on to the manor houses of Crowle and Grimley, to which he had devoted so much attention as prior: he was living in the latter at his death in 1558.[55] So it was that the beneficiaries of this art and architectural disapora reflected the socio-economic breadth of those whose patronage had helped to make the Benedictine houses of the west what they had become by the mid-1530s.

From a certain perspective, then, the patronage of Benedictine art and architecture, like that of other types of monastic property, may be seen to have come full circle. In moving at last to the far side of the Dissolution, this study has also buckled its belt, residing once again with the detritus of art, architecture and documents surveyed in chapter one. It is sobering to stand where we do and look back. Our personal, recurrent experience demonstrates that the images we construct of things anticipated rarely, if ever, survive the revelations of actual acquaintance. We cannot test our images of the later middle ages against the realities of the period, of course; but we realize, nevertheless, how different this past that we study must have been from that which even the best-informed and most open-minded of us can imagine. We must not, then, presume to speak too boldly for, or even about, the later middle ages; that far, 'fair field full of folk'[56] that we fancy we glimpse in the borders of the Luttrell psalter and the naves of Blythburgh and

---

49 *Itinerary*, I, p. 153; *CWA Sherborne*, p. 125: 'Item *paid* to William Wever ffor pullyng downe the vawte off the cloyster, iiijd.'
50 *DNHAFC* 1908, p. lxxii.
51 E.g. Thomas 1991, pp. 115–16, 279, 321, 463–4, 468, 481.
52 Aubrey, p. 33.
53 Horne 1943–46, p. 19. This was apparently identical to 'John Thorne's chair', now at the episcopal palace, Wells (Thorne was one of Glastonbury's martyr monks of November 1539). There may originally have been a set of them.
54 Milner 1794, *passim*. See pp. 412–14 for its importance to the seventeenth-century owners of Old Wardour; p. 416 for a suggested date c.1500.
55 Noake 1866, pp. 204–5; *BRECP*, p. 849.
56 Langland, II, p. 2.

Pickworth. The author of this study hopes to have avoided the charge of doing so; and if he has not, then perhaps these postscriptal comments will intercede on his behalf. What we get right and wrong about the period is important, but what we are ignorant of is liable to be more important still – and certainly more voluminous. With these thoughts as its phylactery, so to speak, this study concludes.

Appendix 1

Houses Covered by the Study

The following list includes all of the Benedictine houses that existed in the region and period covered by this book. Not all of the houses mentioned have been discussed because, for a number of the small ones, no germane information appears to exist. Ellingham (Hants), Livers Ocle, Monkland (both Herefords.), Newent (Gloucs.), and Spettisbury (Dor.) each had an average population of one monk during that portion of the later middle ages for which they endured, and a number of others had either two or three. While the author has no wish to misrepresent the religious integrity of those who staffed such outposts, or their value to local communities, it is fair to say that their institutions existed primarily to collect revenue, not to spend it on art and architecture, and that whatever patronage they exercised will have been minor and mostly mundane. It is certainly obscure. Indeed, some Benedictine cells the existence or status of which is insufficiently attested (e.g. the Bristol 'priories' of St Phillip and St Stephen) have been omitted altogether. The list is based on the information assembled by David Knowles and R. Neville Hadcock (K&H, pp. 52–95, 253–69); whose statistics, if they are not always perfect, are nevertheless the most reliable and relied-upon available.[1] The additional abbreviation 'Ind.', for 'independent', has been introduced. Italics indicate an alien house never made denizen. Approximate incomes are minimum amounts net: for houses with annual net incomes of over £1000, cf. Knowles 1959, pp. 473–4.

Name	County	Approximate income c.1535[2]	Year dissolved	House dependent on
Abbotsbury	Dor.	£ 390	1539	Ind.
Astley	*Worcs.*	*£ 20*	*1414*	*Evreux, St Taurin*
Athelney	Som.	£ 209	1539	Ind.
Avebury	*Wilts.*	*£ 36*	*1378*	*Boscherville, St George*
Barrow Gurney	Som.	£ 24	1536	Ind.
Bath	Som.	£ 617	1539	Ind.
Bristol, St James	Som.	£ 57	1540	Tewkesbury
Cannington	Som.	£ 39	1536	Ind.
Cerne	Dor.	£ 575	1539	Ind.
Clatford	*Wilts.*	*£ 48*	*c.1439*	*St Victor-en-Caux*
Cowick	Dev.	£ 78	1538	Bec-Hellouin/Tavistock[3]
Cranborne	Dor.	£ 55	1540	Tewkesbury
Deerhurst	Gloucs.	£ 134	1540	St Denis/Tewkesbury[4]

[1] On the importance of Knowles and Hadcock's statistics, and some of their shortcomings, see Heale 2004, p. 277.

[2] Or when assessed, if this occurred earlier (as in the case of a number of alien priories).

[3] Transferred to Tavistock in 1464.

[4] Transferred to Tewkesbury in 1467.

Name	County	Approximate income c.1535[2]	Year dissolved	House dependent on
Dunster	Som.	£ 37	1539	Bath
Ellingham	*Hants*	*£ 14*	*1440*	*St Sauveur-le-Vicomte*
Evesham	Worcs.	£1183	1540	Ind.
Ewyas Harold	Herefords.	_____	1359	Gloucester
Exeter, St Nicholas	Dev.	£ 147	1536	Battle
Frampton	*Dor.*	*£ 294*	*1414*	*Caen, St Etienne*
Glastonbury	Som.	£3311	1539	Ind.
Gloucester	Gloucs.	£1430	1540	Ind.
Great Malvern	Worcs.	£ 308	1540	Westminster
Hayling	*Hants*	*£ 144*	*1413*	*Jumièges*
Hereford, St Guthlac	Herefords.	£121	1538	Gloucester
Horton	Dor.	£ 53	1539	Sherborne
Kilpeck	Herefords.	_____	1428	Gloucester
Kington St Michael	Wilts.	£ 25	1536	Ind.
Leominster	Herefords.	£ 448	1539	Reading
Leonard Stanley	Gloucs.	£ 106	1538	Gloucester
Little Malvern	Worcs.	£ 98	c.1537	Worcester
Livers Ocle	*Herefords.*	*£ 24*	*1414*	*Lyre*
Loders	*Dor.*	*£ 80*	*1414*	*Montebourg*
Malmesbury	Wilts.	£ 803	1539	Ind.
Milton	Dor.	£ 578	1539	Ind.
Modbury	*Dev.*	*£ 70*	*1441*	*St Pierre-sur-Dives*
Monkland	*Herefords.*	*£ 11*	*c.1414*	*Conches*
Monk Sherborne	*Hants*	*£ 130*	*1414*	*Cerisy-le-Fôret*
Muchelney	Som.	£ 447	1538	Ind.
Newent	*Gloucs.*	*£ 130*	*1399*	*Cormeilles*
Ogbourne St George	*Wilts.*	*£ 500+*	*1405*	*Bec-Hellouin*
Otterton	*Dev.*	*£ 120*	*1414*	*Mont-St Michel*
Pershore	Worcs.	£ 643	1540	Ind.
Piddletrenthide	Dor.	_____	1345	Winchester-Hyde
Pilton	Dev.	£ 56	1539	Malmesbury
Polsloe	Dev.	£ 164	1538	Ind.
Romsey	Hants	£ 393	1539	Ind.
St Michael's Mount	*Corn.*	*£ 110*	*c.1414*	*Mont-St Michel*
Shaftesbury	Dor.	£1166	1539	Ind.
Sherborne	Dor.	£ 682	1539	Ind.
Spettisbury	*Dor.*	*£ 35*	*c.1324*	*Préaux, St Pierre*
Stogursey	*Som.*	*£ 58*	*1442*	*Lonlay*
Tavistock	Dev.	£ 902	1539	Ind.
Tewkesbury	Gloucs.	£1598	1540	Ind.
Totnes	Dev.	£ 124	1536	Angers, St Serge/Ind.[5]
Tywardreath	Corn.	£ 123	1536	Angers, St Serge/Ind.[6]
Upavon	*Wilts.*	*£ 32*	*1414*	*St Wandrille*
Wherwell	Hants	£ 339	1539	Ind.

[5] Made denizen in 1416, whence it was independent.
[6] Made denizen c.1400, whence it was independent.

Name	County	Approximate income c.1535[2]	Year dissolved	House dependent on
Wilton	Wilts.	£ 601	1539	Ind.
Winchcombe	Gloucs.	£ 759	1539	Ind.
Winchester	Hants	£1507	1539	Ind.
Winchester-Hyde	Hants	£ 865	1540	Ind.
Winchester-Nunnaminster	Hants	£ 179	1539	Ind.
Worcester	Worcs.	£1290	1540	Ind.

Appendix 2

Motives and Misconceptions in the Patronage of Superiors

Reproduction of these documents is intended to illustrate in greater detail points made in chapter three concerning over-attribution of patronage responsibilities to Benedictine superiors. Document 1 is an extract from the chronicle of Evesham abbey. It is typical in its eulogistic tone and ascription of most works to the abbot. Document 2 is an extract from a monastic record which, while dealing with the same campaign, demonstrates the patronage role played by the whole convent in the works. The translation of 1 is largely that of Salzman 1997, pp. 387–8 (by permission of Oxford University Press), with a few authorial interventions based on CAEve., pp. 286–7. The document 2 is extracted from Tindal 1794, pp. 120–1 note.

1. The account given in the Chronicon Abbatiæ de Evesham of the great campaign of building and embellishment carried out at Evesham during the abbacy of John de Brokehampton (1282–1316).

The magnificent achievements and accomplishments of Abbot Brokehampton.

Abbot John de Brokehampton worthily made the chapel of the Blessed Virgin Mary with windows and handsome vaulting and gilded bosses; in which chapel were magnificently depicted the story of the Saviour and stories of various virgins: he also erected there two sumptuous panels, painted and gilded, before and above the altar. He also made the chapter house, ingeniously designed within and without, with excellent vaulting, without a central pillar, beautifully adorned with gilded bosses, and surrounded with glass windows. Which building on account of its spaciousness and beauty is held to be one of the chief chapter houses in this realm. Also, that walk of the cloister opposite the chapter house, over which the monks' studies are built, was erected in his time and with his aid. He also made a good broad dormitory, well and strongly supported on vaults from one end to the other; under which various offices are arranged, namely, the chapel master's chamber, the sacrist's chamber, the misericord and others. The noble infirmary building, also, was erected in his time and with his aid at great expense, where there are now various chambers for the sick, built by the devotion and industry of the monks of this church, as may clearly be seen. He also gave the convent towards building the refectory 100 pounds of silver, with all the timber necessary. Thus, with this God given help, walls, windows, roof and everything was carried through. All these buildings were covered with lead except the infirmary; and of that, the chapel was covered with lead. Also he made the long chamber for those who have been bled, with the vault, over which is built the ambulatory and the privy dormitory. He made also the noteworthy hall of the abbot, of which all the walls were carried out in stone, and he set up over it that roof of remarkable timber construction and covered with lead, and a porch at the door of the hall, with vaulting, and over it a house of receipt, likewise covered with lead. To this hall he attached a kitchen, which he made worthily entirely in stone. He also made a pantry beside the kitchen, and the abbot's chamber painted with the story of Joseph, with a small chapel attached to it; and under this chamber he built a strong vault, where now is the wine-cellar. Likewise, he had the brewhouses and bakehouses strongly and finely built. Moreover, he made two new chambers on the west of the court, with their vaults, for guests, and the cellarer's chamber, with the other joined to it well built upon an arch of stone. Also he made the long stable for guests, on the same side. The long stable on the north side of the court, assigned to the obedientiaries, was built in his time and with his aid. The kitchener's pittancery, with a vault, and over it the hall built for guests, was erected in his time and with his aid; and he built and completed the convent kitchen, adjoining the abbot's kitchen.

2. Division of patronage responsibilities concerning the same campaign of building and embellishment as recorded in the Evesham register now BL MS 3763 Harley (dated 1295).

In the name of the Father, Son and Holy Ghost, Amen. In the year of our Lord 1295, and on the ides of February, the abbot and convent being assembled in chapter, John, abbot of Evesham and of the convent there, having special regard to the finishing of his chapter house then just begun, and also to the reparation of the dormitory, refectory, cloister and infirmary, and further considering that the common fund of the house, to which in matters of this kind chief recourse was to be made, was then very slender and nearly exhausted; with provident consideration and unanimous consent they chose and appointed five of the fraternity, viz. John Strech, Robert de Reckeford, Walter de Blockeleye, Adam de Hauleye, and William de Bengeworth, giving to the said persons full power of providing and ordering how and from whence works of this kind might be best and most easily executed, and the indigence of the community in future be allevi-ated. The prior and the rest of the convent granted, and *bone fide* promised, that they would trust to the provident care and ordering of the said five brethren, and would hold their proceedings good and lawful. The aforesaid five brethren, having then consulted with the abbot and with certain of the fraternity who were chiefly skilled in such matters, resolved that on every year, at the four accustomed quarterly terms, forty shil-lings should be set apart and paid from the priorship. Ten marks from the chamberlain's office. Sixteen marks from the sacristy. Ten marks from the priorship of Penwortham. Forty shillings from the infirmary. Two shillings from the chantry. Ten shillings from the deanery. Twelve shillings from the altar of the Blessed Virgin. Three shillings from the gardener's office. The aforesaid five brethren ordained also, that all the rents of the pittanciary should be given up for this contribution, and those expenses that official should incur in collations and other necessary charges should be made up to him. Like-wise that all the rents of the bursary of the convent, all bequests to the *martilogium*, and those made towards the repairs of the church, should be contributed to the same purpose: excepting only such as were necessary to the expense of that office. And all the offerings to the Cross, excepting those made on the two festivals of the Holy Cross, which belong to the sacristy, should in like manner be contributed. Moreover, that all offerings at the tomb of St Wulsin, and those made at the gate of the church, as well in wax as in money, should be collected for the same uses: excepting only the necessary expenses for supplying the lights. To collect, receive, and faithfully to expend all which, the above five brethren ordained that two monks should be by the prior and convent, in Chapter, deputed, who should demand, collect, receive and deposit in the common chest of the treasury this contribution, keeping it under their care and the prior's key, and should afterward, at the will and disposal of the prior and the rest of the convent, deliver it out and pay it away. And because it seemed to the aforesaid five brethren that each of the offices to be taxed were, *communibus annis*, competent both to the contribution and their own support, they ordained that, if any one of the community who had the care of any of the aforesaid offices to be taxed, should of his own accord, and contrary to the will and assent of the convent, in any way diminish, detract from, or detain any part of the contribution thus provided to the great utility of the church, (which may God avert!) the abbot, at the requisition of the convent, may without delay remove from his office such official, whosoever he be, as an unworthy, useless, and improvident guardian of the property of the church, and by advice of the convent may appoint in his place another more worthy person. – This provision or ordinance the aforesaid abbot has accepted and ratified in all things; to the greater confirmation of which his seal, together with that of the convent, is affixed to it. – Given in the chapter house of Evesham on the day and year aforesaid.

Manuscripts Cited

Cambridge
Fitzwilliam Museum
    MS 2–1957 (hours, Shaftesbury)
Gonville and Caius College
    MS 391 (Hare, *Collectanea*)
Professor S.D. Keynes
    MS 1 (*Gesta Regum* frag. and *tabula*, Glastonbury)
Trinity College
    MS B 3 7 (Stephen Langton, Glastonbury)
    MS B 15 1 (*Legenda Aurea*, Winchester)
    MS R 5 16 (chron. etc. Glastonbury)
    MS R 5 33 (chron. etc. Glastonbury)
    MS R 7 13 (Latin *Brut*, Wm. Malmes., Sherborne)
    MS R 7 14 (French *Brut*)
    MS 0 2 53 (commonplace book, early 16th cent.)
    MS 0 3 59 (illustrated roll of the procession of parliament of 1518)
University Library
    MS Dd 1 17 (misc. vol., Glastonbury)
    MS Dd 8 2 (*Liber vitæ*, offices, Kington St Michael)
    MS Gg 2 18 (*Legenda Aurea*, Winchester)
    MS Additional 6688 (missal, Bromsgrove)

Evesham
Almonry Museum
    Psalter (Evesham)

Exeter
Devon Record Office
    W1258M/G4/53

Gloucester
Cathedral Library
    MS 34 (chron., Gloucester)
    Register C (i) (reg. of Thomas Braunche, Gloucester)
    Register C (ii) (reg. of John Newton, Gloucester)
    Register D (reg. of William Malvern, 1514–28, Gloucester)
    Register E (reg. of William Malvern, 1528–38, Gloucester)

London
British Library
    MS Additional 29943 (Watercolours and drawings by John Carter)
    MS Arundel 2 (reg. of Walter de Monington, Glastonbury)

MS Cotton Domitian A viii, fols 126v–161v (chron., Gloucester)
MS Cotton Faustina A ii, fols 1r–98v (reg. of Sherborne abbey)
MS Cotton Galba E iv (register, Henry of Eastry, C.C.Canterbury)
MS Cotton Nero D iii (misc. reg., Evesham)
MS Egerton 2104(A) (gen. cart., Wherwell)
MS Harley 641 (M. *Polonius*, Glastonbury)
MS Harley 651 (*tabula*, Glastonbury)
MS Harley 960 (psalter, Hyde)
MS Harley 3763 (misc. reg., Evesham)
MS Harley 3776, fols 118r–127v (*Cathalogus sanctorum pausantium in Anglia*)
MS Lansdowne 427 (18th-century extracts from Evesham MSS etc.)
MS Royal B vii (roll) (Western Rebellion, 1497; fines)
MS Additional 17463 (Powell's topographical collections for Somerset)
MS Additional 27866 (psalter, Wherwell)
MS Additional 44949 (psalter, Tywardreath?)
MS Additional 43405–6 (breviary etc. Muchelney)
College of Arms
Muniment 18/19 (Pedigree of Boteler of Sudeley, including the Evesham world map)
Lambeth Palace Library
MS 99, fols 187r–196r (*Cathalogus sanctorum pausantium in anglia*)
MS 179 (historical texts, Gloucester)
MS 3285 (Audley psalter, Shaftesbury)
MS 4513 (Abbotsbury breviary)
Public Record Office
C 150/1 (gen. cart., Gloucester)
E 164/24 (gen. cart., Malmesbury)

Oxford
Balliol College
MS 271 (gen. cart., Hereford, St Guthlac)
Bodleian Library
MS Bodley Rolls 19 (Glastonbury estates, 1539)
MS Lat Misc B 2 (roll) (genealogy Henry VI/pedigree Tewkesbury founders)
MS Rawl liturg f 1 (hours, Gloucester)
MS Top Glouc d 2 (Founders' Book of Tewkesbury)
MS Wood B 1 (Gloucester *Memoriale*)
MS Wood C 10 (Wood, *Collectanea*)
MS Wood D 11 (Wood, *Collectanea*)
MS Wood Empt 1 (gen. cart., Glastonbury)
Corpus Christi College
MS 89 (*Polychronicon*, Gloucester)
The Queen's College
MS 304 (misc. vol., Glastonbury)
MS 367 (chron., Gloucester)

Romsey
Parish (former abbey) church
Psalter (Nunnaminster/Romsey)

Worcester
Cathedral Library
   MS F 129 (Durandus, Worcester)
   MS Register A vi(ii) (priors' reg., Worcester)
   MS Register A vi(iii) (priors' reg., Worcester)
   MS Register A xii (misc. reg., Worcester)
   Muniment C 429

Works Cited

Primary sources

Abbreuiacion	John Capgrave's *Abbreuiacion of Chronicles*, ed. J.P. Lucas, London (EETS, os 285), 1983
Acc.Wor.	*Accounts of the Priory of Worcester for the Year 13–14 Henry VIII. A.D. 1521–2*, ed. J.M. Wilson, Oxford, 1907
AMSA	*Annales Monasterii Sancti Albani a Johanne Amundesham conscripti*, II vols, ed. H.T. Riley, London (RS, 28), 1870–71
Anglia Sacra	*Anglia Sacra*, II vols, ed. H. Wharton, London, 1691
Annales	*Annales Monastici*, V vols, ed. H.R. Luard, London (RS, 36), 1864–69
Aubrey	J. Aubrey, *Collections for Wiltshire, Part 1: North Wiltshire*, ed. J. Britton, London, 1821
Bath Deeds	*Ancient Deeds Belonging to the Corporation of Bath, XIII–XVI Cent.* (vol. IV), ed. C.W. Shickle, Bath, 1921
BBA	*Bridgwater Borough Archives V: 1468–1485*, ed. R.W. Dunning and T.D. Tremlett, Frome (SRS, 70), 1971.
Black Death	*The Black Death*, ed. and trans. R. Horrox, Manchester, 1994
BRECP	*Biographical Register of the English Cathedral Priories of the Province of Canterbury c.1066–1540*, ed. J. Greatrex, Oxford 1997
Brev.Hyde	*The Monastic Breviary of Hyde Abbey, Winchester*, VI vols, ed. J.B.L. Tollhurst, London (Henry Bradshaw Soc., 69–71, 76, 78, 80), 1932–42
Brut	*The Brut or The Chronicles of England*, ed. F.W.D. Brie, II vols, London (EETS, os 131, 136), 1906–08
Bury Wills	*Wills and Inventories from the Registers of the Commissary of Bury St Edmunds and the Archdeacon of Sudbury*, ed. S. Tymms, London (CS, 1st ser. 49), 1850
CABury	*The Chronicle of Jocelin of Brakelond*, ed. and trans. H.E. Butler, London, 1949
CAEve.	*Chronicon Abbatiæ de Evesham ad annum 1418*, ed. W.D. Macray, London (RS, 29),1863
Cart.Bath	*Two Chartularies of the Priory of St. Peter at Bath*, ed. W. Hunt, Frome (SRS, 7), 1893
Cart.Beau.	*The Beauchamp Cartulary*, ed. E. Mason, London (Pipe Roll Soc., ns. 43), 1980
Cart.Cerne	'The Cartulary of Cerne Abbey, Commonly Known as the Red Book of Cerne', ed. and trans. B. F. Lock, *PDNHAFC*, xxviii (1907), pp. 65–95 (I); xxix (1908), pp. 195–224 (II)
Cart.Chichester	*The Cartulary of the High Church of Chichester*, ed. W.D. Peckham, Lewes (Sussex Rec. Soc., 46), 1946

Cart.Glaston.	*The Great Chartulary of Glastonbury Abbey*, III vols, ed. A. Watkin, Frome (SRS, 59, 63, 64), 1945–50
Cart.Much.&Ath.	*Two Cartularies of the Benedictine Abbeys of Muchelney and Athelney in the County of Somerset*, ed. E.H. Bates, Frome (SRS, 14), 1899
Cart.StN.Exon.	'List of the Charters in the Cartulary of St. Nicholas, at Exeter', ed. T. Phillipps, *Collectanea Topographica et Genealogica*, i (1834), pp. 60–5, 184–9, 250–4, 374–88
Cart.Winch.	*Cartulary of Winchester Cathedral*, ed. A.W. Goodman, Winchester, 1927
CCR	*Calendar of the Close Rolls Preserved in the Public Record Office*
CFR	*Calendar of Fine Rolls Preserved in the Public Record Office*
CGA(C)	John of Glastonbury, *The Chronicle of Glastonbury Abbey*, ed. J.P. Carley, trans. D. Townsend, Woodbridge, 1985
CGA(H)	John of Glastonbury, *Chronica sive Historia de Rebus Glastoniensibus*, II vols, ed. T. Hearne, Oxford, 1726
Chapters	*Documents Illustrating the Activities of the General and Provincial Chapters of the English Black Monks 1215–1540*, III vols, ed. W.A. Pantin, London (CS, 3rd ser. 45, 47, 54), 1931–37
Chaucer	Geoffrey Chaucer, *The Canterbury Tales*, ed. N. Coghill, Harmondsworth, 1977
Chron.Lanercost	*Chronicon de Lanercost M.CC.I – M.CCC.XLVI*, ed. J. Stevenson, Edinburgh, 1839
Chron.Oxenedes	*Chronica Johannis de Oxenedes*, ed. H. Ellis, London (RS, 13), 1859
Chron. St Albans	*The St Albans Chronicle: The Chronica maiora of Thomas Walsingham I 1376–1394*, ed. J. Taylor, W.R. Childs and L. Watkiss, Oxford, 2003
CJR	*Chronica Johannis de Reading et anonymi Cantuariensis 1346–1367*, ed. J. Tait, Manchester 1914, 99–186
CLC	*Historical Collections of a Citizen of London in the Fifteenth Century*, ed. J. Gardiner, London (CS, 2nd ser. 17), 1876
CM	*Matthaei Parisiensis monachi Sancti Albani: Chronica majora*, VII vols, ed. H.R. Luard, London (RS, 57), 1872–83
Collectanea	*Collectanea I*, ed. T.F. Palmer, Frome (SRS, 39), 1924
Collectanea Leland	J. Leland, *De Rebus Britannicis Collectanea*, VI vols, ed. T. Hearne, London, 1770
Commentarii	——, *Commentarii de Scriptoribus Britannicis*, ed. T. Hearne, Oxford, 1709
Concilia	*Concilia Magnæ Britanniæ et Hiberniæ*, IV vols, ed. D. Wilkins, 1737
Correspondence	'Correspondence of Bishop Oliver King and Sir Reginald Bray', ed. J.A. Robinson, *PSANHS*, lx (1914), pp. 1–10
Councils & Synods	*Councils and Synods, with other Documents Relating to the English Church, II, A.D. 1215–1313*, II vols, ed. F.M. Powicke and C.R. Cheney, Oxford, 1964
CPR	*Calendar of the Patent Rolls Preserved in the Public Record Office*

CRPer.	'Compotus Rolls of the Monastery of Pershore', ed. F.B. Andrews, *Proceedings of the Birmingham Archaeological Society*, lvii (1935), pp. 1–94
CRWin.	*Compotus Rolls of the Obedientiaries of St. Swithun's Priory, Winchester*, ed. G.W. Kitchin, London, 1892
CRWor.	*Compotus Rolls of the Priory of Worcester of the XIVth. and XVth. Centuries*, ed. S.G. Hamilton, Oxford, 1910
CV	*Chronicon Vilodunense sive de vita et miraculis Sanctæ Edithæ . . .*, ed. G.H. Black, London, 1830
CWA Sherborne	'Post Reformation Churchwardens' Accounts of S. Mary's, Sherborne', ed. J. Fowler, *SDNQ*, xxv (1947–50), pp. 122–6, 169–74
CWA Somerset	*Churchwardens' Accounts of Croscombe, Pilton, Patton, Tintinhull, Morebath, and St. Michael's, Bath*, ed. E. Hobhouse, London (SRS, 4), 1890
CWA Tavistock	*Calendar of the Tavistock Parish Records*, ed. R.N. Worth, Plymouth, 1887
DA	*The Early History of Glastonbury. An Edition, Translation, and Study of William of Malmesbury's De Antiquitate Glastonie Ecclesie*, ed. J. Scott, Woodbridge, 1981
Death and Memory	*Death and Memory in Medieval Exeter*, ed. D. Lepine and N. Orme, Exeter (Devon and Cornwall Rec. Soc., ns. 47), 2003
De Civili Domino	J. Wyclif, *De Tractatus de Civili Domino* (Book III, pt. 1), ed. J. Loserth, London, 1903
Doc. History of Art	*A Documentary History of Art Volume 1: The Middle Ages and the Renaissance*, ed. E.G. Holt, Princeton, 1981
DPP	*Documents Relating to the Priory of Penwortham and other Possessions in Lancashire of the Abbey of Evesham*, ed. W.A. Hulton (Chetham Soc., os 30), 1853
Durandus	*Guillelmi Duranti Rationale divinorum officiorum I–IV*, ed. A. Davril and T.M. Thibodeau, Turnhout (Corpus Christianorum, 140), 1995
Earliest English Wills	*The Fifty Earliest English Wills in the Court of Probate, London*, ed. F.J. Furnivall, London (EETS, os 78), 1882
EBK	*English Benedictine Kalendars after A.D. 1100*, II vols, ed. F. Wormald, London (Henry Bradshaw Soc., 77, 81), 1939–46
Ecclesiastical Docs	*Ecclesiastical Documents*, ed. J. Hunter, London (CS, 1st ser. 8), 1840
EEA XIII	*English Episcopal Acta 13: Worcester 1218–1268*, ed. P.M. Hoskin, Oxford, 1997
EHD	*English Historical Documents* (vols III, IV), ed. D.C. Douglas, London, 1969, 1975
ELW	*Early Lincoln Wills . . . 1280–1547*, ed. A. Gibbons, Lincoln, 1888
English Chronicle	*An English Chronicle of the Reigns of Richard II., Henry IV., Henry V., and Henry VI.*, ed. J.S. Davies, London (CS, 1st ser. 54), 1856
Evesham Wills	'Three Sixteenth Century Evesham Wills', ed. E.A.B. Barnard,

	Notes and Queries Concerning Evesham and the Four Shires, i, 1911, pp. 47–54
Fall of Princes	*Lydgate's Fall of Princes*, IV vols, ed. H. Bergen, London (EETS es 121–4), 1924–27
Foedera	*Foedera. Conventiones, Literæ, et Cujuscunque Generis Acta Publica . . .*, X vols, ed. T. Rymer (3rd edn), London, 1739–45
Froissart	Jehan Froissart, *Chroniques*, ed. G.T. Diller, Geneva, 1972
GA	*Gesta Abbatum Monasterii Sancti Albani*, III vols, ed. H.T. Riley, London (RS, 28), 1867–69
GM	*A Glastonbury Miscellany of the Fifteenth Century*, ed. A. Rigg, Oxford, 1968
Golden Legend	*The Golden Legend of Jacobus de Voragine*, ed. G. Ryan and H. Ripperger (repr. edn), Salem, 1994
Gower	*The Complete Works of John Gower: The French Works*, ed. G.C. Macaulay, Oxford, 1899
GP	*Willelmi Malmesbiriensis Monachi de Gestis Pontificum Anglorum Libri Quinque*, ed. N.E.S.A. Hamilton, London (RS, 52), 1870
GR	'Relics at Glastonbury in the Fourteenth Century. An Annotated Edition of British Library, Cotton Titus D. vii, fols. 2r–13v', ed. J.P. Carley and M. Howley, in *Arthurian Tradition*, pp. 569–616
GRA	William of Malmesbury, *Gesta Regum Anglorum*, II vols, ed. and trans. R.A.B. Mynors, R.M. Thomson and M. Winterbottom, Oxford, 1998–99
GW	Gerald of Wales, *Journey Through Wales and Description of Wales*, ed. and trans. L. Thorpe, Harmondsworth, 1978
Habington	*A Survey of Worcestershire, by Thomas Habington*, II vols, ed. J. Amphlett, Oxford, 1895, 1899
Handlyng Synne	*Robert of Brynne's "Handlyng Synne" A.D. 1303 and Parts of Its Original, William of Waddington's "Manuel des Pechiez"*, ed. F.J. Furnivall, Milwood (EETS, os 119, 123; reprinted as one vol.), 1978
HMC IX:i	Historical Manuscripts Commission, *Ninth Report of the Royal Commission on Historical Manuscripts, Part I: Report and Appendix*, London, 1883
HMC XII:ix	———, *Twelfth Report of the Royal Commission on Historical Manuscripts, Appendix, Part IX*, London, 1891
HMC XIV:viii	———, *Fourteenth Report of the Royal Commission on Historical Manuscripts, Appendix, Part VIII*, London, 1895
HMC Wells	———, *Calendar of the Manuscripts of the Dean and Chapter of Wells*, II vols, London, 1907–14
HMGlouc.	*Historia et Cartularium Monasterii Sancti Petri Gloucestriæ*, III vols, ed. W.W. Hart, London (RS, 33), 1863–67
HRB	*The Historia Regum Britannie of Geoffrey of Monmouth I, Bern, Burgerbibliothek, Ms. 568*, ed. N. Wright, Cambridge, 1984
HRH	D.M. Smith and V.C.M. London, *The Heads of Religious Houses, England and Wales II, 1216–1377*, Cambridge, 2001

Inv.C.C.Cant.	*Inventories of Christ-Church Canterbury*, ed. J.W. Legg and W.H.St J. Hope, Westminster, 1902
Inv.Dioc.Wor.	'Inventories of Church Goods, Diocese of Worcester', ed. M.E.C. Walcott, *AASRP*, xi (1871–72), pp. 303–42
Inv.Kent	'Inventories of (I.) St. Mary's Hospital or Maison Dieu, Dover; (II.) the Benedictine Priory of St. Martin New-Work, Dover, for Monks; (III.) the Benedictine Priory of SS. Mary and Sexburga, in the Island of Sheppey, for Nuns', ed. M.E.C. Walcott, *Archaeologia Cantiana*, vii (1868), pp. 272–306
Inv.Mic.Mt.	'An Inventory of the Property of the Alien Priory of St Michael's Mount, in Cornwall, in the Year 1337 . . .', ed. E. Smirke, *Journal of the Royal Institution of Cornwall*, ii (1866–67), pp. 1–6
Inv.PRO	'Inventories and Valuations of Religious Houses at the Time of the Dissolution from the Public Record Office', ed. M.E.C. Walcott, *Archaeologia*, xliii (1871), pp. 201–49
Inv.Westminster	'Inventories of Westminster Abbey at the Dissolution', ed. M.E.C. Walcott, *Transactions of the London and Middlesex Archaeological Association*, iv (1875), pp. 313–64
Inv.Worc.Lib.	'Two Inventories in the Library of Worcester Cathedral', ed. J.E.H. Blake, *JBAA*, xxxviii (193), pp. 158–82
Itinerary	John Leland, *Itinerary*, V vols, ed. L.T. Smith, London, 1964
Itinerary Worcestre	William Worcestre, *Itineraries*, ed. and trans. J.H. Harvey, Oxford, 1969
Jnl.More	William More, *Journal of Prior William More*, ed. E.S. Fegan, London, 1914
Jos.Lyfe	*Joseph of Arimathie: Otherwise called the Romance of the Seint Graal*, ed. W.W. Skeat (repr. edn), Felinfach, 1996
Kitchener's Roll	'On the Kitchener's Roll of Tewkesbury Abbey', ed. T. Wakeman, *JBAA*, xv (1859), pp. 318–32.
Landboc	*Landboc sive Registrum Monasterii de Winchelcumba*, II vols, ed. D. Royce, Exeter, 1892, 1903
Langland	William Langland, *The Vision of William Concerning Piers Plowman*, V vols in IV, ed. W.W. Skeat, London (EETS os 28, 38, 54, 67, 81), 1867–85
Latimer	*Sermons and Remains of Hugh Latimer*, ed. G.E. Corrie, Cambridge, 1845
LBRJ	Robert Joseph, *The Letter Book of Robert Joseph, Monk-scholar of Evesham and Gloucester College, Oxford 1530–3*, ed. H. Aveling and W.A. Pantin, Oxford, 1967
LDO	*Libellus de Diversis Ordinibus et Professionibus Qui Sunt in Aecclesia*, ed. and trans. G. Constable and B. Smith, Oxford, 1972
L.Hyda	*Liber Monasterii de Hyda*, ed. E. Edwards, London (RS, 45), 1866
Lib.Albus	*The Worcester Liber Albus*, ed. and trans. J.M. Wilson, London, 1920
Lib.Hen.VIII	*The Libraries of King Henry VIII*, ed. J.P. Carley, London (Corpus of Medieval Library Catalogues 7), 2000

Linc.Vis.	*Visitations of Religious Houses in the Diocese of Lincoln*, III vols, ed. A.H. Thompson, London (Canterbury and York Society XVII, XXVI, XXXIII), 1915–27
List Admissions	'An Annotated Edition of the List of Sixty-Three Monks who entered Glastonbury Abbey under Walter de Monington', ed. J.P. Carley, *DR*, xcv (1977), pp. 306–15
Lit.Can.	*Literae Cantuarienses: The Letter Books of the Monastery of Christ Church Canterbury*, III vols, ed. J.B. Sheppard, London (RS, 85), 1887–89
LPHVIII	*Letters and Papers, Foreign and Domestic, of the Reign of Henry VIII*, XXI vols in XXXV, London, 1875–1920
LSK	*Lateinische Schriftquellen zur Kunst in England, Wales and Schottland vom Jahre 901 bis zum Jahre 1307*, V vols, ed. O. Lehmann-Brockhaus, Munich, 1955–60
MA	W. Dugdale, *Monasticon Anglicanum*, VI vols in VIII, ed. J. Caley, H. Ellis and B. Bandinel, London, 1817–30
Mag.Tab.	'Magna Tabula: The Glastonbury Tablets', ed. J. Krochalis, in *Arthurian Tradition*, pp. 435–567.
Mem.Bury	*Memorials of St Edmund's Abbey*, III vols, ed. T. Arnold, London (RS, 96), 1890–96
Mem.Dunstan	*Memorials of Saint Dunstan, Archbishop of Canterbury*, ed. W. Stubbs, London (RS, 53), 1874
Monastic Treasures	*Account of the Monastic Treasures Confiscated at the Dissolution of the Various Houses in England*, ed. J. Williams, London (Abbotsford Club, 1), 1836
MP	William Malvern, 'The Foundation of the Abbey of Gloucester . . .', ed. W. Bazeley, *RGC*, i (1882–83), pp. 148–56
MPLydgate	*The Minor Poems of John Lydgate*, II vols, ed. H.N. MacCracken, London (EETS, es 117, os 192), 1911, 1934
Much.Mem.	*Muchelney Memoranda*, ed. B. Schofield, Frome (SRS, 42), 1927
Off. Eccl. Eve.	*Officium Ecclesiasticum Abbatum Secundum Usum Eveshamensis Monasterii*, ed. H.A. Wilson, London (Henry Bradshaw Soc., 6), 1893
PJH	*Poems of John of Hoveden*, ed. F.J.E. Raby, Durham and London (Surtees Soc., CLIII), 1939
Polychronicon	*Polychronicon Ranulphi Higden monachi Cestrensis*, IX vols, ed. C. Babington and J.R. Lumby, London (RS, 41), 1865–86
PSC	*Proceedings in the Court of Star Chamber in the Reigns of Henry VII. and Henry VIII.*, ed. G. Bradford, Frome (SRS, 27), 1911
RB	*RB 1980. The Rule of St Benedict in Latin and English with Notes*, ed. T. Fry, Collegeville, 1981
RBFox	*Female Monastic Life in Early Tudor England: With an Edition of Richard Fox's Translation of the Benedictine Rule for Women, 1517*, ed. B. Collett, Aldershot, 2002
RCR	*Pecock's Reule of Crysten Religioun*, ed. W.C. Greet, London (EETS, os 171), 1927
RCSWin.	*The Register of the Common Seal of the Priory of St. Swithun,*

	Winchester, 1345–1497, ed. J. Greatrex, Winchester (Hampshire Record Soc., 2), 1978
RD	*Rites of Durham*, ed. J.T. Fowler, London (Surtees Soc., 107), 1903
Reg.Bransford	*The Register of Wolstan de Bransford, Bishop of Worcester 1339–1349*, ed. R.M. Haines, London, 1966
Reg.Bubwith	*The Register of Nicholas Bubwith, Bishop of Bath and Wells 1407–1424*, II vols, ed. T.S. Holmes, London (SRS, 29, 30), 1914
Reg.Chichele	*The Register of Henry Chichele, Archbishop of Canterbury 1414–1443*, IV vols, ed. E.F. Jacob, Oxford (Canterbury and York Society 42, 45–7), 1937–47
Reg.Godstow	*The English Register of Godstow Nunnery near Oxford*, III vols in I, ed. A. Clark, London (EETS os 129, 130, 142), 1911
Reg.Grandisson	*The Register of John de Grandisson, Bishop of Exeter (A.D. 1327–69)*, III vols, ed. F.C. Hingeston-Randolph, London and Exeter, 1894–99
Reg.King	*The Registers of Oliver King, Bishop of Bath and Wells 1496–1503 and Hadrian de Castello, Bishop of Bath and Wells 1503–1518*, ed. H.C. Maxwell-Lyte, Frome (SRS, 54), 1939
Reg.Malmes.	*Registrum Malmesburiense*, II vols, ed. J.S. Brewer and C.T. Martin, London (RS, 72), 1880
Reg.Morton	*The Register of John Morton, Archbishop of Canterbury*, II vols, ed. C. Harper-Bill, Oxford (Canterbury and York Soc.), 1987–91
Reg.Swinfield	*The Register of Richard de Swinfield, Bishop of Hereford (A.D. 1283–1317)*, ed. W.W. Capes, Hereford (Cantilupe Soc.), 1909
Reg.Winchelsey	*Registrum Roberti Winchelsey, Cantuariensis Archiepiscopi A.D. 1294–1313*, II vols, ed. R. Graham, Oxford, 1952–56
Reg.Wolsey	*The Registers of Thomas Wolsey, John Clerke, William Knyght and Gilbert Bourne*, ed. H.C. Maxwell-Lyte, Frome (SRS, 55), 1940
Reg.Woodlock	*Registrum Henrici Woodlock, Diocesis Wintoniensis A.D. 1305–16*, ed. A.W.Goodman, London (Canterbury and York Soc., 43), 1940–41
Relation	*A Relation, or rather, a True Account of the Island of England . . . about the Year 1500*, ed. C.A. Sneyd, London (CS, 1st ser. 37), 1847
Rentalia	*Rentalia et Custumaria Michaelis de Amesbury, 1235–52 et Rogeri de Ford 1252–1261, Abbatum Monasterii Beatæ Mariæ Glastoniæ*, ed. E. Hobhouse, Frome (SRS, 5), 1891
Royal Wills	*A Collection of All the Wills Known to be Extant of the Kings and Queens of England . . .*, ed. J. Nichols, London, 1780
Schaell's Memoir	'Adrian Schaell's Memoir of High Ham Church and Rectory, A.D. 1598', ed. C.D. Crossman, *PSANHS*, xl (1894), pp. 113–22
Short Survey	*A Relation of a Short Survey of the Western Counties Made by a Lieutenant of the Military Company in Norwich, 1635*, ed. J.W. Legg (CS, 3rd ser. 52 pt. 3), 1936
Shorter Catalogues	*English Benedictine Libraries: The Shorter Catalogues*, ed. R.

Sharpe, J.P. Carley, R.M. Thomson and A.G. Watson, London
(Corpus of British Medieval Library Catalogues, 4), 1996

SMW(a)   *Somerset Medieval Wills (1383–1500)*, ed. F.W. Weaver, Frome (SRS, 16), 1901

SMW(b)   *Somerset Medieval Wills (1500–1530), with Some Wills Preserved at Lambeth (1363–1491)*, ed. F.W. Weaver, Frome (SRS, 19), 1903

SMW(c)   *Somerset Medieval Wills (1531–1558)*, ed. F.W. Weaver, Frome (SRS, 21), 1905

Star Chamber   *Select Cases before the King's Council in the Star Chamber . . . A.D. 1477–1509, 1509–1544*, II vols, ed. I.S. Leadam, London (Selden Soc., 16, 25), 1902–10

Suppression Letters   *Three Chapters of Letters Relating to the Suppression of the Monasteries*, ed. T. Wright (CS, 1st ser. 26), 1843

SWE   *Somerset Wills from Exeter*, ed. S.W. Rawlins and I.F. Jones, Frome (SRS, 62), 1952

Test.Vet.   *Testamenta Vetusta: Being Illustrations from Wills . . .*, II vols in I, ed. N.H. Nicholas, London, 1826

Tewkes.Comp.   'A Tewkesbury Compotus', ed. F.W.P. Hicks, *TBGAS*, lv (1933), pp. 249–55

Three Chron.   *Three Fifteenth-Century Chronicles, with Historical Memoranda by John Stowe, the Antiquary*, ed. J. Gardiner, London (CS, 2nd ser. 28), 1880

UANG   *Ungedruckte Anglo-Normannische Geschichtsquellen*, ed. F. Liebermann, Strasburg, 1879

Valor   *Valor Ecclesiasticus Temp. Henry VIII Auctoritate Regis Institutus*, VI vols, ed. J. Caley, London, 1810

Vis.Nor.   *Visitations of the Diocese of Norwich A.D. 1492–1532*, ed. A. Jessopp, London (CS, 2nd ser. 43), 1888

VitaES   *Vita Edwardi Secundi*, ed. N. Denholm-Young, London, 1957

Winch.Anth.   *The Winchester Anthology. A Facsimile of British Library Additional Manuscript 60577*, ed. E. Wilson and I. Fenlon, Cambridge, 1981

Secondary sources

Abrams 1991   L. Abrams, 'A Single Sheet Facsimile of a Diploma of King Ine for Glastonbury', in *Archaeology and History*, pp. 97–133

Alexander & Temple 1985   J.J.G. Alexander and E. Temple, *Illuminated Manuscripts in Oxford College Libraries, the University Archives and the Taylor Institution*, Oxford

Almond 1903   T.L. Almond, 'Somerset Monastic Houses at the Dissolution', *DR*, 2nd ser. iii, pp. 4–21

Andrews 1901   F.B. Andrews, *The Benedictine Abbey of SS. Mary, Peter and Paul at Pershore, Worcestershire*, Birmingham

Andrews 1932   ———, 'Pershore Monastery: Some Chapters in Its Foundation and History', *Laudate*, x, pp. 31–40, 80–7

Anon. 1829   'Altar Piece at Romsey', *Gentleman's Magazine*, pp. 584–6

Anon. 1863   'The Arms of the Nine Worthies and the Tomb of Robert Duke
                     of Normandy', *Herald and Genealogist*, i, pp. 175–82
Anon. 1910–11   'Glastonbury Abbey Excavations', *SDNQ*, xii, pp. 114–16
Anon. 1924–26   'Egelina, Abbess of Shaftesbury', *SDNQ*, xviii, pp. 94–5
Archbold 1892   W.A.J. Archbold, *Somerset Religious Houses*, Cambridge
Astill and Wright   G.G. Astill and M.S. Wright, 'Perceiving Patronage in the
   1993   Achaeological Record: Bordesley Abbey', in M. Carver, ed. *In
                     Search of Cult*, Woodbrige, pp. 125–37
Aston 1973   M. Aston, 'English Ruins and English History. The Dissolution
                     and the Sense of the Past', *Journal of the Warburg and Courtauld
                     Institutes*, xxxvi, pp. 231–55
Atkins 1951   I. Atkins, 'The Effigy at the Back of the Great Altar Screen in
                     Worcester Cathedral', *TWAS*, ns xxviii, pp. 14–22
Atkinson 1935   T.D. Atkinson, 'Figure Sculpture in Winchester Cathedral',
                     Archaeologia, lxxxv, pp. 159–67
Backhouse 1999   J. Backhouse, *The Sherborne Missal*, London
Badham 2004   S. Badham, 'Indents from the Benedictine Priory of St Mary,
                     Coventry', *Monumental Brass Society Bulletin*, xcv, pp. 713–15
Bainbridge 1996   V. Bainbridge, *Gilds in the Medieval Countryside*, Woodbridge
Ballard 1992   R. Ballard, *The History of the Priory Church of St Andrew,
                     Stogursey* (2nd edn), Exeter
Bannister 1902   A.T. Bannister, *The History of Ewias Harold*, Hereford
Barber 1995   P. Barber, 'The Evesham World Map: A Late Medieval English
                     View of God and the World', *Imago Mundi*, xlvii, pp. 13–33
Barker 1994   P. Barker, *A Short Architectural History of Worcester Cathedral*,
                     Worcester
Barker 1997   ———, 'Prince Arthur's Chantry', in P. Barker and C. Guy,
                     eds, *Archaeology at Worcester Cathedral. Report of the Seventh
                     Annual Symposium March 1997*, Worcester, pp. 27–8
Barrett 1789   W. Barrett, *The History and Antiquities of the City of Bristol*,
                     Bristol
Baskerville 1937   G. Baskerville, *English Monks and the Suppression of the Monas-
                     teries*, London
Bassett 1997   *The Origins of the Parishes of the Deerhurst Area* (The Deerhurst
                     Lecture for 1997), Deerhurst
Bates 1904   E.H. Bates, 'Stavordale Priory', *PSANHS*, l, pp. 94–103
Batselier 1981   P. Batselier, *Saint Benedict: Father of Western Civilization*, New
                     York
Baxandall 1972   M. Baxandall, *Painting and Experience in Fifteenth-Century Italy*,
                     Oxford
Bazeley 1882–83   W. Bazeley, 'The History of Prinknash Park', *TBGAS*, vii, pp.
                     267–306
Beacham 1987   M.J.A. Beacham, *West Country Tithe Barns. An Illustrated
                     Checklist of Reputed Tithe Barns in Gloucester, Avon and Somerset*,
                     Studley
Beckett 1995   N. Beckett, 'Henry VII and Sheen Charterhouse', in B.
                     Thompson, ed., *The Reign of Henry VII* (PHS, 1993), Stamford,
                     pp. 117–32

Bell 1933–34 H.I. Bell, 'A Register of Deeds from Shaftesbury Abbey', *British Museum Quarterly*, viii, pp. 18–22

Benedictines and the Book *The Benedictines and the Book* (exhib. cat.), Oxford, 1980

Benedictines in Britain *The Benedictines in Britain*, London, 1980 (various contributors)

Bennett 1830 J. Bennett, *The History of Tewkesbury*, London and Tewkesbury

Bennett 2000 A. Bennett, ' "Modernist" History versus Monastic History: The Continuity of the English Benedictines', *DR*, cxviii, pp. 199–220

Benson & Blanchfield 1997 C.D. Benson and L.S. Blanchfield, *The Manuscripts of Piers Plowman: The B-Version*, Cambridge

Bettey 2003 J. Bettey, 'The Final Years of the Abbey and the Dissolution', in *Tewkesbury Abbey*, pp. 65–74, 294

BGAS 1884–5 'Bristol and Gloucester Archaeological Society. Transactions at Evesham', *TBGAS*, ix, pp. 1–38

Biddle 1993 M. Biddle, 'Early Renaissance at Winchester', in *Winchester Cathedral*, pp. 257–304

Binski 1986 P. Binski, *The Painted Chamber at Westminster*, London

Binski 1987 ———, 'The Stylistic Sequence of London Figure Brasses', in *Earliest English Brasses*, pp. 69–132

Binski 1995 ———, *Westminster Abbey and the Plantagenets. Kingship and the Representation of Power 1200–1400*, London and New Haven

Birch 1887 W. de G. Birch, *Catalogue of Seals in the Department of Manuscripts in the British Museum* (vol. I), London

Bird 1994 N. du Q. Bird, 'A Medieval Inventory from Glastonbury Abbey', *SDNQ*, xxxiii, pp. 310–20

Bird 1995 ———, 'Articles from the Workshop of St Dunstan, Still Existing at Glastonbury in the Thirteenth Century', *SDNQ*, xxxiii, pp. 355–8

Blair 1962 C. Blair, 'An Iconographic Ring Connected with Charles Warne', *PDNHAFC*, lxxxiv, pp. 110–11

Blair 1987 J. Blair, 'English Monumental Brasses before 1350: Types, Patterns and Workshops', in *Earliest English Brasses*, pp. 133–215

Blunt 1898 J.H. Blunt, *Tewkesbury Abbey and Its Associations*, London and Tewkesbury

Bolvig and Lindley 2003 A. Bolvig and P. Lindley, eds, *History and Images: Towards a New Iconology*, Turnhout

Bond 1899 F. Bond, 'On the Comparative Value of Documentary and Architectural Evidence in Establishing the Chronology of the English Cathedrals', *Journal of the Royal Institute of British Architects*, 3rd ser. iv, pp. 17–36

Bond 1913 F.B. Bond, 'Glastonbury Abbey: Sixth Report on the Discoveries made during the Excavations, I. Discovery of St Dunstan's Chapel', *PSANHS*, lix, pp. 56–61

Bond 1915 ———, 'Glastonbury Abbey: Eighth Report on the Discoveries made during the Excavations', *PSANHS*, lxi, pp. 128–42

Bond 1916 F. Bond, *The Chancel of English Churches*, London

Bond 1919 F.B. Bond, 'Glastonbury Abbey (the Loreto Chapel): Ninth

Report on the Discoveries made during the Excavations',
PSANHS, lxv, pp. 76–85

Bond and Weller
1991
C.J. Bond and J.B. Weller, 'The Somerset Barns of Glastonbury
Abbey', in *Archaeology and History*, pp. 57–88

Bony 1979
J. Bony, *The English Decorated Style. Gothic Architecture Transformed, 1250–1350*, Oxford

Bossy 1983
J. Bossy, 'The Mass as a Social Institution, 1200–1700', *Past and
Present*, c, pp. 29–61

Bostick 1998
C.V. Bostick, *The Antichrist and the Lollards. Apocalypticism in
Late Medieval and Reformation England*, Leiden, Boston and Köln

Bowers 1999
R. Bowers, *English Church Polyphony. Singers and Sources from the
14th to the 17th Century*, Aldershot

Brakspear 1913
H. Brakspear, 'Malmesbury Abbey', *Archaeologia*, lxiv, pp.
399–436

Brakspear 1915–16
——, 'On the Dorter Range at Worcester Priory',
Archaeologia, lxvii, pp. 189–204

Brakspear and Parry
1960
—— and H.L. Parry, *St. Nicholas Priory Exeter*, Exeter and
London

Britton 1825
J. Britton, *The History and Antiquities of Bath Abbey Church*,
London

Britton 1829
——, *The History and Antiquities of the Abbey and Cathedral
Church of Gloucester*, London

Brock 1893
E.P.L. Brock, 'Excavation of the Site of Winchcombe Abbey,
Gloucestershire', *JBAA*, xlix, pp. 163–72

Brooke 1963
C.N.L. Brooke, 'St Peter of Gloucester and St Cadoc of
Llancarfan', in N.K. Chadwick, ed., *Celt and Saxon. Studies in
the Early British Border*, Cambridge, pp. 258–322

Brown 1995
A.D. Brown, *Popular Piety in Late Medieval England. The Diocese
of Salisbury, 1250–1550*, Oxford

Brown 2003
S. Brown, 'The Medieval Stained Glass', in *Tewkesbury Abbey*,
pp. 183–96, 306–7

Buchanan 1995
A. Buchanan, 'The Power and the Glory: The Meanings of
Medieval Architecture', in I. Borden and D. Dunster, eds, *Archi-
tecture and the Sites of History. Interpretations of Buildings and
Cities*, New York, pp. 78–92

Bugslag 1980
J.F.P. Bugslag, 'Benedictine Monastic Building in England,
1200–1540' (unpublished M.A. dissertation, University of
Victoria, Canada)

Burgess 1985
C. Burgess, 'For the Increase of Divine Service: Chantries in the
Parish in Late Medieval Bristol', *JEH*, xxxvi, pp. 46–65

Burgess 1987
——, ' "By Quick and by Dead": Wills and Pious Provision in
Late Medieval Bristol', *English Historical Review*, cii, pp. 837–58

Burgess 1988
——, ' "A Fond Thing Vainly Invented": An Essay on Purgatory and Pious Motive in Later Medieval England', in J.S.
Wright, ed., *Parish, Church and People: Local Studies in Lay Religion*, London, pp. 56–84

Burnet 1865
G. Burnet, *The History of the Reformation of the Church of
England*, VII vols, Oxford

Burton 2000   J. Burton, *Monastic and Religious Orders in Britain, 1000–1300*,
                            Cambridge
Butterworth 1890   G. Butterworth, *Deerhurst: A Parish in the Vale of Gloucester*,
                            London
Bynum 1982   C.W. Bynum, *Jesus as Mother. Studies in the Spirituality of the
                            High Middle Ages*, Berkeley and London
Campbell and Steer   L. Campbell and F. Steer, *A Catalogue of Manuscripts in the
    1988   College of Arms Collections* (vol. I), London
Carley 1985   J.P. Carley, 'John Leland and Somerset Libraries', *PSANHS*,
                            cxxix, pp. 141–54
Carley 1996   ———, *Glastonbury Abbey. The Holy House at the Head of the
                            Moors Adventurous*, Glastonbury
Carley 2001   ———, 'A Grave Event: Henry V, Glastonbury Abbey, and
                            Joseph of Arimathea's Bones', in *Arthurian Tradition*, pp.
                            285–302
Carley 2004   ———, 'John of Glastonbury and Borrowings from the Vernac-
                            ular', in R.F. Green and L.R. Mooney, eds, *Interstices: Studies in
                            Middle English and Anglo-Latin Texts in Honour of A.G. Rigg*,
                            Toronto, pp. 55–73
Carpenter 1986   C. Carpenter, 'The Fifteenth-Century English Gentry and their
                            Estates', in M. Jones, ed., *Gentry and Lesser Nobility in Late Medi-
                            eval Europe*, Gloucester, pp. 36–60
Carus-Wilson 1957   E. Carus-Wilson, 'The Significance of the Secular Sculptures in
                            the Lane Aisle, Cullompton', *Medieval Archaeology*, i, pp.
                            104–17
Catalogue Augsburg   *Die Handschriften der Staats-und Stadtbibliotek Augsburg* (vol. III),
                            ed. H. Spilling, Wiesbaden, 1984
Catalogue CUL   *A Catalogue of the Manuscripts Preserved in the Library of the
                            University of Cambridge*, V vols + index, ed. C. Hardwick and
                            H.R. Luard, Cambridge, 1856–67
Catalogue Exhibits   'Catalogue of Objects of Interest Exhibited at the
    1883   Conversazione', *RGC*, i, pp. 81–96
Catalogue OBL   *A Summary Catalogue of Western Manuscripts in the Bodleian
                            Library at Oxford*, VII vols in VIII, ed. F. Madan et al.,
                            1895–1953
Catalogue PML   *Catalogue of Manuscripts and Early Printed Books . . . Now
                            Forming a Portion of the Library of J. Pierpont Morgan*, London,
                            1906
'Catalogue of Rolls'   'Catalogue of Certain Rolls in the Archives of the Dean and
                            Chapter of Worcester', ed. J.H. Bloom, in S.G. Hamilton, ed.
                            Collectanea, London, 1912, pp. 91–136
Catalogue Royal MSS   G.F. Warner and J.P. Gilson, *Catalogue of Western Manuscripts
                            in the Old Royal and King's Collections*, IV vols, London, 1921
Catalogus OQC   *Catalogus Codicum MSS. Collegii Reginensis*, Oxford, n.d.
Catto 1985   J. Catto, 'Religious Change under Henry V', in G.L. Harriss,
                            ed., *Henry V: The Practice of Kingship*, Oxford, pp. 97–115
Cave 1904–09   C.J.P. Cave, 'A List of Hampshire Brasses', *Transactions of the
                            Monumental Brass Society*, v, pp. 247–91, 295–325, 343–71

Cave 1929   ———, 'The Roof Bosses in the Nave of Tewkesbury Abbey',
                       Archaeologia, lxxix, pp. 73–84
Chandler 1979   P.E. Chandler, 'The Bishop's Palace, Gloucester', *TBGAS*,
                       xcvii, pp. 81–3
Cheetham 2003   F. Cheetham, *Alabaster Images of Medieval England*, Woodbridge
Chope 1920–21   R.P. Chope, 'The Order of Brothelyngham', *DCNQ*, xi, pp.
                       62–4
Chope 1922–23   ———, 'Proposed Religious Houses at Clovelly', *DCNQ*, xii,
                       pp. 311–12
Christie 1936   A.G.I. Christie, *English Medieval Embroidery*, Oxford
Clanchy 1999   M. Clanchy, *From Memory to Written Record. England
                       1066–1307* (2nd edn), Oxford
Clapham 1934   A.W. Clapham, 'Howden Minster', *AJ*, xci, pp. 398–9
Clark 2001   J. Clark, 'The St Albans Monks and the Cult of St Alban: the
                       Late Medieval Texts', in M. Henig and P.G. Lindley, eds, *Alban
                       and St Albans* (BAACT, 24), Leeds, pp. 218–30
Clark 2002(a)   ———, 'The Religious Orders in Pre-Reformation England', in
                       idem, ed., *The Religious Orders in Pre-Reformation England*,
                       Woodbridge, pp. 3–33
Clark 2002(b)   ———, 'Monastic Education in Late Medieval England', in
                       C.M. Barron and J. Stratford, eds, *The Church and Learning in
                       Later Medieval Society: Essays in Honour of R.B. Dobson* (PHS,
                       1999), Donington, pp. 25–40
Clark-Maxwell   Revd Prebendary Clarke-Maxwell, 'Some Letters of Confrater-
   1924–25   nity', *Archaeologia*, lxxv, pp. 19–60
Clark-Maxwell 1929   ———, 'Some Further Letters of Fraternity', *Archaeologia*, lxxix,
                       pp. 179–216
Clarke 1904–05   K.M. Clarke, 'The Conventual Houses of Exeter and the Neigh-
                       bourhood', *DCNQ*, iii, pp. 129–51
Clayton 1927–29   C.E. Clayton, 'Glastonbury in 1635', *SDNQ*, xxix, pp. 80–2
Coates 1999   A. Coates, *English Medieval Books: The Reading Abbey Collection
                       from Foundation to Dispersal*, Oxford
Cobb 1980   G. Cobb, *English Cathedrals: The Forgotten Centuries*, London
Coldicott 1989   D.K. Coldicott, *Hampshire Nunneries*, Chichester
Coldstream 1976   N. Coldstream, 'English Decorated Shrine Bases', *JBAA*, cxxix,
                       pp. 15–34
Coldstream 1989   ———, 'St Peter's Church, Howden', in C. Wilson, ed., *Medi-
                       eval Art and Architecture in the East Riding of Yorkshire* (BAACT,
                       9), Leeds, pp. 109–20
Cole 1993   W. Cole, *A Catalogue of Netherlandish and North European Roun-
                       dels in Britain* (Corpus Vitrearum Medii Aevi: Great Britain,
                       Summary Catalogue I), Oxford
Collinson 1791   J. Collinson, *The History and Antiquities of the County of
                       Somerset*, III vols, Bath
Colvin 1999   H. Colvin, 'Recycling the Monasteries: Demolition and Reuse
                       by the Tudor Government, 1536–47', in idem, *Essays in English
                       Architectural History*, London and New Haven, pp. 52–67

Condon 2003 · · · · · M. Condon, 'The Last Will of Henry VII: Document and Text', in *Westminster Abbey*, pp. 99–140

Cook 1947 · · · · · G.H. Cook, *Mediaeval Chantries and Chantry Chapels*, London

Cook 1956 · · · · · ———, *The English Mediaeval Parish Church*, London

Cook 1959 · · · · · ———, *English Collegiate Churches of the Middle Ages*, London

Coppack 1996 · · · · · G. Coppack, 'Some Descriptions of Rievaulx Abbey in 1538 and 1539: The Disposition of a Major Cistercian Precinct in the Early Sixteenth Century', *JBAA*, cxxxix, pp. 100–33

Cottle 1988 · · · · · B. Cottle, 'Cults of the Saints in Medieval Bristol and Gloucestershire', *TBGAS*, cvi, pp. 5–18

Cotton 1925 · · · · · C. Cotton, 'A Contemporary List of the Benefactions of Thomas Ikham, Sacrist, to St. Austin's Abbey, Canterbury, *circa* 1415', *Archaeologia Cantiana*, xxxvii, pp. 152–9

Coulson 1982 · · · · · C. Coulson, 'Heirarchism in Conventual Crenellation. An Essay in the Sociology and Metaphysics of Medieval Fortification', *Medieval Archaeology*, xxvi, pp. 69–100

Coulton 1928 · · · · · G.G. Coulton, *Art and the Reformation*, Oxford

Coulton 1936 · · · · · ———, *Five Centuries of Religion Vol. III: Getting and Spending*, Cambridge

Cox 1980 · · · · · D.C. Cox, *Evesham Abbey and Its Parish Churches*, Gloucester

Cox 1988 · · · · · ———, *The Battle of Evesham: A New Account*, Evesham

Cox 1990 · · · · · ———, 'The Building, Destruction and Excavation of Evesham Abbey: A Documentary Account', *TWAS*, 3rd ser. xii, pp. 123–46

Crick 1989 · · · · · J.C. Crick, *The Historia Regum Britannie of Geoffrey of Monmouth, vol. III: A Summary Catalogue of the Manuscripts*, Cambridge

Crick 1991 · · · · · ———, 'The Marshalling of Antiquity: Glastonbury's Historical Dossier', in *Archaeology and History*, pp. 217–43

Crick 2001 · · · · · ———, 'Offa, Ælfric and the Re-Foundation of St Albans', in M. Henig and P.G. Lindley, eds, *Alban and St Albans* (BAACT, 24), Leeds, pp. 78–84

Crook 1982 · · · · · J. Crook, 'The Pilgrims' Hall, Winchester', *PHFCAS*, xxxviii, pp. 85–101

Crook 1991 · · · · · ———, 'The Pilgrims' Hall, Winchester: Hammerbeams, Base Crucks, and Aisle Derivative Roof-Structures', *Archaeologia*, cix, pp. 129–59

Crook 1993 · · · · · ———, 'St Swithun of Winchester', in *Winchester Cathedral*, pp. 57–68

Crook 1994 · · · · · ———, 'A Worthy Antiquity: the Movement of King Cnut's Bones in Winchester Cathedral', in A. Rumble, ed., *The Reign of Cnut, King of England, Denmark and Norway*, London, pp. 165–93.

Crook 1999 · · · · · ———, 'The "Rufus Tomb" in Winchester Cathedral', *Antiquaries Journal*, lxxix, pp. 187–212

Crook and Kusaba 1993 · · · · · ——— and Y. Kusaba, 'The Perpendicular Remodelling of the Nave: Problems of Interpretation', in *Winchester Cathedral*, pp. 215–30

Crossley 1987	P. Crossley, 'English Gothic Architecture', in *AoC*, pp. 60–73
Cunich 1997	P. Cunich, 'The Dissolution', in D. Rees, ed., *Monks of England: The Benedictines in England from Augustine to the Present Day*, London, pp. 148–66
Daniel 1902	P. Daniel, 'The Accounts of St John's Church, Glastonbury', *PSANHS*, xlviii, pp. 11–21
Davidson 1884	S.B. Davidson, 'On the Charters of King Ine', *PSANHS*, xxx, pp. 1–31
Davies 1908–09	W. Davies, 'Some Notes on the Ancient Records Preserved in Kingsbridge Church', *DCNQ*, v, pp. 94–118
Davies 1991	R.G. Davies, 'Lollardy and Locality', *TRHS*, 6th ser. i, pp. 191–212
Davis 1834	E. Davis, *Gothic Ornaments Illustrative of Prior Birde's Oratory in the Abbey Church, Bath*, London
Davis 1958	G.R.C. Davis, *Medieval Cartularies of Great Britain: A Short Catalogue*, London
Davis 1993	V. Davis, *William Waynflete: Bishop and Educationalist*, Woodbridge
Deacon and Lindley 2001	R. Deacon and P.G. Lindley, *Image and Idol: Medieval Sculpture*, London
Dennison and Rogers 2002	L. Dennison and N. Rogers, 'A Medieval Best-Seller: Some Examples of Decorated Copies of Higden's *Polychronicon*', in C.M. Barron and J. Stratford, eds, *The Church and Learning in Later Medieval Society: Essays in Honour of R.B. Dobson* (PHS, 1999), Donington, pp. 80–99
Deshman 1995	R. Deshman, *The Benedictional of Æthelwold*, Princeton
Devenish 1924–26	W.H. Devenish, 'Prior Cantlow', *SDNQ*, xviii, pp. 49–53
Dickens 1972	A.G. Dickens, *The English Reformation*, London
Dickens 1994	———, *Late Monasticism and the Reformation*, London
Dicker 1908	C.W.H. Dicker, 'The Architectural History of the Parish Church of St Mary at Cerne', *PDNHAFC*, xxix, pp. 1–7
Dickinson 1950	J.C. Dickinson, *The Origins of the Austin Canons and their Introduction into England*, London
DNHAFC 1903	'Dorset Natural History and Antiquarian Field Club. Shaftesbury Meeting', *PDNHAFC*, xxiv, pp. liii–lxi
DNHAFC 1908	'Dorset Natural History and Antiquarian Field Club. Glastonbury Meeting', *PDNHAFC*, xxix, pp. lxx–lxxii
Dobson 1950	D.P. Dobson, 'Stone Pulpits in North Somerset Churches', *PSANHS*, xciv, pp. 71–80
Dobson 1973	B. Dobson, *Durham Priory 1400–1450*, Cambridge
Dobson 1990	———, 'The English Monastic Cathedrals in the Fifteenth Century', *TRHS*, 6th ser. i, pp. 151–72
Dodd 1999	D. Dodd, *Dunster Castle, Somerset*, London
Douglas 1987	M. Douglas, *How Institutions Think*, London
Dow 1992	H.J. Dow, *The Sculptural Decoration of the Henry VII Chapel, Westminster Abbey*, Edinburgh, Cambridge and Durham
Downing 2002	M. Downing, 'Medieval Military Effigies up to 1500 Remaining in Worcestershire', *TWAS*, xviii, pp. 133–209

Draper 1981	P. Draper, 'The Sequence and Dating of the Decorated Work at Wells', in N. Coldstream and P. Draper, eds, *Medieval Art and Architecture at Wells and Glastonbury* (BAACT, 4), Leeds, pp. 18–30
Driver 1995	M.W. Driver, 'Nuns as Patrons, Artists, Readers: Bridgettine Woodcuts in Printed Books Produced for the English Market', in C.G. Fisher and K.L. Scott, eds, *Art into Life: Collected Papers from the Kresge Art Museum Medieval Symposia*, East Lansing (Mich.), pp. 237–67
Du Boulay 1970	F.R.H. Du Boulay, *An Age of Ambition: English Society in the Late Middle Ages*, London
Duffy 1992	E. Duffy, *The Stripping of the Altars. Traditional Religion in England 1400–1580*, New Haven and London
Duffy 2001	———, *The Voices of Morebath. Reformation and Rebellion in an English Village*, New Haven and London
Duffy 2003	'Late Medieval Religion', in *Gothic*, pp. 56–67
Duffy, M. 2003	M. Duffy, *Royal Tombs of Medieval England*, Stroud
Dufty 1947	A.R. Dufty, 'Place Farm, Tisbury', *AJ*, civ, pp. 168–9
Dunning 1991	R.W. Dunning, 'The Tribunal, Glastonbury, Somerset', in *Archaeology and History*, pp. 89–93
Dunning 2000	———, 'John Stowell, Freemason of Wells', xxxiv, *SDNQ*, p. 398
Dunning 2001	———, *Somerset Monasteries*, Stroud
Dunning 2002	———, 'The Abbot of Glastonbury Saves Money', *SDNQ*, xxxv, pp. 51–2
Dyer 1998	C. Dyer, *Standards of Living in the Later Middle Ages. Social Change in England c.1200–1520* (rev. edn), Cambridge
Eames 1980	E.S. Eames, *Catalogue of Medieval Lead-Glazed Earthenware Tiles in the Department of Medieval and Later Antiquities, British Museum*, II vols, London
Eeles 1927–29	F.C. Eeles, 'Alabaster Table at Shaftesbury', *SDNQ*, xix, pp. 113–14
Elliott 1986	B. Elliott, 'The Appropriation of Parish Churches', *DR*, civ, pp. 19–24
Emery 1996–2000	A. Emery, *Greater Medieval Houses of England and Wales*, II vols, Cambridge
Engel 2000	U. Engel, *Die Kathedrale von Worcester*, Munich and Berlin, 2000
Erlande-Brandenburg 1975	A. Erlande-Brandenburg, *Le roi est mort. Étude sur les funérailles, les sepultures et les tombeaux des rois de France jusqu'à la fin du XIIIe siècle*, Geneva
Evans 1949	J. Evans, *English Art 1307–1461*, Oxford
Everett 1934–35	A.W. Everett, 'Polsloe Priory: A Remarkable Architectural Feature', *DCNQ*, xviii, pp. 170–1
Farley 1990	J. Farley, *The Misericords of Gloucester Cathedral*, Gloucester and Cheltenham
Farmer 1987	D.H. Farmer, *The Oxford Dictionary of Saints*, Oxford

Ferris 2001 I.M. Ferris, 'Excavations at Greyfriars, Gloucester, in 1967 and 1974–5', *TBGAS*, cxix, pp. 95–146

Finberg 1951 H.P.R. Finberg, *Tavistock Abbey: A Study in the Social and Economic History of Devon*, Cambridge

Finberg 1953 ———, 'Sherborne, Glastonbury and the Expansion of Wessex', *TRHS*, 5th ser. iii, pp. 101–24.

Fleming 1984 P.W. Fleming, 'Charity, Faith and the Gentry of Kent 1422–1529', in T. Pollard, ed., *Property and Politics. Essays in Later Medieval English History*, Gloucester, pp. 36–58

Fleming 1987 ———, 'The Hautes and their "Circle". Culture and the English Gentry', in D. Williams, ed., *England in the Fifteenth Century* (PHS, 1986), Woodbridge, pp. 85–102

Fletcher 1922 J.M.J. Fletcher, 'The Black Death in Dorset 1348–1349', *PDNHAFC*, xliii, pp. 1–14

Flower 1912 C.T. Flower, 'Obedientars' Accounts of Glastonbury and Other Religious Houses', *Transactions of the St Paul's Ecclesiological Society*, vii, pp. 50–61

Fowler 1951 J. Fowler, *Medieval Sherborne*, Dorchester

French 1997 K.L. French, 'Competing for Space. Medieval Religious Conflict in the Monastic-Parochial Church at Dunster', *Journal of Medieval and Early Modern Studies*, xxvii, pp. 215–44

Fryer 1917 A.C. Fryer, 'Monumental Effigies in Somerset (Part III)', *PSANHS*, lxiii, pp. 1–20

Fryer 1922 ———, 'Monumental Effigies in Somerset (Part VIII)', *PSANHS*, lxviii, pp. 27–63

Fryer 1924 ———, 'Monumental Effigies in Somerset (Part X)', *PSANHS*, lxx, pp. 45–85

Fryer 1925 ———, 'Monumental Effigies in Somerset (Part XII), *PSANHS*, lxxi, pp. 38–66

Fulbrook-Leggatt 1946–48 L.E.O.W. Fulbrook-Leggatt, 'Medieval Gloucester. II', *TBGAS*, lxvii, pp. 217–306

Gaignières Drawings J. Adhémar with G. Dordor, 'Les tombeaux de la collection Gaignières: dessins d'archéologie du XVIIᵉ siècle', II vols, *Gazette des Beaux-Arts*, 6th ser. lxxxiv (1974), pp. 2–192; lxxxviii (1976), pp. 3–128

Gardner 1940 A. Gardner, *Alabaster Tombs of the Pre-Reformation Period in England*, Cambridge

Gardner 1951 ———, *English Medieval Sculpture*, Cambridge

Gasquet 1892 F.A. Gasquet, 'List of Glastonbury Monks and Others of Their Household in A.D. 1377', *DR*, xi, pp. 150–1

Gee 2002 L. Gee, *Women, Art and Patronage from Henry III to Edward III 1216–1377*, Woodbridge

Gem 2001(a) R. Gem, 'The Reconstructions of St Augustine's Abbey, Canterbury, in the Anglo-Saxon Period', in *idem*, *Studies in English Pre-Romanesque and Romanesque Architecture* (vol. I), London, pp. 253–76

Gem 2001(b) ———, 'The English Parish Church in the Eleventh and Early Twelfth Centuries: A Great Rebuilding?', in *idem*, *Studies in*

	English Pre-Romanesque and Romanesque Architecture (vol. II), London, pp. 712–45
Georgius 1824	'Georgius' (George May), 'Effigies, &c. from Tewkesbury Abbey', *Gentleman's Magazine*, pp. 306–7
Gerould 1917	G.H. Gerould, 'The Legend of St. Wulfhad and St. Ruffin at Stone Priory', *Publications of the Modern Language Association of America*, xxxii, pp. 323–37
Gibbs 1904–05	R. Gibbs, 'The Memorials of Bishop Lacy', *DCNQ*, iii, pp. 113–19
Gibbs and Lang 1962	M. Gibbs and J. Lang, *Bishops and Reform 1215–1272, with Special Reference to the Lateran Council of 1215*, Oxford
Gittos 2002	B. and M. Gittos, 'Motivation and Choice: The Selection of Medieval Secular Effigies', in P. Coss and M. Keen, eds, *Heraldry, Pageantry and Social Display in Medieval England*, Woodbridge, pp. 143–67
Given-Wilson 1996	C. Given-Wilson, *The English Nobility in the Late Middle Ages*, London
Given-Wilson 2004	———, *Chronicles: The Writing of History in Medieval England*, London
Goodall 1990	J.A. Goodall, 'Rolls of Arms of Kings: Some Recent Discoveries in the British Library', *Antiquaries Journal*, lxx, pp. 82–94
Goodall 1997	———, 'Heraldry in the Decoration of English Manuscripts', *Antiquaries Journal*, lxxvii, pp. 179–220
Goodall 2001	———, 'The Glastonbury Abbey Memorial Reconsidered', in *Arthurian Tradition*, pp. 185–92
Graham 1927	R. Graham, 'The Benedictine Priory of St Nicholas at Exeter', *JBAA*, xxxiii, pp. 58–69
Graham 1929	———, 'Four Alien Priories in Monmouthshire', *JBAA*, xxxv, pp. 102–21
Graham 1960	———, 'An Essay on English Monasteries', in G. Barraclough, ed., *Social Life in Early England*, London, pp. 51–95
Gransden 1974	A. Gransden, *Historical Writing in England: I, c.550–1307*, London
Gransden 1982	———, *Historical Writing in England: II, c.1307 to the Early Sixteenth Century*, London
Gransden 1985	———, 'The Legends and Traditions Concerning the Origins of the Abbey of Bury St Edmunds', *English Historical Review*, c, pp. 1–24
Gransden 1992	———, *Legends, Traditions and History in Medieval England*, London and Rio Grande
Gray 1926(a)	H.St.G. Gray, 'The Abbot's Fish House, Meare', *PSANHS*, lxxii, p. xli
Gray 1926(b)	———, 'The Abbot's Manor House, Meare', *PSANHS*, lxxii, p. xlii
Greatrex 1977	J. Greatrex, 'A Fourteenth-Century Injunction Book from Winchester', *Bulletin of the Institute of Historical Research*, l, pp. 242–6

Greatrex 1980   ———, 'Monastic or Episcopal Obedience: The Problem of the Sacrists of Worcester' (*Worcester Historical Society Occasional Publications*, 3), Worcester

Greatrex 1993   ———, 'St Swithun's Priory in the Later Middle Ages', in *Winchester Cathedral*, pp. 139–66

Greatrex 1998   ———, 'Benedictine Sermons: Preparation and Practice in the English Monastic Cathedral Cloisters', in C. Muessig, ed., *Medieval Monastic Preaching*, Leiden, pp. 257–78

Greatrex 1999   ———, 'Rabbits and Eels at High Table: Monks of Ely at the University of Cambridge, c.1337–1539', in B. Thompson, ed., *Monasteries and Society in Medieval Britain* (PHS, 1994), Stamford, pp. 312–28

Greatrex 2002   ———, 'After Knowles: Recent Perspectives in Monastic History', in J. Clark, ed., *The Religious Orders in Pre-Reformation England*, Woodbridge, pp. 35–47

Green 1796   V. Green, *The History and Antiquities of the City and Suburbs of Worcester*, II vols, London

Green 1933   A.R. Green, 'The Romsey Painted Wooden Reredos, with a Short Account of Saint Armiel', *AJ*, xc, pp. 306–14

Gunton 1686   S. Gunton, *The History of the Church of Peterburgh*, London

Guy 1991   C. Guy, 'Worcester Castle', in P. Barker and C. Guy, eds, *Archaeology at Worcester Cathedral. Report of the First Annual Symposium on the Precinct, 1991*, pp. 3–4

Haigh 1950   G. Haigh, *The History of Winchcome Abbey*, London

Haines 1989   R.M. Haines, 'The Appointment of a Prelate (a): The Election of an Abbot of Tewkesbury' in *idem, Ecclesia Anglicana. Studies in the English Church of the Later Middle Ages*, Toronto, pp. 15–25

Hall 1904   H. Hall, 'Notes on the Tiles at Tewkesbury Abbey', *The Ancestor*, ix, pp. 46–64

Hamburger 1997   J. Hamburger, *Nuns as Artists. The Visual Culture of a Medieval Convent*, Berkeley

Hammond 1910–11   E.P. Hammond, 'Two Tapestry Poems by Lydgate', *Englische Studien*, xliii, pp. 10–26

Hare 1992   M. Hare, *The Two Anglo-Saxon Minsters at Gloucester*, Deerhurst

Hare 1997   ———, 'Kings and Crowns and Festivals: The Origins of Gloucester as a Royal Ceremonial Centre', *TBGAS*, cxv, pp. 41–78

Harper-Bill 1980   C. Harper-Bill, 'Cistercian Visitation in the Late Middle Ages: the Case of Hailes Abbey', *Bulletin of the Institute of Historical Research*, liii, pp. 103–14

Harper-Bill 1996(a) ———, *The Pre-Reformation Church in England 1400–1530*, London

Harper-Bill 1996(b) ———, 'The English Church and English Religion After the Black Death', in M. Omrod and P.G. Lindley, eds, *The Black Death in England*, Stamford, pp. 79–121

Harvey 1956   J.H. Harvey, 'Notes on the Architects of Worcester Cathedral', *TWAS*, xxxiii, pp. 23–7

Harvey 1978   ———, *The Perpendicular Style*, London

Harvey 1984	———, *English Medieval Architects: A Biographical Dictionary down to 1550* (2nd edn), Gloucester
Harvey 1988	B.F. Harvey, *Monastic Dress in the Middle Ages: Precept and Practice*, Canterbury
Harvey 1995	———, *Living and Dying in Medieval England 1100–1540: The Monastic Experience*, Oxford
Harvey 2002	———, *The Obedientiaries of Westminster Abbey and their Financial Records, c.1270–1540*, Woodbridge
HCE	*Heralds' Commemorative Exhibition 1484–1934* (exhib. cat.), London, 1970
Heale 1994	N. Heale, 'Religious and Intellectual Interests at St Edmunds Abbey at Bury and the Nature of English Benedictinism, c.1350–1450' (D.Phil. dissertation, University of Oxford)
Heale 1997	———, 'Rottenness and Renewal in the Later Medieval Monasteries', in D. Rees, ed., *Monks of England: The Benedictines in England from Augustine to the Present Day*, London, pp. 135–47
Heale 2001	M.R.V. Heale, 'The Dependent Cells of the Benedictine Monasteries of Medieval England, 1066–1540' (unpublished Ph.D. dissertation, Cambridge University)
Heale 2003	———, 'Monastic-Parochial Churches in England and Wales', *Monastic Research Bulletin*, ix, pp. 1–19
Heale 2004	———, *The Dependent Priories of Medieval English Monasteries*, Woodbridge
Heath 1990	P. Heath, 'Between Reform and Reformation. The English Church in the Fourteenth and Fifteenth Centuries', *JEH*, xli, pp. 647–78
Heighway 2003	C. Heighway, 'Tewkesbury before the Normans', in *Tewkesbury Abbey*, pp. 1–10, 290–1
Henderson 1937	A.E. Henderson, 'Plan of Glastonbury Abbey Church Dedicated to the Blessed Virgin Mary and St. Peter and St. Paul. Restored to the Year 1539, Showing Suggested Arrangements', *Transactions of the St Paul's Ecclesiological Society*, x, pp. 107–10
Herbert 1920	J.A. Herbert, *The Sherborne Missal*, Oxford, 1920
Heslop 1980	T.A. Heslop, 'English Seals from the Mid Ninth Century to c.1100', *JBAA*, cxxxiii, pp. 1–16
Heslop 1987	———, 'Attitudes to the Visual Arts: the Evidence from Written Sources', in *AoC*, pp. 26–32
Hewett 1988	C. Hewett, 'English Medieval Cope Chests', *JBAA*, cxli, pp. 105–23
HKW	H.M. Colvin, et al., *The History of the King's Works. Vols I, II, The Middle Ages; Vol. III, Pt. 1, 1485–1660*, London, 1963–75
Holdsworth 1991	C. Holdsworth, *The Piper and the Tune. Medieval Patrons and Monks* (The Stenton Lecture for 1990), Reading
Holt 1985	R. Holt, 'Gloucester in the Century after the Black Death', *TBGAS*, ciii, pp. 149–61
Hope 1890(a)	W.H.St J. Hope, 'On the Sculpted Alabaster Tablets called St. John's Heads', *Archaeologia*, lii, pp. 669–708

Hope 1890(b)   ———, 'Notes on the Benedictine Abbey of St Peter, Gloucester', *RGC*, iii, pp. 90–134

Hope 1906   ———, 'The Obituary Roll of John Islip, Abbot of Westminster, 1500–1532, with Notes on other English Obituary Rolls',
Vetusta Monumenta, vii, pp. 39–51

Hope 1907   ———, 'The Episcopal Ornaments of William of Wykeham
and William of Waynfleet', *Archaeologia*, lx, pp. 465–92

Hope 1913   ———, *Windsor Castle: An Architectural History*, II vols + plans,
London

Hope 1914   ———, 'The Funeral, Monument, and Chantry Chapel of King
Henry V', *Archaeologia*, lxv, pp. 129–86

Hope 1917   ———, 'Quire Screens in English Churches with Special Reference to the Twelfth-Century Screen Formerly in the Cathedral
Church of Ely', *Archaeologia*, xviii, pp. 43–110

Hope 1925   ———, *The History of the London Charterhouse from Its Foundation until the Suppression of the Monastery*, London

Horne 1943–46   E. Horne, 'The Original Glastonbury Chair', *SDNQ*, xxiv, pp.
19–21

Howell 1982   M. Howell, 'Abbatial Vacancies and the Divided *Mensa* in
Medieval England', *JEH*, xxxiii, pp. 173–92

Hudson 1910   C.H.B. Hudson, 'The Founders' Book of Tewkesbury Abbey',
TBGAS, xxxiii, pp. 60–6

Hugo 1858   T. Hugo, 'Muchelney Abbey', *PSANHS*, viii (1858), pp. 76–132
Hugo 1863–64   ———, 'Mynchin Barrow Priory', *PSANHS*, xii, pp. 46–147
Hugo 1897   ———, 'Athelney Abbey', *PSANHS*, xliii, pp. 94–165

Hutchins *Dorset*   J. Hutchins, *The History and Antiquities of the County of Dorset*
(3rd edn), IV vols, ed. W. Shipp and J.W. Hodson, London,
1861–74

Hutchinson 1942   F.E. Hutchinson, 'The Medieval Effigies in the Cathedral
Church of Worcester', *TWAS*, 2nd ser. xix, pp. 25–36

Irvine 1890   J.T. Irvine, 'Description of the Remains of the Norman Cathedral at Bath', *JBAA*, xlvi, pp. 84–94

Jackson 1858   J.E. Jackson, 'Kington St Michael', *WAM*, iv, pp. 36–128
James 1900–02   M.R. James, *The Western Manuscripts in the Library of Trinity
College, Cambridge*, III vols, Cambridge

James 1912   ———, *A Descriptive Catalogue of the Manuscripts in the Library
of Corpus Christi College, Cambridge*, II vols, Cambridge

James and Jenkins   ——— and C. Jenkins, *A Descriptive Catalogue of the Manu-
1930–32   scripts in the Library of Lambeth Palace*, Cambridge

James & Tristram   ——— and E.W. Tristram, 'The Wall Paintings in Eton
1928–29   College Chapel and in the Lady Chapel of Winchester Cathedral', *Walpole Society*, xvii, pp. 1–43

Jeffery 2004   P. Jeffery, *The Collegiate Churches of England and Wales*, London
Jervis 1993   S. Jervis, 'The Venerable Chapel Armoire', in *Winchester Cathedral*, pp. 207–14

Jones 1889   W. Jones, 'Curious Inscription in the Chancel of Spreyton
Church, and Contributions to the History of the Parish', *Notes
and Gleanings*, ii, pp. 23–7

Jones and Traskey 1997	S. Jones and P. Traskey, *Milton Abbey*, Derby
Jordan 1959	W.K. Jordan, *Philanthropy in England 1480–1660: A Study of the Changing Patterns of English Social Aspirations*, London
Kauffmann 2001	C.M. Kauffmann, 'Lansdowne Ms. 383: The Shaftesbury Psalter?', in P. Binski and W. Noel, eds, *New Offerings, Ancient Treasures. Studies in Medieval Art for George Henderson*, Gloucester, pp. 256–78
Keen 2002	M. Keen, *Origins of the English Gentleman. Heraldry, Chivalry and Gentility in Medieval England, c.1300–c.1500*, Stroud
Keil 1959–60	I. Keil, 'The Garden at Glastonbury Abbey 1333–4', *PSANHS*, civ, pp. 96–101
Keil 1961–67(a)	———, 'The Archdeaconry of Glastonbury in the Later Middle Ages', *SDNQ*, xxviii, pp. 129–33
Keil 1961–67(b)	———, 'Mills on the Estates of Glastonbury Abbey in the Later Middle Ages', *SDNQ*, xxviii, pp. 181–4
Keil 1963	———, 'Some Taxation Assessments of the Income of Glastonbury Abbey', *SDNQ*, xxviii, pp. 159–61
Keil 1964(a)	———, 'Corrodies of Glastonbury Abbey in the Later Middle Ages', *PSANHS*, cviii, pp. 113–31
Keil 1964(b)	———, 'The Abbots of Glastonbury in the early Fourteenth Century', *DR*, lxxxii, pp. 327–48
Kellock 1989	A. Kellock, 'Abbot Sebrok's Pavement: A Medieval Tile Floor from Gloucester', *TBGAS*, cvii, pp. 171–88
Kendrick 1950	T.D. Kendrick, *British Antiquity*, London
Kennett 1818	W. Kennet, *Parochial Antiquities Attempted in the History of Ambrosden, Burchester and other Adjacent Parts . . .*, II vols, Oxford
Kerr 1985	J. Kerr, 'The East Window of Gloucester Cathedral', in T.A. Heslop and V. Sekules, eds, *Medieval Art and Architecture at Gloucester and Tewkesbury* (BAACT, 7), Leeds, pp. 116–29
Kershaw 1976	I. Kershaw, 'The Great Famine and Agrarian Crisis in England, 1315–22', in R.H. Hilton, ed., *Peasants, Knights and Heretics. Studies in Medieval English Social History*, Cambridge, pp. 85–132
Keynes 2001	S. Keynes, 'The Cartulary of Athelney Abbey Rediscovered', *Monastic Research Bulletin*, vii, pp. 2–5
K&H	D. Knowles and R.N. Hadcock, *Medieval Religious Houses: England and Wales*, Harlow, 1996
King 1985	P.M. King, 'The Iconography of the "Wakeman Cenotaph" in Tewkesbury Abbey', *TBGAS*, ciii, pp. 141–8
Kingsford 1913	C.L. Kingsford, *English Historical Literature in the Fifteenth Century*, Oxford
Knowles 1948	D. Knowles, *The Religious Orders in England*, Cambridge
Knowles 1950	———, *The Monastic Order in England*, Cambridge
Knowles 1955	———, *The Religious Orders in England II: The End of the Middle Ages*, Cambridge
Knowles 1959	———, *The Religious Orders in England III: The Tudor Age*, Cambridge

Lagorio 2001   V. Lagorio, 'The Evolving Legend of St Joseph of Glastonbury',
                      in *Arthurian Tradition*, pp. 55–81
Lake 1867–72   W. Lake, *Parochial History of the County of Cornwall*, IV vols,
                      London and Truro
Lander 1983   J.R. Lander, *Government and Community. England 1450–1509*,
                      London
Lapidge 2001   M. Lapidge, 'The *Vera Historia de Morte Arthuri*: A New
                      Edition', in *Arthurian Tradition*, pp. 115–41
Lee 1908   E.H.H. Lee, 'Hilton Church', *PDNHAFC*, xxix, pp. 111–18
Leedy 1980   W.C. Leedy, *Fan Vaulting. A Study of Form, Technology and
                      Meaning*, Santa Monica
Lega-Weekes   E. Lega-Weekes, 'Exeter Clerical Subsidies', *DCNQ*, iv, pp.
   1906–07(a)   271–80
Lewis 1926   L.S. Lewis, 'The Church of St John the Baptist, Glastonbury',
                      PSANHS, lxxii, pp. xxxii–xxxvii
Lindley 1951   E.S. Lindley, 'St. Arild of Thornbury', *TBGAS*, lxx, pp. 152–3
Lindley 1986   P.G. Lindley, 'The Great Screen of Winchester Cathedral I',
                      Burlington Magazine, cxxxi, pp. 604–17
Lindley 1988   ———, 'The Sculptural Programme of Bishop Fox's Chantry
                      Chapel', *WCR*, lvii, pp. 33–7
Lindley 1993(a)   ———, 'The Medieval Sculpture of Winchester Cathedral', in
                      Winchester Cathedral, pp. 97–122
Lindley 1993(b)   ———, 'The Screen of Winchester Cathedral Part II: Style and
                      Date', *Burlington Magazine*, cxxxv, pp. 796–807
Lindley 1995   ———, 'The Tomb of Bishop William de Luda: an Architec-
                      tural Model at Ely', in *idem, Gothic to Renaissance. Essays on
                      Sculpture in England*, Stamford, pp. 85–96
Lindley 1996   ———, 'The Black Death and English Art: The Debate and
                      Some Assumptions', in M. Omrod and P.G. Lindley, eds, *The
                      Black Death in England*, Stamford, pp. 125–46
Lindley 2003(a)   ———, ' "The singular mediacions and praiers of al the holie
                      companie of Heven": Sculptural Functions and Forms in Henry
                      VII's Chapel', in *Westminster Abbey*, pp. 259–93
Lindley 2003(b)   ———, 'The Later Medieval Monuments and Chantry
                      Chapels', in *Tewkesbury Abbey*, pp. 161–82, 303–6
Lindley (forthcoming) ———, ' "Disrespect for the Dead"? The Destruction of Tomb
                      Monuments in Mid-Sixteenth-Century England', *Church
                      Monuments*
Liveing 1906   H.G.D. Liveing, *Records of Romsey Abbey*, Winchester
Lloyd 1873   R. Lloyd, *An Account of the Altars, Monuments, & Tombs
                      Existing in Saint Alban's Abbey*, Saint Albans
Lockyer 1991   R. Lockyer, *Henry VII* (2nd edn), London and New York
Long 1922(a)   E.T. Long, 'Ancient Stained Glass in Dorset Churches',
                      PDNHAFC, xliii, pp. 44–56
Long 1922(b)   ———, 'Dorset Church Woodwork', *PDNHAFC*, xliii, pp.
                      15–32
Long 1928(a)   ———, 'English Alabaster Tables in Dorset', *PDNHAFC*, xlix,
                      pp. 101–13

Long 1928(b)	———, 'Ancient Mural Paintings in Dorset Churches', *PDNHAFC*, l, pp. 97–108
Long 1931	———, 'The Religious Houses of Dorset', *PDNHAFC*, liii, pp. 16–50
Lowe, Jacob & James 1924	W.R.L. Lowe, E.F. Jacob and M.R. James, *Illustrations to the Life of St Alban in Trin. Coll. Dublin Ms. E. i. 40*, Oxford
Luce 1979	R. Luce, *The History of the Abbey and Town of Malmesbury*, Minety
Lunn 1973	D.M. Lunn, 'Benedictine Reform Movements of the Later Middle Ages', *DR*, xci, pp. 275–89
Luxford 2000	J.M. Luxford, 'In Dreams: the Sculptural Iconography of the West Front of Bath Abbey Church Reassessed', *Religion and the Arts*, iv, pp. 313–37
Luxford 2002(a)	———, '*Auro et Argento Pulcherrime Fabricatum*: New Visual Evidence for the Feretory of St Dunstan at Glastonbury and its Relation to the Controversy over the Relics', *Antiquaries Journal*, lxxxii, pp. 105–24
Luxford 2002(b)	———, 'The Great Rood of Glastonbury Abbey', *PSANHS*, cxlv, pp. 83–7
Luxford 2002(c)	———, 'A Previously Unlisted Manuscript of the Latin *Brut* Chronicle with Sherborne Continuation', *Medium Ævum*, lxxi, pp. 286–93
Luxford 2002(d)	———, 'Art and Ideology on the Eve of the Reformation: The Monument of Osric and the Benedictines of Gloucester', *TBGAS*, cxx, pp. 177–211
Luxford 2002(e)	———, 'The Patronage of Benedictine Art and Architecture in the West of England during the Later Middle Ages (1300–1540)' (unpublished Ph.D. dissertation, Cambridge University)
Luxford 2003(a)	———, 'More on the Sculptural Iconography of the West Front of Bath Abbey: Christ of the Charter and Antichrist', *Religion and the Arts*, vii, pp. 299–322
Luxford 2003(b)	———, 'A Leiston Document from Glastonbury', *Proceedings of the Suffolk Institute of Archaeology and History*, xl, pp. 278–88
Luxford 2003(c)	———, 'The Founders' Book', in *Tewkesbury Abbey*, pp. 53–64, 293–4
Luxford 2004(a)	———, 'Sculpture as Exemplar: The Founders' Book of Tewkesbury Abbey and Its Sculptural Models', *Sculpture Journal*, xii, pp. 4–21
Luxford 2004(b)	———, 'Flourishing the Register: The Worcester Monk-Artist Thomas Blockeley at Work', *TWAS*, xix, pp. 141–8, 248
MacKenzie 1997	I. MacKenzie, 'Some Tremors at the Foundation of Prince Arthur's Chantry', in P. Barker and C. Guy, eds, *Archaeology at Worcester Cathedral. Report of the Seventh Annual Symposium March 1997*, Worcester, pp. 24–7
McAleer 2001	J.P. McAleer, 'The Tradition of Detached Bell Towers at Cathedral and Monastic Churches in Medieval England and Scotland (1066–1539)', *JBAA*, cliv, pp. 54–83

McClure 1912   E. McClure, 'Some Remarks on Prince Arthur's Chantry
                      Chapel in Worcester Cathedral', *AASRP*, xxxi, pp. 539–69
McFarlane 1973   K.B. McFarlane, *The Nobility of Later Medieval England*, Oxford
McFarlane 1981   ———, *England in the Fifteenth Century*, ed. G.L. Harriss,
                      London
McGinn 2000   B. McGinn, *Antichrist. Two Thousand Years of the Human Fasci-
                      nation with Evil*, New York
McHardy 1991   A.K. McHardy, 'Some Patterns of Ecclesiastical Patronage in
                      the Later Middle Ages', in D.M. Smith, ed., *Studies in Clergy and
                      Ministry in Medieval England*, York, pp. 20–37
Major 1946   K. Major, 'The Thornton Abbey Chronicle (Bodleian Library.
                      Tanner Ms. 166), with Extracts Relating to the Fabric of the
                      Abbey', *AJ*, ciii, pp. 174–8
Malden 1901   A.R. Malden, *The Canonization of St. Osmund*, Salisbury
Manco 1993   J. Manco, 'The Buildings of Bath Priory', *PSANHS*, cxxxvii, pp.
                      75–109
Manco 1998   ———, *The Spirit of Care. The Eight-Hundred-Year Story of St
                      John's Hospital, Bath*, Bath
Manual   A.E. Hartung and J.B. Severs, gen. eds, *A Manual of the Writings
                      in Middle English 1050–1500*, XI vols, New Haven, 1967–98
Marks 1974   R. Marks, 'The Stained Glass Patronage of Sir Reginald Bray',
                      *Report of the Society of the Friends of St George's and the Descen-
                      dants of the Knights of the Garter*, v, pp. 199–202
Marks 1993   ———, *Stained Glass in England during the Middle Ages*, London
Marks 2004   ———, *Image and Devotion in Late Medieval England*, Stroud
Marret 1970–72   P. Marret, 'The Use of the Pontificalia by the Priors of
                      Worcester in the Fourteenth Century', *TWAS*, 3rd ser. iii, pp.
                      61–2
Martindale 1995   A. Martindale, 'Patrons and Minders. The Intrusion of the
                      Secular into Sacred Spaces during the Late Middle Ages', in D.
                      Wood, ed., *The Church and the Arts* (Studies in Church History
                      28), Oxford, pp. 143–78
Martindale 1998   ———, 'The Wall-paintings in the Chapel of Eton College', in
                      C. Barron and N. Saul, eds, *England and the Low Countries in the
                      Late Middle Ages* (Stroud, 1998), pp. 133–52
Mason 1984   E. Mason, 'St Wulfstan's Staff: A Legend and Its Uses', *Medium
                      Ævum*, liii, pp. 157–79
Matheson 1998   L.M. Matheson, *The Prose Brut. The Development of a Middle
                      English Chronicle*, Tempe
Maxwell-Lyte 1909   H.C. Maxwell-Lyte, *A History of Dunster, and the Families of
                      Mohun and Luttrell*, II vols, London
Mayo 1894   C.H. Mayo, 'Shaftesbury', *PDNHAFC*, xv, pp. 36–51
Michael 1997   M. Michael, 'The Privilege of "Proximity". Towards a
                      Re-Definition of the Function of Armorials', *Journal of Medieval
                      History*, xxiii, pp. 55–74
Milner 1794   J. Milner, 'Observations on an Ancient Cup, formerly belonging
                      to the Abbey of Glastonbury', *Archaeologia*, xi, pp. 411–24

MLGB	N. Ker, *Medieval Libraries of Great Britain: A List of Surviving Books* (2nd edn), London, 1964
MLGB Supp.	A.G. Watson, *Medieval Libraries of Great Britain: Supplement to the Second Edition*, London, 1987
MMBL	N. Ker, et al., *Medieval Manuscripts in British Libraries*, IV vols, Oxford, 1969–92
Molyneux & McGregor 1997	A.D. Molyneux and J.E. McGregor, *The Medieval Tiles at Great Malvern Priory*, Great Malvern
Monckton 1999	L. Monckton, 'Late Gothic Architecture in South-West England' (unpublished Ph.D. dissertation, University of Warwick)
Monckton 2000	——, 'The Late Medieval Rebuilding of Sherborne Abbey: A Reassessment', *Architectural History*, xliii, pp. 88–120
Monckton 2004	——, 'Fit for a King? The Architecture of the Beauchamp Chapel', *Architectural History*, xlvii, pp. 25–52
Moore 1887	S.A. Moore, 'Documents Relating to the Death and Burial of King Edward II', *Archaeologia*, l, pp. 215–26
Morganstern 2000	A.McG. Morganstern, *Gothic Tombs of Kinship in France, the Low Countries and England*, Princeton
Morris 1974	R.K. Morris, 'Tewkesbury Abbey: the Despenser Mausoleum', *TBGAS*, xciii, pp. 142–55
Morris 1978	——, 'Worcester Nave: From Decorated to Perpendicular', in *Medieval Art and Architecture at Worcester Cathedral* (BAACT, 1), Leeds, pp. 116–43
Morris 1979	R. Morris, *Cathedrals and Abbeys of England and Wales*, London
Morris 2003(a)	R.K. Morris, 'The Monastic Buildings', in *Tewkesbury Abbey*, pp. 143–60, 300–3
Morris 2003(b)	——, 'The Gothic Church: Vaulting and Carpentry', in *Tewkesbury Abbey*, pp. 131–42, 299–300
Morris 2003(c)	——, 'Master Masons at Gloucester Cathedral in the 14th Century', *Friends of Gloucester Cathedral Annual Report*, lxvii, pp. 10–17
Morris and Kendrick 1999	—— and D. Kendrick, *Roof Bosses in the Nave of Tewkesbury Abbey*, Tewkesbury
Morris with Luxford 2002	——, with J. Luxford, 'Fragments from Tewkesbury Abbey', in S. Boldrick, D. Park and P. Williamson, eds, *Wonder: Painted Sculpture from Medieval England*, Leeds, pp. 86–91
Morris with Thurlby 2003	——, with M. Thurlby, 'The Gothic Church: Architectural History', in *Tewkesbury Abbey*, pp. 109–30, 297–9
Nightingale 1881	J.E. Nightingale, 'On the Succession of the Abbesses of Wilton, with Some Notice of Wilton Seals', *WAM*, xix, pp. 342–62
Nilson 1998	B. Nilson, *Cathedral Shrines of Medieval England*, Woodbridge
Noble 2001	C. Noble, 'Aspects of Life at Norwich Cathedral Priory in the Late Medieval Period' (unpublished Ph.D. dissertation, University of East Anglia)
Nott 1896	J. Nott, *Malvern Priory Church: A Descriptive Account of Its Ancient Glass, Old Tombs, Tesselated Pavements, and Other Antiquities*, Malvern, 1896

Oates 1958   J.C.T. Oates, 'Richard Pynson and the Holy Blood of Hayles', *The Library*, 5th ser. xiii, pp. 269–77

O'Grady 1901   The Hon. Mrs O'Grady (first name not specified), 'Bishop Cobham 1317–1327: His Monument and Work in Worcester Cathedral', *AASRP*, xxvi, pp. 232–40

Oliver 1846   G. Oliver, *Monasticon Dioecesis Exoniensis*, Exeter

Oliver 1937   V.L. and V.F.M. Oliver, 'Cerne Abbey', *PDNHAFC*, LIX, pp. 15–24

Oman 1957   C. Oman, *English Church Plate, 597–1830*, Oxford

Orme 1984   N. Orme, 'A School Notebook from Barlinch Priory', *PSANHS*, cxxviii, pp. 55–63

Orme 1986(a)   ———, *Exeter Cathedral as It Was, 1050–1550*, Exeter

Orme 1986(b)   ———, 'Two Saint-Bishops of Exeter: James Berkeley and Edmund Lacy', *Analecta Bollandiana*, civ, pp. 403–18

Orme 1987–91(a)   ———, 'Music and Teaching at Tywardreath Priory, 1522–36', *DCNQ*, xxxvi, pp. 277–80

Orme 1987–91(b)   ———, 'Warland Hospital, Totnes, and the Trinitarian Friars in Devon', *DCNQ*, xxxvi, pp. 41–8

Orme 1990   ———, 'Saint Walter of Cowick', *Analecta Bollandiana*, cviii, pp. 387–93

Orme 2004   ———, 'The Dead Beneath Our Feet', *History Today*, liv, pp. 19–25

Ormrod 1989   W.M. Ormrod, 'The Personal Religion of Edward III', *Speculum*, lxiv, pp. 849–77

Oswald 1966   A. Oswald, 'Milton Abbey, Dorset', *Country Life*, pp. 1586–9, 1650–4, 1718–22

Owst 1926   G.R. Owst, *Preaching in Medieval England: An Introduction to Sermon Manuscripts of the Period c.1350–1450*, Cambridge

Pächt & Alexander 1966–73   O. Pächt and J.J.G. Alexander, *Illuminated Manuscripts in the Bodleian Library*, III vols, Oxford

Pantin 1929   W.A. Pantin, 'Abbot Kidderminster and Monastic Studies', *DR*, xlvii, pp. 198–211

Pantin 1950   ———, 'Some Medieval English Treatises on the Origins of Monasticism', in V. Ruffer and A.J. Taylor, eds, *Medieval Studies Presented to Rose Graham*, Oxford, pp. 189–215

Pantin 1955   ———, *The English Church in the Fourteenth Century*, Cambridge

Pantin 1957   ———, 'Medieval Priests' Houses in South-west England', *Medieval Archaeology*, i, pp. 118–46

Pantin and Rouse 1955   ——— and E.C. Rouse, 'The Golden Cross, Oxford', *Oxoniensia*, xx, pp. 46–89

Park 1996   D. Park, 'The Giffard Monument', in P. Barker and C. Guy, eds, *Archaeology at Worcester Cathedral. Report of the Sixth Annual Symposium March 1996*, Worcester, pp. 20–1

Park 1998   ———, 'Rediscovered 14th-Century Sculptures from the Guesten Hall', in C. Guy, ed., *Archaeology at Worcester Cathedral. Report of the Eighth Annual Symposium March 1998*, Worcester, pp. 18–21

Park and Welford 1993	—— and P. Welford, 'The Medieval Polychromy of Winchester Cathedral', in *Winchester Cathedral*, pp. 123–38
Parkes 1997	M.B. Parkes, 'Archaizing Hands in English Manuscripts', in J.P. Carley and C.G.C. Tite, eds, *Books and Collectors 1200–1700. Essays Presented to Andrew Watson*, London, pp. 101–41
Payne and Payne 1994	M.T.W. Payne and S.E. Payne, 'The Wall Inscriptions of Gloucester Cathedral Chapter House and the de Chaworths of Kempsford', *TBGAS*, cxii, pp. 87–104
Pearce 1916	E.H. Pearce, *The Monks of Westminster*, Cambridge
Pearsall 1995	D. Pearsall, 'Chaucer's Tomb: The Politics of Reburial', *Medium Ævum*, lxiv, pp. 51–73
Pepin 1980	P.B. Pepin, *The Monumental Tombs of Medieval England, 1250–1350*, Ann Arbor
Perkins 1907	T. Perkins, *A History and Description of Romsey Abbey*, London
Pevsner 1958(a)	N. Pevsner, *The Buildings of England. North Somerset and Bristol*, Harmondsworth
Pevsner 1958(b)	——, *The Buildings of England. South and West Somerset*, Harmondsworth
Pevsner 1968	——, *The Buildings of England. Worcestershire*, Harmondsworth
Pevsner and Cherry 1975	—— and B. Cherry, *The Buildings of England. Wiltshire*, Harmondsworth
Pevsner and Cherry 1989	——, *The Buildings of England. Devon*, Harmondsworth, 1989
Pevsner and Lloyd 1967	—— and D. Lloyd, *The Buildings of England. Hampshire and the Isle of Wight*, Harmondsworth
Pevsner and Newman 1972	—— and J. Newman, *The Buildings of England. Dorset*, Harmondsworth
Piper 1998	A.J. Piper, 'The Historical Interests of the Monks of Durham', in D. Rollason, ed., *Symeon of Durham: Historian of Durham and the North*, Stamford, pp. 301–32
Platt 1969	C. Platt, *The Monastic Grange in Medieval England*, London
Platt 1984	——, *The Abbeys and Priories of Medieval England*, London
Playne 1915	A.T. Playne, *A History of the Parishes of Minchinhampton and Avening*, Gloucester
Postan 1975	M.M. Postan, *The Medieval Economy and Society: An Economic History of Britain in the Middle Ages*, Harmondsworth
Pounds 2000	N.J.G. Pounds, *A History of the English Parish*, Cambridge
Powell 1973	K.G. Powell, 'The Social Background to the Reformation in Gloucestershire', *TBGAS*, xcii, pp. 96–120
Power 1922	E. Power, *English Medieval Nunneries c.1275–1535*, Cambridge
Preston 1935	A.E. Preston, 'The Demolition of Reading Abbey', *The Berkshire Archaeological Journal*, xxxix, pp. 107–44
Price 1979	E.G. Price, 'Survivals of the Medieval Monastic Estate of Frocester', *TBGAS*, xcviii, pp. 73–88
Prideaux 1907	W.C. Prideaux, 'The Ancient Memorial Brasses of Dorset, IV: Milton Abbey and Melbury Sampford', *PDNHAFC*, xxviii, pp. 225–44

Prideaux 1934–35	F.B. Prideaux, 'Inquisitio Post Mortem on Hugh de Courtenay, Earl of Devon (1377)', *DCNQ*, xviii, pp. 114–20, 161–5, 202–5
Raban 1974	S. Raban, 'Mortmain in Medieval England', *Past and Present*, lxii, pp. 3–26
Raban 1982	———, *Mortmain Legislation and the English Chruch 1279–1500*, Cambridge
Radford 1932–3	E.L. Radford, 'The Buildings of Tavistock Abbey after the Dissolution', *DCNQ*, xvii, pp. 195–203
Ralegh-Radford 1986	C.A. Ralegh-Radford, 'Cowick Priory', *DCNQ*, xxxiv, pp. 383–4
Ramsay and Sparks 1988	——— and M. Sparks, *The Image of St Dunstan*, Canterbury
RCHM *Dorset* 1952	Royal Commission on Historical Monuments. *Dorset* (vol. I: West Dorset), London
RCHM *Dorset* 1970	——— (vol. III, pt. 2: Central Dorset), London
RCHM *Dorset* 1972	——— (vol. IV: North Dorset), London
RCHM *Hereford*	Royal Commission on Historical Monuments. *An Inventory of the Historical Monuments in Herefordshire*, III vols, London, 1931–34
Rea 1924–25	C. Rea, 'Medieval Latin', *DCNQ*, xiii, pp. 307–8
Reyner 1626	C. Reyner, *Apostolatus Benedictorum in Anglia, siue disceptatio historica, de antiquitate ordinis congregationisque monachorum nigrorum S. Benedicti in regno Angliae*, Regensburg
Richardson 1951	L. Richardson, 'The Stone of the Canopy of Edward II's Tomb in Gloucester Cathedral', *TBGAS*, lxx, pp. 144–5
Richmond 1991	C. Richmond, 'The English Gentry and Religion, c.1500', in C. Harper-Bill, ed. *Religious Belief and Ecclesiastical Careers in Late Medieval England* (Proceedings of the Conference held at Strawberry Hill, Easter 1989), Woodbridge, pp. 121–50
Richmond 1996	———, 'Religion', in R. Horrox, ed., *Fifteenth-Century Attitudes. Perceptions of Society in Late Medieval England*, Cambridge, pp. 183–201
Riddy 2001	F. Riddy, 'Glastonbury, Joseph of Arimathea and the Grail in John Harding's Chronicle', in *Arthurian Tradition*, pp. 269–84
Ridsdale 1884–85	E.S. Ridsdale, 'The Almonry of Evesham Abbey', *TBGAS*, ix, pp. 128–33
Rigold 1965	S.E. Rigold, 'Froucester Court Tithe Barn', *AJ*, cxxxiii, pp. 209–11
Robbins 1963–64	R.H. Robbins, 'Wall Verses at Launceston Priory', *Archiv*, cc, pp. 338–43
Roberts and Clarke 1998	E. Roberts and K. Clarke, 'The Rediscovery of Two Major Monastic Buildings at Wherwell', *PHFCAS*, liii, pp. 137–53
Rogers 1983	N.J. Rogers, 'The Cult of Prince Edward at Tewkesbury', *TBGAS*, ci, pp. 187–9
Rogers 1984	———, 'Books of Hours Produced in the Low Countries for the English Market in the Fifteenth Century' (II vols: unpublished M.Litt. dissertation, University of Cambridge)

Rogers 1987   ———, 'English Episcopal Monuments, 1270–1350', in *Earliest English Brasses*, pp. 8–68

Rogers 1999   ———, 'Monuments to Monks and Monastic Servants', in B. Thompson, ed., *Monasteries and Society in Medieval Britain* (PHS, 1994), Stamford, pp. 262–76

Roper 1993   S.E. Roper, *Medieval English Benedictine Liturgy. Studies in the Formation, Structure and Content of the Monastic Votive Office, c.950–1540*, New York and London

Rosenthal 1972   J.T. Rosenthal, *The Purchase of Paradise. Gift Giving and the Aristocracy 1307–1485*, London

Rose-Troup 1913   F. Rose-Troup, *The Western Rebellion of 1549*, London

Rose-Troup 1936–37   ———, 'The Five Prebends of Cullompton', *DCNQ*, xix, pp. 139–41

Rouse and Varty 1976   E.C. Rouse and K. Varty, 'Medieval Paintings of Reynard the Fox in Gloucester Cathedral, and Some Other Related Examples', *AJ*, cxxxiii, pp. 104–17

Rowntree 1981   C.B. Rowntree, 'Studies in Carthusian History in Later Medieval England with special reference to the Order's Relations with Secular Society' (unpublished Ph.D. dissertation, York University)

Rowntree 1990   ———, 'A Carthusian World View: Bodleian Ms. E Museo 160', *Analecta Cartusiana*, xxxv:9, pp. 5–72

RSTC   A.W. Pollard and G.R. Redgrave, *A Short-Title Catalogue of Books Printed in England, Scotland and Ireland and of English Books Printed Abroad 1475–1640* (rev. edn, ed. W.A. Jackson, F.S. Ferguson and K.F. Pantzer), III vols, London, 1976–91

Rudder 1781   S. Rudder, *The History and Antiquities of Gloucester*, Cirencester

Rushforth 1921   G.McN. Rushforth, 'The Glass of the East Window of the Lady Chapel in Gloucester Cathedral', *TBGAS*, xliii, pp. 191–218

Rushforth 1922   ———, 'The Great East Window of Gloucester Cathedral', *TBGAS*, xliv, pp. 293–304

Rushforth 1924   ———, 'The Glass in the Quire Clerestory of Tewkesbury Abbey', *TBGAS*, xlvi, pp. 289–324

Rushforth 1925   ———, 'The Burial of Lancastrian Notables in Tewkesbury Abbey After the Battle, A.D. 1471', *TBGAS*, xlvii, pp. 131–49

Rushforth 1936   ———, *Medieval Christian Imagery as Illustrated by the Painted Windows of Great Malvern Priory Church, Worcestershire*, Oxford

Salzman 1997   L.F. Salzman, *Building in England Down to 1540: A Documentary History*, Oxford

Sandler 1986   L.F. Sandler, *Gothic Manuscripts 1285–1385*, II vols, London (Survey of Manuscripts Illuminated in the British Isles, 5), 1986

Sauerländer 2002   W. Sauerländer, 'Images Behind the Wall', *The New York Review of Books*, April 25, 2002, pp. 40–2

Saul 1980   N.E. Saul, 'The Religious Sympathies of the Gentry in Gloucestershire, 1200–1500', *TBGAS*, xcviii, pp. 99–109

Saul 2002   ———, 'Bold as Brass: Secular Display in English Medieval Brasses', in P. Coss and M. Keen, eds, *Heraldry, Pageantry and Social Display in Medieval England*, Woodbridge, pp. 169–94

Sayers 1976   J. Sayers, 'Monastic Archdeacons', in C.N.L. Brooke, D.E. Luscombe, G.H. Martin and D. Owen, eds, *Church and Government in the Middle Ages. Essays Presented to C.R. Cheney on his 70th Birthday*, Cambridge, pp. 177–204

Sayers 1990   ———, 'Violence in the Medieval Cloister', *JEH*, xli, pp. 533–42

Scarth 1883   H.M. Scarth, 'Note on a Tomb at Barrow Gurney', *PSANHS*, xxix, p. 117

Scase 1989   W. Scase, *Piers Plowman and the New Anticlericalism*, Cambridge

Scott 1996   K.L. Scott, *Later Gothic Manuscripts 1390–1490*, II vols, London (Survey of Manuscripts Illuminated in the British Isles, 6)

Sekules 2000   V. Sekules, 'Dynasty and Patrimony in the Self-Construction of an English Queen: Philippa of Hainault and Her Images', in J. Mitchell and M. Moran, eds, *England and the Continent in the Middle Ages. Studies in Memory of Andrew Martindale* (PHS, 1996), Stamford, pp. 157–74

S.F. 1968–70   S.F. (full name not supplied), 'Otterton Priory and Mont St. Michel Its Motherhouse', *DCNQ*, vi, pp. 1–10

Sharpe 2001   R. Sharpe, *A Handlist of the Latin Writers of Great Britain and Ireland before 1540*, Turnhout

Sheppard 1912   L. Sheppard, 'The Franciscans or Grey Friars of Worcester', *AASRP*, xxxi, pp. 243–58

Sherlock 1955–60   R.J. Sherlock, 'The Glastonbury Ring', *SDNQ*, xxvii, pp. 125–6

Shickle 1907   C.W. Shickle, 'Cardinal Adrian, Bishop of Bath and Wells', *Proceedings of the Bath Natural History and Antiquarian Field Club*, xi, pp. 75–81

Short 1946–48   R.D. Short, 'Graffiti on the Reredos of the Lady Chapel of Gloucester Cathedral', *TBGAS*, lxvii, pp. 21–36

Singer and Anderson 1950   D.W. Singer and A. Anderson, *Catalogue of Latin and Vernacular Plague Tracts*, London

Smith 1942   R.A.L. Smith, 'The *Regimen Scaccarii* in English Monasteries', *TRHS*, 4th ser. xxiv, pp. 73–94

Smith 1951   R.A. Smith, 'The Organization and Financing of Monastic Building in England in the Later Middle Ages' (unpublished M.A. dissertation, University of London)

Smith 1988(a)   A. Smith, 'The Chantry Chapel of Bishop Richard Fox', *Winchester Cathedral Record*, lvii, pp. 27–32

Smith 1988(b)   ———, 'The Life and Building Activity of Bishop Richard Fox, c.1448–1528' (unpublished Ph.D. dissertation, University of London)

Smith 1993   K.A. Smith, 'History, Typology and Homily. The Joseph Cycle in the Queen Mary Psalter', *Gesta*, xxxii, pp. 147–59

Smith 1996   A. Smith, *Roof Bosses of Winchester Cathedral*, Winchester

Snape 1926   R.H. Snape, *English Monastic Finances in the Later Middle Ages*, Cambridge

Snell 1967   L.S. Snell, *The Suppression of the Religious Foundations of Devon and Cornwall*, Marazion

Southern 1990   R.W. Southern, *Western Society and the Church in the Middle Ages*, Harmondsworth

Spalding 1914   M.C. Spalding, *The Middle English Charters of Christ*, Bryn Mawr

Stephenson 1926   M. Stephenson, *A List of Monumental Brasses in the British Isles*, London

Stone 1972   L. Stone, *Sculpture in Britain: The Middle Ages*, Harmondsworth

Stones and Keil 1976 E.G.L. Stones and I. Keil, 'Edward II and the Abbot of Glastonbury: A New Case of Historical Evidence Solicited from Monasteries', *Archives*, xii, pp. 176–82.

Strange 1904   E.F. Strange, *Worcester: The Cathedral and See*, London

Stratford 1983   N. Stratford, 'Glastonbury and Two Gothic Ivories in the United States', in F.H. Thompson, ed. *Studies in Medieval Sculpture* (Society of Antiquaries of London Occasional Paper, n.s. III), London, pp. 208–16

Strauss 1959   H. Strauss, 'The History and Form of the Seven-Branched Candlestick of the Hasmonean Kings', *Journal of the Warburg and Courtauld Institutes*, xxii, pp. 7–16

Summerson 1963   J. Summerson, 'Heavenly Mansions. An Interpretation of Gothic', in *idem*, *Heavenly Mansions and other Essays on Architecture*, New York, pp. 1–28

Swanson and Lepine   R. Swanson and D. Lepine, 'The Later Middle Ages, 1268–
  2000   1535', in G. Aylmer and J. Tiller, eds, *Hereford Cathedral: A History*, London, pp. 48–86

Tanner 1787   T. Tanner, *Notitia Monastica*, Cambridge

Tanner 1984   N.P. Tanner, *The Church in Late Medieval Norwich 1370–1532*, Toronto

Tatton-Brown 2003   T. Tatton-Brown, 'The Building History of the Lady Chapels', in *Westminster Abbey*, pp. 189–204

Taylor 1966   J. Taylor, *The Universal Chronicle of Ranulph Higden*, Oxford

Thomas 1736   W. Thomas, *A Survey of the Cathedral-Church of Worcester*, London

Thomas 1974   I.G. Thomas, 'The Cult of Saints' Relics in Medieval England' (unpublished Ph.D. dissertation, University of London)

Thomas 1991   K. Thomas, *Religion and the Decline of Magic*, Harmondsworth

Thompson 1917   A.H. Thompson, 'Notes of Colleges of Secular Canons in England', *AJ*, xxiv, pp. 139–239

Thompson 1925   ———, 'Muchelney Abbey', *PSANHS*, lxxi, pp. xxvii–xxx

Thompson 1926   ———, 'The Church of the Blessed Virgin Mary, Meare', *PSANHS*, lxxii, pp. xliii–xlv

Thompson 1989   B. Thompson, '*Habendum et Tenendum*. Lay and Ecclesiastical Attitudes to the Property of the Church', in C. Harper-Bill, ed. *Religious Belief and Ecclesiastical Careers in Late Medieval England* (Proceedings of the Conference held at Strawberry Hill, Easter 1989), Woodbridge, pp. 197–238

Thompson 1994   ———, 'Monasteries and their Patrons at Foundation and Dissolution', *TRHS*, 6th ser. iv, pp. 103–25

Thomson 2001   R.M. Thomson, *A Descriptive Catalogue of the Medieval Manuscripts in Worcester Cathedral Library*, Cambridge

Thurlby 1996	M. Thurlby, 'The Abbey Church, Pershore: An Architectural History', *TWAS*, 3rd ser. xv, pp. 147–210
Thurlow 1979	G. Thurlow, 'The Bells of Gloucester Cathedral', *TBGAS*, xcvii, pp. 5–7
Tindal 1794	W. Tindal, *The History and Antiquities of the Abbey and Borough of Evesham*, Evesham
Tolley 1988	T.S. Tolley, 'The Use of Heraldry in an English Illuminated Manuscript of the Early Fifteenth Century', *The Coat of Arms*, ns vii, pp. 122–33
Tout 1921	T.F. Tout, 'The Captivity and Death of Edward of Carnarvon', *Bulletin of the John Rylands Library*, vi, pp. 69–114
Tracy 1987	C. Tracy, *English Gothic Choirstalls 1200–1400*, Woodbridge
Tracy 1993(a)	———, 'The 14th-Century Choir-Stalls', in *Winchester Cathedral*, pp. 193–206
Tracy 1993(b)	———, 'The Lady Chapel Stalls', in *Winchester Cathedral*, pp. 231–46
Trapp 1981–82	J.B. Trapp, 'Pieter Meghen 1466/7–1540, Scribe and Courtier', *Erasmus in English*, xi, pp. 28–35
Traskey 1978	J.P. Traskey, *Milton Abbey: A Dorset Monastery in the Middle Ages*, Tisbury
Trenholme 1927	N.M. Trenholme, *The English Monastic Boroughs*, Columbia, Mo.
Trevelyan 1838	W.C. Trevelyan, 'Names of Pilgrims from England to Rome in the years 1504–1507, 1581–1587; With Some of Earlier Date', *Collectanea Topographica et Genealogica*, v, pp. 62–88
Tristram 1955	E.W. Tristram, *English Wall Painting of the Fourteenth Century*, London
Tudor-Craig 1974	P. Tudor-Craig, 'Fragment of a Panel of the Flagellation in the Possession of Canterbury Cathedral and the Martyrdom of St Erasmus belonging to the Society of Antiquaries', *Antiquaries Journal*, liv, pp. 289–90
VCH Dorset	*The Victoria History of the County of Dorset*
VCH Gloucester	*The Victoria History of the County of Gloucester*
VCH Hampshire & I.W.	*The Victoria History of the County of Hampshire and the Isle of Wight*
VCH Lincoln	*The Victoria History of the County of Lincoln*
VCH Somerset	*The Victoria History of the County of Somerset*
VCH Suffolk	*The Victoria History of the County of Suffolk*
VCH Wiltshire	*The Victoria History of the County of Wiltshire*
VCH Worcester	*The Victoria History of the County of Worcester*
Verey 1970	D. Verey, *The Buildings of England. Gloucestershire*, II vols, Harmondsworth, 1970
Vince 1977	A. Vince, 'The Medieval and Post-Medieval Ceramic Industry of the Malvern Region. The Study of Ware and Its Distribution', in D.P.S. Peacock ed., *Pottery and Early Commerce*, London, pp. 257–305
Vince 2003	———, 'The Medieval Tile Pavements', in *Tewkesbury Abbey*, pp. 197–204, 307–8

Vince and Wilmott 1991 ———— and Wilmott, 'A Lost Tile Pavement at Tewkesbury Abbey, and an Early Fourteenth-Century tile Factory', *Antiquaries Journal*, lxxi, pp. 138–73

Vincent 2001 N. Vincent, *The Holy Blood. King Henry III and the Westminster Blood Relic*, Cambridge

Vivian-Neal 1959–60 A.W. Vivian-Neal, 'Cannington Court', *PSANHS*, civ, pp. 62–86

Walcott 1866 M.E.C. Walcott, 'A Benedictine Monastery in the Thirteenth Century (Westminster)', *The Ecclesiastic*, xxviii, pp. 533–82

Walker 1999 J. Walker, *Romsey Abbey through the Centuries*, Romsey

Warren n.d. J. Warren, *St. Peter's Church Hereford*, Hereford

W.A.S. 1952 W.A.S. (full name not supplied), 'A Finger-Ring from Minchin Buckland', *PSANHS*, xcvi, pp. 235–7

Watkin 1914–17 H.R. Watkin, *A History of Totnes Priory and Medieval Town, Devonshire*, II vols, Torquay

Watkin 1948 A. Watkin, 'Last Glimpses of Glastonbury', *DR*, lxvii, pp. 76–86

Webster 1943–46 D.K. Webster, 'A Bath Cartulary', *SDNQ*, xxiv, pp. 243–4

Weil-Garris 1977 K. Weil-Garris, *The Santa Casa di Loreto. Problems in Cinquecento Sculpture*, II vols, New York and London

Welander 1985 D. Welander, *The Stained Glass of Gloucester Cathedral*, Gloucester

Welander 1991 ————, *The History, Art and Architecture of Gloucester Cathedral*, Stroud

Were 1911 F. Were, 'Tombs and Tiles Adjoining Barrow Gurney Church', *PSANHS*, lvii, pp. 120–5

Whalley 1969 J.I. Whalley, *English Handwriting 1540–1830: An Illustrated Survey Based on Material in the National Art Library, Victoria and Albert Museum*, London

White 1993 J. White, *Art and Architecture in Italy: 1250–1400* (3rd edn), Harmondsworth

Williams 1993–98 D.H. Williams, *Catalogue of Seals in the National Museum of Wales*, II vols, Cardiff

Williamson 1995 P. Williamson, *Gothic Sculpture 1140–1300*, New Haven and London

Williamson 1996 ————, ed., *The Medieval Treasury. The Art of the Middle Ages in the Victoria and Albert Museum*, London

Willis 1718 B. Willis, *An History of the Mitred Parliamentary Abbies and Conventual Cathedral Churches . . .*, II vols, London

Willis 1863 R. Willis, 'The Architectural History of the Cathedral and Monastery of Worcester', *AJ*, xx, pp. 83–133, 255–72, 301–18

Willis 1998 ————, *The Architectural History of Winchester Cathedral*, (repr. edn), Winchester

Wilson 1911 J.M. Wilson, 'The Library of Printed Books in Worcester Cathedral', *The Library*, 3rd ser. ii, pp. 1–33

Wilson 1980 C. Wilson, 'The Origins of the Perpendicular Style and Its Development to c.1360' (unpublished Ph.D. dissertation, University of London)

Wilson 1990	———, *The Gothic Cathedral. The Architecture of the Great Church 1130–1530*, London
Wilson 1995	———, 'The Medieval Monuments', in P. Collinson, N. Ramsay and M. Sparks eds, *A History of Canterbury Cathedral*, Oxford, pp. 451–510
Wilson 2003(a)	———, 'The Functional Design of Henry VII's Chapel: A Reconstruction', in *Westminster Abbey*, pp. 141–88
Wilson 2003(b)	———, ' "Excellent, New and Uniforme": Perpendicular Architecture c.1400–1547', in *Gothic*, pp. 98–119
Witts 1882–83 (a)	F.E.B. Witts, 'Old Bells in Gloucestershire Belfries', *TBGAS*, vii, pp. 56–68
Witts 1882–83(b)	———, 'The Bells and Bell-Founders of Gloucester Cathedral', *RGC*, i, pp. 127–39
Wolffe 1981	B. Wolffe, *Henry VI*, London
Wood 1955	S. Wood, *English Monasteries and Their Patrons in the Thirteenth Century*, Oxford
Wood 1994	M. Wood, *The English Medieval House*, London
Woodforde 1946	C. Woodforde, *Stained Glass in Somerset 1250–1830*, London
Wood-Jones 1956	R.B. Wood-Jones, 'The Rectorial Barn at Church Enstone', *Oxoniensia*, xxi, pp. 43–6
Wood-Legh 1934	K.L. Wood-Legh, *Studies in Church Life Under Edward III*, Cambridge
Wood-Legh 1965	———, *Perpetual Chantries in Britain*, Cambridge
Woodman 1996	F. Woodman, 'The Gothic Campaigns', in I. Atherton et al., eds, *Norwich Cathedral: Church, City and Diocese 1096–1996*, London and Rio Grande, pp. 158–96
Wooley 1930	E. Wooley, 'The Ramryge Chantry', *St Albans and Hertfordshire Architectural and Archaeological Society Transactions for 1930*, pp. 31–6
Wormald 1959	F. Wormald, *The Benedictional of St Æthelwold*, London
Wormald and Giles 1982	——— and P.M. Giles, *A Descriptive Catalogue of the Additional Illuminated Manuscripts in the Fitzwilliam Museum*, II vols, Cambridge
W.S.W. 1851	W.S.W. (full name not supplied), 'Original Documents Relating to Property at Totnes, Devon', *AJ*, viii, pp. 307–12
Wylie 1894	J.H. Wylie, *History of England under Henry the Fourth* (vol. II), London
Yeo 1986	G. Yeo, 'Where was Cowick Priory?', *DCNQ*, XXXIV, pp. 321–6
Yeo 1987	———, *The Monks of Cowick Priory*, Cowick
Youings 1971	J. Youings, *The Dissolution of the Monasteries*, London
Zarnecki 1984	G. Zarnecki, ed., *English Romanesque Art 1066–1200*, London

Index

Other volumes in
Studies in the History of Medieval Religion

Lightning Source UK Ltd.
Milton Keynes UK
UKOW04f1542060717

304758UK00001B/91/P